P9-DDJ-048

WORLD RELIGIONS

A CANADIAN CATHOLIC PERSPECTIVE

Theologian and Editor-in-Chief
Dr. John van den Hengel, SCJ

Authors
Char Deslippe
Religious Education Consultant for the
Catholic Independent Schools, Diocese of Victoria

Michael Harrison
Program Consultant: Religious Education, Faith Formation & Integrated Arts
Dufferin-Peel Catholic District School Board

John van den Hengel, SCJ
Professor Emeritus, Saint Paul University, Ottawa

Les Miller
Coordinator: Religious Education, Family Life Education & Equity
York Catholic District School Board

Seán Stokes
Teacher, St. Michael's College School, Toronto

Michael Way Skinner
Consultant: Faith Leadership and Student Engagement
York Catholic District School Board

Religious Education Consultant
Sharron McKeever
Consultant for Religious and Family Life Education
for the Durham Catholic District School Board (retired)

NOVALIS

NELSON EDUCATION

NOVALIS

NELSON EDUCATION

World Religions
A Canadian Catholic Perspective

Theologian and Editor-in-Chief
Dr. John van den Hengel, SCJ

Authors
Char Deslippe, Michael Harrison, John van den Hengel, Les Miller, Seán Stokes, Michael Way Skinner

Religious Education Consultant
Sharron McKeever

Novalis Publishing Inc.

Publishing Director
Joseph Sinasac

Editorial Consultant
Dr. Michael O'Hearn

Editorial Director, Parish and School Resources
Grace Deutsch

Managing Editor
Anne Louise Mahoney

Director, Sales and Marketing
Lauretta Santarossa

Nelson Education Limited

General Manager and Publisher, Catholic Resources
Carol Stokes

Publisher
Doug Panasis

Managing Editor, Development
Karin Fediw

Senior Program Manager
Laura Jones

Product Managers
Linda Krepinsky, Doug Morrow

Editor
Norma Pettit

Assistant Editor
Kimberly Murphy

Editorial Assistant
Jordana Camerman

Bias Review
Nancy Christoffer

Fact Checker
Lynne Hussey

Senior Production Coordinator
Sharon Latta Paterson

Design Director
Ken Phipps

Interior Design
Glenn Toddun

Cover Design
Sasha Moroz

Printer
Transcontinental Printing Inc.

Focus Strategic Communications Inc.

Project Manager
Adrianna Edwards

Copyeditor
Susan McNish

Editorial and Production Assistant
Tracey Peck

Proofreaders
Linda Szostak, Linda Cahill

Index
Ron Edwards

Compositor
Valentino Sanna

Photo Research and Permissions
David Strand

COPYRIGHT © 2011 by
Novalis Publishing Inc. and
Nelson Education Ltd.

ISBN-13: 978-0-17-624245-9
ISBN-10: 0-17-624245-7

Printed and bound in Canada
2 3 4 13 12 11 10

For more information contact
Novalis Publishing Inc.
10 Lower Spadina Avenue
Suite 400
Toronto, Ontario, M5V 2Z2.
Or you can visit our Internet site.

Nelson Education Ltd.,
1120 Birchmount Road,
Toronto, Ontario, M1K 5G4.
Or you can visit our Internet site.

ALL RIGHTS RESERVED. No part of this work covered by the copyright herein, except for any reproducible pages included in this work, may be reproduced, transcribed, or used in any form or by any means—graphic, electronic, or mechanical, including photocopying, recording, taping, Web distribution, or information storage and retrieval systems—without the written permission of the publisher.

For permission to use material from this text or product, submit all requests online to the Cengage permissions website.

Every effort has been made to trace ownership of all copyrighted material and to secure permission from copyright holders. In the event of any question arising as to the use of any material, we will be pleased to make the necessary corrections in future printings.

Acknowledgments

This program was initiated by and developed in collaboration with the Assembly of Catholic Bishops of Ontario. In plenary assembly, the bishops of Ontario recognized that the content of this program is faithful to the teaching of the Church and conforms to the *Ontario Catholic Secondary Curriculum Policy Document for Religious Education, Revised 2006* of the Assembly of Catholic Bishops of Ontario. Each diocesan bishop maintains the right and duty to approve specific catechetical texts in his own diocese.

Imprimatur
\+ Most Reverend Thomas Collins
Archbishop of Toronto
November 26, 2009
President of the Assembly of Catholic Bishops of Ontario

Novalis-Nelson Advisory Panel

Gerry Blake
Retired Executive Director
Catholic Curriculum Corporation

Jozef Gal
Religious Education Specialist
Teacher, St. Joseph-Scollard Hall CSS
Nipissing-Parry Sound CDSB

Bronek Korczynski
Coordinator of Religious and Family Life Education
Algonquin and Lakeshore CDSB

Paul McKenna, MA
Interfaith Department
Scarboro Missions

Ovey N. Mohammed, S.J.
Professor Emeritus, Regis College
University of Toronto

John Podgorski
Visiting Professor
Faculty of Education
University of Ottawa

Eva Solomon, CSJ, D.Min.
Sister of St. Joseph of Sault Ste. Marie
Assembly of Western Catholic Bishops—Standing Committee on Aboriginal Affairs

Dr. Larry Trafford
Faculty of Education
York University

Assembly of Catholic Bishops of Ontario (ACBO) Education Commission

Most Reverend Paul-André Durocher
(Chair), Bishop of Alexandria-Cornwall

Most Reverend Gerard P. Bergie
Auxiliary Bishop of Hamilton

Most Reverend Fred J. Colli
Bishop of Thunder Bay

Most Reverend Ronald Fabbro
Bishop of London

Most Reverend Michael Mulhall
Bishop of Pembroke

Father Rémi Lessard
(Associate Member)
Transfiguration Parish, Cochrane

Assembly of Catholic Bishops of Ontario (ACBO)/Institute for Catholic Education (ICE) *World Religions* Advisory Panel

Sister Joan Cronin, g.s.i.c.
Executive Director, ICE

Alphonse Ainsworth
Past General Secretary, ACBO

Most Reverend Gerard P. Bergie
Auxiliary Bishop of Hamilton

Angelo Bolotta
Past Principal, Cardinal Carter Academy for the Arts, Toronto CDSB

Josephine Lombardi
Assistant Professor, Pastoral and Systematic Theology
St. Augustine's Seminary

Luciano (Lou) Piovesan
General Secretary, ACBO

Bernadette Provost
Superintendent, Lakeland Catholic Separate School District #150, AB

Bernard Smyth
Former Principal and Teacher of Religious Education and Family Life
CDSBEO

ICE *World Religions* Pedagogical Advisory Panel

Robert Cartwright
Notre Dame CSS
Durham CDSB

Paige Forsyth
St. Dominic CSS
Simcoe Muskoka CDSB

Patricia Murphy
Sacred Heart CHS
York CDSB

Susan Peterson
St. Joseph CSS
Dufferin-Peel CDSB

Deirdre Vance
Sacred Heart CHS
York CDSB

Faith Reviewers

Who Are Catholics?

Dr. Reid B. Locklin
Associate Professor and
Programme Coordinator
Christianity and Culture
Saint Michael's College
University of Toronto

Aboriginal Spirituality

Brenda Davis
Education Consultant
Six Nations of the Grand River

Judaism

Arliene Botnick
Director of Education
Solel Congregation of Mississauga

Rabbi Dow Marmur
Rabbi Emeritus
Holy Blossom Temple, Toronto

Rabbi Reuven Bulka
Congregation
Machzikei Hadas, Ottawa

Christianity

Catherine E. Clifford, Ph.D.
Associate Professor and Vice Dean
Faculty of Theology
Saint Paul University

Fr. John A. Jillions, D.Min., Ph.D.
Associate Professor
Sheptytsky Institute of
Eastern Christian Studies
Saint Paul University

Rev. Professor Kevin Flynn
Director of Anglican Studies Program
Saint Paul University

Islam

Imam Abdul Hai Patel
Interfaith Director
Canadian Council of Imams, Toronto

Shaikh Habeeb Alli
Secretary
Canadian Council of Imams, Toronto

Naheed Syed
Teacher of Islamic Studies
Karachi Grammar School, Karachi

Hinduism

Pandit Roopnauth Sharma
Spiritual Leader, Ram Mandir,
Mississauga

Buddhism

Chai Setsaenmo
Theravada Buddhist,
Bracebridge

Sikhism

Dr. Mohinder Singh Grover, with Tanbir Grover and Dr. Harpreet Grover
Founding member; Former Vice-President, Education; Member, Executive Committee (2004–2008); and Interfaith Relations Coordinator,
Gursikh Sabha Canada Gurdwara, Scarborough

The publishers would like to thank the following individuals for their support of, and contributions to this Student Book:

Catholic Association of Religious and Family Life Educators of Ontario (CARFLEO)

Religious Education and Family Life Consultants

Catholic Curriculum Organizations

Michael Bator
Executive Director
Catholic Curriculum Corporation

Lorne Keon
Executive Director
Eastern Ontario Catholic Curriculum Cooperative

Suzanne Wishak
Executive Director
Northern Ontario Catholic Curriculum Cooperative

Western Provinces

The Editorial Board and the Advisory Panel would like to thank the **Most Reverend Frederick B. Henry**, Bishop of Calgary, representing the Alberta Bishops, and **Stefan Michniewski**, Executive Director, Alberta Catholic School Trustees' Association for their support.

Editorial Board

Bernadette Provost
Superintendent, Lakeland Catholic Separate School District #150

Advisory Panel

Angela Auger
Calgary RCSSD #1

Kathy Inglis
Red Deer CRD #39

Michael Marien
St. Thomas Aquinas RCSRD #38

Mark Nixon
Holy Spirit RCSRD #4

Russ Snoble
Grand Prairie RCSSD #28

Sandra Talarico
Edmonton CSSD #7

Field Test Teachers

Penny Authier
Regina Mundi CSS, London, ON

Bill Bazinet
Patrick Fogarty CSS, Orillia, ON

Daniel Berthiaume
St. Joseph-Scollard Hall CSS
North Bay, ON

Carol Bomans
Catholic Central CSS, London, ON

Brian Butlin
St. Joseph's CSS, Cornwall, ON

Angelita Donatelli
St. Jean de Brebeuf CSS
Hamilton, ON

Grazyna Farmus
St. Joseph College School
Toronto, ON

Jozef Gal
St. Joseph-Scollard Hall CSS
North Bay, ON

Monica Godin
St. Joseph College School
Toronto, ON

Sean Grimes
All Saints High School
Kanata, ON

Peter Huczek
Notre Dame Secondary School
Brampton, ON

Martha Joyce
Regina Mundi CSS, London, ON

Marie McDade
St. Anne's CSS, Clinton, ON

Margie O'Connor
Catholic Central CSS, London, ON

Dan Reis
St. Mary's High School
Kitchener-Waterloo, ON

Mark Shaw
Notre Dame CSS, Burlington, ON

Fran Tignanelli
St. Joseph-Scollard Hall CSS
North Bay, ON

Sara Van Dommelen
John Paul II CSS, London, ON

Cornelia Verwer
John Paul II CSS, London, ON

Tara Warren-Vrbanac
St. Michael CSS, Stratford, ON

Kathi Zappala
St. Joseph-Scollard Hall CSS
North Bay, ON

Table of Contents

NEL

ASSEMBLY OF CATHOLIC BISHOPS OF ONTARIO

ASSEMBLÉE DES ÉVÊQUES CATHOLIQUES DE L'ONTARIO

Dear Students,

We are pleased to offer as part of your Religious Studies program a learning resource entitled

World Religions: A Canadian Catholic Perspective.

As you undertake your World Religions course, it is our profound hope that this resource will help you to better understand and deepen your faith, and to appreciate how important faith in God is in becoming fully human. At the same time, it offers you learning opportunities to acquire an understanding and appreciation for other faith traditions.

Finally, we are confident that your Religious Studies program will support your formation as "a discerning believer formed in the Catholic Faith community who celebrates the signs and sacred mystery of God's presence." *

Sincerely yours in Christ,
The Catholic Bishops of Ontario
January, 2010

*Ontario Catholic School Graduate Expectations

How to Use This Book

In *World Religions: A Canadian Catholic Perspective*, you will find the following features that will help deepen your understanding of your own faith and that of other religions.

Each chapter
- introduces some of the main features or aspects of the religion with an opening visual and a scriptural quotation
- profiles a young person from that faith who describes the challenges and rewards of living his or her faith in Canada today
- gives demographic statistics about the religion in Canada
- surveys important historical events
- presents each religion through its
  - rituals and ways of marking time
  - life-cycle ceremonies such as birth, marriage, and death
  - festivals and holy days
  - family and community life
  - central beliefs and scriptures
  - moral life
- discusses the attempts of the Catholic Church to engage in dialogue with the religion
- concludes with a prayer from that religion

1

What You Will Learn

In this chapter, you will learn about

- where Buddhism is practised, and Buddhism in Canada
- the founder of Buddhism, the history of the religion, and its development into different types of Buddhism
- Buddhist rituals (including meditation) and festivals
- central beliefs of Buddhism: the Three Jewels, the Four Noble Truths, the Eightfold Path
- Buddhist morality: the Five Precepts and Buddhist values
- family life and daily life for Buddhists
- the Catholic Church and Buddhism

1. *What You Will Learn* introduces the chapter's key ideas.

2. Questions help you consolidate, extend, and reflect on your learning.

2

Check Your Understanding

1. Explain why Buddhists meditate, and describe three techniques that help them meditate.

Think About It

2. Why do you think a close bond has developed between some Catholic and Buddhist monks and nuns?

Making It Personal

3. Many religions include meditation. For example, Christians might use the Aramaic word *Maranatha*, from one of the earliest Christian prayers, in their meditations. *Maranatha* means "Come, Lord." Have you ever used a repeated word in prayer? Which one do you use and how does it help you pray?

3. Key terms are highlighted when they first appear in the text and are defined in the margin for easy reference.

3

Buddhists, like Hindus, use the term ***karma*** related to *samsara* and reincarnation. Buddhism understands *karma* as being directly related to intentions and to the Buddhist concept of merit. For Buddhists, intention is central.

Karma
The law of cause and effect, of one's actions having an impact on one's future life

Catholic Connection

The title "the Buddha" is applied to Siddhartha Gautama in the same way as the title "the Christ" is applied to Jesus. The title means the "Enlightened One." Siddartha Gautama was never considered divine as Jesus is.

4

Fast Fact

The Buddha's remains, such as his teeth, were divided among his followers. These remains (called relics) were placed in special stone burial mounds called *stupas*, which became centres of Buddhist devotion.

5

4. *Catholic Connections* point out similarities and differences between world religions and Catholicism.

5. *Fast Facts* present interesting information related to the main topic.

A Closer Look

In Buddhism, the ideas of "right," "good," "evil," and "wrong" are relative. The intention behind a deed and its effect on oneself and others are critical in determining whether it is right or wrong.

6

6. *A Closer Look* allows you to explore a topic in more depth.

Make It Your Own: The Life of the Buddha

7

It is hard to know the historical accuracy of accounts of the life of the Buddha:

- We know that he lived about 2500 years ago, and we also know that some parts of his story are more legendary than factual.
- Certain parts of his life provide lessons to his followers about the choices we make in life. Maybe that is why they were included in his biographies.
- Also, when we look at somebody who lived 2500 years ago, we look at his life through present-day eyes. It is not easy for us to understand what life was like in his time.

These conditions make it difficult to know the historical situation of the Buddha. Nevertheless, the story of the Buddha makes fascinating reading.

Activities

1. Create an illustrated timeline or a multimedia presentation of the life of the Buddha. Illustrate the dates and events with pictures or photographs or slides.
2. Find songs or video clips that represent key moments in the Buddha's life. Explain why you made these selections.

7. *Make It Your Own* features allow you to express your learning in creative, hands-on ways, through independent and partner work.

Skill Focus: Meditation

8

Many people in the West have become interested in meditation as it is practised in religions such as Buddhism and Hinduism. Meditation has many benefits: it focuses the mind and helps one to remain calm under stress. Learning and adapting some of the techniques from Buddhist meditation can help you study for a test, prepare for an oral presentation, perform onstage before an audience, or compete in a sports event. Meditating is difficult, but there are some guidelines for beginners.

1. Make a habit of meditating at the same time each day. Start with small periods of time from 5 to 15 minutes.
2. Have a purpose for meditating. Choose a subject, mantra, or virtue to meditate on. If you are preparing for some stressful event (for example, a school or driving test, a performance, a job interview, a competition), you might wish to meditate on courage or on staying calm. If you are having trouble getting started on a difficult task (for example, studying, writing an essay, doing a chore), you may wish to meditate on the virtue of persevering.
3. Choose a place where you will be comfortable and where you will not be interrupted or distracted. Turn off your cellphone, the computer, and the TV.
4. You may wish to meditate with your eyes closed, but if that is too difficult, choose an object to look at. The object should be something that is meaningful and calming for you to contemplate (for example, a religious object, a photograph).
5. Pay attention to your breathing as you meditate. Take long, slow breaths in and exhale slowly. Slow breathing helps to slow down the heart rate and helps concentration.

8. *Skill Focus* features provide tips for applying the skill highlighted in the chapter performance task.

9

What I Have Learned

In this chapter, I learned about

- where Buddhism is practised, and Buddhism in Canada
- the origins of Buddhism as an offshoot of Hinduism, the history of Siddhartha Gautama and the religion, and its development into different schools of Buddhism
- Buddhist rituals (including meditation), symbols, and festivals
- the concepts of *samsara*, nirvana, enlightenment, *karma*, merit, *dukkha*, *metta*
- central beliefs of Buddhism—the Three Jewels, the Four Noble Truths, the Eightfold Path
- Buddhist morality: the Five Precepts and Buddhist values (self-determination, compassion, loving-kindness, and detachment)
- similarities, differences, and interreligious dialogue between Catholics and Buddhists

9. *What I Have Learned* summarizes the chapter's key ideas.

10. The Glossary makes finding the definitions of unfamiliar terms fast and easy.

Samsara The law of birth, death, and rebirth, or the process of reincarnation

10

11. The Pronunciation Key will help you to learn and use unfamiliar terminology when you discuss concepts in class and present orally.

Dukkha **dū** kə

11

Chapter 1

World Religions and Religious Pluralism

"I truly understand that God shows no partiality, but in every nation anyone who fears him and does what is right is acceptable to him."
(Acts of the Apostles 10:34–35)

Earth from Outer Space. This photograph of Earth was taken on December 7, 1972, by the astronauts of *Apollo 17* on their way to the Moon. "May the dawn from on high break upon us ... to guide our feet into the way of peace" (Luke 1:78–79). At any given moment in the twenty-first century, 30 to 40 wars are being waged on Earth. **Why can't the peoples on Earth live together in peace and work out their differences?**

What You Will Learn

In this chapter, you will learn about

- the possibility of diverse peoples living together peacefully in Canada
- living together peacefully in societies with religious pluralism
- the Catholic Church's position on interreligious and ecumenical dialogue
- a brief history of Christian evangelization
- dialogue as a new way for believers of different world religions to live together
- four ways of participating in the dialogue of world religions

Personal Recollection

I knew almost nothing about Myint-San. She just was there one day, sitting at a seat by the window at the back of the class, looking nervous and uncomfortable. The teacher had told us that she was a Karen from Myanmar (Burma) who had spent three or four years in a refugee camp in Thailand. I'd never heard of the Karens. I hardly knew where Myanmar was on the map. She and her family had been allowed into Canada as refugees. Canada is her new country now.

Myint-San is not alone in our class. There are several other students like her who have come from other countries to Canada. I wasn't surprised that she seemed uncomfortable, shy, and scared. I wondered what her story was.

I talked with her at lunchtime that day. Over the next few months we became friends. I learned that Karens were Catholics and that they were a minority in Myanmar, which is mainly a Buddhist country. I learned a lot about the Karens and Myanmar. I also developed a better understanding of what it is like to come to a new and unfamiliar country and to try to fit in to a new school.

—**Danielle K.**

The Face of Canada. Canada is a nation of immigrants, built upon the foundation of the Aboriginal peoples, the French, and the British.

Religious Pluralism in Canada

Baisakhi Parade. Sikh children chant songs as they parade through the streets of Vancouver, British Columbia, during the annual Baisakhi Parade, which celebrates the Sikh New Year.

Good Friday Procession. On Good Friday, parishioners of St. Francis of Assisi Church stage a procession through Toronto's Little Italy neighbourhood. They have been doing so for more than 40 years.

Fast Fact

The 2006 census lists more than 200 cultures that can now be found in Canada. Canada is one of the most ethnically diverse countries in the world.

The Al-Rashid Mosque. Built in 1938 in Edmonton, Alberta, the Al-Rashid Mosque is North America's oldest mosque.

Danielle's experience of sharing a classroom with students from cultures and religions different from her own is more and more common in Canada. Canada's diversity of cultures and faiths is the result of two related facts:

- Canada has a history of immigration and a policy of multiculturalism.
- Canada's Charter of Rights and Freedoms guarantees "freedom of conscience and religion."

From the time of Confederation in 1867, Canada has changed from a country of around 3 million people—mainly Aboriginal, French, and British peoples—to one of approximately 34 million people of tremendous diversity. Canadians speak many languages, practise many religions, and come from many cultures and ethnic groups. As a result, Canada is considered **multicultural**.

The Canadian policy of **multiculturalism** seeks to define how all Canadians—whatever their ethnic, cultural, linguistic, or religious background—make up the fabric of the nation and its identity. By law, all are to participate equally in every aspect of Canadian life while at the same time preserving their cultural heritage.

Over the years, the Canadian government and the courts have addressed issues of citizenship that include the following:

- the rights and obligations of Canadian citizens
- languages
- cultural heritage
- racism and race relations
- how Canadian society can accommodate the wishes of religious minorities or cultures
- other issues that affect how a diverse Canada functions

Since the *Multicultural Act* was passed in 1988, the federal government has broadened the rights that all Canadians share. Canada today is an exciting venture of living together as one people with many differences.

Multicultural

Consisting of multiple ethnic groups, cultures, languages, and religions

Multiculturalism

A policy and law that recognizes and supports the diversity of a nation's or province's population

Check Your Understanding

1. Describe Canada's policy of multiculturalism in your own words to a classmate.
2. Explain why Canada's policy of multiculturalism was necessary.

Think About It

3. Find examples in the mass media (news reports, movies, TV shows, posters, and so on) of Canadian diversity, the roles and rights of citizens, or issues that relate to these subjects. Make note of the examples you find and your ideas about what each example means for living peacefully in Canada.
4. Do you agree with the policy of multiculturalism? Give reasons to support your viewpoint.

Making It Personal

5. Identify an example in your community of the policy of multiculturalism in action. Explain how this example reflects the policy.
6. Does the policy of multiculturalism affect your life? Explain.

History of Religious Pluralism

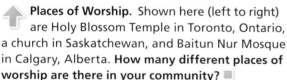

Places of Worship. Shown here (left to right) are Holy Blossom Temple in Toronto, Ontario, a church in Saskatchewan, and Baitun Nur Mosque in Calgary, Alberta. **How many different places of worship are there in your community?**

Since Confederation, Canada has mostly been a Christian country. Even most Aboriginal peoples have become Christian. Although around 72 percent of Canadians still identified themselves with the Christian faith in 2001, other faiths were becoming increasingly visible. Today, one in sixteen Canadians belongs to a faith other than Christianity. If immigration continues at the current rate, this number will grow. Canada is increasingly a country where **religious pluralism** is practised.

At the beginning of the twenty-first century, more and more Christian Canadians can count Jews, Muslims, Sikhs, Buddhists, Jains, Hindus, Bahais, and followers of Aboriginal spirituality and traditional Chinese religions among their neighbours, friends, and family. If immigration continues at the 2006 rate, the number of such interactions will be more frequent.

Of all the differences between people, religious differences are the most enduring. Although religious traditions and beliefs may evolve or

Religious pluralism

The co-existence of many religions in a society; Canada, India, and the United States are examples of countries where religious pluralism exists

Distribution of World Religions in Canada, 2001

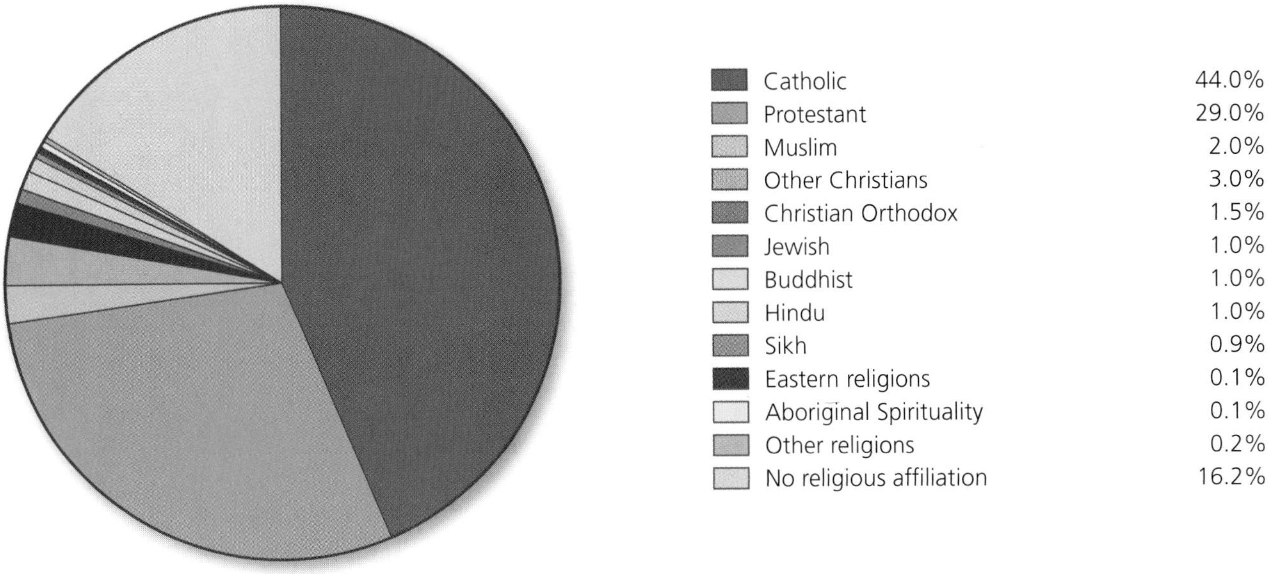

World Religions in Canada. This pie graph demonstrates the diversity of religions in modern Canada. (Note: numbers have been rounded off.) **Does any of the data surprise you? How does the percentage of people with no religious affiliation compare to the total percentage of people who listed their religious affiliation?**

be transformed, they still operate at subconscious levels after thousands of years because they touch people's souls.

The symbols, rituals, and beliefs of religion play a key role in how people perceive and live their lives. Each religion claims that its identity is divinely approved. Because of these strongly held beliefs, religions have not always lived peacefully side by side. Today, more than ever, believers from different religions need to learn how to live together.

To accomplish this task, we all must develop some ground rules for living together. Four ground rules will be discussed under the following headings:

1. Respect the Faith and Religion of Others
2. There Is No Neutral Stance
3. The Truth of Other Religions
4. Accept the Importance of Religion

1. Respect the Faith and Religion of Others

The first ground rule for dialogue is to learn to respect the faith and religion of other peoples. To say "I believe" means "I pledge myself." When Muslims pray the Shahadah ("I bear witness that there is no God but Allah. And I bear witness that Muhammad is the Messenger of Allah"), or when Jews pray the Shema ("Hear, O Israel, the Lord is our God, the Lord is one"), or when Catholics pray the Apostles' Creed ("I believe in God ..."), they express their deepest convictions. They express what they believe is true.

A Closer Look

Serious conflicts between followers of different religions—such as Muslims and Christians in Iraq, Hindus and Muslims in India, Jews and Muslims in Israel and the Palestinian Territories, Hindus and Christians in India—are part of the world's recent history. Serious conflicts also occur between followers of the same religion, including Christians.

Prayer. In prayer, humans touch a core of themselves that wants to talk to God. Here the most fundamental things about life are said. Prayer is a conversation with a Reality upon whom we depend to the depths of our being.

The Cross and the Resurrection. The cross and the resurrection of Jesus are central to the Catholic faith. Catholics bring these beliefs to their interactions with members of other religions. **Discuss how these beliefs might affect how Catholics relate with members of other religions.**

This truth has held for them for centuries without change. It has withstood the test of time. These confessions of faith are sacred to these religions and are repeated in their rituals and liturgies. Since these confessions touch the heart of a person's identity, they call for the utmost respect.

2. There Is No Neutral Stance

The second ground rule for religious dialogue is to acknowledge that we cannot be neutral observers of other religions. For example, if we are Catholic and profess the Catholic faith, we live with Buddhists in Canada as Catholics. Non-believers will live with Buddhists as non-believers. (After all, non-believers believe something. If they believe that religion is an illusion or superstition, they will relate to religions as if they are superstitions.)

Everyone has a particular stance or perspective—a starting point. Everyone has certain presuppositions, certain beliefs about God or the Supreme Spirit and the meaning and purpose of life; everyone also has certain prejudices.

This textbook takes its position from a Christian, and, more specifically, a Catholic perspective. It asks how Catholics ought to live with members of other religions. What does it mean for someone living the Catholic way of life to interact with members of other religions?

To enter into dialogue with another religion, Catholics need a strong sense of themselves and their Catholic identity. They must be aware of their beliefs and opinions, for these will colour the relationships they have with others.

3. The Truth of Other Religions

For believers of a religion, their faith explains for them how the world works and how reality holds together. At a practical level, members of each religion believe their religion to be true. That is what all religions celebrate: the truth of what they believe. To this truth believers pledge themselves. The third ground rule for religious dialogue is therefore to express respect for the truth of other religions. A Muslim, for example, holds as true that the Qur'an is literally the word of God as revealed to Muhammad. When a Muslim *imam* (leader) reads the Qur'an at Friday services, those present hear and understand it as the word of Allah.

In performing their rituals, the members of a religion make present what they believe. For example, Muslims understand the reading of the Qur'an to be Allah's word to them. For them, their faith is the truth. When a Catholic and a Muslim encounter each other, it is important for each to appreciate what the other holds as true. Catholics and Muslims may disagree about the roles of Muhammad and Jesus, but they must start by recognizing how important Jesus and Muhammad are to each other's religions. Each must respect what the other holds to be true.

4. Accept the Importance of Religion

The fourth ground rule for interreligious dialogue is the acceptance of religion—even with its different forms—as important for human beings. Some people propose abolishing religion because they think that the world would be better off without it. They blame religion for violence and tensions among people. Without religion, they claim, there would be greater peace and harmony in the world.

It may also be argued that religion—even a course on world religions like this one—leads to harmony and peace by promoting ways of living peacefully together and promoting social justice, for example. It can also be claimed that the greatest violence has come from those who deny religion. After all, some of the most deadly violence of the twentieth century was carried out by the fascist National Socialists (the Nazis) of Germany and by secular communist governments in the Soviet Union (Russia), China, and Cambodia.

Other people suggest that religions drop all their differences and seek one religion—a so-called one-size-fits-all solution. But, whose differences ought to be dropped? And are differences the problem? Are differences among people not part of the richness of human life? The same is true for religions.

The differences among religions are a sign of the wealth of diversity of humans. Religious diversity is their glory, not their failure. Differences are important, even though they may cause tensions at times. The challenge is to shape harmony amid all the diversity.

For Catholics, the source of unity amid diversity is their belief in one God who is Father, Son, and Holy Spirit. In God there is a unity with difference: the more the three persons in God are distinct, the more they are one. In a similar way, harmony among religions does not mean doing away with all the differences.

In the Catholic tradition, for instance, clear distinctions exist between the Roman Church and the Eastern Churches. Yet, they still form one Church. To be one does not mean to be the same. Diversity does not mean division or disunity. The intent of studying other religions is not to create a sort of **syncretism** of religions, but to appreciate and celebrate our differences and to learn from one another.

The Word of God. Catholic priests (top) and Jewish rabbis both proclaim the Word of God. **How is the Bible the Word of God for both Catholics and Jews? What does this suggest about the relationship between Jews and Catholics?**

Syncretism
The attempt to blend the beliefs and practices of different religions into one system

Check Your Understanding

1. Define religious pluralism.
2. In your own words, state the four ground rules, outlined above, for religions to live together.

Think About It

3. There is one human race but a great number of cultures, ethnic groups, languages, customs, foods, types of music, and religions. In a small group, discuss this question: Have you ever thought about what the world would be like without these differences? Name one difference for each category that you think is a positive thing.

Making It Personal

4. What attitudes or virtues do people need to live together with many ethnic groups in one country?
5. Describe any attempts you have seen in your school or community by people of different faiths to take active steps to live together in harmony. What steps might you personally take?

The Goals of Dialogue

What Is Tolerance?

Canadians like to think of themselves as a tolerant people, accepting that people are different and respecting those differences. We tend to hesitate to interfere with the beliefs and values of others. We feel that to respect others' beliefs, we must leave them alone and never question them. Some feel that to question another's beliefs indicates a lack of respect and a refusal to accept differences.

Tolerance

An attitude that recognizes the right of others to think, live, or worship according to their own beliefs

This kind of **tolerance** of difference is tolerance for the sake of peace. It reflects an assumption that we must do everything we can to avoid causing hard feelings or tension.

But tolerance does not mean always agreeing with others. In fact, tolerance comes into play when there *are* disagreements. At such times, we do not have to act as if we agree. At the same time, we do not have to speak out forcefully, except when what is being promoted is intolerable, such as slavery, racism, and physical or sexual abuse.

We practise tolerance in the face of such differences as dress (for example, the *hijab*, worn by many Muslim women), the wearing of symbols (for example, the *kirpan*, worn by many Sikh boys and men), or foods people eat (for example, kosher laws followed by many Jews).

Religions Must Interact with Each Other

Our relationship with other religions must go beyond tolerance. It is not enough to respect others and leave them in peace. Religions deal with ultimate matters such as the meaning and purpose of life and one's sense of identity. Religions cannot just live side by side making absolute claims without asking questions of each other. They must interact. So, in addition to living together and respecting each other, religions must talk with each other.

The Catholic Church has done so from its beginning. To understand how the Catholic Church has interacted with other religions, it is worthwhile to give a brief history of the Church's understanding of its mission.

The Parable of the Weeds among the Wheat (Matthew 13:24–30). In the parable, Jesus speaks of the human condition, where good and bad people, enemies and friends—radically diverse people—live together. He compares the human condition to the farmer's experience of finding weeds among wheat. He warns his disciples not to try to root out what they consider to be weeds, but to live with them until the harvest. In the end, it will all be sorted out. As long as humans live on Earth, they are not to act as judges of others; God is the only judge who knows the truth about others. **Find situations around you (such as in your family, school, or neighbourhood) that fit this parable.**

Skill Focus: How to Engage in Dialogue

In its simplest meaning, a dialogue is a conversation between two or more people. It can also mean an exchange of ideas, especially between two groups of people who have very different or even opposing viewpoints.

There will be many opportunities to engage in dialogue with your classmates as you study world religions. Before you begin, remember that there are some ground rules for dialogue.

1. Always be respectful of another person's point of view, even if you disagree with it.
2. Listen carefully to the other participants. A dialogue is a conversation, not a speech.
3. Before you speak, wait until you are sure that the other person has finished. Then acknowledge the validity of the other person's point of view when you begin speaking.
4. Summarize the other person's viewpoint to ensure that you have understood it. If your summary is inaccurate, then you can ask questions to clarify.

Christianity and Evangelization

Fast Fact

"Evangelization" comes from a Greek word meaning "to proclaim good news." It refers to the Church's mission to bring the good news of Jesus and his love to people in places where the Gospel has not been heard before or where it has been forgotten. Matthew, Mark, Luke, and John, the writers of the Gospels, are called evangelists for the same reason.

Why does the Church see it as its mandate to bring the name of Jesus to all peoples? There are two basic reasons.

First, Jesus revealed in a unique way who God is. The disciples of Jesus were deeply impressed by the intimate relation of Jesus to God, whom he called Abba (Father). They asked Jesus to teach them to pray to God as he did. Through Jesus, they came to know a God who healed people, loved the poor and the outcast, raised the dead to life, and set people free. In Jesus's death on the cross and in his resurrection, they experienced how faithful Jesus was to this God who loved people and how God raised Jesus from the dead. The disciples felt compelled to bear witness to others about this God of Jesus. For them, Jesus was the only access to this God. Jesus was the way to God.

Second, Catholics proclaim Jesus to all peoples because they believe that in the resurrection, Jesus was revealed to the disciples as the very Word of God. Jesus was in God. Jesus was the incarnation of God. This meant that the One God was Trinitarian (three persons): Father, Son, and Spirit. Catholics feel compelled to proclaim Jesus Christ because, by talking about Jesus, they talk about God. When Catholics talk about God, they do so by telling the story of Jesus.

Statue of Jesus. Detail of a statue of Christ. The message of faith in a God of love, who cared for all without distinction, had great appeal among people everywhere.

Early Evangelization: The Great Commission

The impulse for Christians to reach out to others came from Jesus himself. At the end of the Gospel of Matthew, before Jesus left his disciples, he gave them the great commission. He said to them:

> *All authority in heaven and on Earth has been given to me. Go therefore and make disciples of all nations, baptizing them in the name of the Father and of the Son and of the Holy Spirit, and teaching them to obey everything that I have commanded you. And remember, I am with you always, to the end of the age.*
> (*Matthew 28:18–20*)

NEL

The disciples did as Jesus asked. They began a world mission to tell people about Jesus and the God he proclaimed. First, they went to their own people: the Jews. Then they went to anyone who was willing to hear.

The disciples told people what they had experienced in following Jesus: how Jesus had been open to others, how he loved the poor, how he made the outcast and the sinner feel that they belonged, how God forgives freely and asks his followers to do the same. They presented Jesus as the prophet of God's love who loves everyone, even enemies, and talked about how God acted in this world through the death and resurrection of Jesus. Life was to be a gift of service to others, no matter who they were.

The work the disciples did was revolutionary. What Jesus proclaimed often did not fit the cultures of the time. To people in the Roman Empire, Christians were dangerous. Their lord was Jesus, not the emperor. They refused to worship the emperor. In particular, they wanted to turn upside down the usual relationships between Jews and Romans, Greeks and barbarians, the free and the slaves, rich and poor, men and women. Humans were to be brother and sister to each other in the name of Jesus. To many people in the Roman Empire, this view did not make sense.

The second-century Roman historian Suetonius saw Christians as followers of a "new and dangerous superstition." Others called them "vain and insane," or said that they were "filled with hatred of the human race." Many Christians were hunted down and martyred, killed for their faith. Yet, Christianity grew into a powerful movement.

Christians attracted people by their example, by their new understanding of God, and by their love, which broke down many of the barriers that existed between people in the Roman Empire.

Yet, even though the very first Christians were Jews, Christians and Jews did not succeed in maintaining good relationships with one another. For all sorts of reasons, Jews and Christians soon came to a parting of the ways. Some of the bitterness Christians felt toward the Jews at times shows through in the Gospels.

A Closer Look

During its first 300 years, Christianity was an illegal religion in the Roman Empire. Christians suffered great persecution. In order to survive, Christianity became a secret religion. To recognize each other, Christians used to wear the symbol of a fish. The letters of the Greek word for fish—*ichthus*—formed an acronym for "Jesus Christ, God's Son, Saviour."

Fast Fact

The Roman Empire was the world power at the time of Jesus's life and for some 400 years after. Its leader was the emperor, who was worshipped as a god.

Check Your Understanding

1. Explain what Jesus meant when he gave his disciples the great commission.
2. Describe how the disciples carried out the great commission.

Think About It

3. The idea of being called insane or being killed for one's faith would seem outrageous to most people today. In writing or in a drawing, respond to the threat Christians faced in the first centuries of the religion.

Making It Personal

4. State what you think a Catholic might say and do to bring the Gospel of Jesus to people.

The Spread of Christianity, 100 CE–600 CE

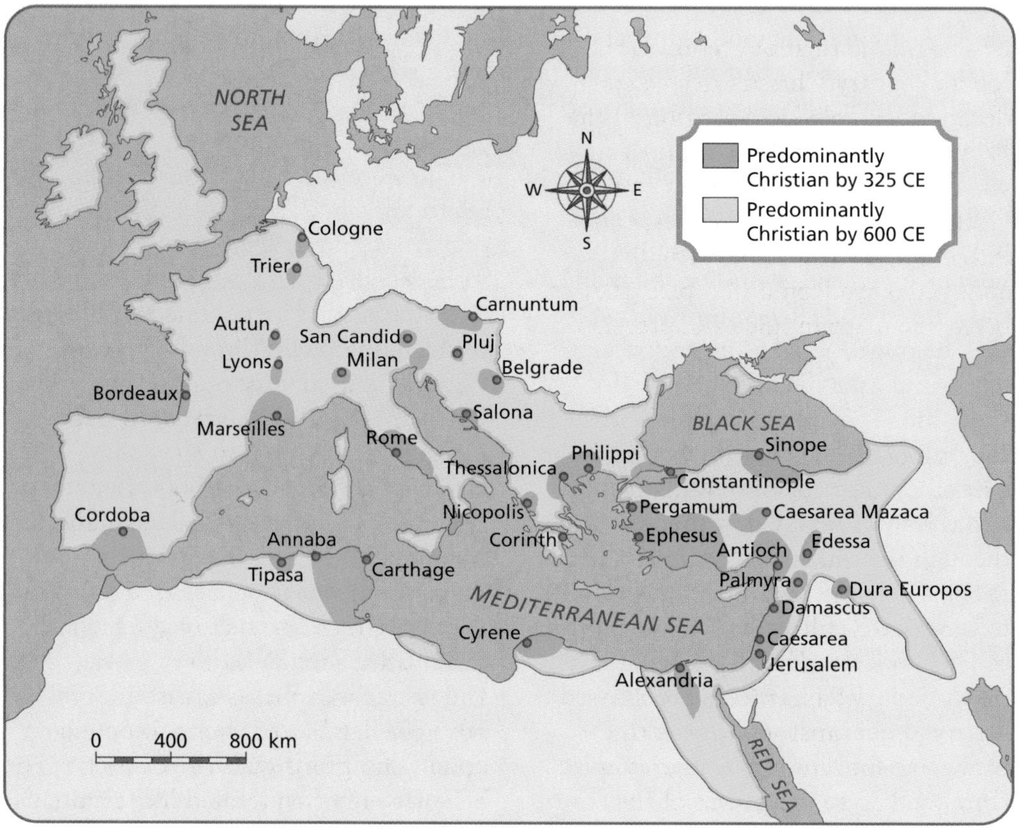

The Spread of Christianity. As Christianity spread, the early approach to community changed. The Christian community became more organized, more like an institution. This development was unavoidable, because so many people from all over the empire were joining. However, the ideal remained the same. Christianity was to be a community of love.

Tertullian. Tertullian was one of the first Roman Christian theologians. A lawyer and writer, he was instrumental in making Christianity an important movement in the Roman Empire in the late first and early second centuries. He coined the word "Trinity" to describe the three persons of God.

Christianity and the Roman Empire

The first stage of Christianity's outreach was done by the disciples, following the example of Jesus. The second stage started in the second century, when Christianity began to make inroads into the Roman Empire.

By the beginning of the second century, preachers and healers had already gone into many of the cities of the empire. People were drawn to Christianity by the example of these preachers and healers. They healed the sick and formed powerful communities. But, Christians were outsiders, strangers in the Roman Empire, a minority of simple people, most of whom had little education.

A Religion of the Learned

Things changed after the second century. From the third century on, some great scholars joined the Christian movement. They were able to translate the Christian message into the language of Greek philosophy, the dominant philosophy of the Roman Empire. Their knowledge and their schools became popular. Gradually, Christianity became the religion not only of the poor and uneducated, but also of the learned. Christians became the cultured people, the intellectuals. They became the driving force of the empire. Over time, Christians began to feel like insiders, like true citizens of the empire.

Those who were not Christians came to be seen as inferior, not just in religious terms, but often also socially and economically. The old Roman religion lost its power. People stopped identifying with it and became Christian, even though Roman emperors continued to persecute Christians.

Christianity: The Religion of the Empire

In a dramatic turn of events, in the fourth century Christianity was declared the sole legal religion of the Roman Empire. In later centuries, whenever other groups, such as the Goths or the Germanic tribes, came into contact with and eventually conquered the Roman Empire, they became Christian. (See Chapter 5, The Story of Christianity.)

A Mission to the World

The fall of the Roman Empire and Christianity's new status changed the social structure of Christianity. With the empire weakened and disappearing in the West, the institutional structures of the Church filled the void. Bishops became civic leaders, judges, and even rulers. In the East, where the Roman Empire was transformed into the Byzantine Empire, the Church was closely allied to the power of the court, which came to be seen as a reflection of the heavenly kingdom.

In both cases, attention became focused more on the Church and its internal structures and dynamics. The ideal was to make the Church a holy place, a holy people, so that those who gathered there could share in the love of God. Slowly, the belief arose that those who did not gather in this way could not share in God's love and salvation.

The Middle Ages

How did Christianity relate to other religions during the Middle Ages? Between 600 and 1500, Christianity became the dominant religion of Europe. From the Roman Empire, Christianity spread north and east, into the Scandinavian countries and far into Russia. Most of this evangelization was the work of monks who set up monasteries across Europe. They kept alive the tradition of welcoming others to Christianity.

Goths. The Roman Empire fell because of tribes such as the Goths from Eastern Europe. These tribes invaded the empire a number of times and finally conquered Rome. The tribes that swept across the empire became the basis for the Europe that emerged after the fall of Rome. This photograph is a mosaic of a Goth king found in a palace in Constantinople.

Once it was established throughout Europe, Christianity became an intellectual, cultural, and spiritual powerhouse as great universities, monasteries, and cathedrals were opened. The Church also became a strong political force.

The belief that one had to recognize Jesus as God's Messiah in order to be saved led Church leaders to pressure, and sometimes force, those who did not believe this to convert. People who openly disagreed with the Church's beliefs were often treated like criminals.

European Cathedrals. As Christianity became stronger and more widespread throughout Europe, the Church created the great institutions of Western civilization, such as universities, cities, trade halls, guilds, monasteries, and churches. Among these institutions, people still prize the massive, ornate cathedrals found in most European cities, such as this one in Rheims, France. **Why do you think building huge and highly decorated cathedrals was so important to Christians during this period?**

Kazimierz, Poland. This painting shows Kazimierz, now a district of Krakow, Poland, sometime during the 1800s. It was once a separate city and the site of a Jewish community from the fourteenth century until the Second World War.

Relations with Other Religions in the Middle Ages

In the Middle Ages, Christians had little contact with members of other religions. The two exceptions were Jews and Muslims.

Catholics and Jews

Jews lived among Christians in many parts of Europe. They had formed communities around the Mediterranean many centuries before Christ was born. After the destruction of Jerusalem by the Roman Empire in the second century, Jews no longer had a geographical centre of faith. As a minority in many parts of Europe, their lives were not easy. In certain cities, they were forced to live in separate neighbourhoods, called ghettos. They sometimes had to wear distinctive clothing. During the crusades to recapture the Holy Land, which had been seized by Muslims, some Christian soldiers attacked and destroyed Jewish towns along the Danube and Rhine rivers. Such attacks continued in later centuries.

Catholics and Muslims

The relations between Catholics and Muslims were mostly a story of armed conflict. Most of the conflicts were political ones. In the eighth century, Muslim armies attacked and conquered northern Africa, which at the time was nearly all Christian. They then attacked Christian Europe from the south, through Spain, which became an Islamic country, as well as from the east, through what is now Turkey. Christian armies succeeded in stopping their advances. In his desire to keep the holy city of Jerusalem accessible to Christian pilgrims and to help the Byzantine Christians in Constantinople, the pope called for crusades against the Muslim armies. Nine such crusades took place between 1095 and 1272.

Christian armies were successful for a time and held Jerusalem. In the end, however, the Muslims recaptured the Holy Land in 1291.

The Siege of Antioch in the First Crusade (1098). Huge armies of Christians from across Europe gathered to do battle with Muslims.

By 1453, Muslims had conquered Constantinople. They then advanced to the gates of Vienna in 1529.

Until they were decisively stopped in 1683, Muslim armies were seen as a constant threat to Christian Europe. A number of Christian writers of the time, including Raymond Lull (thirteenth century), St. Francis of Assisi (thirteenth century), and William of Tripoli (thirteenth century) tried to engage Islam in dialogue, but such attempts were rare. In Spain, after the Catholic King Ferdinand and Queen Isabella managed to recapture their territory from the Muslim armies, they expelled all Muslims and Jews from their land.

A Closer Look

In 1219, Francis of Assisi travelled to Egypt during one of the crusades to preach peace. There is a story of Francis passing through the armies of the crusaders to speak to the sultan of Egypt. In order to convince the sultan of the truth of Christianity, Francis engaged him and his Muslim scholars in a wager by fire. Francis proposed that whoever should survive the test by fire could claim his religion to be true. Francis said that he would go first. If he came out unharmed, the sultan would have to accept Christ as the true God. The test never took place, but the sultan was so impressed that he allowed Francis to preach about Jesus in Egypt.

St. Francis of Assisi. This fresco by the Italian painter Giotto (1267–1337) portrays St. Francis of Assisi and his ordeal by fire before the sultan of Egypt.

Check Your Understanding

1. Make your own timeline of events from the time Christianity entered into the Greek culture around the Mediterranean until the end of the Middle Ages.

Think About It

2. In a small group, discuss the high and low points of Christianity during the Middle Ages.

Making It Personal

3. Compare the challenges of living as Catholics today with the challenges Christians faced in the Middle Ages.

Akbar. Akbar, the great mogul (ruler) of India (1556–1605) and a Muslim, showed keen interest in world religions. He invited Catholic Jesuit priests to come and debate with him. European Christians were excited about his invitation. They hoped to bring Jesus's message of love to the people of India. But, Akbar was not interested in becoming a Christian. He was simply curious about many things, including religions. He was a good model for dialogue.

A Closer Look

With the separation in the Church, working for unity among the Christian churches became necessary. The dialogue among the churches to arrive at unity is called ecumenical dialogue. You will explore the Reformation and dialogue among Christians in Chapter 5.

Modern Times: 1500–1950

Christian Europe underwent some dramatic changes around the year 1500. These changes were to lead to the birth of a whole new world: the modern world. For Christianity, modern times began with a serious and painful separation in the Church through the Protestant Reformation. Some groups called for major changes or reforms to the Church. The tension in the Church grew so much that some groups broke away from the Church to create the Lutheran, Reformed, Anglican, and Anabaptist communities. The Church was no longer united. Princes and kings felt forced to choose sides. Then wars erupted between Catholics and Protestants, with various political undercurrents, making everything even more complicated.

Colonization and the Spread of Christianity

The Reformation happened just as a whole new world opened up before European Christianity—a world that no one could have imagined before. It began with a new awareness of lands beyond Europe. In 1492, Christopher Columbus set out to find a shorter route to India and "discovered" America. Other such journeys of exploration followed.

Christians were shocked to learn that the millions of people in these faraway places had never heard of Christ. Since these people were not baptized, Christians thought they would be barred from heaven.

As European nations vied with each other to claim these new areas as colonies, they also felt duty-bound to preach the Gospel and make these new peoples Christian. Right behind the colonizers of the Americas, Asia, and Africa came Christian missionaries wishing to evangelize the people. In this era, at the beginning of modern times, Christians felt that people belonging to other religions needed to be converted to Christianity in order to know God's salvation in Christ. In their eyes, other religions were simply "false" religions.

The Age of Dialogue: 1950–Present

By the middle of the twentieth century, the missionary approaches to other religions started to change. The Church no longer wanted to be identified with the colonial practices of European nations. This insight led to new approaches in missionary work and new kinds of relationships with other world religions. Mutual condemnation was slowly replaced by dialogue.

The Catholic Church first entered this dialogue through the missionaries who were living in the various countries around the world. Here are some of the changes that occurred in the approach to other religions:

- There was a realization that there were good, worthy elements in other religions.
- There was a renewed emphasis on bringing not just the message of the Gospel to other nations, but also its impact, by focusing on the well-being of other peoples and providing socio-economic development in the areas of education, medicine, and social aid.
- Salvation was understood as being not only for the next world, but for this world also.
- The focus was not only on the individual, but also on the community and society.

A more public and official involvement began through the Second Vatican Council, a gathering of the world's Catholic bishops in Rome between 1962 and 1965. A number of documents emerged from the Council that dramatically changed the Church's relationship to other religions. We will spend the rest of the chapter exploring these changes.

Dialogue with Christians and Buddhists. Cardinal Jean-Louis Tauran, president of the Pontifical Council on Interreligious Dialogue (right), meets with Master Xuecheng, vice-chairman of the Buddhist Association of China, at the World Conference on Dialogue.

A Closer Look

An ecumenical council is the highest exercise of the Church's power. All the bishops of the Church come together with the pope, the bishop of Rome, to decide on issues of importance for the whole Church. In the 2000-year history of the Church, there have been 21 ecumenical councils. The councils are identified by the places where they are held. The most recent ecumenical council—Vatican II—was held between 1962 and 1965 at Vatican City in Rome.

Check Your Understanding

1. Explain to a partner what happened when European nations began their journeys of "discovery."
2. What is colonialism? How did the Christian Church use a colonial approach to religion?
3. Summarize how the Church began to change its approach to other religions after 1950.

Think About It

4. In the nineteenth century, many religious communities were set up in Europe and in North America by Catholic missionaries. In your opinion, what made the missionaries leave their families and their countries of birth to preach the Gospel?

Making It Personal

5. Think about something you did in the past that had a negative impact. What changes would you make if you could do it all over again?

Catholics and Other Religions in the Twentieth and Early Twenty-First Centuries

A Closer Look

Pope John Paul II spoke to young Muslims at Casablanca, Morocco, on August 19, 1985. Here is an excerpt from his speech:

> People do not accept their differences.
> They do not know each other sufficiently.
> They reject those who have not the same civilization.
> They refuse to help each other.
> They are unable to free themselves from egoism and from self-conceit.
> But God created all [people] equal in dignity, though different with regard to gifts and to talents.
> [Humanity] is a whole where each one has [a] part to play;
> the worth of the various peoples and of the diverse cultures must be recognized.
> The world is as it were a living organism;
> each one has something to receive from the others, and has something to give to them.

In many ways, the world became smaller in the twentieth century. Telephone, radio, television, long-distance air travel, the Internet, communication satellites, and a host of other technological advances alerted people within hours or even minutes about events happening in the farthest corners of Earth. Everything was becoming both global and local.

These trends also had an impact on world religions. The Catholic Church's relations with other religions changed dramatically. One of the most significant changes was the growing awareness that all human beings of Earth form one human race, one world.

Religions had more and more contact with each other. Until the mid-twentieth century, they had often been strangers to each other. But, as the century progressed, they began to show a desire to understand one another. They realized that they must understand their differences so that they might work together to make the world more livable. Thus began the long and difficult process of removing the prejudices, distrust, and historical memories that had been such sources of conflict in the past.

We realize today that the work of dialogue has just begun. Religions have started to speak with one another. For Catholics, the first real steps were made at the Second Vatican Council. Some bishops, especially bishops from Asia, who daily rubbed shoulders

Dialogue with Sikhs and Jews. Mohinder Singh (left) and René Sirat from the Sikh and Jewish delegations, respectively, talk about peace during the Peace Summit in Assisi.

Second Vatican Council. Led by Pope John XXIII, the meeting of the worldwide Catholic clergy from 1962 to 1965 took place in St. Peter's Basilica in Vatican City, Rome. It is known as the Second Vatican Council.

with people of other religions and struggled to interact with them, demanded that the topic be discussed at the Council. At their insistence, it was added to the agenda of the Council. From these first steps, the dialogue has continued to grow.

What are the guidelines that the Second Vatican Council concluded should be considered in dialogue with other religions? We will look at them under the following headings:

- God's Salvation Is Offered to All People
- Jesus Christ Is Present in Other Religions
- The Holy Spirit Is at Work in Other Religions
- Dialogue Is Part of the Church's Mission

God's Salvation Is Offered to All People

Since Vatican II, the Catholic Church has taught that all human beings can be saved, even if they are not baptized or do not believe in Christ. This is because Catholics believe God—Father, Son, and Spirit— is the creator of all humanity. All humans are images of the same God. Human beings are one in spite of all their differences. According to the Catholic tradition, therefore, there is only one way of **salvation**. It comes as a gift from God, offered to all.

Implication

For Catholics, other religions are ways of life that are filled "with a profound religious sense" (*On the Relation of the Church to Non-Christian Religions,* #2). They can lead to salvation—as all humans can attain salvation by following their conscience. Here is what the Church says: "Those also can attain to salvation who through no fault of their own do not know the Gospel of Christ or His Church, yet sincerely seek God" (*The Constitution on the Church,* #16).

The fact that all human beings find their origin as well as their ultimate happiness in God unites them in a deep and powerful way, whatever their religion. This unity of origin and purpose expresses itself in a universal quest for meaning: all people, whether

A Closer Look

The documents of the Catholic Church are usually given the title of the first two words of the text. The texts are usually written in Latin. For example, the first two words in Latin of *On the Relation of the Church to Non-Christian Religions* are *Nostra aetate*, which means "In this age of ours." The Latin title of another document, *Ad gentes*, means "To the nations." The English title is *On the Mission Activity of the Church. The Dogmatic Constitution on the Church* is the English title of *Lumen gentium*, which means "Light of the nations."

Salvation

A word meaning, literally, "made whole" or "made healthy"; Catholics use this term to describe how people are made whole in Christ and freed from the power of sin and death; salvation is a gift from God, not something that people can obtain for themselves they realize it or not, are looking for God. And all religions are an expression of that quest. This is why Catholics can see "whatever good is in the minds and hearts of men, whatever good lies latent in the religious practices and cultures of diverse peoples" (*The Constitution on the Church*, #17).

Jesus Christ Is Present in Other Religions

The first reason why Catholics find themselves connected to people who belong to other religions is that Catholics believe God to be the creator of all human beings. The Christian God is Father, Son, and Holy Spirit. And so, if all human beings, created by God, are in the image of God, they are the image of the Trinity. That means that they also reflect Jesus Christ, who for Christians is the Son of God.

What makes interreligious dialogue difficult is that for Christians, Jesus is the only way to God. Does that mean that for Christians, other religions are obstacles to the search for God or are not ways of holiness? Here the Church is very careful. The Church believes that God wants all people to be saved, including those who are not members of the Church. The Church also believes that there is one universal plan of salvation. In other words, whether they realize it or not, all humans take part in that plan of God. In looking at other religions, the bishops gathered at the Second Vatican Council said that, in some manner, Christ was present in other religions.

Vatican II said that all authentic religions have something in them that reflects Jesus Christ. It does not say that the fullness of Christ is in them. That fullness, the Church says, can be found only where Jesus is fully worshipped and followed. However, other authentic religions contain "a ray" of the truth who is Christ. In other religions, the Church says, we can find "seeds of the Word." In a mysterious way, then, Jesus is active in these other religions. What we know of Christ through the Gospels and the teaching of the Church is sometimes reflected in these religions. In other words, for Catholics, what in other religions is a reflection of God's way of salvation cannot contradict or replace what was said and revealed through Jesus of Nazareth. Jesus remains the way, the truth, and the life (*On the Relation of the Church to Non-Christian Religions*, #2, and *On the Mission Activity of the Church*, #11).

For this reason, all people of goodwill are "partners in the Paschal Mystery of Christ." Sincere believers in other religions are somehow caught up in that Paschal Mystery, in the life, death, and resurrection of Christ. The love that shines in them is not separate from the love that God has for all humanity in Christ.

A Closer Look

"Paschal" comes from the Greek word *pascha*. It refers to Easter. The Paschal Mystery is the celebration of the life, death, and resurrection of Jesus, the central symbol of God's love for humanity.

Implication

Other religions do not understand themselves as Catholics see them. If Catholics see some elements of other religions as "a ray" of Christ or a "seed" of the Word, it is not because other religions acknowledge the presence of Christ in their religion. Though Catholics may speak of these rays of truth, they are often hidden, seen only by those Catholics who have intense contact with these religions. Learning about another religion is like learning a new language. It takes time and a lot of real communication to discern Christ's presence in these religions.

If Christ is present in other religions, Catholics will want to speak openly about Christ in all their conversations with other religions. Speaking openly about Christ may show where there are points of similarity and unity between Christianity and another religion. That is why Catholics are never to hide their faith in Jesus Christ.

NEL

Dialogue with Christians and Muslims. Pope Benedict XVI meeting Mustafa Ceric, the Muslim religious leader of Bosnia. The pope has frequently met with Muslims to increase mutual trust. **Do you think that meetings such as these are worthwhile? Why or why not?**

Faith in Christ is what Catholics want others to understand about Christianity. Christ is the great mystery of God's love at the centre of Catholic faith. This is the message that Catholics will bring to the conversation, a message they themselves will understand more as they enter into dialogue.

The Holy Spirit Is at Work in Other Religions

If God the Father and the Son are present in other religions, how is the Holy Spirit at work in them?

Catholics attribute to the Holy Spirit the mission of guiding all people toward the image of Christ. The Holy Spirit completes and realizes what Jesus Christ set in motion during his life on Earth. What needed to be completed? For one thing, Jesus was at first known only to a small group. Jesus's story needed to be told everywhere. As Jesus said on that night to the disciples who were at the table with him, "I still have many things to say to you, but you cannot bear them now" (John 16:12). The full meaning of the message and deeds of Jesus was not yet clear to the disciples. It would unfold in a way as yet unknown to them. He told them this was the task of the Holy Spirit. Jesus called the Spirit an advocate, a guide to lead everyone "into all truth" (John 15:13).

Catholics believe that this guide, the Holy Spirit, works within each person. The Vatican Council expressed this belief when it stated that "the Holy Spirit in a manner known only to God offers to every man the possibility of being associated with this paschal mystery." Acknowledging this action of the Spirit in the hearts of all people leads the Church to recognize that there is "much that is good, true and holy" in other religions.

Implication

Catholics keep in mind that "[the Spirit's] presence and activity are universal" (*On the Relation of the Church to Non-Christian Religions*, #28). The Spirit is everywhere. The mission of the Spirit is to complete the work of Jesus and lead people to the full truth of Jesus—truths that Jesus's disciples could not yet bear. Today, Catholics believe that they may also come to a fuller truth about Jesus by listening to the workings of God in all religions.

The same Holy Spirit lives in other religions. There is only one Holy Spirit. There is not one Holy Spirit for the Church and another for other religions. What the Spirit does in other religions will not contradict what the Spirit makes flourish in the Church. The task of Catholics is to discover what the Spirit brings alive in other religions. It is the intent of interreligious dialogue, therefore, to discern where the Spirit is flourishing in the other religions.

While many differences may exist among people, these differences "are less important than the unity, which by contrast, is radical, basic and decisive" (Pope John Paul II, December 22, 1986).

A Closer Look

Be careful! What Catholics say about the presence of Christ and the Spirit in other religions is not how other religions understand themselves. Speaking in these terms is the way Catholics want to respect what God is doing in other religions. That is why dialogue with religions is so important for Catholics: it strengthens their own faith in God's activity.

Dialogue Is Part of the Church's Mission

Interreligious dialogue is itself an act of the Holy Spirit leading people to the truth. As the Second Vatican Council said, "All [people] are called to be part of this catholic unity of the people of God … And there belong to or are related to it in various ways, the Catholic faithful, all who believe in Christ, and indeed the whole of [humanity], for all [human beings] are called by the grace of God to salvation" (*Dogmatic Constitution on the Church*, #13).

Catholics believe that the Holy Spirit "flourishes" in the Church (*Catechism of the Catholic Church*, #749). That is, it comes to life especially in the Church.

Implication

If the Spirit is indeed at work in religions, there are many implications. First, it means that these gifts of the Spirit must be found and appreciated. Also, it means that these gifts must be received by the Church. It is the Church's mission to listen intently to what other religions have to say and to discern what is of God and what is not of God. Here, dialogue becomes essential.

The Church accepts that God may be found in the prayers, practices, insights, and traditions of other religions. Only in intense dialogue will it be possible to hear what they bear as wisdom within them. If the Church fails to be receptive to other religions, it may be failing in its own mission to proclaim Christ. As Pope John Paul II said, "Every form of the Spirit's presence is to be welcomed with respect and gratitude" (*On the Church's Missionary Mandate*, #30).

Check Your Understanding

1. Explain what it means to say that God wants to save all people.
2. Describe how Catholics might discover traces of Christ in other religions.
3. Explain the role of the Holy Spirit in the Catholic faith. How is the Spirit active in other religions?

Think About It

4. With a partner, discuss why you think that Catholics must participate in interreligious dialogue.

Making It Personal

5. How should you interact with people from other religions if you believe that God is at work within Muslims, Hindus, Jews, and others?

Proclamation and Mission

The history of the Catholic Church through the centuries is full of good and courageous works, and of holy and faithful people. In its zeal, it has also at times lost sight of the dignity of all people and of the possibility that God is already at work in the hearts of those who belong to other religions.

Today, Catholics still firmly believe that what God did through Jesus Christ is essential for human life to flourish. For this reason, the Church must and always will proclaim the Good News of the Gospel. The Church would not be the Church unless it proclaimed Jesus Christ. That is why the mission of evangelization, of bringing the Gospel to others, must continue.

In fact, new efforts are being made to bring the Gospel to countries, particularly in the West, where people have given in to doubt and skepticism. But, it needs to be proclaimed in a new way. Pope John Paul II called for a "new evangelization"—new in its ardour, its method, and its expression. He explained, "This should be done however with the respect due to the different paths of different people and with sensitivity to the diversity of cultures in which the Christian message must be planted, in such a way that the particular values of each people will not be rejected but purified and brought to their fullness" (Pope John Paul II, "At the beginning of the New Millenium").

Part of the new way of evangelization is entering into dialogue with other religions. The first aim of this dialogue is not conversion, but mutual understanding.

A Closer Look

A sign of the importance of this dialogue for the Catholic Church is the existence of a Pontifical Council for Interreligious Dialogue at the Vatican. The Council explains its methodology this way: "Dialogue is a two-way communication. It implies speaking and listening, giving and receiving, for mutual growth and enrichment. It includes witness to one's own faith as well as an openness to that of the other. It is not a betrayal of the mission of the Church, nor is it a new method of conversion to Christianity."

World Day of Prayer. On October 27, 1986, Pope John Paul II met with religious leaders from various Christian churches and other world religions to pray for peace. He underlined the fundamental unity of the human race, in its origin and its destiny, and the role of the Church as an effective sign of this unity. He emphasized the importance of interreligious dialogue, while at the same time reaffirming the Church's duty to announce Jesus Christ to the world.

Superficial. Canadian artist Michel de Broin's 2004 sculpture is of a rock partially covered with mirrors in the middle of a forest. Called *Superficial*, this sculpture is a great image of dialogue. All of us are part rock. There is something solid in us that is our foundation, our deepest self. At the same time, our deepest self is also open to others: reflecting the others from whom we receive our identity. We are forever bouncing between the one and the other. Dialogue is like that. We receive and we give. **Draw your own interpretation of dialogue.**

Four Types of Interreligious Dialogue

How do Catholics become part of this dialogue? Interreligious dialogue is not only the task of scholars and experts. All Catholics are part of it. After all, the dialogue's aim is not merely to arrive at mutual understanding and friendly relations. It reaches deeper. All Catholics can give witness to what they believe. All can deepen their religious commitment. All can seek to understand the other's way of life.

In 1991, the Church's Pontifical Council for Interreligious Dialogue outlined four ways of achieving this dialogue.

1. The Dialogue of Everyday Life

The population of Canada is now so diverse that Canadians are likely to meet someone from another religion nearly every day. The dialogue of everyday life is the dialogue of courtesy, openness, and becoming good neighbours. Human beings share much in common. We can be joyful or sorrowful with others. We can be ready to help others when they are in need. We can seek to enter into their world and understand the challenges they may have living in Canada, where they are part of a minority religion and culture.

2. The Dialogue of Action

The Church's mission is not only to proclaim the Gospel of Jesus. The Gospel of Jesus also aimed to create a new humanity, to take care of the poor and the sick, to bring back those who are excluded, to liberate those who are unfree and addicted. This concern for others, for their full development as persons and their need for freedom, is shared with other religions, as you shall see as you explore the rituals and beliefs of other religions or spiritual beliefs in this resource.

As Christians, Catholics are encouraged to work with members of other religions for the well-being of humanity: to safeguard the rights of individuals, to promote people's aspirations for happiness, to protect nature, to show solidarity with the victims of injustice, and to struggle for peace and justice.

3. The Dialogue of Theological Exchange

It is equally important that Church leaders and theologians take part in serious intellectual dialogues. We need to understand each other's religious traditions, ways of life, and spiritual values. Taking a course such as this one is one way to get involved in the issues and questions.

Once mutual trust has been gained, these exchanges can tackle more difficult issues: bitterness from past actions, inconsistencies in each other's positions, prejudices, and human rights. Catholics will find certain aspects of other religions unacceptable—such as reincarnation, the worshipping of several deities, polygamy, and the caste system.

These difficult areas must become part of what Pope Benedict XVI called the dialogue of truth. But, we must also remember what Pope John Paul II said: the differences that exist between people "are less important than the unity, which, by contrast, is radical, basic and decisive."

4. The Dialogue of Religious Experience

In several parts of Canada, people from different religious traditions come together to speak with each other about their spirituality. Here, Catholics may explain to Hindus or Muslims their prayer life or how they meditate. They may talk about their beliefs and how they search for God. Their dialogue partners share their own practices. This type of spiritual dialogue can lead not only to a deep appreciation of what moves members of other religions, but also to a deeper appreciation of our own faith.

Interfaith Action for Peace. Muslim and Jewish members of the Jerusalem-based Interfaith Encounter Association share a kosher Ramadan meal they jointly prepared for the Muslim holy month of Ramadan. The meal was prepared with kosher food and utensils out of respect for the Jewish participants. These sorts of interfaith groups have made serious efforts to heal the hostilities between Christians, Jews, and Muslims.

Listening Circle. As part of the Sulha Peace Project, Israeli Jews and Palestinian Muslim youth gather in a listening circle (Sulhita) at the Gaza border in 2007.

Check Your Understanding

1. Explain why the Church must continue to perform its mission of evangelization in today's world.
2. In your own words, describe the four types of dialogue.

Think About It

3. Research listening circles. What are the ground rules for participating in a listening circle? Who takes part in them? What kinds of communities use them? Compare a listening circle with some other form of dialogue, for example, a debate.

Making It Personal

4. Have you ever taken part in any of the four types of dialogue—such as with strangers, friends, co-workers or classmates, or on a committee or team? Describe your experience.

What I Have Learned

In this chapter, I learned about

- the Canadian experience of living together with others
- Canadian legislation regarding multiculturalism
- the Canadian experience of religious pluralism
- some ground rules for living together with other religions
- the need to go beyond living together: the call to dialogue
- a brief history of Christianity and its relationship to other religions
  - the "great commission of Jesus" to teach and baptize
  - Christianity's interaction with the Greek and Roman worlds
  - Christianity as the religion of the Western world
  - Christianity in the age of colonialism and modern times
  - the new interaction with world religions: interreligious dialogue
- how Catholics view other religions
  - God's salvation is offered to all people
  - Jesus Christ is present in other religions
  - the Holy Spirit is at work in other religions
  - dialogue is part of the Church's mission
- the four types of interreligious dialogue
- the continued mission to proclaim the Gospel to the world

A Prayer for Dialogue

Dear friends, let our sincere dialogue and cooperation inspire all people to ponder the deeper questions of their origin and destiny. May the followers of all religions stand together in defending and promoting life and religious freedom everywhere. By giving ourselves generously to this sacred task—through dialogue and countless small acts of love, understanding and compassion—we can be instruments of peace for the whole human family.

—Pope Benedict XVI, in a meeting with representatives of other religions, Washington, D.C. (April 17, 2008)

Chapter 2 Who Are Catholics?

Catholic Beliefs. The Creed exists in various forms. Below is the form of the Creed said on Holy Saturday. **How would you answer the question "Who are Catholics?" What are some of the beliefs that unite all Catholics across Canada and around the world?**

The Creed

From the liturgy of the Easter Vigil, these questions are addressed to adult candidates for baptism:

"Do you believe in God the Father almighty, creator of heaven and earth?
I do.
Do you believe in Jesus Christ, his only Son, our Lord, who was born of the Virgin Mary, was crucified, died, and was buried, rose from the dead, and is now seated at the right hand of the Father?
I do.
Do you believe in the Holy Spirit, the holy catholic Church, the communion of saints, the forgiveness of sins, the resurrection of the body, and the life everlasting?
I do."

What You Will Learn

To undertake a dialogue with other religions, you must know your own faith tradition as a starting point. For this reason, this book starts by studying the Catholic tradition as a religion.

In this chapter, you will learn about

- Catholics in Canada
- the roots of Catholicism in Jesus of Nazareth
- the power of rituals to introduce people into a religion
- the way rituals shape time, beliefs, and morality
- the Catholic central rituals: the liturgy and the sacraments
- the Catholic way of living time: the feasts
- the core Catholic beliefs: the scriptures and the Creed
- the heart of Catholic moral life: the Sermon on the Mount
- Catholic family life

Personal Recollection

Laura Dufour. Laura Dufour is a student at St. Paul High School in Ottawa.

I am a Roman Catholic Christian. I was baptized when I was five weeks old and since then have celebrated the sacraments of reconciliation, confirmation, and first Eucharist. I go to Mass every Sunday with my family. We give thanks to God before each meal and we grew up saying prayers together before going to bed. Within my family, we have our own special traditions for each of the main liturgical seasons, Advent–Christmas and Lent–Easter.

To live a Christian lifestyle, we must try to follow Jesus's example of loving service. When I was seven years old, my family moved to Waupoos Farm near Ottawa as a resident family for two years. There we helped with the day-to-day operations of the farm, which offers vacation opportunities for families in need. Every week, I saw Christian service in action. I learned that every person has dignity and should be treated with respect. I also learned that the Gospel message has to be put into action.

Since that time, I have tried to use my gifts to serve others. At church, I am a lector (I read from the lectionary or book of readings at Mass), and I help at children's liturgy (the Liturgy of the Word for children). At school, I have been involved with youth ministry and peer helping.

Recently, I went on a Third World awareness trip to the Dominican Republic. This experience has helped me to see my neighbours in the global community with new eyes. This summer, I am returning to the Dominican Republic with my family, as part of a mission trip to build houses.

My faith is the foundation of all that I do.

— **Laura Dufour**

Catholicism in Canada

! A Closer Look

In this book, we use the words "Catholic" and "Christian." Everyone who is baptized in Christ is a Christian. Because there are many Christian traditions, each baptized person also belongs to a particular family of Christians, such as Anglicans, United Church, or Baptists. Catholics are Christians who belong to the Latin or the Eastern Catholic Churches. All Christians are, however, catholic (with a small "c"), because Christ is present in all Christian churches. The word "catholic" means "universal" or "to the whole world": wherever Christ is, all Christians are (*Catechism of the Catholic Church*, #834).

We will explore the traditions of non-Catholic Christians in Chapter 5, The Story of Christianity.

You read in the introduction to this book that you will study world religions through their ritual life. The Catholic tradition—both the Latin Church and the Eastern Churches—has a rich and diverse ritual life.

French Catholics were among the first European settlers to come to Canada, over 400 years ago.

Samuel de Champlain led an expedition to the New World in 1605. He built the first permanent settlements in what is now Nova Scotia. From there, the French spread east and north into what today are Québec, eastern Ontario, and northern Ontario. A majority of French Catholics settled in Québec. As a result, the Catholic Church became very influential in Québec. It was present in every aspect of daily life. It helped to set up the first social services—feeding the hungry, serving the poor, and taking care of orphans and elderly people. It built the first hospitals, and it set up schools so that settlers and their children could be educated.

The Catholic Church became vitally present in the rest of the country as well. Aboriginal peoples who converted to Catholicism, Irish and Scots, and later Italians, Ukrainians, Portuguese, Filipinos, and other Catholic people from countless other countries formed Catholic communities across the land.

Catholics in Canada Today

Although religion, including the Catholic Church, does not play as dominant a role in society today as it did in earlier times, people who state that they are Christians still make up 78 percent of the total population of Canada. Forty-three percent of Canadians are Catholics. Nearly half of these are French-speaking. Because one of every four immigrants to Canada is Roman Catholic, the percentage of Catholics in Canada has stayed fairly stable over the past few decades, even though the birth rate among Canadian-born Catholics is declining. Today, about 75 percent of Catholics in Canada live in Québec, eastern Ontario, the Greater Toronto Area, and New Brunswick (see map on page 33). The other 25 percent live in the other provinces and territories.

Bishop François Montmorency de Laval. François de Laval, 1623–1708, the first bishop of Québec. Bishop Laval organized the Church in Québec and began a seminary (school) where people could study theology. That school eventually grew into Laval University, where thousands of students now study everything from biology to literature.

Percentage of Canadians Who Are Catholic

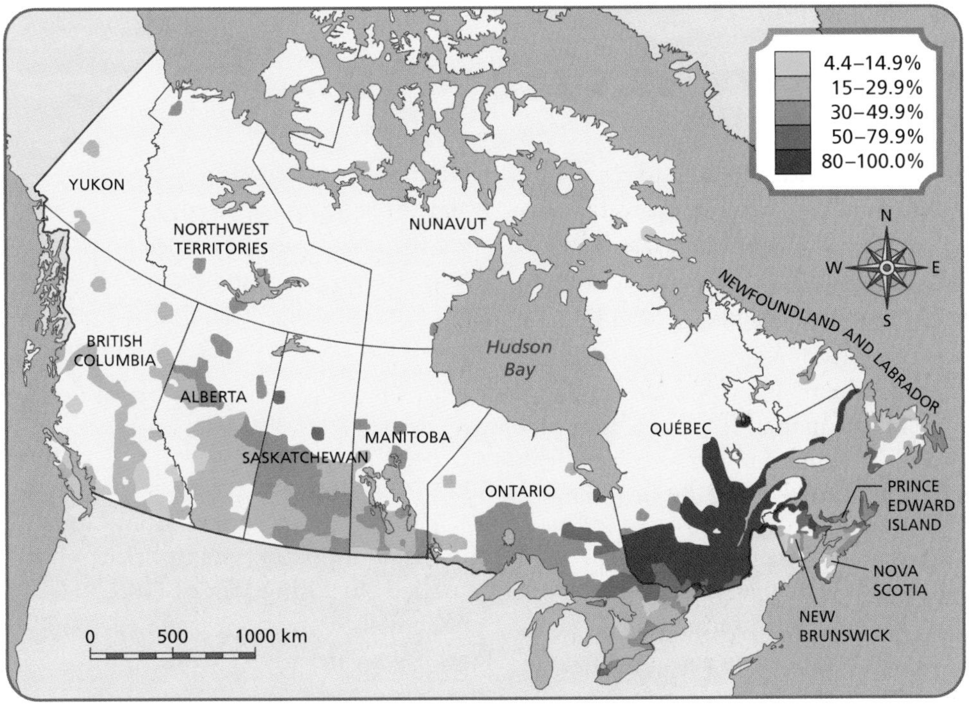

Distribution of Catholics. This map shows the distribution of Catholics in Canada in 2001.

Check Your Understanding

1. When did Catholicism arrive in Canada?
2. Where do we find the greatest number of Catholics in Canada? Why?

Think About It

3. With a partner or in a small group, research and discuss the contributions of the Catholic Church to the early development of social and educational life across Canada.
4. Why do you think the Catholic Church was so influential in Québec when it was first established?

Making It Personal

5. Where did your ancestors come from? When did they arrive in Canada and where did they first settle? Why did they settle where they did?

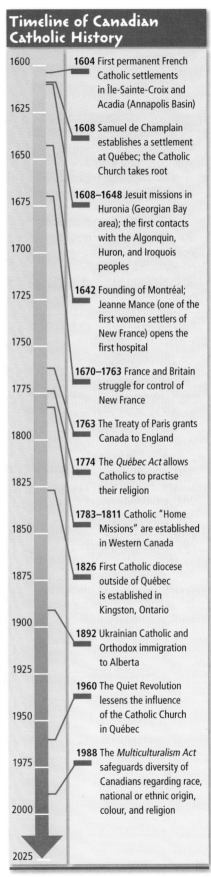

Timeline of Canadian Catholic History

1600, 1625, 1650, 1675, 1700, 1725, 1750, 1775, 1800, 1825, 1850, 1875, 1900, 1925, 1950, 1975, 2000, 2025

1604 First permanent French Catholic settlements in Île-Sainte-Croix and Acadia (Annapolis Basin)

1608 Samuel de Champlain establishes a settlement at Québec; the Catholic Church takes root

1608–1648 Jesuit missions in Huronia (Georgian Bay area); the first contacts with the Algonquin, Huron, and Iroquois peoples

1642 Founding of Montréal; Jeanne Mance (one of the first women settlers of New France) opens the first hospital

1670–1763 France and Britain struggle for control of New France

1763 The Treaty of Paris grants Canada to England

1774 The *Québec Act* allows Catholics to practise their religion

1783–1811 Catholic "Home Missions" are established in Western Canada

1826 First Catholic diocese outside of Québec is established in Kingston, Ontario

1892 Ukrainian Catholic and Orthodox immigration to Alberta

1960 The Quiet Revolution lessens the influence of the Catholic Church in Québec

1988 The *Multiculturalism Act* safeguards diversity of Canadians regarding race, national or ethnic origin, colour, and religion

The History of Catholicism

Fast Fact

"BCE" stands for "Before the Common Era" and covers the same time period as BC ("Before Christ"). "CE" stands for "Common Era," and covers the same time period as AD (*"Anno Domini,"* or Year of the Lord).

Fast Fact

Jesus entered public ministry around 28 CE during the reign of Emperor Tiberius. Jesus was crucified in Jerusalem by the Romans in 30 CE. Many calendars are dated from the birth of Jesus in 1 CE. However, the calculation of Jesus's birth date in the sixth century was incorrect. Today, scholars put Jesus's birth four to six years earlier, in 6 to 4 BCE.

Jesus of Nazareth

Where does the Catholic faith come from? Catholics trace their origins to Jesus of Nazareth, whom they acknowledge to be the Son of God.

Jesus came from a small village called Nazareth in the region of Galilee in the Holy Land (see map). He was the son of Mary and Joseph, who was a carpenter. We know next to nothing about Jesus until he was about 30 years of age. Around the year 28 CE, he travelled to the Jordan River to be baptized by his cousin, a fiery prophet known as John the Baptist. The Gospel of Mark tells us that as Jesus was coming out of the water after being baptized, the heavens were torn apart and the Holy Spirit descended on Jesus like a dove. A voice from heaven said, "You are my Son, the Beloved; with you I am well pleased" (Mark 1:9–11).

After his baptism, Jesus went to Galilee and began a ministry of healing and preaching. What was most striking was the way Jesus spoke about God. His whole ministry was to bring what he called the "kingdom of God." He said that this kingdom was near—in fact, it was already at work in his deeds and works.

Historic Map of Israel

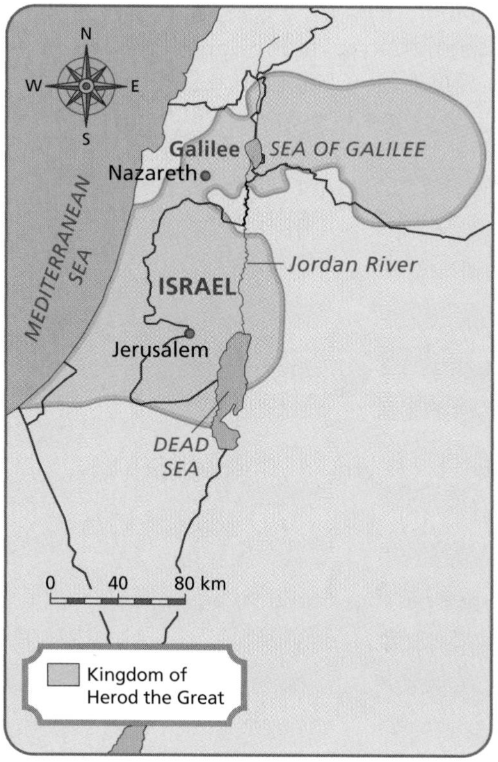

Israel in New Testament Times

Jesus's Death and Resurrection

Jesus attracted many people. Great crowds came to hear him and to witness his healings and to listen to his stories. From among his disciples, he chose 12 for a special mission. He sent them to all the towns and villages of Galilee to proclaim the kingdom of God and to heal people.

The 12 disciples were far from perfect. At times they were impulsive, competitive, and jealous. They did not always understand Jesus's teachings or his mission.

Jesus's message was not well received by Jewish religious leaders. As well, his impact on the unstable political situation in Judea made the Roman authorities uneasy. As a result, Jesus was condemned to death in the year 30 CE. The followers of Jesus were devastated. However, on the third day after his death, some women followers went to his tomb to anoint his body, as was the custom of the time. The tomb was empty!

IF THE RESURRECTION HAPPENED TODAY...
NO BODY... TRACE EVIDENCE OF DNA, NO PROOF OF ANY CRIMINAL MISCHIEF...YEP, I'D SAY YOU HAVE YOURSELF A RESURRECTION!
JERUSALEM CRIME LAB
ARTIZANS.COM

If the Resurrection Happened Today... Physical evidence for the resurrection of Jesus is not available. The belief in the resurrection of Jesus is not based on physical proof but on faith in God.

Catholic Connection

For Christians, Jesus is the incarnation of God: in Jesus, the second person of the Trinity took on a human body. This is why Jesus is considered divine.

That same day, Jesus himself came to meet the frightened and despairing disciples. Jesus wished them peace. He asked for food and ate with them. Their doubts and fears faded away; their faith and courage returned. In experiencing the risen Jesus, the disciples realized that Jesus was from God and was indeed the Messiah. They began to spread this message in Jerusalem and soon in all the major cities of the Roman Empire. From their preaching Christianity was born.

Jesus had promised to send the Holy Spirit as their helper. He repeated that promise during his appearance to the 12 disciples after his resurrection. Fifty days later, the Holy Spirit descended upon them in tongues of fire. Christians celebrate this day as the beginning of the Church.

Catholic Connection

The first meaning of "Church" is assembly or congregation. Christians believe that the Church is the body of Christ, the beginning of God's gathering of all the peoples of the Earth (*Catechism of the Catholic Church,* #751–752).

Jesus as a Member of Many Different Races. Through the Holy Spirit, Christians believe Jesus lives in every believer. For this reason, artists from various nations have pictured him as a member of many different races. **Do these images remind you of images you see at home or at church? How would you explain any differences?**

Make It Your Own: The Crucifix

The two major symbols in the Catholic tradition are the crucifix and the Resurrected Body of Christ. These are the symbols of the Paschal Mystery. The Paschal Mystery refers to the life, death, and resurrection of Jesus. "Paschal" refers to "lamb": Jesus is the Lamb of God who offered himself for us.

A crucifix is an image of a cross with the body of Christ attached. It is a symbol used mainly by Catholic and Orthodox churches. The cross is a symbol that does not have the body of Jesus attached to it. It is mainly used in other Christian churches. The crucifix is a reminder of the ultimate sacrifice and suffering of Christ. The image of the resurrection is a reminder that Jesus conquered death and lives forever. The Paschal Mystery teaches that death and suffering are not the end. Hope, life, and liberation come through suffering and challenges. When Christians feel despair, they can be connected to Jesus. He suffers as well. But, when Christians feel good, and see beauty in the world, they see the resurrection.

Christians live in and can see the coldness and darkness of the world—poverty, war, injustice, suffering, and death. However, Christians are an Easter people: they live in the certain hope of a world of abundance, peace, justice, and even triumph over death. In a spirit of trust, Christians help to bring about the change for which they hope.

In the deepest experiences of poverty, people like Mother Teresa and Archbishop Oscar Romero step forward as hope and comfort. In the face of a culture of death, our Church speaks a message of life. In the name of faith, Catholic men and women all over the world shelter the widow and the orphan, give food to those who are hungry, and water to those who thirst. In the name of Jesus and the Church, faith-filled Catholics clothe the naked, comfort the dying, and shelter the homeless poor.

Christians are not people who wallow in the crucifixion, but who dance in the light of the resurrection. The Passion of our Lord ends with the empty tomb. Such hope is Christianity's gift to the world. From death, life and healing emerge. From pain and suffering come deep peace and understanding. Such virtues fuel just action in the world.

Crucifix. In the Christian tradition, the cross was used from early on as a symbol of Christianity. It is a paradoxical image of God: How can God be connected with an instrument used to execute criminals? Hence the cross is a symbol of the mystery of God.

Activities

1. Draw a large crucifix on Bristol board. Then, draw a large image of the resurrected Jesus on another piece of Bristol board. Using images found in magazines, newspapers, and from Internet sources, cover the body of Jesus on the crucifix with images and words that show suffering and negativity in our world. Then cover the body of the resurrected Jesus with images and/or words of hope, goodness, and bounty in our world. Display the collages together in your classroom or throughout the school.
2. Write a one-page reflection describing the images you used and your thoughts about them. Be sure to include a discussion of one example of crucifixion and one example of resurrection. How do these images relate to the notion of moving from death to life?

Check Your Understanding

1. What is the story of Jesus's life? What was his main message?
2. What attracted people to Jesus?
3. Explain how Christianity began.

Think About It

4. How do different images of Jesus reflect the incarnation of God?
5. How do the two major symbols of the Catholic Church, the crucifix and the Resurrected Body of Jesus, help you understand Catholicism more deeply?

Making It Personal

6. What is your favourite image of Jesus Christ?

Rituals

The Catholic tradition, as part of Christianity, is structured as and acts as a religion. This makes it possible for us to find similarities between the Catholic religion and other religions. One of the main points of comparison is ritual structure. All religions use rituals to enact what they live and believe.

Each of the following sections, looking at time, community, beliefs, moral life, and family life, begins with a reflection on the power of rituals, and then shows how rituals function in Catholicism.

Rituals: The Building Blocks of Religion

The Need for Religion

A Chinese family enters a restaurant in Vancouver's Chinatown. They sit at a large round table, leaving an empty chair and an extra place set where no one sits. The Wong family always sets an extra place. "You can't leave out our ancestors," Nelly Wong explains. "They need to be cared for in the afterlife and they help us." Before she serves a meal, Nelly always briefly places the food before a picture of her grandfather, who died some years earlier, and kneels and touches the ground with her forehead. What the Wongs do as part of their meals is one way Chinese people venerate (honour) their ancestors. It is a religious action or ritual.

We human beings would not have become who we are without religion. We need religion because it gives our lives meaning. Two capabilities set us apart from all other life forms: language and ritual actions.

The Importance of Stories

Humans have created meaningful explanations about their place on Earth, usually in the form of stories called **myths**. From this set of meanings, cultures are formed. Myths tell us about persons, events, or actions by relating stories about their origins. A myth of the creation of the first man or woman tells us a truth about man and woman, their origin in God, their relationship, marriage, children, and so on. This type of story is neither history nor fiction, but a myth: a way of telling a deep truth.

The Importance of Rituals in Religion. The central ritual of Christianity is the receiving of communion, when the participants eat and drink the gift of the Body and Blood of Christ.

Myths
Stories of how things came to be

Holy
Describes what is spiritually whole, sound, virtuous, or acceptable to God

Religion has played a key role in creating these stories and cultures. In expressing the meaning of their lives, humans acknowledge that their lives are bonded to something **holy**, something that is much bigger than they are.

Rituals: The Holy and Identification

The actions and the language that bond people to the holy are called rituals. Rituals are at the heart of all religions. Religious rituals help us discover who we are. These actions identify someone as, for example, a First Nations person, as a Catholic Christian, or as a Muslim, among many possibilities. They help give us our identity.

Countless religious rituals exist. Here are some examples.

Religious Rituals

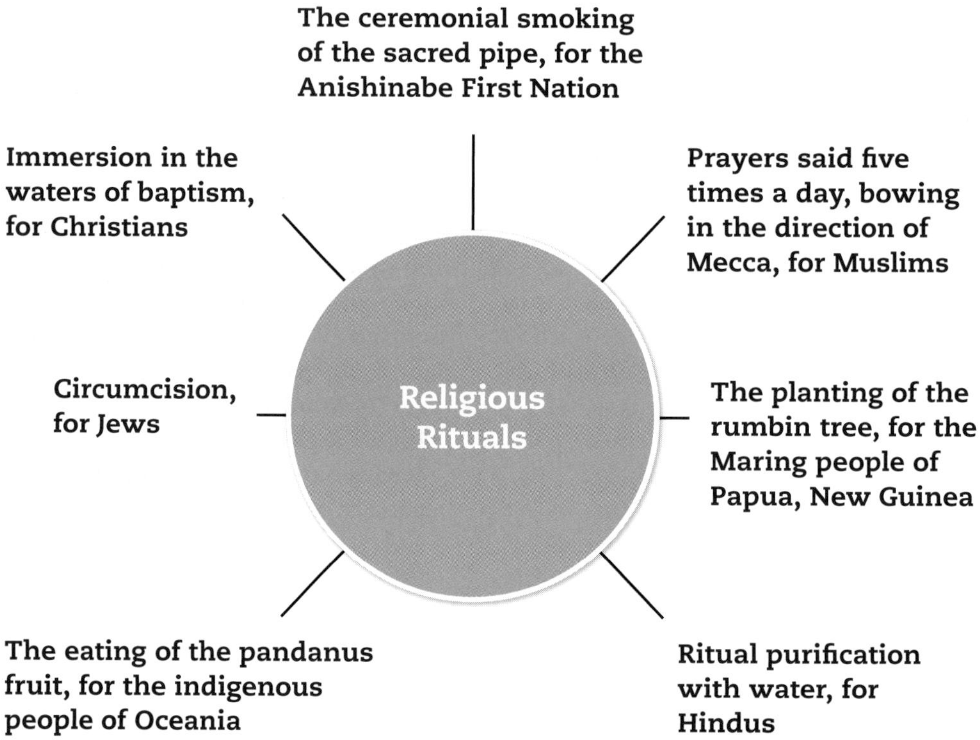
Religious Rituals
The ceremonial smoking of the sacred pipe, for the Anishinabe First Nation
Prayers said five times a day, bowing in the direction of Mecca, for Muslims
The planting of the rumbin tree, for the Maring people of Papua, New Guinea
Ritual purification with water, for Hindus
The eating of the pandanus fruit, for the indigenous people of Oceania
Circumcision, for Jews
Immersion in the waters of baptism, for Christians

Religious Rituals. The photos below show various rituals in different religions: prayer, purification, and life-cycle rituals. By participating in these rituals, people show that they are Aboriginal, Muslim, Maring, Hindu, indigenous persons from Oceania, Jewish, or Christian. One becomes what one ritualizes. **Do you have a favourite religious ritual? Describe it and its meaning.**

Similarities among Religious Rituals

Sociologists, who study how human societies originate and develop, recognize a number of elements that are common to all rituals:

- They are believed to have begun long ago, sometimes at the dawn of human memory.
- They follow set rubrics (rules of conduct of a ritual) that change very little over time.
- They have clear beginnings and ends.
- They do not seem to have practical results in the world.
- They say something about the individuals who participate in them.
- They say something about who we are as human beings, about our Earth, about time, about the holy, about God or other sacred beings.

Rituals express our understanding of where we came from, who we are, and where we are going. Together, ritual and story spell out the way of life of the participants. They express certain beliefs about many things.

In other words, participating in religious rituals gives life to a particular view of the world and tells us what it means to live in the world.

Differences among Religious Rituals

Religions do rituals differently. That is how we can tell one religion from another. The rituals give shape to the many understandings of human existence, of the holy, of time, of the divine. That is why rituals are **sacred** for religions. The rituals give people access to what they consider to be holy and to what helps make them holy.

Religious rituals also help to create relationships, as individuals and as a believing community, with what is ultimately most important in people's faith traditions. For this reason, it is normally improper to take part in the rituals of another religion. To participate in a ritual is to say, "I accept what this religion considers sacred; I say yes to the world that ritual seeks to bring into being."

Religious rituals also help us to understand another person's religion.

Catholic Connection

For Catholics, rituals are religious acts to God, performed for the sake of honouring God.

Sacred

Describes what has been set aside as holy in a religious ritual, such as the water blessed in baptism and made holy by the words of the priest

Significance of Rituals

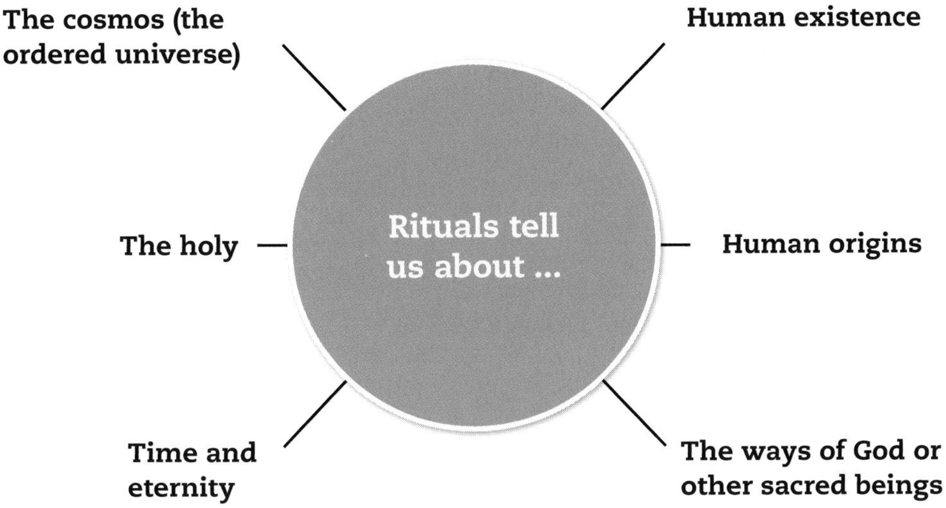

Significance of Rituals. In many ways, rituals connect human lives with the mysteries of human existence.

Profile: Bishop Paul-André Durocher

In July 2007, Paul-André Durocher, Bishop of Alexandria–Cornwall, Ontario, walked part of the ancient pilgrimage route to Santiago de Compostela, Spain. For many centuries, people have made pilgrimages, for all sorts of reasons. Often, a pilgrimage triggers a turning point in people's lives. When we are separated from our ordinary lives, new ideas or attitudes become possible. Here is Bishop Durocher's reflection on his pilgrimage.

> Twenty-five kilometres a day for 30 days: that's the distance I walked on the pilgrimage route to the tomb of Saint James the Apostle in Compostela, Spain. People have been walking this route for over a thousand years. I met all sorts of people—believers and non-believers. I met a 12-year-old girl walking with her dad; a 70-year-old sailor who was doing the route for the third time; four teenagers who were walking with their grandparents, a donkey carrying their tents and packsacks. I got blisters on my toes. I got exhausted climbing mountains. I got cold in the rain and hot in the sun. But I felt what nearly everyone feels when they walk this path: a presence, a spirit, a deep, quiet peacefulness. A sign on the road said it well: "In the silence, you can hear what is essential."

Bishop Durocher. Bishop Paul-André Durocher during his pilgrimage.

Skill Focus: Journal Writing

As you work through this textbook, you will have many opportunities to write about your personal experiences and reflections. One tool for reflecting and writing on your own experiences is the journal. When you prepare to write a journal entry, ask yourself the following questions:

1. What do I already know (or think I know) about the topic?
2. What questions would I like to answer, or what issues would I like to find out more about in this chapter?

These questions will help you focus on meaningful ideas and information as you read, research, and participate in class discussions and other activities.

When you have finished learning about a topic, ask yourself one final question:

3. What have I learned? Did I find the answers to my questions? Did I learn more about the issues I was curious about? Did I learn anything new or unexpected?

Check Your Understanding

1. What are religious rituals? Identify three examples and explain why they are religious rituals.
2. What role do rituals play in people's lives and why are rituals important? Share your answers with a partner.
3. What is a person saying when he or she takes part in a ritual?

Think About It

4. Describe any non-religious rituals you may follow. For example, common non-religious rituals might include getting a driver's licence or graduating from elementary or high school. How are these non-religious rituals different from religious rituals?
5. Briefly research some of the rituals used in another religion of your choice. Compare and contrast three of these rituals with three rituals used in the Catholic Church.

Making It Personal

6. How often do you participate in religious rituals? Explain what taking part means to you. If you do not do so, describe some non-religious rituals you participate in and explain what these rituals mean to you.

Catholic Rituals: Sacraments and Liturgy

Sacraments

Catholics have many rituals, among which are the sacraments. The celebration of these sacraments is called liturgy. The most important liturgy for Catholics is the Sunday Mass.

What are sacraments? Christians believe that God encounters them in the rituals of the sacraments. Catholics believe that there are seven sacraments (all Christians accept baptism, but not all accept the other sacraments).

The Church believes that these sacraments have their source in Jesus Christ. What Jesus did is at work for Christians today in the sacraments by the action of the Holy Spirit. The sacraments bring the person of Jesus into the lives of Christians in the twenty-first century.

Catholic Sacraments

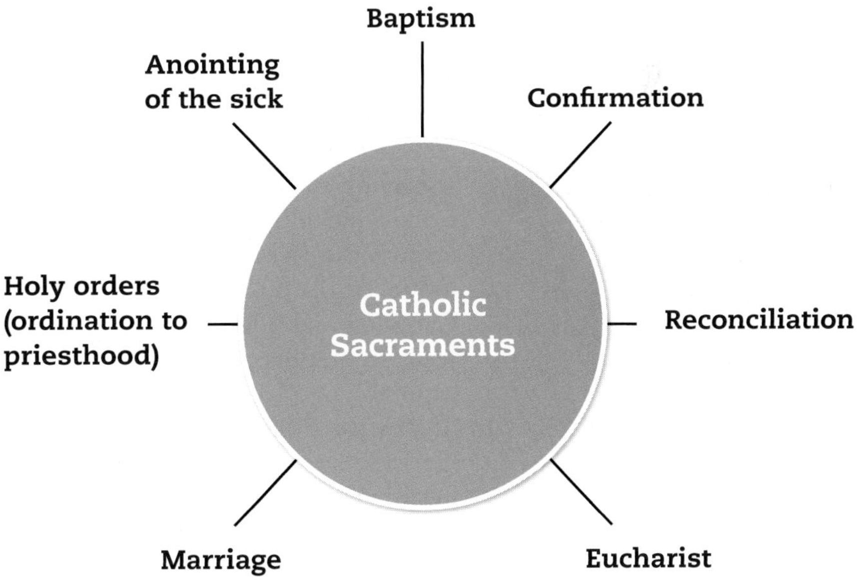

Catholic Sacraments. Catholic sacraments connect individual lives and special occasions in life with the work and person of Jesus Christ. In this way, human lives become filled with the life of Christ. Christ's love gradually becomes our love.

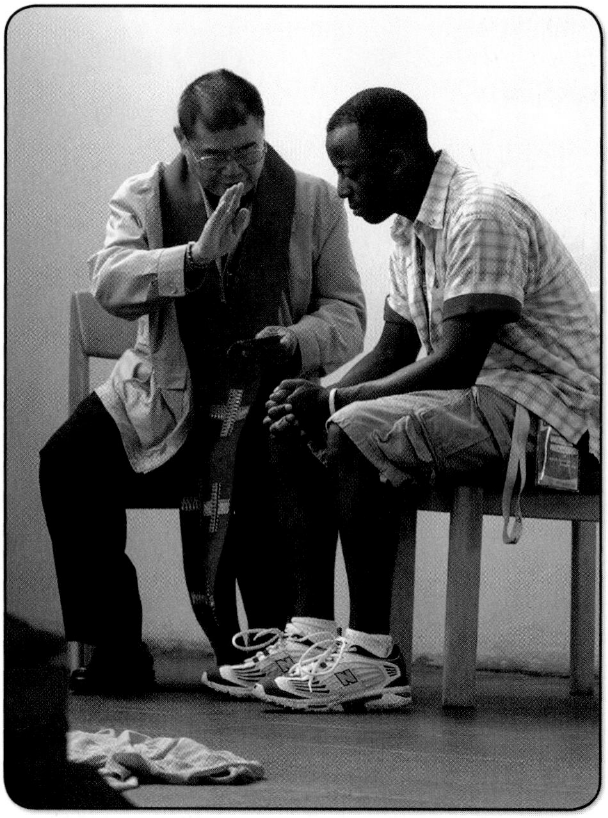

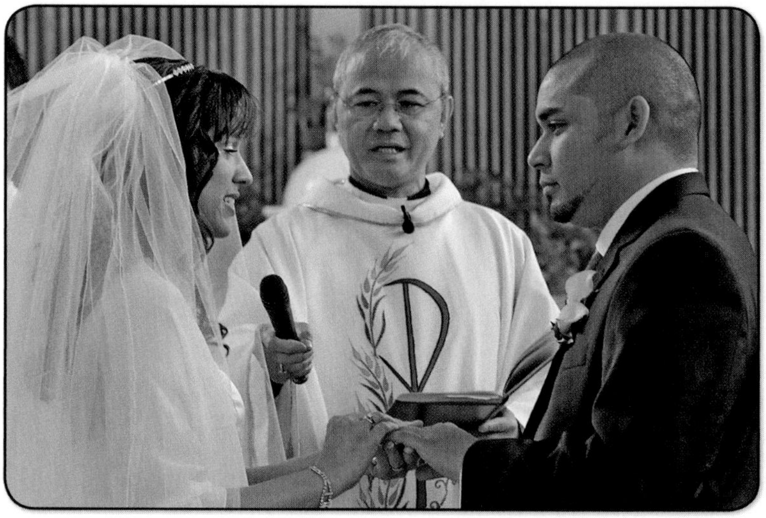

Celebrating Sacraments. Catholics mark important life stages with various sacraments such as reconciliation (top left), holy orders (top right), and marriage (bottom right).

Fast Fact

Laying on of hands is a ritual gesture of extending one's hands over a person. The ritual makes the Holy Spirit present for someone. Anointing is a symbol of the Holy Spirit. Oil is used throughout the Bible to empower people.

All important life experiences have rituals, including birth and growth, forgiveness, sickness, and vocation in life. At the different stages of life, Catholics and other Christians turn to Jesus so that his death and resurrection can have an effect on all areas of life. By the rituals of the sacraments, Christians enter into the deeper meaning of life. In the sacraments, Christians encounter Jesus in the important moments of their lives.

Liturgy

The liturgy of a sacrament always makes present something that Jesus said or did. That is why a reading about Jesus from the Bible is part of each sacrament. These scripture passages about Jesus are always accompanied by a ritual action. For example, in the sacrament of the anointing of the sick, the priest reads a story of Jesus healing someone. Then the priest lays hands on the sick person and anoints the person's head and hands with oil. In the sacrament of marriage, a story from the Bible about love and commitment is followed by a man and a woman's words of commitment to each other. Together, the word of God and the ritual action effectively make the two into a married couple.

In the rituals of the liturgy, Christians turn to Jesus so that his death and resurrection can enter into all the areas of life. That is why participating in liturgy is so powerful. Through the participants, God's work in Christ comes alive in people today.

Check Your Understanding

1. Explain what liturgy is and why it is important.
2. If you had to explain to someone what a sacrament is, how would you do it? How do sacraments connect someone with Jesus?
3. Why does the liturgy involve people's minds, words, and bodies?

Think About It

4. Choose one of the sacraments. How does this sacrament bring the person of Jesus into our lives?
5. How can involving the mind, words, and body help people to find meaning in a ritual such as the liturgy?

Making It Personal

6. What particular elements of the liturgy (for example, music, quiet time, readings, appropriate decorations, and so on) help make the liturgy most meaningful for you?

Chrismation
When a baptized person is confirmed by anointing the person with chrism (holy oil)

Rite of Initiation

How does someone become a Catholic? The story of Laura at the beginning of the chapter tells us. When she was an infant, her parents took her to church to be baptized. Through the ritual actions and words of baptism, she became a Christian and a member of the Catholic Church. For full initiation into the Church, a person is baptized, is confirmed (**chrismated**), and receives the Eucharist.

Baptism

In its most basic form, baptism involves a priest or deacon pouring water over the person's head and saying, "I baptize you in the name of the Father, and of the Son, and of the Holy Spirit." This action and these words make real what they signify: the baptized person receives a new identity and new life in God—he or she becomes Christian.

Baptism. In baptism, a person is immersed in the death and resurrection of Christ. **Have you ever witnessed a baptism? Describe what happened.**

Confirmation. As his family, godparents, and members of the congregation of this Canadian church bear witness, a young Catholic is confirmed. Here, the bishop puts his hand on the boy's head, praying for him to receive the gifts of the Holy Spirit. He then makes the sign of the cross on his forehead with chrism—a holy mixture of oil and balm used for anointing—to strengthen the boy in his ability to follow Jesus Christ and to take part in his mission. **Have you or one of your friends been confirmed? Describe what happened.**

Assembly

For Christians, a gathering of baptized people for liturgy or worship in the name of Christ; the assembly is also called the "congregation" or the "Church"

The Ritual of Eucharist. The Eucharistic ritual uses the gifts of bread and wine to bring about a deep unity between Christ and the participants. The ritual intends to transform participants into the image of Christ. **If religious rituals make participants holy, how does a ritual like the Eucharist make participants holy?**

Confirmation

The sacrament of confirmation is celebrated through the laying on of hands and the anointing with perfumed oil to signify the gift of the Holy Spirit. It completes baptism (*Catechism of the Catholic Church*, #1288–1289).

Eucharist

Baptism and confirmation are the first steps of initiation into the Catholic faith. Initiation is completed and continued in the Sunday Mass. The Catholic Church calls the Mass or Eucharist the "fount and apex of the whole Christian life" (*Constitution on the Church*, #11). Living a fully Christian life takes a lifetime; it is a never-ending journey. The Sunday Mass is the constant companion on this journey.

The liturgy of the Mass has hardly changed since the third and fourth centuries. The structure of the Mass is both simple and complex. It consists of two parts: the Liturgy of the Word and the Liturgy of the Eucharist. The leader of the **assembly** is first the bishop and, in his absence, the priest.

During the Eucharist, everyone who is present participates. At the beginning of the Eucharistic Prayer, the priest (or bishop) says to the people, "Lift up your hearts." The people respond, "We lift them up to the Lord." In other words, they say, "We are ready!" People stay active throughout the prayer, responding aloud to the words of the priest and singing "Amen" at the end. Through the Eucharistic Prayer, the whole Church prays that the Holy Spirit will unite all people in one body and one spirit and heal all divisions among people. The highlight of participation is the rite of Communion, where the people eat and drink the gift of the Body and Blood of Christ. By participating in the Eucharist, Catholics are affirming and committing themselves to God's great act of saving and reshaping the world in the image of Jesus Christ.

Communion. These young people, who are members of a Canadian church, are receiving Communion. Receiving Communion in the Eucharist is a way of sharing in the person of Christ. For Catholics, they become what they eat and drink. Here, too, the ritual of Communion does what it signifies. **Why are Catholics so concerned about who partakes of Communion?**

Check Your Understanding

1. Describe the main liturgical actions of baptism.
2. Describe the two main parts of the Mass and what happens during each part.

Think About It

3. How do baptism and Eucharist shape the identity of someone who is Catholic?
4. Research the rite of baptism in another religion. How are the rituals in this religion similar to and different from the rituals of baptism in the Catholic Church?

Making It Personal

5. If possible, give some examples from your own experience of how you participate in Mass. Or, ask a friend who has participated in Mass to describe his or her actions, and make notes.

A Closer Look

Over the centuries, the Sunday gathering of Catholics has been called by many names.

- **Eucharist:** from the Greek, meaning "an action of thanksgiving"
- **The Memorial of the Paschal Mystery:** remembering the passion (suffering), death, and resurrection of Jesus
- **The Lord's Supper:** recalling the Last Supper of Jesus with the disciples
- **The Breaking of Bread:** referring to what Jesus did at the Last Supper, a sign that he would give his life for all the next day
- **The Holy and Divine Liturgy:** referring to the act of celebrating the *sacred mysteries* (sacraments) of the faith
- **Holy Communion:** indicating the moment when the faithful share in Christ's Body and Blood
- **Holy Mass:** "Mass" comes from the Latin word *missa*, which means "sent": the people are sent out into the world at the end of the liturgy

(*Catechism of the Catholic Church*, #1329–1332)

Marking Time

The Menhirs of Brittany. The menhirs in Carnac (Carnac Stones) in Brittany, France, are lined up, perhaps astronomically, to form a single line at sunrise at the summer solstice. It is not clear what made the pre-Celtic people of Brittany haul these massive stones into this arrangement in the Neolithic period (3500 BCE). Some say that the arrangement expresses a belief in an afterlife.

Fast Fact

Among the Maring people, the ritual cycle, which includes the planting of rumbin trees in large gardens, the raising of pigs, a sacrifice of the pigs to the ancestors, and the uprooting of the rumbin trees, takes 10 to 20 years to complete.

Time is a mysterious thing. It governs our lives and affects everything we do. Yet, if we were to ask, "What is time?" we would find it hard to answer the question.

Time pervades everything, including religion. Countries organize time by setting workweeks and time for leisure, civic holidays, and days of remembrance. For countries, and for people, who work to benefit society and to earn money to survive, it is largely the economy that shapes time. In contrast, religions organize time through rituals. Rituals shape how we mark time, how we live out our traditions, and what we expect for the future. Rituals show what people think is important, what preoccupies them.

For religions, the sacred shapes time. Each religion has a certain time set aside for the sacred: for example, for Muslims, it is Friday; for Jews, it is Shabbat (Saturday); for Christians, it is Sunday. A religion may follow five-day weeks, seven-day weeks, or nine-day weeks. It has "high" times or seasons, with special feasts and celebrations, and "low" times, when nothing out of the ordinary happens. Some of these special times are marked by the Sun, others by the Moon. Rituals highlight these times and allow participants to celebrate them. The rituals marking sacred times return in cycles, whether that is once a year or every 20 years.

The regular recurrence of sacred times, and the repetition of rituals, makes sacred time appear unchanging; it is time out of time. Although the rituals do not change, over time the participants do. They change because their constant participation in the rituals makes them become more and more what their religion is all about. This rhythm of time enables people to grow to maturity as a member of their religion.

Catholics and the Marking of Time

As members of a historical religion, Catholics celebrate time—sacred and ordinary—in many ways. For Catholics, time is not all about making money, being successful in school, being popular, or having a good job. Time has a deeper purpose. It is intended to develop one's relationship to God and to fashion a world that reflects the compassionate and loving God. For Catholics, time is also for the unfolding of the mystery of Jesus in one's life (*Catechism of the Catholic Church*, #1163). Here are some examples of how time is lived in Catholicism.

The Liturgical Year

Over the centuries, the Church has created a detailed calendar of seasons, feasts, festivals, holy days, and saints' days. These events give a sacred structure to the entire year. The Christian calendar (called the liturgical year) is organized around the story of Jesus. It starts on the first Sunday of Advent—the Sunday nearest November 30. The first great feast of the liturgical year is the birth of Jesus Christ on December 25. During the year, Catholics remember all the major events of the life and death and resurrection of Jesus. The end of the Catholic calendar leads Catholics out of time: the last Sundays before Advent look forward to the second coming of Christ.

The chart of the liturgical year, below, shows the rhythm of Sacred and Ordinary Time during the year. The colours of the chart represent the liturgical colours of each season.

Fast Fact

Advent is a four-week season of preparation for the feast of Christmas. The Advent season begins on the Sunday nearest November 30.

The Liturgical Year

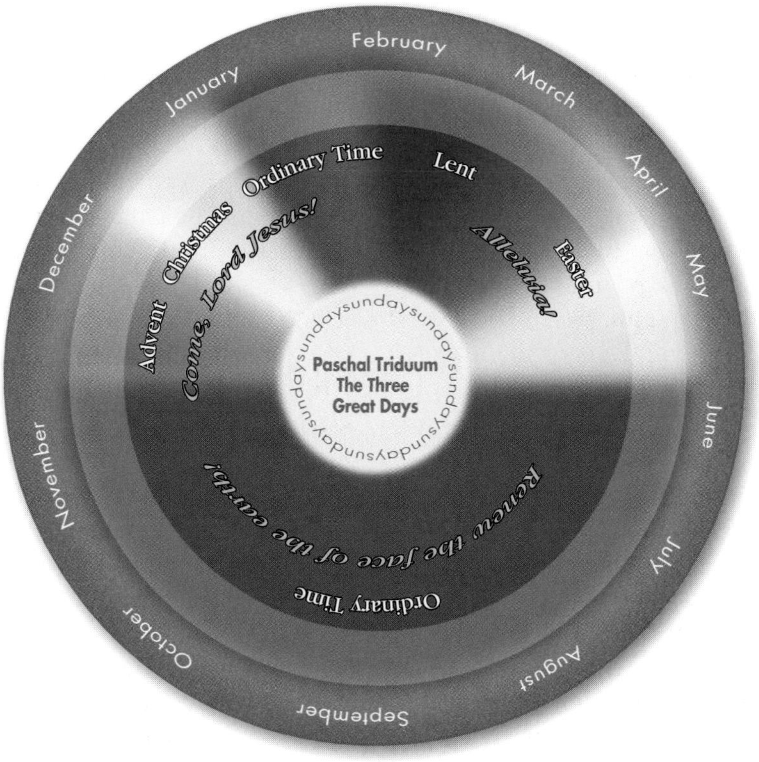

The Liturgical Year. This graphic art shows the colours that are used during the seasons of the liturgical year. This calendar of Ordinary and Sacred Time determines the colours of the priest's vestments, the altar cloth, wall hangings and banners, and so on. Green is the liturgical colour of Ordinary Time. Purple is the colour of Advent, Lent, and Good Friday. White is the colour of Holy Thursday, Easter, and Christmas.

The Resurrection. *Christ Risen from the Tomb,* by Italian painter Gaudenzio Ferrari (1475–1546). **How does the artist show that this is the risen Christ? Why is the resurrection so important to Catholics?**

Fast Fact

"Sunday is the day of the Resurrection, it is the day of Christians, it is our day" (St. Jerome, c. 347–420 CE). For Catholics, Sunday is "the fundamental feast day, established not only to mark the succession of time, but to reveal time's deeper meaning" (Pope John Paul II, *The Lord's Day,* #2). Sunday is sometimes called the "eighth day." It is the day after the Jewish Sabbath, God's day of rest. For Catholics, the day of Jesus's resurrection becomes the day when creation is renewed (*Catechism of the Catholic Church,* #1166).

The Importance of Sunday

The first followers of Jesus were Jewish. At first, they continued to celebrate the Jewish Sabbath, the seventh day of creation when the Lord rested. For Christians, the Sabbath was the day when Jesus "rested" in the tomb. However, they saw the "first day of the week"—Sunday, the day of the resurrection—as more important, so early Christians began to celebrate the resurrection every Sunday. Sunday, known as the "Lord's Day," is the main marker of time for Christians. Easter Sunday, the most solemn of Christian feasts, has been called the "Sunday of Sundays," the "feast of feasts." That is why going to Mass on Sunday is so important for Catholics.

Marking the Times of the Day

Jesus taught us to "pray always." For this reason, Catholics set aside different times of the day to pray. In general, they are encouraged to pray in the morning, in the evening, and before meals.

Check Your Understanding

1. In small groups, discuss the following questions:
   a) How does our society organize time?
   b) How do religions order time?

Think About It

2. How do Catholics organize time? How does this compare with how other religions organize time?
3. Use a Venn diagram to compare the Catholic liturgical calendar with the Jewish calendar. What patterns do you see? How are the calendars similar to each other (for example, both celebrate religious festivals)? How are they different from each other (for example, the celebration of the beginning of the year)?

Making It Personal

4. How much does your faith influence how you think about time?

Easter

In the Western Churches, Easter is celebrated on the first Sunday after the full Moon following the spring equinox. Because of the importance of the death and resurrection of Jesus, the celebration of the Paschal Mystery begins with Mass on Holy Thursday evening and ends with evening prayer on Easter Sunday. This celebration is called the **Triduum**.

The most solemn liturgy takes place on Holy Saturday night. It is called the Easter **Vigil**. It begins with the lighting of the Paschal candle. During the Vigil, new members are baptized, confirmed, and admitted to Eucharist. The Vigil begins in darkness until the light of the risen Christ is brought into the church.

On Easter Sunday, Catholics greet each other with "Christ is risen! Alleluia!" The response is "He is risen indeed! Alleluia!" Because Easter is so important, the Easter season lasts for 50 days. It ends with the feast of Pentecost, when Jesus sent the gift of the Holy Spirit.

Paschal Mystery. *Paschal Mystery,* 1993, by Saskatoon artist Gisele Bauche. Through her paintings, Bauche seeks to reveal the richness of scripture and Christianity, and to nurture and enrich the way people worship and look at the world. **Draw your own version of the Paschal Mystery. Share it with a classmate and explain your thought processes as you made your version.**

Fast Fact

The word "paschal" comes from the Jewish Passover. For Jews, it refers to the Lord passing over the houses of the Hebrews in Egypt, sparing their firstborn sons from death. For Christians, "paschal" refers to Jesus passing over death at Easter and is symbolized by the Paschal candle. "Paschal Mystery" means the mystery of the life, death, and resurrection of Jesus.

Triduum

The three days of Holy Thursday, Good Friday, and Easter

Vigil

A time of staying awake and waiting before a great feast; at the Easter Vigil, Christians stay awake with Jesus in the tomb to be present at his resurrection

Fast Fact

Pentecost is Greek for "fiftieth day."

The Easter Vigil. At the Easter Vigil, Catholics welcome Christ in the symbol of the Paschal candle. **How is Christ a light for our world?**

Nativity Scenes. A nativity scene. The display of Christmas crèches, or nativity scenes, was started by St. Francis of Assisi in the twelfth century. Some crèches can be very elaborate, recreating whole villages, with the house of Mary and Joseph at the centre.

Fast Fact

The Magi are symbols of all the peoples of Earth.

Christmas–Epiphany (Theophany)

The other major feast after Easter is Christmas–Epiphany, which celebrates the birth of Jesus and the arrival of the Magi to pay homage to him. In the Western Church, the birth of Jesus is celebrated on December 25. The Eastern Church, using the Julian calendar, celebrates it on January 7.

This feast is by far the most popular of the Christian feasts. It continues to be celebrated as a feast of gift-giving and of the family in Western countries for Christians, and for many people who are non-practising Christians.

Fast Fact

Martyrs are people who died because of their faith in Christ.

Feasts of Mary and the Saints

Because God's call for Mary to be the mother of Jesus connects her intimately to the ministry and person of Jesus, the Church celebrates a number of feast days honouring Mary. In Mary, the Church sees the best example of what the work of Christ can do in a human being. In Mary, Catholics see what they hope to be (*Catechism of the Catholic Church*, #1172).

Alongside Mary, the Church remembers the martyrs and other saints who lived as Christ did. Among them are a number of Canadian saints: the Canadian Martyrs (eight Jesuit priests killed by the Iroquois in the 1640s), St. Marguerite d'Youville, St. Marguerite Bourgeoys, Blessed Marie de l'Incarnation, Blessed Kateri Tekakwitha, and Blessed François de Laval.

Because saints resemble, in different ways, the person of Christ, Catholics often turn to the saints in prayer to intercede with God. The saints remain part of the Church. Together with all the baptized, they form the communion of saints.

Crucifixion

"Do not weep for me, Mother,

When I am in my grave."

A choir of angels glorified the hour,
the vault of heaven was dissolved
in fire.

"Father, why hast thou forsaken me ..."

"Mother, I beg you, do not weep
for me ..."

Mary Magdalene beat her breasts
and sobbed, his dear disciple,
stone-faced, stared.

His mother stood apart.

No other looked into her secret eyes.

No one dared.

—Anna Akhmatova

The Virgin Mary. *Mary, A Mother's Sorrow,* by American artist Janet McKenzie. **How do you picture Mary?**

Check Your Understanding

1. Explain how the Catholic Church marks time.
2. What is the main feast for Christians? Why?
3. Find the feasts honouring Mary and explore their meaning.

Think About It

4. With a partner, choose a martyr or saint and research his or her life. Explain why he or she was martyred or made a saint. Prepare a brief presentation of your findings to share with the class.
5. Read the poem "Crucifixion" by Anna Akhmatova on this page. What message do you think the author is trying to communicate?

Making It Personal

6. Do you or a Catholic friend have a favourite Catholic feast? Why is it a favourite?

Rituals and Community

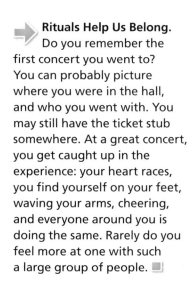

Rituals Help Us Belong. Do you remember the first concert you went to? You can probably picture where you were in the hall, and who you went with. You may still have the ticket stub somewhere. At a great concert, you get caught up in the experience: your heart races, you find yourself on your feet, waving your arms, cheering, and everyone around you is doing the same. Rarely do you feel more at one with such a large group of people.

A concert is a kind of ritual. It gathers people together and bonds them through a common experience. As we know from going to concerts, rituals do more than shape time. They also create community.

As we saw earlier, liturgical time is measured not in seconds but in hours, days, weeks, or even months and years. Liturgical life helps people to stand still and focus on what is at the heart of being human. Liturgical time wants to envelop us. It takes time to form community through the celebration of rituals.

As we enter into rituals, we set aside our moods or emotions and join the larger group. The longer a ritual lasts and the more often it is repeated, the more the entire gathering moves as one. In this way, rituals shape communities. That is why communities stand on a common ground. They are bonded together by their ritual actions.

Catholic Rituals Strengthen a Person's Belonging to the Church

The Eucharist Makes the Church

The Catholic tradition sees community as very important. In fact, the Church understands itself as a large movement in which God gathers people from every nation into a community with God. This gathering of all peoples into a community is called the Church.

The ritual that creates the Catholic Church is the Sunday Mass. Catholics celebrate that, in a broken world, God acts among

NEL

Worshippers Celebrate Mass around the World. Young people pray and sing at Sunday Mass in an urban church in Ontario (top right). Iraqi Chaldean Catholics pray at a Eucharist in Baghdad, Iraq (top left). An Ethiopian Orthodox priest conducts Sunday morning Mass in Lalibella, Ethiopia (bottom left). **What is similar about each of these images? What is different?**

them to overcome all divisions and to make all of humanity one. That is why, more than any other rite, the Eucharist makes the Church become what it is: a sign and a symbol of God's community. Even though Catholics often fail, they celebrate that God continues to form them into a community. For Catholics, the symbols of this unity are the bishops, especially the Bishop of Rome, who is the pope. By presiding at the Eucharist, the bishop oversees this gathering of all the believers into communion or community.

The final prayer of Jesus was a prayer for unity of his followers. That is why the division of Christianity into churches that do not accept each other, have fought each other over the centuries, and have not been able to celebrate Mass together has been so tragic. The divisions are obstacles to the mission of Christians to be one as God is one. Because it is God who gathers people together, Catholics believe that in the Eucharist, God gathers in one family all who believe in Christ wherever they live in the world. All of humanity is part of the family of God.

Make It Your Own: Teaching About the Mass

School Atrium. In this small atrium, you can see an altar with art, candle, flowers, and a crucifix. There is a lectern and a stool as well.

Maria Montessori believed that children learn best when they learn in a beautiful setting where they can touch and interact with items that help them learn. The **Catechesis** of the Good Shepherd was developed in the Toronto area as a way of using the teaching methods of Maria Montessori to help children learn about the Bible, Jesus (the Good Shepherd), the Mass, and the Catholic faith.

Many years ago, an atrium was a gathering place between the Church and the street that was used for teaching people who wanted to be baptized Catholic. In the Catechesis of the Good Shepherd, a special room or space, called an atrium, is set up for the children who may be too young to read. It is a sacred space with simple yet beautiful materials that children can touch and interact with in order to learn. In the atrium, young children can set a small altar, stand at a small lectern, or even hold small versions of a priest's vestments. By working with the items in the atrium, children can learn and reflect.

Activity

1. In your classroom, set up an atrium that can be used to teach children about the Mass. You will need the following:
   - a table for the altar
   - a tablecloth
   - flowers
   - a sample tabernacle
   - a podium or lectern
   - a Bible or a lectionary or a sacramentary
   - a large Paschal candle and two altar candles
   - banners
   - a chalice and ciborium
   - Bible stories for children

Catechesis

Word meaning "teaching"; a catechist is a person who teaches about the faith

Check Your Understanding

1. Explain what a religious community is and how it is formed.

2. How does the Eucharist make the community of the Church?

Think About It

3. Research ways in which the division of Christianity into churches has acted as an obstacle to the mission of Christians. What implications does this have for you as a Catholic?

Making It Personal

4. Have you ever been to an event that made you and the crowd feel like one big family? What was it? What did it feel like to be part of this community?

5. How does your church or place of worship make you feel like part of a community? Is it the same kind of feeling you get when you attend a concert or similar event?

Central Beliefs

Rituals Shape the Beliefs of a Religion

By now, it is obvious that rituals communicate something important. They contain a message. Those who take part in rituals act out this message. The Chinese family described earlier in this chapter left a place open at the table for an ancestor in order to symbolize a belief. For the Chinese, setting a place at the table for their ancestors is a central religious ritual.

Rituals seek to communicate things that words alone cannot convey. For this reason, rituals always involve both words and actions. To signify the importance of and their belief in the Trinity, Catholics sign themselves with the sign of the cross.

Religious beliefs are usually learned by participating in rituals. Over time, they become part of life. By entering into the rituals of religion, we enter the world where the rituals make sense.

Liturgical rituals help us look beyond our everyday lives. They reveal truths that transcend us, that are bigger than we are. They reveal the holy. The sound of choir and organ, or guitar and flute; the church bells; the light shining through the stained glass windows; the prayers; the statues of saints and biblical figures; the open space; the incense; the taste of the transformed bread and wine at Communion—all these point to something out of the ordinary. In these moments, religions express their deepest convictions about what is ultimately true.

The Blessed Trinity. This painting, *The Blessed Trinity,* was created by Peter Paul Rubens (1577–1640). For Catholics, God is the Trinity: Father, Son, and Holy Spirit. Father, Son, and Spirit are so intimately related that they are one. This is the central mystery of Christian faith. **How does this image represent God? How would you represent God? Do you think God should be represented in images? Why or why not?**

Fast Fact

Most of what Catholics believe is expressed in the Sunday Mass. All the mysteries of Christ and the most important parts of the scriptures are remembered on Sundays during the liturgical year.

Reading Scripture at Mass. A major part of the liturgy consists of reading from the Bible, especially from the New Testament. For Christians, the Bible is the Word of God.

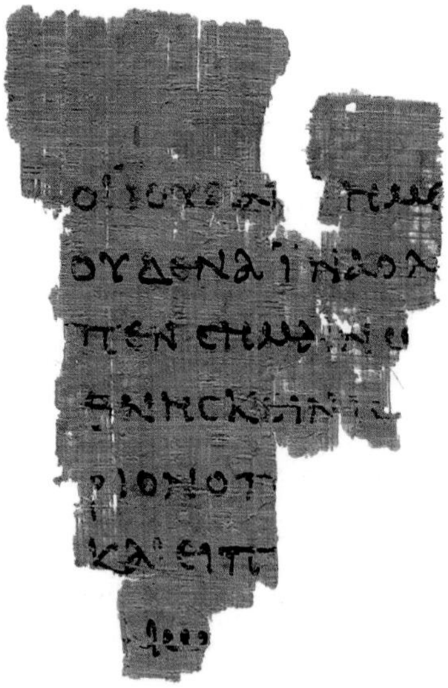

The Gospel of John. This fragment from the Gospel of John is the oldest fragment of the New Testament. It is dated at 125 CE. It contains parts of John 18:31–33 and 37–38. The stories and teachings of the New Testament are the main source of Catholic beliefs.

Catholic Liturgy Shapes Catholic Beliefs

Catholics express and affirm their beliefs in their ritual celebrations. This happens particularly in the Sunday Mass, during the Liturgy of the Word. The primary source of their beliefs is found in the Bible and in the interpretations of the Bible. During the Liturgy of the Word, passages from the Bible—both the Old Testament and the New Testament—are read and explained. The proclamation of the Gospel about Jesus is the high point of the Liturgy of the Word.

The Creed

During the Mass, the Creed sums up the Bible's story of God. Catholics recite the Creed each Sunday after the homily to express what they believe and who they are as a faith community. The Creed is like a story with three parts.

A Closer Look

The word "creed" comes from the Latin word *credo*, which means "I believe."

In the Western Church, two creeds may be used in the Mass. The Apostles' Creed dates back to the year 340. A bishop named Marcellus wrote this creed for Pope Julius I to show him that the church in Ancyra (present-day Ankara, Turkey) held the same beliefs as the Church of Rome. The Nicene Creed comes from the councils of Nicaea in 325 and Constantinople in 381. It is common to all the great churches of the East and the West (*Catechism of the Catholic Church,* #194–195).

Council of Nicaea. In 325, the Roman Emperor Constantine called the bishops together in the town of Nicaea (in present-day Turkey) to deal with a conflict about the divinity of Jesus Christ. Out of the deliberations came the Nicene Creed. The church in which the council was held is now a ruin. At one time, it was also a mosque.

I believe

We tend to interpret "I believe" to mean "I accept that something is true." But, that is not the original meaning. To say "I believe in God" does not mean "I believe that there is a God." To say "I believe in God" is more like a promise or a pledge. It means "I promise or I pledge that from this moment I set my life, love, heart, and mind, my whole being, on God and on God alone." People make this promise because they love and trust God.

I believe in God, the Father almighty, creator of heaven and earth.

I believe in Jesus Christ, his only Son, our Lord.
He was conceived by the power of the Holy Spirit and born of the Virgin Mary.

He suffered under Pontius Pilate, was crucified, died and was buried.

He descended to the dead.

On the third day he rose again.

He ascended into heaven, and is seated at the right hand of the Father.

He will come again to judge the living and the dead.

I believe in the Holy Spirit,
the holy catholic Church,
the communion of saints,
the forgiveness of sins,
the resurrection of the body,
and the life everlasting. Amen.

I believe in God, the Father almighty, creator of heaven and earth ...

First, Catholics pledge themselves to the Father. The name "Abba" (an Aramaic word), or "Father," is the name Jesus used when he spoke to God in prayer. Jesus's whole ministry was about revealing who the Father is.

For Jesus, God (Abba, Father) is a Father like no other. "Call no one your father on Earth," he said, "for you have one Father—the one in heaven" (Matthew 23:9). For Jesus, God (Abba, Father) is a parent who loves his children fiercely and will always care for them. This God is the creator of heaven and Earth, the maker of all things, visible and invisible.

I believe in Jesus Christ, his only Son, our Lord ...

The heart of the Creed is about Jesus Christ. The Creed sums up what the scriptures say about Jesus. Jesus is the Father's only Son and the Lord. The Creed highlights Jesus's life in six points. Catholics pledge themselves to Jesus Christ because he is the Word of the Father, the one through whom God is revealed. In other words, there is nothing more to see in God than what we see in Jesus Christ. He is the full appearance of God.

Notice that the Creed speaks only about the beginning and the end of the story of Jesus. The emphasis is on his death and resurrection. Here, the mystery of God is revealed for Catholics. Here, God entered into the human drama of suffering and death. Catholics see the cross of Jesus as the symbol of God's love.

I believe in the Holy Spirit ...

The third part of the Creed is about the Church's commitment to the Holy Spirit. The Spirit is the bond of love between the Father and the Son. It is the Spirit of God that dwells in human hearts and acts in the rest of creation. The Spirit is known as "the gift."

The Nicene Creed—the longer creed that Catholics say at Mass—calls the Spirit "the Lord and giver of life." That is why the Spirit is also called love. The Spirit is where love happens.

Icon of the Trinity. Images of the Trinity in the form of icons are found in Eastern or Orthodox Churches. They are crafted with great care. They are usually paintings but sometimes, as in this icon, they are in bas relief. Because the Bible forbids graven images of God, the bas relief is never more than two centimetres thick.

The Spirit as God's power of love is revealed when two people can finally forgive each other; when people find joy again in living; when life overcomes death. The Spirit makes alive today in the community of Catholics what Jesus brought to life in his time: God's kingdom of justice, peace, and joy. When Catholics pledge themselves to the Holy Spirit in the Creed, they also promise to respect, protect, and promote all living things.

Check Your Understanding

1. Explain how the three parts of the Creed express belief in God.
2. Explain why Jesus is the centre of Catholic beliefs.
3. Where do Catholics believe the Spirit is active?

Think About It

4. Why do you think Catholics emphasize the teachings in the New Testament?

Making It Personal

5. What are your faith beliefs? Try to sum them up in one or two sentences. What is at the centre of your beliefs?

Morality

Fast Fact

Torah is the heart of the Jewish Bible. It consists of the first five books of the Bible (see Chapter 4, The Story of Judaism).

As we just saw, the rituals of religion express people's ultimate beliefs. They also teach people how to act. In some religions, moral teachings are quite explicit, and sometimes there are many of them. In Judaism, for example, the Torah contains 613 laws. Moral teachings make it clear how a religion sees the world. They tell believers how to live in the world. They also tell what kind of people they should become.

If in a ritual we pledge ourselves to the holy, we are expected to live in a way that is holy. All religions expect this commitment from the people who take part in their rituals. Practising Muslims are expected to live as faithful Muslims. Practising Catholics are expected to live as faithful Catholics.

Morality is an important part of the rituals of a religion. Each religion follows a moral order that is unique to that religion. The ritual or liturgical life of each religion shapes that religion's moral teachings in a certain way.

Human Morality. To be a moral human being is to act in such a way that life together is good. What is proclaimed in religious rituals helps the participants to know and live what is good. **According to you, what is the highest moral norm for living together?**

Catholic Liturgy and Morality

The Catholic faith, too, promotes a specific moral or ethical view of life through its rituals, especially the Mass. In the Mass, the teachings on morality are mostly found in the readings from scripture.

Catholic moral teaching is based on both **philosophy** and **theology**: on philosophical positions and theological reflections (see *Catechism of the Catholic Church,* #1877–1942). Here are three examples of the Catholic tradition and morality as shaped through the scriptures:

1. Catholicism is first of all a celebration of God's love of humans and the world. The focus is not on human sin, although the Church admits sin is there. The focus is on God's grace, God's reaching out in love to people. The scriptures say that God has an intense desire for human well-being and health. To express this idea, the scriptures use the word "salvation." God wants all to be saved, that is, made whole and complete.
2. The main attitude of Catholics is to be grateful for the gift of love at the heart of all existence. Catholic worship or liturgy is to give praise and thanks and to live a life of thanksgiving and generosity, mirroring for others the love God has for them. They are to be generous to others—especially the poor—as God is generous.
3. The highest expression of this response is found in the Sermon on the Mount (Matthew 5:1–7:29). Followers of Jesus must "be perfect ... as your heavenly Father is perfect" (Matthew 5:48).

A Closer Look

Catholics believe that when they do something to another person or to themselves that breaks their relationship with God and with the other, they can be forgiven. Sins are forgiven in the power of God's love. This happens in the ritual of reconciliation. Catholics are invited to take part in this sacrament when they repent of their sins.

Philosophy
Literally, "love of wisdom"; the study of what is true, good, and beautiful in human existence, the use of reason to seek truth and knowledge

Theology
The study of God

Moses and Jesus. Jesus is like Moses. Both went up a mountain to reveal what is in the heart of God. For both, it was summed up in the word "love": Love God and show that love by loving your neighbour as yourself. **Read the Sermon on the Mount (Matthew 5:1–7:29) and summarize in your own words the main message of Jesus.**

Make It Your Own: The Beatitudes

The Beatitudes of Jesus call us to humility, charity, and love. The Beatitudes inspire us to look at the "attitudes" we need to have to find true happiness or blessedness. The "Be Attitudes" are the good attitudes we need to live as Christians in the world. They challenge the "Bad Attitudes" that keep us from living the life God wants for us.

- To be poor of spirit and humble challenges the hurtful attitude of conceited pride.
- To be gentle, kind, and meek challenges the violence and selfishness of our world.
- To seek truth and righteousness keeps us from lying to and deceiving others.
- To be merciful means having compassion for others and mourning with those who suffer. This opposes the Bad Attitudes of disdain and apathy for others.
- To be pure of heart requires that we eliminate self-serving attitudes.
- To be a peacemaker means eliminating strife in our relationships and society in general.
- To have courage enables us to stand up for what is right, even in the face of persecution. We refuse to allow fear to control us.

When we practise the Be Attitudes, we prevent the Bad Attitudes from causing harm to us, our relationships, and our world.

Activities

1. Read the Beatitudes in Matthew 5:3–10. Who are the people in your life who show you examples of each of these Be Attitudes? Write a set of your own Beatitudes that show how these people demonstrate how to live the Beatitudes.
2. With a partner, discuss which Beatitude you think relates most closely to engaging in dialogue with others.

A Closer Look

The Sermon on the Mount contains what we call the Golden Rule: "Do to others as you would have them do to you" (Luke 6:31). See page 369 where this Golden Rule is echoed in other religions.

Love and Justice

Catholics believe justice to be a very important moral value. In justice, we give others what is due to them: adequate food, shelter, security, and whatever they need to lead a life of dignity, worthy of honour and respect. Just as Catholics are fed through the scriptures and Communion at Sunday Mass, they are told to feed others. No one is to be excluded; all are brothers and sisters.

The Catholic Church teaches that this moral goal is achieved through the doctrine of social justice. Teachings on social justice related to business and industry were developed in the nineteenth and twentieth centuries to help working people who suffered because of industrialization. At that time, many people left their farms to work in factories and cities. The work

Jean Vanier and L'Arche. Two of the 1700 high school students from southern Ontario who spent the day with Jean Vanier in October 2007. Vanier founded L'Arche in 1964. It is a worldwide organization that assists people with disabilities, from many different faiths, to live and work together to create homes. The first Canadian community was founded in 1969 in Richmond Hill, Ontario.

was hard and often unsafe, and the workers were not always treated fairly. Many could not feed their families. The Church spoke out against these unjust practices. It pointed out that all people deserve to be respected and treated well because they were created by God. God's desire for justice for all is also found in the Spirit's presence in the world's religions.

Love and Respect for Life

Catholics believe that human life has great value and dignity—that, in fact, life is a gift from God. The Church proclaims a "gospel of life," especially for those who are vulnerable and unable to defend themselves. Catholics believe that life is sacred from the moment of conception until the moment of natural death. The life of every person—those who are not yet born, those who have disabilities, those who are terminally ill, those who are criminals—is sacred to God.

Christ teaches about respecting life in all people. He told his followers this parable to help them understand what it means to follow him:

Then the King will say to those at his right hand, "Come, you that are blessed by my Father, inherit the kingdom prepared for you from the foundation of the world; for I was hungry and you gave me food, I was thirsty and you gave me something to drink, I was a stranger and you welcomed me, I was naked and you gave me clothing, I was sick and you took care of me, I was in prison and you visited me." Then the righteous will answer him, "Lord, when was it that we saw you hungry and gave you food, or thirsty and gave you something to drink? And when was it that we saw you a stranger and welcomed you, or naked and gave clothing? And when was it that we saw you sick or in prison and visited you?" And the King will answer them, "Truly, I tell you, just as you did it to one of the least of these who are members of my family, you did it to me" (Matthew 25:34–40).

A Closer Look

Over the centuries, the Catholic Church has developed a teaching on peace and war. Peace, it states, is the result of justice and charity (*Catechism of the Catholic Church*, #2304). One must always be a creator of peace and reconciliation. If relations between peoples become so tense that war threatens, certain clear conditions for a legitimate defensive war must be maintained. For example, all other means to resolve the conflict must have been exhausted before resorting to military force as a way to defend oneself (see *Catechism of the Catholic Church*, #2309).

Feeding the Hungry. Soup kitchens have become common in our society. The things done to help the weak and the poor are called the Corporal Works of Mercy because they tend to people's bodily needs.

Fast Fact

"Corporal" comes from the Latin word for "body."

Make It Your Own: The Corporal Works of Mercy

The Mass ends with the words "Go in peace to love and serve the Lord." As Roman Catholics, we place a great emphasis on faith in action. We believe that it is not enough to say we have faith in Jesus. We are called to be a people of justice, making the world a better place. We see ourselves as a people who must stand up for what is right, and help those who are suffering or who have been wronged.

In our Catholic tradition, we are told about the Corporal Works of Mercy. All Catholics are called to do the following:

1. Feed the hungry.
2. Give drink to the thirsty.
3. Clothe the naked.
4. Shelter the homeless.
5. Care for the sick.
6. Visit those in prison.
7. Bury the dead.

Many activities and organizations ensure that this work is being done in our world and society. Our task is to think about the gifts and abilities we have, and how we can use them to make life better for others.

Activities

1. List the groups or activities in your school that provide opportunities for performing the Corporal Works of Mercy. What does each group do? When? What can you do to help?
2. Create a poster to promote participation in a school group that performs Corporal Works of Mercy.

Check Your Understanding

1. Explain what is the first aim of Christian morality.

2. Describe how rituals and liturgy are linked to morality.

Think About It

3. "I was in prison and you visited me" (Matthew 25:37). Explore what this means by studying the sixth Corporal Work of Mercy: to visit the imprisoned.

Making It Personal

4. How do you personally show respect for life?

5. God asks us to care for the sick. How can you do this in your life?

Family Life

Catholics and Family Life

Although much of Catholic faith is centred on the parish, where most ritual life (baptism, Eucharist, weddings, and funerals) takes place, the family and the home also play key roles. In the Catholic tradition, marriage is a sacrament. This means that a Catholic couple—in their life together and with their family—are to show both the faithfulness of Christ and the sort of love that Jesus had for people. For Catholic families, the Gospel of Jesus acts as a trusted guide.

The Second Vatican Council called the family a "domestic church" (*Constitution on the Church*, #11). From the first moment of life, a child learns how to love through the love he or she receives from parents, siblings, and relatives. The home is sometimes portrayed as the school of faith, hope, and love. Catholic parents are encouraged to teach their young children how to live, love, and pray, and, when they are ready, how to take part in the Sunday Eucharist and in the life of the Church.

A Catholic Home

A Catholic home does not always look different from other homes. But, often Catholic symbols will be prominently displayed in it: a cross or crucifix on the wall, a palm branch left over from Palm Sunday, an icon, a little shrine with house patron saints, a statue of Mary or a favourite saint, a rosary. Some families use symbols when celebrating the great feasts of the Church, especially Easter and Christmas. At Easter, they may paint Easter eggs; at Christmas, they may set up a nativity scene and decorate their home with lights.

Family Prayer. Catholic families mark important life moments at church, at home, and in the world. **What is one of your favourite memories of your home? Explain.**

Ukrainian Easter Eggs. Designs are "written" on a *pysanka*, or Ukrainian Easter egg, in hot beeswax with a stylus. In fact, *pysanka* comes from the Ukrainian word for "to write." The parts not to be dyed are waxed, similar to the method used in batik. Then the raw egg is dipped in dye to add colour, and the process is repeated. At the end, the wax is melted off to reveal a beautifully coloured *pysanka*. The eggs are often given as gifts at Easter, as a symbol of life.

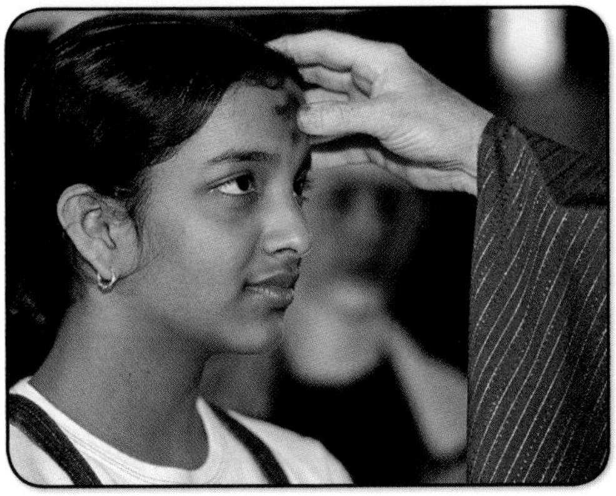

Ash Wednesday. Ashes are a sign of repentance. During Lent, Catholics are asked to turn away from sin and toward God.

As well as showing their faith through visible symbols, Catholics are urged to pray together. Many families pray before meals, because every meal is a memory of the Eucharistic meal, where Christ gave himself to his followers. Many homes also have a bedtime ritual where parents tell stories and say prayers with their children. A ritual such as this strengthens the bonds between family members and, at the same time, strengthens each person's relationship with God.

Catholic Education

Religion, for Catholics, is a public act that aims to touch all life and learning. The Catholic Church says that parents have the right to choose their children's education. In many countries—including some Canadian provinces—parents can educate their children in the Catholic faith by sending them to a Catholic school. In the 1960s, the pope and the world's Catholic bishops prepared a famous document in which they said, "The future of humanity lies in the hands of those who are strong enough to provide coming generations with reasons for living and hoping" (*The Church in the Modern World*, #31). Catholic schools work to contribute to society in this way.

Office of Catholic Youth. Students gather at Martyrs' Shrine in Midland, Ontario, for a World Youth Day celebration event sponsored by the Office of Catholic Youth (OCY) in Toronto. **What activities or events identify your school as Catholic?**

What I Have Learned

In this chapter, I learned about

- Jesus as the origin of Christianity
- the importance of rituals to understand religion
- the central ritual for Catholics: the Sunday Mass
- religious rituals and the marking of time: the importance of Sunday for Catholics
- religious rituals and the shaping of communities: the importance of Church for Catholics
- religious rituals and the shaping of moral life
- the Catholic home as the cradle of faith

The most important prayer for Catholics is the prayer that Jesus taught his disciples. After Jesus had prayed for a whole night, the disciples asked him to teach them to pray. The prayer is called the Lord's Prayer. Catholics pray it at Mass to begin the Communion rite.

The Lord's Prayer

Our Father,
who art in heaven,
hallowed be thy name;
thy kingdom come;
thy will be done on earth as it is in heaven.
Give us this day our daily bread;
and forgive us our trespasses
as we forgive those who trespass against us;
and lead us not into temptation,
but deliver us from evil. Amen.

Chapter 3

The Story of Canadian Aboriginal Spirituality

"O Great Spirit, whose voice I hear in the winds, and whose breath gives life to the world, hear me. I come to you as one of your many children. I am small and weak. I need your strength and your wisdom. May I walk in beauty. Make my eyes ever behold the red and purple sunset. Make my hands respect the things that you have made and my ears sharp to hear your voice. Make me wise so that I may know the things you have taught your children, the lessons you have hidden in every leaf and rock. Make me strong, not to be superior to my brothers, but to be able to fight my greatest enemy, myself. Make me ever ready to come to you with straight eyes, so that when life fades as the fading sunset, my spirit may come to you without shame."

(Attributed to Chief Yellow Lark)

Angel of the North. In this painting, *The Angel of the North* by Ojibwa artist Blake Debassige, we can see how some First Nations artists are integrating the spiritual traditions of their own people with those of the Christian tradition. The painting also reveals the connection between the natural world and the spiritual world. **What familiar symbols can you find? What elements in the painting show the importance of the natural world to Aboriginal peoples?**

What You Will Learn

In this chapter, you will learn about

- Aboriginal peoples in Canada, including their great diversity
- contributions of Aboriginal peoples to Canadian society
- the history of the spiritual traditions of Aboriginal peoples in Canada
- some of the practices and rituals of Aboriginal spiritual traditions, including prayer and ceremonies
- spiritual beliefs and moral life of Aboriginal peoples in Canada
- family life of Aboriginal peoples in Canada
- examples of missions to, and dialogue with, Aboriginal peoples
- contemporary efforts for reconciliation and renewal

Personal Recollection

Candace Sutherland. Candace Sutherland is an Aboriginal student who lives in Winnipeg with her sibling, aunt, and uncle.

My name is Candace Sutherland. I am Aboriginal Canadian. At age 8, I took to running long distance. On my way to the gym one day in winter, I noticed a lot of homeless people standing around, huddled against a heating vent to keep warm. A voice appeared to me and told me that this is my journey. I must take a journey where I can make a difference to our poor. Since I had experienced poverty already, I decided to combine this experience with my ability to run. I started running competitions that offered prize money. With the prize money that I was winning—because my Creator made sure that I would win—I was able to buy food to give to the homeless.

I challenged people, large groups, and companies to join me in matching my donations. Other children were taking notice and wanted to join me in fighting poverty. People started to notice that I was only 10 years old and if I could do it, they could, too. It all started with me, one person, and now well over 3000 people have joined my causes.

My spiritual journey is not about what I do. It's all about what we can do. To do this work is my reward. It's the importance of caring, sharing, loving, giving from the heart. Our Creator is a loving Creator, and his words are words of love. I have seen and felt poverty. When somebody helped me, it made me happy to be able to eat.

I came into this world with nothing.
I will live in this world with nothing.
I will leave this world with nothing.
But what I leave behind is something.

— **Candace Sutherland**

Aboriginal Peoples in Canada Today

Aboriginal Peoples in Canada

Aboriginal Peoples in Canada. The 2006 census identified 1 172 790 people in Canada as Aboriginal peoples. Not all Aboriginal people take part in the census, however, so the numbers might be even higher. **What definitions of the terms "First Nations," "Métis," "Inuit," and "Aboriginal peoples" do you know? Write your own definitions, and then discuss them in the class.**

According to Statistics Canada (2006), more than 1 million people in Canada are Aboriginal. That might seem a small proportion of Canada's total population of 31.62 million, but the number of Aboriginal people is growing at a fast rate—it grew by 45 percent from 1996 to 2006, compared with an 8 percent growth in the non-Aboriginal population during the same time period.

Of the Aboriginal population in Canada, most Aboriginal people (8 out of 10) live in Ontario and the Western provinces. Although Aboriginal people are less likely to live in urban centres than non-Aboriginal people, over half of Aboriginal people (54 percent) do live in urban centres; in contrast, about 80 percent of non-Aboriginal Canadians live in urban centres.

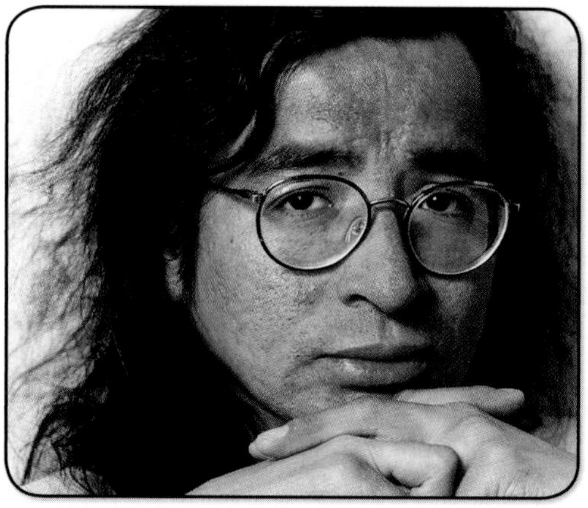

Tomson Highway. Playwright Tomson Highway was born near the Cree community of Brochet, Manitoba, and spoke mainly Cree during his childhood. He has written plays and novels in English, and children's books in both Cree and English. Two of his best-known plays are *The Rez Sisters* and *Dry Lips Oughta Move to Kapuskasing*. He has received the Order of Canada and a National Aboriginal Achievement Award. He is now trilingual (speaking Cree, English, and French) and lives in Ontario.

Aboriginal Teenagers in Winnipeg. Ten percent of Winnipeg's population (about 68 380 people) is Aboriginal.

As you read this chapter, keep in mind that "Aboriginal peoples" is a broad term referring to people who are First Nations, Métis, and Inuit. Beyond these terms, you will find a variety of terms and names in this chapter. Where possible, the text is specific—for example, identifying the Squamish people rather than using the broader term "First Nations people." You will also find contrasts between names given by others versus those used by the people themselves. Finally, as you read this and other texts, you will find some variations in spellings because spoken terms were written down in many forms—for example, Anishinabeg, Anishinabe, Nishnawbe.

Aboriginal People in Atlantic Canada. A young Aboriginal girl in traditional dance dress performs in Dartmouth, Nova Scotia.

Fast Fact

Many Aboriginal peoples identify themselves with a term that means "the people" in their language. For example, "Inuit" means "the people" in Inuktitut, the Inuit language. Similarly, "Anishinabe" means "the people" or "good people."

Métis in Western Canada. Young Métis paddlers on the Assiniboine River in Manitoba follow the historic fur trade route.

Aboriginal People in the North. Young people play soccer in Iqaluit, Nunavut. A traditional igloo is in the background.

The History of Aboriginal Spirituality

The Aboriginal peoples of Canada have a long, rich, and varied context for their spiritual traditions. Aboriginal peoples in the land that is now Canada were—and are—diverse. They live in diverse environments and have a great variety of rituals, symbols, and practices. However, the spiritual traditions are deeply connected to the physical environment in which the Aboriginal peoples have traditionally lived—including the animals and plants of the environments—and life is seen as interconnected.

Until very recently, Aboriginal cultures have been oral ones. Traditionally, Aboriginal peoples have relied on memory and memory keepers—people who have received the sacred teachings from the **elders** and other spiritual leaders. As a result, the history of Aboriginal spiritual traditions is contained in teachings and practices passed down orally through the centuries as well as those shown in some archaeological findings.

Aboriginal peoples have a long tradition of seasonal food growing and gathering, hunting, fishing, and spiritual and cultural activities. Their oral traditions reflect the knowledge and wisdom of generations.

Some First Nations, like the Tsleil-Waututh Nation of the Burrard Inlet area on the West Coast, have described their origins in written form in the Declaration of the Tsleil-Waututh Nation.

Fast Fact

The word "religion" is not one that most indigenous people use to describe their spiritual practices. For some Aboriginal peoples of Canada, the terms "spirituality" and "spiritual traditions" are preferred.

Elders

Aboriginal men or women who are recognized, respected, and consulted for their wisdom, experience, knowledge, background, and insight; an elder is not necessarily one of the oldest people in the community

Fast Fact

Today, some sacred ceremonies and teachings are not considered appropriate to pass on in written form.

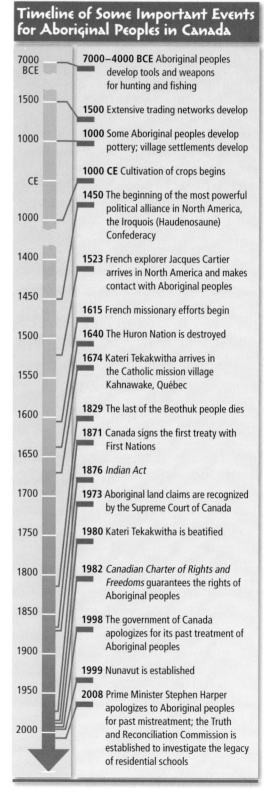

Timeline of Some Important Events for Aboriginal Peoples in Canada

7000 BCE, 1500, 1000, CE, 1000, 1400, 1450, 1500, 1550, 1600, 1650, 1700, 1750, 1800, 1850, 1900, 1950, 2000

7000–4000 BCE Aboriginal peoples develop tools and weapons for hunting and fishing

1500 Extensive trading networks develop

1000 Some Aboriginal peoples develop pottery; village settlements develop

1000 CE Cultivation of crops begins

1450 The beginning of the most powerful political alliance in North America, the Iroquois (Haudenosaune) Confederacy

1523 French explorer Jacques Cartier arrives in North America and makes contact with Aboriginal peoples

1615 French missionary efforts begin

1640 The Huron Nation is destroyed

1674 Kateri Tekakwitha arrives in the Catholic mission village Kahnawake, Québec

1829 The last of the Beothuk people dies

1871 Canada signs the first treaty with First Nations

1876 *Indian Act*

1973 Aboriginal land claims are recognized by the Supreme Court of Canada

1980 Kateri Tekakwitha is beatified

1982 *Canadian Charter of Rights and Freedoms* guarantees the rights of Aboriginal peoples

1998 The government of Canada apologizes for its past treatment of Aboriginal peoples

1999 Nunavut is established

2008 Prime Minister Stephen Harper apologizes to Aboriginal peoples for past mistreatment; the Truth and Reconciliation Commission is established to investigate the legacy of residential schools

Ojibwa Rock Painting. This Ojibwa rock painting is found at Agawa Bay, in Lake Superior Provincial Park, Ontario. Some of the 35 rock paintings in this area are estimated to be at least 1500 years old. According to one interpretation, some paintings show the spirit of the Ojibwa sea monster Mishipizheu (a spirit also called Great Horned Lynx), and one of a fleet of canoes that was able to cross the dangerous eastern Lake Superior with the spirit's blessing.

A Closer Look

"The traditional way of education was by example, experience, and storytelling. The first principle involved was total respect and acceptance of the one to be taught, and that learning was a continuous process from birth to death. It was total continuity without interruption. Its nature was like a fountain that gives many colours and flavours of water and that whoever chose could drink as much or as little as they wanted to whenever they wished. The teaching strictly adhered to the sacredness of life whether of humans, animals, or plants."

—Art Solomon, Ojibwa Elder

There is great diversity among Aboriginal peoples of Canada and the environments of their traditional lands, yet their worldviews are similar to those of **indigenous** peoples everywhere on Earth. The traditional worldview shows a deep sense that all that exists—trees, plants, animals, humans, the earth, even certain rocks—is alive.

Petroglyphs in Nova Scotia. These petroglyphs can be seen in Kejimkujik National Park, Nova Scotia. They are part of the legacy from 4000 years of the Mi'kmaq people's spiritual relationship to this land.

Indigenous

Refers to native, original, or earliest known inhabitants of a region

Petroforms in Manitoba. Petroforms are arrangements of rocks or boulders made by Aboriginal people and understood to be for teaching, healing, and other spiritual practices. Some petroforms show turtles, humans, fish, and a giant serpent. This petroform at Whiteshell Provincial Park in Manitoba may date back to the same time a nearby camp was created—500 CE.

Aboriginal Language Families of Canada, Showing Their Approximate Location at the Time of European Contact

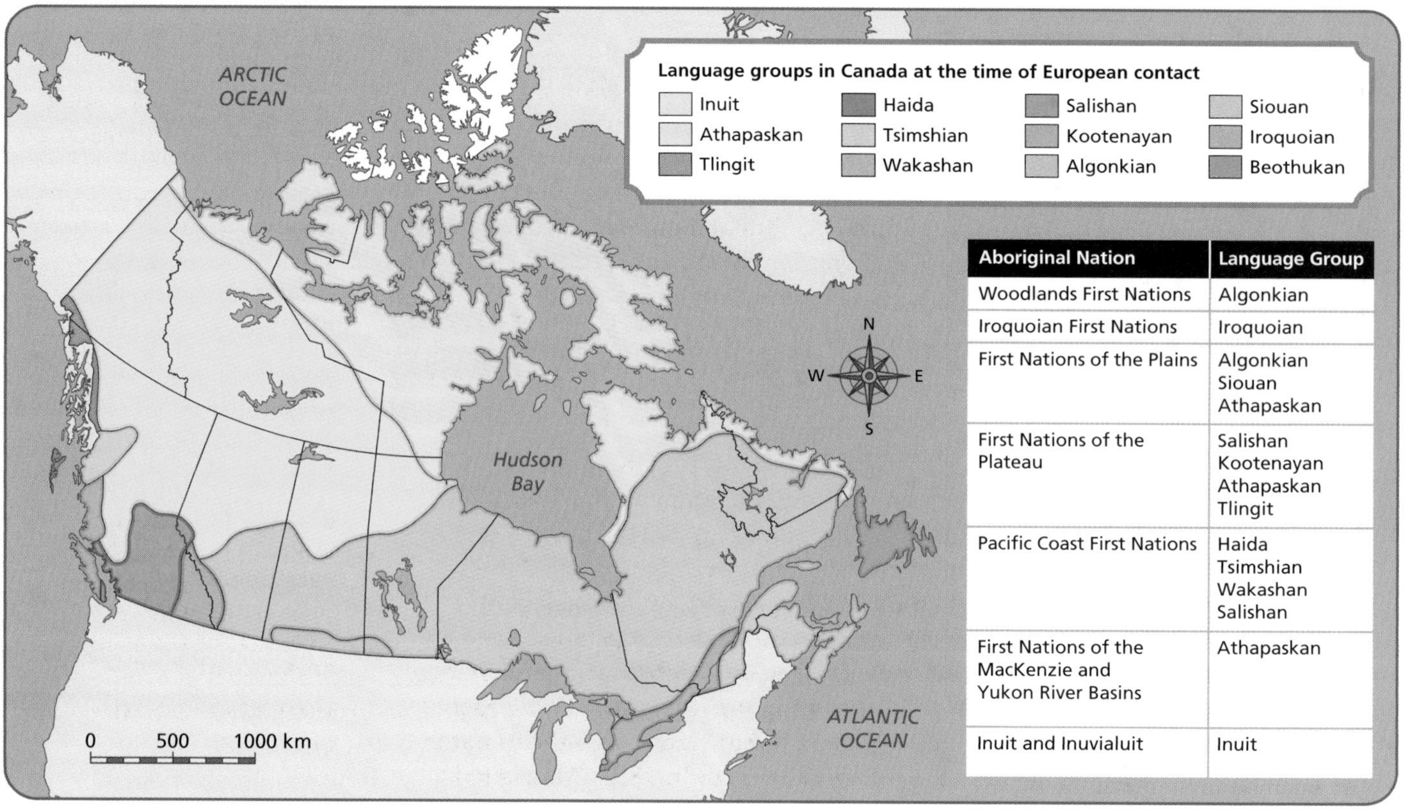

Aboriginal Nation	Language Group
Woodlands First Nations	Algonkian
Iroquoian First Nations	Iroquoian
First Nations of the Plains	Algonkian Siouan Athapaskan
First Nations of the Plateau	Salishan Kootenayan Athapaskan Tlingit
Pacific Coast First Nations	Haida Tsimshian Wakashan Salishan
First Nations of the MacKenzie and Yukon River Basins	Athapaskan
Inuit and Inuvialuit	Inuit

Aboriginal Nations in Canada. Each of the Aboriginal nations at the time of contact in 1534 had its own language, spiritual beliefs, and practices. There are now more than 60 Aboriginal languages and dialects in Canada.

Check Your Understanding

1. Define the term "Aboriginal peoples" and describe the recent trend in Aboriginal population growth in Canada.
2. How have spiritual traditions been passed down from one generation to the next?

Think About It

3. Review the pages you have read in this chapter so far. What key ideas and questions do you have to this point? How might you find answers to your questions?

Making It Personal

4. Aboriginal spiritual traditions are very connected to the physical environment. In what ways is your own religion or faith connected to the natural world? What might that fact mean in your natural environment? Express your ideas in an illustration, collection of photos, or journal entry.
5. Looking at the map above, identify which Aboriginal peoples in 1534 lived closest to where you live now. What do you know about the Aboriginal history of your community?

NEL

Buffalo Meat Drying. Many early Métis hunted buffalo and made pemmican with the meat. They supplied pemmican to European traders. This painting shows Métis drying buffalo meat.

European Contact and Aboriginal Spiritual Traditions

As you read in Chapter 2, the Europeans came to North America as explorers, traders, colonizers, settlers, and missionaries. Over time, the contact between Europeans and Aboriginal peoples had a range of impacts. In some cases, for example, Aboriginal peoples helped early Europeans by teaching them survival skills. As you read below about some of the attitudes and actions of the Europeans, think about the possible effects on the Aboriginal spiritual traditions you have read about so far in this chapter.

- Many Europeans considered their own ways "civilized" but Aboriginal ways "uncivilized." They believed that Aboriginal peoples should give up their own traditions.
- As early as 1701, treaties were signed to define promises, obligations, and benefits. They covered land, hunting and fishing rights, and other issues concerning Aboriginal peoples and Europeans.
- Reserves were created, which set aside parcels of land for specific First Nations peoples to use.
- *The Gradual Civilization Act* (1857) was passed to **assimilate** Aboriginal peoples into European culture.
- *The Indian Act* (1876) set out the federal government's responsibility for education of Status Indian children aged 6 to 18. It allowed for the setting up of residential schools run by Anglican, United, Presbyterian, and Catholic churches.
- Starting in 1885, one West Coast Aboriginal ceremony—the potlatch—was banned. In 1895, Aboriginal ceremonies, dances, and festivals were banned.

In the words of Black Elk, a Sioux spiritual leader and a Catholic, the arrival of the Europeans broke the sacred circle of life: "The Wasichus [white men] have put us in these square boxes. Our power is gone and we are dying, for the power is not in us anymore." What do you think Black Elk might mean by "square boxes"?

Fast Fact

"Status Indian" is a term used in the *Indian Act*. Registered Status Indians are entitled to services from the federal government.

Assimilate

Absorb one group into the culture of another

Aboriginal Residential Schools. These Aboriginal children are in class at a residential school on the Stoney Reserve, Morley, Alberta, around 1950. Many Aboriginal children were taken far distances away from their families for many years at a time. Many residential schools did not allow students to speak Aboriginal languages.

Recent History

Through the twentieth century and into the twenty-first century, Aboriginal peoples in Canada have faced many challenges and made many changes. Here are some examples that relate to Aboriginal spiritual traditions.

- Many banned Aboriginal ceremonies continued in private. The ban was officially lifted in 1951.
- The creation of the territory of Nunavut in 1999 was the largest land claim settlement in Canada's history. Nunavut has three official languages (Inuktitut, English, and French) and a territorial government that favours making decisions by consensus—a traditional practice among Inuit.
- Elder Noel Knockwood has been active in reviving Aboriginal spirituality in Nova Scotia and New Brunswick. For example, he has published a book titled *Mi'kmaq Teaching and Prayers*, helped Aboriginal spirituality become recognized as an official religion in Nova Scotia, and participated in the Eagle Feather project, which allows for the eagle feather to be used in the provincial justice system in place of a Bible.
- After the Canadian public became aware of the cultural, physical, emotional, and sexual abuse that had occurred at residential schools, the schools were eventually closed. Both the federal government and the churches involved apologized to Aboriginal peoples. In 2008, the federal government set up a Truth and Reconciliation Commission to document the legacy of the residential schools.
- In 1982, the *Canadian Charter of Rights and Freedoms* guaranteed the rights of Aboriginal peoples and had a powerful and positive effect on legal issues relating to Aboriginal peoples.

Federal Government Apology to Aboriginal Peoples. In 2008, on behalf of the government of Canada, Prime Minister Stephen Harper asked "the forgiveness of the Aboriginal peoples of this country for failing them so profoundly," and added, "We are sorry." He is shown here presenting a citation to Assembly of First Nations Chief Phil Fontaine.

Meeting between the Pope and Aboriginal Elders. In April 2009, Pope Benedict XVI expressed his sorrow over the abuse suffered by some at residential schools. Assembly of First Nations Chief Phil Fontaine, Aboriginal elders, and survivors met with the pope.

Aboriginal Peoples in Canada Today

Today, Aboriginal peoples in Canada are a fast-growing group. Many Aboriginal peoples are trying to address the negative impacts of contact, recover and revive traditional practices, and move toward a stronger future. Recognizing and taking pride in Aboriginal achievements is part of this movement. Another part is the revival of Aboriginal spiritual traditions.

The history of the encounter between Aboriginal peoples and European colonizers of Canada made it difficult for Aboriginal peoples to express their ancient spiritual traditions. In part, the federal government's apology to Aboriginal peoples was due to the increasing interest and success of many Aboriginal people in rediscovering their traditional spiritual roots.

For Aboriginal peoples reviving Aboriginal spiritual traditions, this can mean

- embracing once again the healing spiritual values and practices of their ancestors after decades of treatment as second-class citizens
- reviving spiritual traditions in the midst of an increasingly secular Canada
- integrating Aboriginal spiritual heritage with Christianity

For Aboriginal Canadians who are Christian, this revival can mean struggling with the question of whether they can be true to their own Aboriginal spiritual traditions while remaining faithful to the Gospel as followers of Christ. This is an *intra-religious dialogue*—a dialogue within a religion. There are no easy answers.

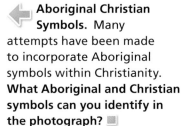

Aboriginal Christian Symbols. Many attempts have been made to incorporate Aboriginal symbols within Christianity. **What Aboriginal and Christian symbols can you identify in the photograph?**

Aboriginal Culture, Tradition, and History. In 1998, Joe and Josephine Crowshoe were honoured with a National Aboriginal Achievement Award. As elders of the Piegan Nation in southern Alberta, they worked to educate Aboriginal and non-Aboriginal peoples about Aboriginal culture, tradition, and history, and to promote a harmonious relationship between Aboriginal and non-Aboriginal peoples.

The First Legislature of Nunavut. In this photo of the interim legislature of Nunavut, taken in 1999, the members of the legislature are being sworn in. Unlike other legislatures, the Nunavut legislature is set up as a ring in which all members are joined, rather than having members sit on opposite sides from each other. **What does this set-up tell you about how the Inuit view decision making?**

Make It Your Own: The Talking Feather

In many Aboriginal cultures, people use a talking feather, stick, or stone to help them talk and listen respectfully. Only the person holding the feather, stick, or stone may talk: other people in the group must listen attentively and respectfully. When the speaker is finished, he or she passes the feather, stick, or stone to the next person who wishes to speak. In this way, everyone has an opportunity to speak and a right to be heard with respect.

There is a well-known teaching about how the talking feather came to symbolize the power of words and communication. Crow and Magpie argued so loudly that they disturbed all the villagers. A villager asked Eagle to frighten the squabbling birds into silence, but they were too busy arguing to notice Eagle. During their dispute, one of the birds bumped into Eagle, causing one of his feathers to fall out. Both birds were ashamed of their actions, and realized that they could solve their argument by talking instead of fighting. Eagle gave the feather to the people and from then on, when the people gathered, only the one who held the talking feather could speak.

Activity

1. With your classmates, create your own version of a talking feather, stick, or stone to use during discussions or debates in the class. Then, create a list of rules for how to use it. How can you and your classmates show respect for this powerful symbol?

Sacred Eagle Feathers. Many Aboriginal peoples consider eagle feathers sacred because the eagle is viewed as a divine messenger. Its feathers represent power and protection. Because the eagle soars high in the skies, it is the only creature believed to have touched the face of the Creator.

Skill Focus: Making Decisions through Consensus

Aboriginal peoples make decisions through a process of consensus, that is, of coming to agreement as a group. If an issue requires discussion and debate, it is discussed by all the members of the group. All opinions are respected and listened to. If members disagree about the course of action, the most skilled negotiators in the group try to help the group reach a compromise.

These principles can apply to group discussions and group work in class, as well.

1. All group members are responsible for contributing to the discussion.
2. To ensure that everyone contributes, sit in a circle and go around the group. Everyone speaks in turn according to his or her position in the circle. If your group has made a talking stick or feather, use it to determine who will speak.
3. While someone is speaking, all other group members must listen respectfully, without interrupting.
4. Accept all ideas brought forward at this point in the discussion.
5. As a group, assign the role of note taker to one or more group members. If your group has more than one note taker, combine your notes at the end of the discussion.
6. Once you have gone around the circle and everyone has had a chance to contribute, identify where you have agreed or disagreed.
7. If your group disagrees about an issue, the next step is to discuss the disagreement more fully.
   - How do the two viewpoints differ?
   - Are there any areas of agreement? Can your group build on those?
   - Can another member suggest a compromise between both viewpoints?

Making decisions by consensus can be a long process, but in the end all members of the group achieve some of their goals.

Check Your Understanding

1. a) Describe at least three ways in which contact with Europeans affected Aboriginal peoples.

b) Describe two recent positive changes in the situation of Aboriginal peoples in Canada.

Think About It

2. Create a timeline or clock to mark dates for archaeological evidence, traditional teachings, and key events noted on pages 70 to 74. How would you describe the history of Aboriginal spiritual traditions?

3. Where have you gained most of your knowledge about the Aboriginal peoples of Canada? How do your sources influence your understanding of Aboriginal peoples, their contributions to Canadian society, and their spiritual traditions?

Making It Personal

4. Consider your own belief systems. If you were not allowed to practise rituals, speak your first language, or feel pride in your heritage, how would that affect you? How would you face that challenge?

5. In 2008, Canada's prime minister made a statement of apology to the Aboriginal peoples of Canada on behalf of the Canadian government. If you could add your own personal statement, what would you add?

Rituals

Inuksuk. In the Far North, Inuksuit might be used for navigation and communication. They also have spiritual meaning.

As you read earlier, Aboriginal peoples, their traditional environments, and their traditional practices are diverse within Canada. However, traditional spiritual practices have the following in common:

- their strong relationship to the physical environment
- their underlying belief that life is interconnected

Some rituals, such as prayer, may be everyday actions. Some rituals mark special events in a person's life, or they mark seasonal or community events.

The Sacred in Daily Life and Environment

In traditional Aboriginal worldviews and spiritual beliefs, all is sacred and everything is connected. Everything is pervaded by spirit power. All life is a manifestation of spiritual reality. Everything comes from the spirit. When we leave this life, we return to the world of the spirit. Spirit is what connects all living things.

For these reasons, traditionally, every action involves the sacred and every aspect of a person's physical environment holds power. Being attentive to the physical environment—as someone must be to live from the resources of the land—helps one to see the power in the environment. As Walking Buffalo, a Sioux, said, "Do you know that trees talk? Yes, they talk; they talk among themselves and to you if you take pains to listen."

Prayer has always been an important part of Aboriginal spiritual practices. God is understood as the Creator. The purpose of praying is to recognize God's greatness and to express thanks for all the Creator's gifts. Individuals, families, and groups celebrate with a variety of sung and spoken prayers, usually spontaneously, from the heart. Some prayers can involve offering a gift or sacrifice.

Fast Fact

Four plants are considered especially sacred to the Aboriginal peoples of Canada: cedar, sage, tobacco, and sweetgrass. Which of these plants might grow naturally in your environment?

A Prayer of Thanks is used to communicate with the Creator before and after actions such as waking, sleeping, hunting, planting, and harvesting. In earlier periods, time was often set aside to pray, fast, and make sacrifices to charm the evil spirits that played havoc with the hunt or caused sudden storms to arise.

When I was 10 years old, I looked at the earth and the rivers, the sky above, and I could not but realize that they had been created by a great power.

I was so curious to understand this power that I questioned the trees and the brooks, and it seemed to me that the flowers looked at me, and I wanted to ask them: "Who created you?" I looked at rocks covered with moss; some seemed to have the features of a man, but they could not answer me. Then I had a dream, and in the dream one of the small round rocks appeared to me, and it said the creator of the whole universe was "*Wakan Tanka*" and that to honour him, I ought to honour his works in nature.

All my life I have been faithful to the sacred rocks. I have lived according to their principles, and they have helped me in my problems ... I know that I am not worthy of talking directly to *Wakan Tanka*. I talk to the rocks, and they intercede for me.

—Brave Buffalo (Sioux)

Aboriginal Peoples and the Church. Much Aboriginal spirituality is derived from nature, but many Aboriginal people now do not live "on the land." In fact, more and more Aboriginal people are living in cities, where their connection to the natural environment is harder to maintain. In the cities, including in urban Catholic parishes, Aboriginal peoples are making great efforts to revive spiritual traditions. In this photo, First Nations representatives from Ojibwa, Mohawk, Cree, and Algonquin Nations celebrate the installation of Archbishop Terry Prendergast in Ottawa. The First Nations people are members of the Kateri Native Ministry of Ottawa. The Kateri Native Ministry works to improve relations between Aboriginal peoples and the Church, and to incorporate Aboriginal spiritual traditions into the Catholic tradition.

Smudging

Smudging is a holy act that is a part of many rituals. Sacred herbs are burned in a shell or earthen bowl, and then the smoke is brushed or washed over the eyes, mouth, ears, hands, heart, and whole being of each participant. The cleansing smoke from smudging can be used to purify people and places, for example, before an important event such as a wedding, powwow, or healing. Because smudging is a holy act, the ashes are holy, too. Traditionally, as a sign of respect, after the ceremony the ashes are returned to the earth in an area where they will not be walked on.

Fast Fact

Many Aboriginal peoples perform smudging ceremonies, using a variety of different plants. Meetings of Métis people often open and close with a prayer and smudging ceremony.

Stirring a Smudge Pot. Terry McGurrin of Edgewood Farms near Brockville, Ontario, stirs a smudge pot with an eagle feather during a blessing ceremony.

Fast Fact

For some Aboriginal peoples, many ceremonies are considered sacred and not to be photographed or taped. In some cases, however, a community's elders may give permission to do this for the good of the community.

Sacred Pipe Ceremony

The Sacred Pipe ceremony is one of the most powerful and sacred spiritual rituals for Aboriginal peoples in Canada. The pipe symbolizes the unity and harmony of the world. To smoke the pipe in a ritual is to give back to the world its unity, peace, and harmony. Before lighting the pipe, the pipe carrier prays that the whole universe and all it contains be transferred to the pipe. When lit, all that the pipe contains is delivered over to the fire, which is the Great Spirit. Everything is dissolved into the cosmic unity of the Great Spirit.

The stone bowl of the pipe represents truth. The stem represents the way we are to live in harmony and balance with all of creation. The bowl, with its hole for accepting the wooden stem, represents the woman; the stem represents the man. Joining the bowl to the stem symbolizes a union and a balance between male and female aspects of the world. Because smoking the sacred pipe involves all the elements of earth, fire, air, and water (condensation in the stem), it again stresses the oneness and unity of all creation.

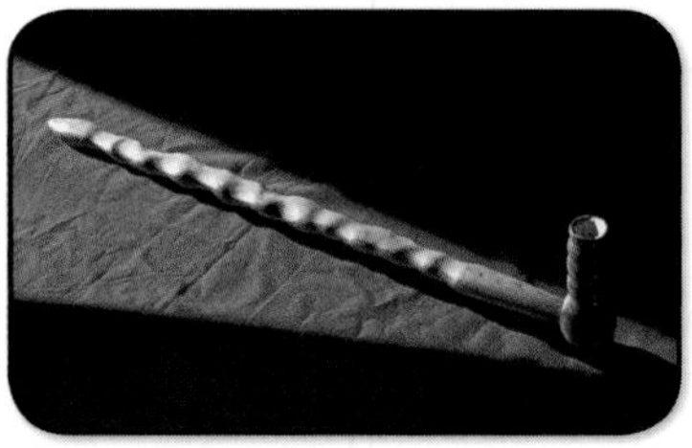

Sacred Pipe. The carved wooden pipe bowl and stem used by Algonquin First Nations. It was sometimes referred to as the peace pipe.

The Sweat Lodge

Many Aboriginal cultures have a form of sweat lodge. The sweat lodge ceremony aims to purify the body, mind, spirit, and heart, and to restore right relationships with self, others, the Creator, and all of creation. For this reason, the sweat lodge is considered a sacred space, a place of spiritual refuge and healing. It is sometimes called the womb of Mother Earth.

A sweat lodge is a closed structure built around a pit into which heated rocks are placed during the ceremony. The sweat leader pours water onto the hot rocks to create steam. In this dark, moist setting, participants return to the womb and the innocence of childhood. Here they sing, pray, talk, meditate, sit in silence, or reflect on creation stories. Sweat lodge ceremonies can last for several hours.

Sweat Lodge. This photo shows a sweat lodge with a teepee in the background.

NEL

Life-Cycle Rituals

Birth and Naming Rituals

Most Aboriginal people go to great lengths to give the right name to each child. To learn the right name of a child, the name-giver (often the child's grandparent or an elder) enters into a time of fasting, meditation, prayer, or dreaming. The name revealed by the Spirit is then given to the child in a special ceremony, which the child's family, relatives, and friends attend. As a person matures, this name may change. The name expresses the identity of the person, which consists of his or her relation to the spirit power.

Puberty

In most Aboriginal communities, young people go on a vision quest—an intense, solitary spiritual experience for those seeking direction in life. Young people prepare for about a year and go on the vision quest only when parents or elders believe they are ready. Traditionally, young people must undertake the vision quest to be accepted as adults in the community.

Catholic Connection

At the beginning of his ministry, after Jesus was baptized by John, "Jesus, full of the Holy Spirit, returned from the Jordan and was led by the Spirit in the wilderness, where for forty days he was tempted by the devil. He ate nothing at all during those days ..." (Luke 4:1–2). During his stay in the desert, Jesus had a spiritual experience that prepared him for his mission. How is this experience similar to the vision quest?

Location for a Vision Quest. The circle sets off the space for the vision quest. A person in search of spirit helpers will spend three to four days in a spot such as this without food, with a little water, trying to stay awake. Dreamer's Rock on the Whitefish River Reserve near Manitoulin Island in Ontario (shown here) is a place often used for vision quests.

Make It Your Own: The Vision Quest

During a vision quest, the young person prays and goes without food and sleep, and eventually encounters a spirit helper through a dream, vision, or phenomenon of nature. The spirit gives insights into the person's future life role. The spirit helper may appear in various forms—often in the form of an eagle, a bear, or another animal. After the vision quest, an elder interprets the vision.

Activity

1. Based on this understanding of a vision quest (and possibly additional research), create a storyboard to tell about one young person's vision quest. Be sure to include the following:
   - a special or sacred location
   - fasting and prayer
   - the vision: the arrival of the spirit helper and the spirit helper's teachings
   - the return home
   - the elder's interpretation

Aboriginal Hair. Long, uncut, braided hair worn by Aboriginal people is often a spiritual or cultural statement about belonging to a particular First Nation.

Hair

Some Aboriginal peoples consider long, uncut hair, worn by men and women, to be sacred. Generally, hair is braided, and among some men, three braided strands signify the body, mind, and spirit. The length and style are not uniform, but braids or uncut hair generally signify that the style worn is of spiritual and cultural importance to the individual and reinforces his or her sense of belonging to a particular First Nation. For some, cut hair is a sign of mourning. In what other traditions do you know about hair having special significance? For example, covered, long, short—what might it mean among people you know?

Death

Death rituals, and the beliefs that underpin them, vary among Aboriginal peoples. Some examples are described below.

Those who have died also need to relearn what it is to be a spirit. The time required for this transition is slightly different for each person, but tradition requires a waiting period of one year. At that time, a Death Feast is held for the spirit of the person who has left.

Today, the Ojibwa celebrate the Feast of the Dead each autumn to remember all who died during the previous year. Among traditional Ojibwa, each family who has lost someone during the past year holds a banquet for the entire village. The food is placed not necessarily on the table, but in an open area outside. A place is set for the deceased, whose spirit remains with the family.

Cree, who honour the circle of life, also honour death. In their tradition, the body undergoes physical transformations, but the spirit remains unchanged. It ascends into another realm to join the ranks of the ancestors who preceded it in death.

Separation from the body does not mean that all ties to people are gone. Cree believe spirits have the power to reveal themselves and communicate with humans in dreams or visions, or when called upon to do so in sacred ceremonies, such as the sweat lodge or sun dance.

Thanks for Successful Hunt. Typically, when an animal dies—including when it has been hunted for food—traditional belief requires giving a prayer of thanks.

Great Plains Death Ceremony. In earlier times, when a Great Plains member died, his or her body was placed on a platform. During this time, it was believed that the person's spirit journeyed into the next world. The body was then wrapped in animal skins or fur and buried with the feet pointing southward (the direction of the next world). Food and tools for the journey to the next world were buried with the deceased. Small buildings were sometimes constructed over the grave to shelter the spirit.

The wake, a ceremony for returning the body to Mother Earth, and the round dance, a ceremony to commune with spirits who have passed to the spirit world, are important parts of the Cree grief and healing process.

The round dance is celebrated so that the family and friends who remain behind will allow the spirit of the deceased to fly free so that it can dance with the other spirits who make up the northern lights.

Northern Lights. The Cree believe that the northern lights (aurora borealis) are the spirits of dead relatives dancing.

A Fancy Shawl Dance. A Blackfoot fancy shawl dancer performs at Fort McLeod, Lethbridge, Alberta. The fancy shawl dance refers to the shawl worn by the women.

Seasonal and Community Rituals

Harvest Feast

Each year at harvest time, Aboriginal peoples traditionally celebrate the harvest from the field and forest. This is a way of recognizing the spirits that acted on their behalf to give them food, and of renewing the earth by prayers, chants, and dances. This feast, celebrated particularly by Aboriginal peoples who are farmers, was adopted by non-Aboriginal peoples, who call it "Thanksgiving." Similar celebrations follow a successful hunt or fishing expedition.

The Powwow

The powwow is a dance of renewal for the restoration of right relationships and the healing of all of creation. It is a community celebration, a time to get together to sing and dance, and to celebrate one's identity, heritage, and language. As in all Aboriginal rituals, the powwow takes place in a circle. Always blessed by a spiritual leader, the space within the circle is holy.

Generally, the dancers and singers enter the circle from the east, where the Sun rises, and move in a clockwise direction—in the same direction as the Sun moves. The drumbeat that accompanies many events is symbolic of the solemn rhythm of creation, the heartbeat of Mother Earth and the rhythm of the mother's heartbeat that all hear in the womb.

Sun Dance

The sun dance ceremony is celebrated by peoples of the Prairies in June or July, at the time of the full Moon.

Sun Dance Ritual. Blackfoot First Nations perform the sun dance in 1908.

According to tradition, the sun dance began when a warrior's vision quest showed him a new way to pray to the Great Spirit. The purpose of the sun dance became the renewal of dedication to the Great Spirit. Participants take part in four annual dances to prepare themselves for the final stage of the rite.

Four days before the ceremony, the dancers purify themselves (for example, with a sweat lodge ceremony) and prepare. The sun dance itself takes another four days, during which time the dancers fast. The final stage of the rite involves piercing the body and, in a dance, tearing away from the piercing to symbolize a renewal of the quest for the spirit in one's life.

Giveaways and the Potlatch

A common festival is the giveaway. This ceremony might celebrate a special event, such as a birth or wedding, or it may commemorate a death. The event involves giving gifts of blankets, beadwork, or crafts to family, friends, or visitors plus ceremonial dancing and singing.

On the West Coast, Aboriginal peoples, such as the Haida, have potlatches. These are like giveaways in that they mark significant events in a family, such as the birth of a child, the death of a relative, or a chief taking office. However, they also increase the host's standing in the community and highlight the host's generosity, wealth, and power.

Potlatch. A potlatch in Kispiox Skeena Valley, British Columbia, is a celebration to redistribute wealth in a community. It highlights the important value of equality among Aboriginal peoples.

Fast Fact

When the Canadian government banned potlatches in 1887, officials believed that they contributed to poverty among coastal nations. The ban was lifted in 1951, when the government recognized that the potlatch was the main cultural, social, religious, and political institution of the people, and therefore was important to their ability to maintain solidarity and a sense of identity.

Check Your Understanding

1. With a partner or in a small group, create a chart summarizing and categorizing the rituals described on pages 78 to 85.

Think About It

2. Consider the government ban on Aboriginal spiritual ceremonies. From your perspective now, why did this happen? Would it ever be reasonable for a government to ban a spiritual practice? In a class discussion, use a talking feather, stick, or stone to have a respectful discussion of these questions.
3. Research spiritual practices and rituals of Aboriginal peoples living in or near your community. If possible, ask to interview an elder. Present your findings respectfully to your classmates.

Making It Personal

4. One theme running through Aboriginal spiritual rituals is respect for Earth. Is this a theme in your life and rituals? On a poster, or in a short blog or interview, comment on this theme, your beliefs, and those you have read about so far in this chapter.

Central Beliefs and Morality

Catholic Connection

In the Judeo-Christian tradition, the power that pervades all creation is called "wisdom" in the Old Testament (Proverbs 8:22–30). "Wisdom" is seen as a power present when God made all things. In the New Testament, this power is identified with Christ: "In him [Christ] all things in heaven and on earth were created ... all things have been created through him and for him. He himself is before all things, and in him all things hold together" (Colossians 1:16–17).

As you have read, the Aboriginal worldview sees the sacred in all creation—in every aspect of humans and the environment. As well, all life is seen as interconnected. However, Aboriginal peoples believe that the world around them is always changing from within. The forces of this transformation, which live among us and within us, seem to work independently of one another. They show themselves in the rising of the Sun, in the movement of the clouds, in the coming of the first frost, and in the growth of plants and trees. In this way, the universe is a complex assembly of powers or spirits—small and great, beneficial and dangerous. Humans do not control these spirits. To live, humans must ally themselves to these spiritual powers to keep harmony between them. That is why humans need to learn how these powers act.

For Aboriginal peoples, all power comes from a common origin. In other words, the same energy inhabits all things.

- The Siouan peoples of the plains call this energy *Wakan. Wakan Tanka* or *Wakonda* is the Great Spirit.
- The Haudenosaune (Iroquois) call it *Orenda. Orenda* is a distinct spirit that, from time to time, attaches itself to an object or animal.
- The Algonkian-speaking peoples call it *Manitou. Manitou* is the "Great Mystery," "the Great Mysterious One," or the "Great Spirit."

Some things have a greater quantity of this spirit or energy, while other things have less of it. A certain tree, a certain mountain, a certain animal may have more power than others. Learning the power of each thing is central to Aboriginal life.

The Great Spirit

Aboriginal peoples believe in the pervasiveness of spirit in all things. Some non-Aboriginal peoples have suggested that this is a form of animism—the identification of the spirit with the objects it inhabits. But, for most

The Healing Rock. *The Healing Rock* by Métis artist Natalie Rostad stands at the entrance to an Aboriginal burial ground on South Point at the fork where the Red and Assiniboine rivers meet in Winnipeg. It is covered with 100 paintings and Aboriginal symbols. It is found beside the Oodena Celebration Circle, a site that is 3000 years old.

Aboriginal peoples, the spirit force is fluid. It is there at specific moments. For example, it is there when the eagle is in flight high in the sky, but not when the eagle is asleep. Asked whether stones are alive, or touched by spirit, an Ojibwa elder replied, "No! but some are."

Aboriginal peoples believe in a Great Spirit who inhabits all things: rocks, land, water, plants, animals, fish, birds, and people. They often address this Great Spirit as the Creator. There appears, therefore, to be a highest God, the Creator, who is one.

This Spirit reveals itself in its many manifestations in nature. That is why Aboriginal peoples will also talk about spirits. These are the powers they encounter in everything, particularly the unusual around them. These they encounter when they find their spirit helpers in their vision quests. Like the angels of the Christian tradition, the spirits become the guardians of people's spirit lives.

The Trickster

Many sacred teachings include a figure who plays an important role in the creation of the world but is not the Creator. The figure is generally called the Trickster and is often credited with giving Earth the form it has today. The Trickster can be both mean and generous. He (because most forms of the Trickster are male) is impulsive, a bungler, a joker or buffoon. He acts as if there is no moral value. He is often a pleasure-seeking figure, a troublemaker.

The Ojibwa Trickster Nanabush was useful in that he stole fire for humans; he calmed dangerous winds; he invented strategies for hunting. He also helped to restore Earth after the great flood and taught the people how to live again according to the original instructions given to them by the Creator. He is at times helpful—quite often accidentally. He at times has great power, somewhere between the human and the divine.

Fast Fact

God is understood as the Creator. Prayer is a significant ritual in Aboriginal spiritual traditions and is usually spontaneous and personal. The purpose of praying is to recognize God's greatness and to express thanks for all the Creator's gifts.

The Haida Trickster Raven. In this sculpture, *The Raven and the First Men* (1980), by Haida artist Bill Reid, Raven is shown helping deliver the first humans (the Haida), who emerged from a clam shell.

Trickster

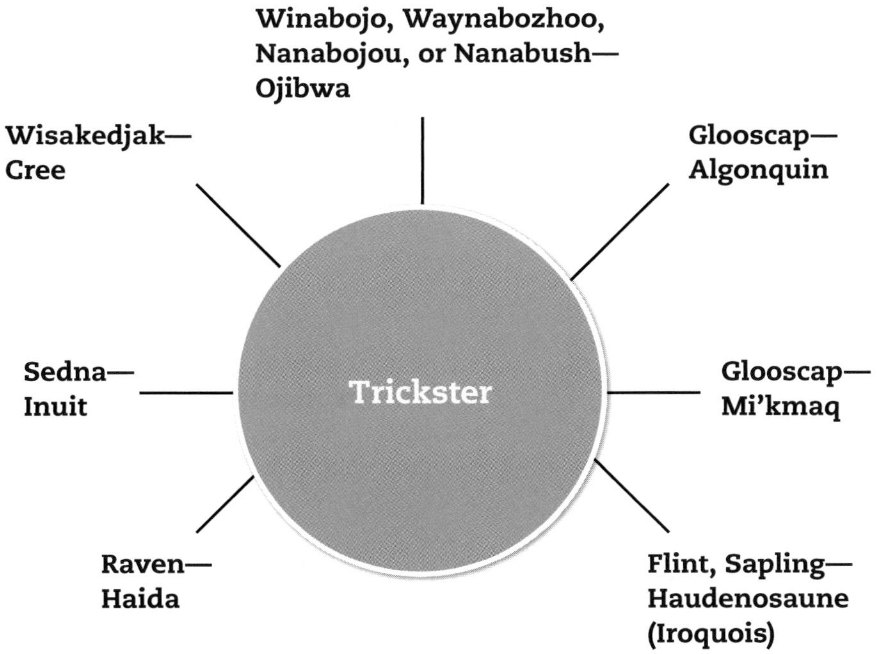

Tricksters from Different Aboriginal Cultures. The presence of tricksters in many Aboriginal spiritual traditions reflects a belief that the world is a mixture of good and bad but also that, through the sometimes painful actions of tricksters, good may result.

Make It Your Own: The Grandfather Teachings

The Seven Grandfather Teachings were the teachings given to the Anishinabeg early in their history. The first elder was given gifts of knowledge by the seven grandfathers to help the people live a good life and respect the Creator, Earth, and each other.

Wisdom is to cherish knowledge.

Love is to know peace.

Respect is to honour all of the Creation.

Bravery is to face the foe with integrity.

Honesty is to be sincere when facing a situation.

Humility is to know oneself as a sacred part of the Creation.

Truth is to know all of these things and live them.

Activities

1. Create a poster that compares the Seven Grandfather Teachings to the Eight Beatitudes. Show how each of the Grandfather Teachings matches a Beatitude of Jesus.
2. Create a poster that displays seven wise sayings that your elders (parents, guardians, grandparents, aunts, and uncles) offer you to help you live a good life.

Catholic Connection

The notion of an intermediary or helper to the Creator in the creation of the world is widespread. In Christianity, the priest Arius (from Alexandria in Egypt, in the third and fourth centuries) proclaimed that Christ was such an intermediary. Christianity rejected his position. The Church could not accept Christ as someone between the human and the divine. Christ is both fully human and fully divine.

Shaman

An Aboriginal spiritual leader

Spiritual Teachers and Leaders

Aboriginal people pass on to each other their knowledge of the spirit powers through teachings—mainly oral teachings. In addition, they perform a number of rituals that keep the world in balance. Certain men and women possess a greater quantity of power than others. They are more able to deal with these powers than other people in the community are. Such a person is known as a **shaman** or, in some areas, a medicine person.

Traditionally, the shaman uses these powers for the benefit of the community: helping hunters find their prey, making it rain for farmers, making love charms, but especially healing the sick. The shaman functions as a physical and spiritual healer and performs ceremonies for healing, and for the spiritual needs of the people, using special knowledge of appropriate medicines and herbs.

The shaman also remembers and tells the spiritual teachings of the community—for example, by telling in a chant how Earth was created. These are sacred teachings; often Aboriginal peoples will let non-Aboriginal peoples know their creation teachings, but will not train them in how to chant the teachings. It is as if the shaman in his or her chant is presiding over the creation of Earth. It is like an incantation or formula. In the ritual, Earth is recreated.

Spiritual Teachings

In Aboriginal spiritual traditions, beliefs and sacred teachings are generally passed on within communities and within families orally and through example. The many Aboriginal peoples who live in Canada have diverse traditions. Discussed below are some examples:

The Medicine Wheel

In the medicine wheel

- the circle represents the continuous cycle of life and the connection among all species
- the cross points in the four directions

The powers of the four directions organize everything that exists: the seasons (winter, spring, summer, fall);

the races (red, white, yellow, black); the elements of the universe (water, fire, air, earth); the stages of life (child, youth, adult, elder); the aspects of the human personality (spiritual, physical, mental, emotional); and more.

Elders use the medicine wheel as a tool for teaching younger generations about who they are, where they come from, their place in the world, and how they are related to each other and to all that lives and breathes.

Time, Shelters, Drums, and More Circles

Time is considered to be circular—divided into its four seasons. The circular symbolism of the cosmos is found everywhere. Encampments are generally circular. Meetings involve forming a circle. Traditional shelters (for example, igloos, teepees, and wigwams) are circular. These encampments mirror the universe, and each shelter is a replica of it.

Drums are sacred objects of different sizes, types, and purposes, and are used in ceremonies. They represent the heartbeat of the nation and of Mother Earth, the pulse of the universe. The heart and the drum share the same purpose and responsibility: providing life through its beat.

The circle is sacred. Dancing intended for the renewal of all creation is done in a circle. The sacred pipe is passed from one to the next in a circular motion. Aboriginal peoples see the circle everywhere because they see the powers of the universe operating as a circle.

Ethics

What distinct ethics (moral principles) guide life for many Aboriginal peoples in Canada? According to some sources, here are some core ethics:

- **Do not interfere.** Modelling behaviour and showing by example are valued. Ordering, giving advice, cajoling, telling someone what to do, and interfering with someone's behaviour in a demanding way are not.
- **The community is important.** Community members are expected to do their jobs—and do them well—for the community.
- **Everything is shared.** One takes only what one needs from the environment to survive, ensuring that there is enough left over for others in the community to use. Similarly, everyone is equal, not to be left out.

Catholic Connection

Catholics believe that when priests perform certain actions with certain words (for example, in the ritual of baptism), then the person who receives these actions is changed. In the case of baptism, he or she is now a Christian. But, it is Christ's Spirit that is acting to bring about the change, not the priest's personal power.

Douglas Cardinal. Architect Douglas Cardinal designed the Canadian Museum of Civilization. It is located in Gatineau, Québec.

The Majorville Medicine Wheel in Southern Alberta. Physical medicine wheels, or sacred hoops, consist of stones placed in a particular pattern on the ground. The most common pattern resembles a wagon wheel: a centre of stones connected by spoke-like lines of stones to an outer ring of stones.

Check Your Understanding

1. In point form, describe Aboriginal beliefs about spirit, the Great Spirit, and the Trickster.
2. What are three additional central beliefs, and who teaches them?

Think About It

3. From pages 86 to 89, choose two or three central beliefs. In daily life, what might be examples of living these central beliefs? What similarities and differences do you see compared to some central beliefs you know well?
4. How could you learn more about the central beliefs in a specific Aboriginal community?

Making It Personal

5. Have you, or has anyone you know, ever experienced what Aboriginal peoples call "power" or "spirit"? Describe the experience.

Family Life

Fast Fact

Traditions vary from one part of the country to another. For example, in northern climates, when an Inuit boy killed his first seal or caribou, the family might hold a modest feast.

In traditional Aboriginal life, before the Europeans arrived, how families lived depended on the traditions developed within their nations and in response to their environments. For example:

- People of the Plains (for example, Piegan, Blood, Blackfoot) lived in small groupings in the winter, then joined in a communal hunt in the spring, and gathered for the sun dance in the summer. Women and men had distinct roles, and girls and boys learned these from an early age. The women made, owned, and set up the teepees that were so important to the communal hunts and gatherings.
- In contrast, in what is now southern Ontario, five or six families might live in each Iroquoian longhouse in a village of a hundred longhouses. The people hunted, fished, and gathered, but also grew food crops, so family life and spiritual traditions involved planting these crops.

Wherever they lived, children would observe family members and elders, learning by example and through sacred teachings and cultural practices, such as the vision quest. In general, men would marry when they could provide for a family; women typically married when they reached puberty, by which time they had learned their traditional tasks.

Aboriginal Agriculture. Sacred teachings tell about the Three Sisters planted near the longhouses: corn, squash, and beans.

String Games. During the long winters, Inuit played string games and told the stories that went with them.

Recent Changes

In recent centuries, family life has changed in many Aboriginal communities. Like many Catholic leaders, Aboriginal elders complain about the indifference among the youth. What are the reasons?

The recent trend toward more First Nations, Métis, and Inuit living in cities has had an effect as Aboriginal families are less connected to the environments and practices that are at the root of their spiritual practices. Also, Aboriginal communities have faced some of the same challenges that all Canadians face, such as the following:

- youth being more influenced by popular culture (for example, movies, TV, mobile phones, the Internet) than by family, elders, and traditional teachings
- increasing secularism in Canada (See Chapter 10 for more about secularism.)

However, Aboriginal families have undergone some specific changes because of colonization and modernization. An example is the impact of residential schools, including the decline in the use of traditional languages, loss of traditional skills, and tremendous pain and grieving over abuse and loss of cultures. In some cases, the traditional life is no longer an option for young people of a community because of loss of lands or environmental degradation. The effects have been felt by many generations, and many Aboriginal Canadians have had a hard time finding meaning in the traditions of the elders; many have not even had opportunities to experience them.

Premier Eva Aariak. In 2008, Eva Aariak became the premier of Nunavut. As language commissioner for Nunavut, she chose the Inuktitut word for "the Internet": *ikiaqqivik*. The Inuktitut word means "travelling through layers" and refers to the traditional spiritual concept of a shaman travelling through time and space to find answers. In choosing that word, Aariak made a bridge between traditional beliefs and language, and new technologies.

Dorothy Betz. Ojibwa grandmother Dorothy Betz cooks traditional bannock on the *Loving Spoonfuls* cooking series on W Network (formally WTN). Betz helped develop Native Friendship Centres. They are now in more than 100 cities across Canada. Aboriginal people moving to cities can go to these centres to get information, find out about work and education opportunities, and socialize.

Many Aboriginal peoples in Canada are looking toward the future with resilience and are reviving many traditional practices. They have also found new ways to create community. An example is the Friendship Centres they have established in many cities.

Check Your Understanding

1. Create a timeline with the headings Past, Recent Past and Present, and Future Hopes. On the timeline, note in point form details of family life for Aboriginal peoples in Canada.

Think About It

2. Research to find an example of "resilience" among Aboriginal peoples of Canada and develop a way to present your example creatively to the class.

Making It Personal

3. Working with a partner, brainstorm and discuss ideas for how families might revive or deepen their spiritual traditions or practices. With another pair of students, share and discuss ideas. Finally, choose one idea to develop into a proposal to present to the class.

The Seven Fires

In the oral tradition of the Ojibwa, prophecies announced a period of time in which the people would suffer and forget the way they had received fire from the beginning of creation and how they would recover their fire. The narrative, known as "The Seven Fires," tells how seven prophets came to the Anishinabe when they were living a full and peaceful life on the northeastern coast of America. These prophets left the people with seven predictions about their future. Each prophecy was called a fire, and each fire referred to a particular time to come. In the narrative, Aboriginal peoples express their hope and confidence about the return of Aboriginal traditions and about the way this tradition could live alongside non-Aboriginal traditions.

This prophecy has given new life and a new sense of responsibility to many. Charlie Patton of the Mohawk Trail Longhouse (Kahnawake, Québec) expresses it well:

> We are now responsible for our nations, our spirituality, our relations with the Creator; we bear it on our shoulders. We have the mandate to take this on today, at this very moment. Our languages, our spirituality and all that we are has been given us by our ancestors. When they were no longer able to take this responsibility and they departed to the world of the spirits, they left this task to us by saying: "Now, it is you who are real persons. You must accept this responsibility." Today they are in the world of the spirits. They are our past. And now, we must assume this responsibility because we have been told that there will be seven other generations after ours. These generations to come, they are our future.

(From the *Report of the Royal Commission on Aboriginal Peoples*, Vol. 1, p. 680.)

NEL

Dialogue

Almost since the beginning of contact between Aboriginal peoples and Europeans, Christian mission and dialogue have been part of the relationship. While the historical relationship has had times of mutual benefit and co-operation, it is also a history of colonization and attempted assimilation. Now, many Aboriginal peoples in Canada are reviving Aboriginal spiritual traditions. In some cases, they are doing so as Aboriginal Christians.

The dialogue, then, is complex—for example:

Kateri Tekakwitha. Kateri Tekakwitha was beatified in 1980 by Pope John Paul II, the first Aboriginal person to be declared blessed. This group of Aboriginal teenagers from Kitchitwa Kateri Anamewgamik Parish in Thunder Bay, Ontario, is carrying a banner showing Kateri Tekakwitha.

Dialogue

Dialogue

- **A dialogue between Christians and Aboriginal peoples of diverse, rich, and long spiritual traditions**
- **A dialogue between Catholics and Aboriginal Catholics**
- **A dialogue between Christian missionaries and Aboriginal peoples who responded to the Gospel**
- **A dialogue about reconciliation and the future**
- **A dialogue among Canadians looking back on historical oppression and harm—including broken treaties, the reserve system, the extremely painful and disastrous attempt to assimilate Aboriginal peoples to Western ways through government policies and residential schools, unsettled land claims, conflict over using or stewardship of land**

Dialogue. There are many areas in the relations between Aboriginal peoples and others (non-Aboriginal Canadians and Aboriginal and non-Aboriginal Christians) where dialogue is necessary.

In the following paragraphs, we will look at a range of historical and present-day faith dialogues that add to what you have read earlier in this chapter about the history of Aboriginal spiritual traditions in Canada.

The Blessed Kateri is the patron of the Tekakwitha Conference. The conference is an annual gathering of Aboriginal Catholics in the United States and Canada and was started in 1939. Its goal was to begin a discussion of how the Catholic Church could better respond to traditional Aboriginal beliefs and practices. Half a million Aboriginal Catholics from 300 nations are members. Over the years, the conference has looked at all the ways in which Aboriginal Catholics can remain both Aboriginal and Catholic.

The most famous of the Catholic missionaries in Canada are the early Jesuit missionaries who worked among the Hurons and were martyred between 1642 and 1649. They had succeeded in befriending the Hurons. As the *Jesuit Relations* reports in 1649: "The little settlement of Trois Rivières is so slightly defended that the French are in daily peril of their lives; but all connected with the mission—not only the priests, but their servants—are ready to lay down their lives, if need be, for the sake of the little Indian church which they have there founded." In Midland, Ontario, the place where most of them lost their lives, a shrine is dedicated to the martyrs.

In the late twentieth and early twenty-first centuries, the Church's relationship with Aboriginal peoples shifted to dialogue. Great efforts have been made to respect Aboriginal traditions and bring some Aboriginal rituals into the Church.

The Midland Martyrs. The Midland Martyrs were eight Jesuit priests who were killed in the mid-seventeenth century near what is now Midland, Ontario.

Pope John Paul II at Midland. During his visit to Midland in 1985, Pope John Paul II encouraged this integration of Aboriginal rituals. He himself took part in a sweetgrass ceremony.

Profile: René Fumoleau

Born in France in 1926, René Fumoleau came to northern Canada as an Oblate priest (a member of the Oblates of Mary Immaculate) in 1953. Since then, he has chronicled the Dene way of life and his own experiences in poems, stories, films, and photographs. When he retired, he took up residence in the Dene community of Lutsel K'e (formerly known as Snowdrift), in the Northwest Territories.

Fumoleau/NWT Archives/N-1995-002: 1547

Father René Fumoleau. Father René Fumoleau has chronicled the Dene way of life in the Northwest Territories since he arrived there from France in 1953.

Missionary

I was telling stories to a large audience in Calgary,
and a man asked me:
"What is a missionary for you?"
I replied:
"I don't know a precise definition,
but I'll tell you an old, old story:
A long time ago,
a missionary was sent
to unknown people
in a faraway land.
The missionary learned
a new language,
strange customs,
original do's and don'ts,
unusual ways of working,
of relating,
of travelling.
The missionary experienced
unfamiliar family structures,
tribal traditions,
political institutions,
secular and religious customs.
The missionary shared
the people's highs and lows,
joys and sorrows,
good days and bad days,
hopes and frustrations,
listening,
learning,
understanding,
guessing, too.
It took the missionary years and years,
in fact as long as thirty years.
And one day,
after thirty years,
the missionary said:
'I thank you for everything you shared with me.
I, too, have something beautiful to share with you.'"

It is clear now that many Aboriginal Christians did not leave their cultures behind to become Christian. They interpreted Christianity in a way that made sense to their cultures. Their traditional ways were so strongly embedded within them that they could not be suppressed. And so it is that for many Aboriginal peoples, the Christian and traditional Aboriginal ways live side by side. In many ways, Aboriginal peoples live like other Christians, participating in Christian rituals: at the same time, they celebrate fully their own traditions and model them for their children.

In the poem "The Renaissance" on page 96, Arthur Solomon (an Ojibwa elder and spiritual leader) presents a look at the future from a different perspective.

The Renaissance

The nature of the spiritual and cultural rebirth
of Native people is not easy to describe, but I
will use this way that seems the easiest.
The nature of the rebirth is like this, when the
sun comes up in the morning it shines on the
higher ground first, it warms up the ground,
and the air and the plants and the people.
They see it and feel it and understand it.
But on the lower ground it comes later.
And in the deep shade the perception comes very
slowly and very poorly.
The ones on the higher ground are the leaders,
the elders and the spiritual people.
They are the ones who see and feel and
understand the nature of "The Bundle"
that has been left behind.
It is they who understand the nature and the
meaning and the power of those sacred ways.
That "Bundle" contains the original instruction
and the sacred teachings that were given
to our people so that they could conduct
themselves in honour and reverence toward
the Creation.
The nature of the renaissance is like the sun coming
up in the morning.
And there is no man who has the power to stand
there and say to the sun, "Don't come up just
yet because I am not ready."
The rebirth is an imperative which has its source
and power and direction from the great
mystery, the Creator who created the four
colours of man, four sacred colours.
God created all humans equal and it was never
in God's plan that one colour of man should
oppress another, whether by economic slavery
or whatever form of domination.
The imperative which drives us will overcome all
obstacles no matter how formidable, because
there is no power that can stand in the way of
the Supreme Power.

—Arthur Solomon, Ojibwa Elder

Check Your Understanding

1. What is the significance of
a) the Midland Martyrs' Shrine? b) the Tekakwitha Conference?

2. Summarize the points of view of
a) Father Fumoleau b) Arthur Solomon

Think About It

3. Reflect on Father Fumoleau's statement: "I thank you for everything you shared with me. I, too, have something beautiful to share with you." What did he mean?

4. Using a talking feather, stick, or stone, hold a respectful class discussion about what it means to "conduct [oneself] in honour and reverence toward the Creation."

Making It Personal

5. In a journal entry, reflect on the impact this chapter has had on you personally, including your thoughts, your feelings, the questions you have, and what action you could take.

NEL

What I Have Learned

In this chapter, I learned about

- Aboriginal peoples in Canada, including their great diversity and resilience
- examples of Aboriginal achievement
- the history of the long spiritual traditions of Aboriginal peoples in Canada, changes since the beginning of contact with Europeans, recent history, and hopes for the future
- some of the practices and rituals of Aboriginal spiritual traditions, including prayer and ceremonies—for example, smudging, the Sacred Pipe ceremony, naming and death rituals, the vision quest, the sun dance, the potlatch
- spiritual beliefs and moral life of Aboriginal peoples in Canada
- family life of Aboriginal peoples in Canada, traditionally and in the recent past and present, including some challenges families face
- examples of mission to, and dialogue with, Aboriginal peoples
- contemporary efforts for reconciliation and renewal

Aboriginal Prayer

Everything an Indian does is in a circle,
Because the power of the world
Always works in circles,
And everything tries to be round
The sky is round,
And the earth is round like a ball,
And so are the stars.
The wind, in its greatest power whirls.
Birds make their nests in circles,
For their religion is the same as ours.
The sun comes forth and goes down again
in a circle.
The moon does the same, and both are round.
Even the seasons form a great circle
In their changing,
And always come back again to where
they were.
Human life is a circle
From childhood to childhood
And so it is in everything where power moves.

—Black Elk, Oglala Sioux

Chapter 4 The Story of Judaism

"Hear, O Israel, the Lord is our God, the Lord is one. You shall love the Lord your God with all your heart and with all your soul and with all your strength. Take to heart these instructions with which I charge you this day. Impress them upon your children. Recite them when you stay at home and when you are away. Bind them as a sign on your hand and let them serve as a symbol on your forehead; inscribe them on the doorposts of your house." (Deuteronomy 6:4–9)

(From the Shema, the central profession of faith recited during the morning and evening service)

Passover. A family celebrates Passover. This family is celebrating Passover with a special meal called the Seder. The Seder commemorates the escape of the children of Israel from captivity in Egypt. In this photo you can see many of the elements of the feast: the central Seder plate with its symbolic foods, cups of wine, and pillows. The family members are reading from the Haggadah, the religious text that describes the rituals to be used during the Seder.

What You Will Learn

In this chapter, you will learn about

- the origins of Judaism as we know it today
- the Tanakh and Talmud as key elements of the Jewish tradition
- key parts of Torah
- the Jewish Holocaust (the Shoah) and the founding of Israel in the twentieth century
- ritual prayer on holy days and festivals expressing the Jewish people's deep relationship with the Lord
- living in a Jewish family that actively observes Jewish law
- why Judaism must be the first dialogue partner of the Catholic Church

Personal Recollection

One of the bravest things my 13-year-old self ever did happened during my bat mitzvah when I was standing on the *bima* (raised platform) at my synagogue chanting my Torah portion. I was leaning into the microphone so the gigantic room full of people could hear me, and I was so nervous that my voice quavered and shook horribly, which sounded much worse amplified. *This isn't what I sounded like practising last night,* I moaned in my head. *I'm a good singer!*

I could feel my rabbi on one side of me and my cantor, whose voice had guided me through the memorization of the piece, on the other. Both were there to help me. I realized then that, even though I wasn't going to sound perfect, I had to keep going because I had committed to it. I had to be an adult. In fact, the purpose of this rite of passage is to be welcomed into the Jewish community as an adult, so my little lesson could not have come at a more appropriate time.

Most of my non-Jewish friends who came to the party that night told me they wished they could have had a bat mitzvah, too, but I don't think they completely understood. Although afterwards I was still treated like a kid—I was only 13—I started to like going to synagogue on Saturdays after that. I felt like I belonged there; that I had chosen and earned my place.

— **Jessica Rose**

Jessica Rose. Jessica's bat mitzvah was an act of commitment to follow Jewish tradition. At the heart of this tradition is the Torah, the revealed word of the God of Israel. By reading from the Torah, Jessica entered into the story of God and of her people, and became part of that story. It is now her story, too. **How do Catholics become members of the Church? When do they commit themselves to follow Jesus?**

A Closer Look

"Israel" has two main meanings.

- Today, Israel is a country in the Middle East. The modern state of Israel was established as a Jewish homeland in 1948.
- In the Bible, however, "Israel" describes the Hebrew people or nation with whom God made a covenant. This is the meaning used most often in this chapter.

Judaism in Canada

Holocaust
The systematic killing of over six million Jews before and during World War II

Canada has the fourth-largest Jewish population in the world, after the United States, Israel, and France. Many of the approximately 330 000 Canadian Jews who now live here trace their origins back to Russian and Eastern European Jews who emigrated to escape persecution during the late nineteenth and early twentieth centuries. Others are associated with the 40 000 **Holocaust** survivors who came to Canada in 1945, after World War II. Another wave of Jewish immigrants arrived here in the 1950s. They emigrated from the French colonies in North Africa. Most settled in large cities such as Montréal and Toronto.

Kirkland Lake Synagogue. This synagogue in Kirkland Lake, Ontario, was dedicated in 1929. Rabbi Joseph Rabin brings in the scroll of the Torah. Canada's first synagogue was built in Montréal in 1768. **Where is the synagogue nearest your home? When was it built or when did it become a synagogue?**

Jewish Population in Canada

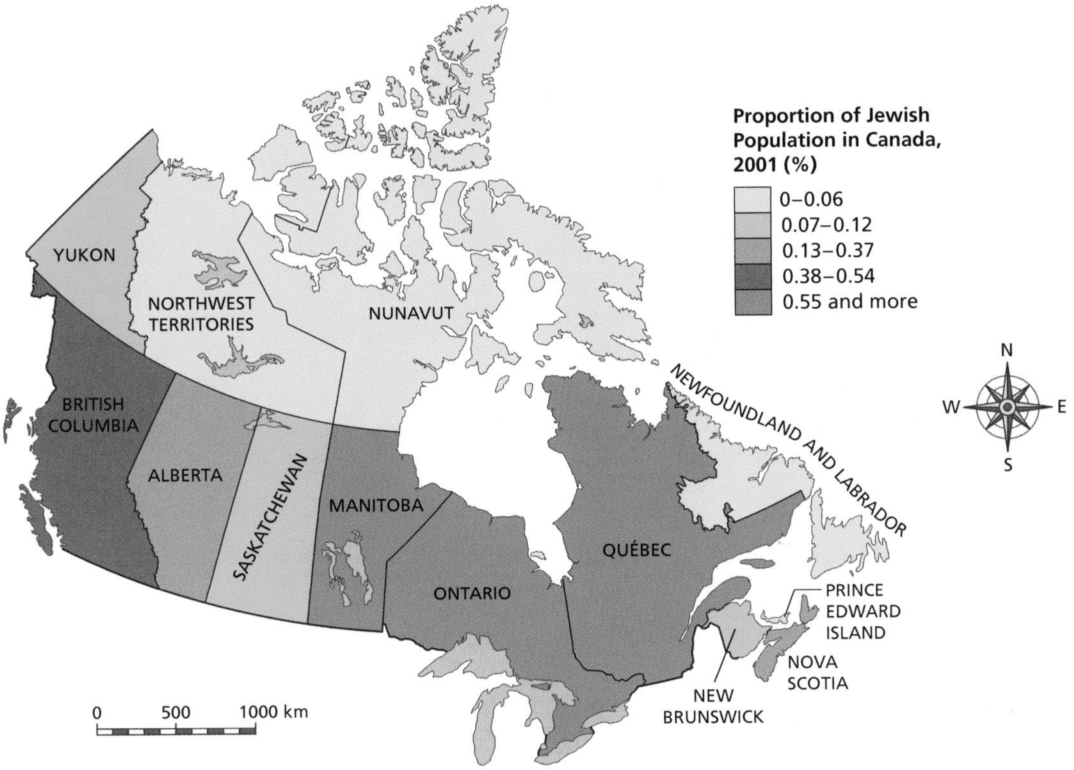

Distribution of Jewish Population in Canada. Many of the first Jewish Canadians were either fur traders or members of the British army stationed in what is now the province of Québec. Today, the largest number of Jews in Canada live in Toronto and Montréal. Vancouver, Ottawa, Winnipeg, and Calgary also have large Jewish communities.

Naomi Klein. Naomi Klein is a Canadian journalist and social activist.

A Closer Look

Since the first Jewish emigrants arrived in Canada, many members of the Jewish community have had a far-reaching impact on Canadian life. Well-known Jewish Canadians include singer/songwriters Leonard Cohen and Steven Page; writers Mordecai Richler and Sharon Pollack; media magnate Moses Znaimer; humanitarian Stephen Lewis; and activists and writers Judy Rebick and Naomi Klein.

The History of Judaism

Origins of Judaism

Judaism traces its origins back 3800 years to Abraham and Sarah, the patriarch and matriarch of a people called the Hebrews (or Israelites). The story of Abraham, Sarah, and their descendants is told in the Jewish scriptures. It is a story of a **covenant** or promise made between God and Abraham.

Covenant

An agreement of mutual faithfulness, like a contract or alliance, between two parties; "I will be your God and you shall be my people"; the agreement binds the parties together with mutual privileges and obligations

Now the Lord said to Abram,
"Go forth from your native land
and from your father's house
to the land that I will show you.
I will make of you a great nation,
and I will bless you; I will make
your name great, and you shall
be a blessing."

(Genesis 12:1–2)

Links to the Past

The area that we now know as Israel was once divided into two kingdoms: the kingdom of Israel (the northern kingdom) and the kingdom of Judah (the southern kingdom). The religion that began with Abraham among the Hebrew people is called Judaism because the Jewish people of today trace their heritage to the Hebrew people who lived in the southern kingdom of Judah.

Throughout its sacred texts, which you will learn more about later in this chapter, Judaism has maintained continuity with its distant past. But, even though Judaism's roots date back to ancient times, over the centuries it has evolved and changed from the practices of the early Hebrews.

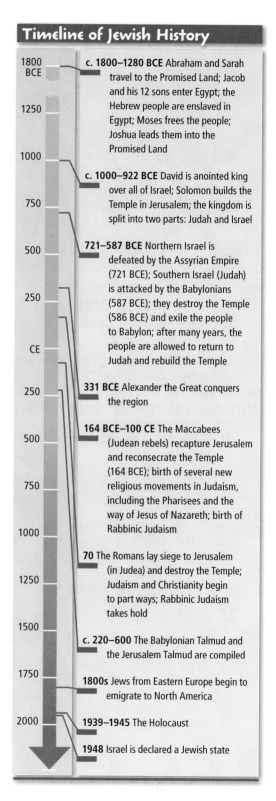

Timeline of Jewish History

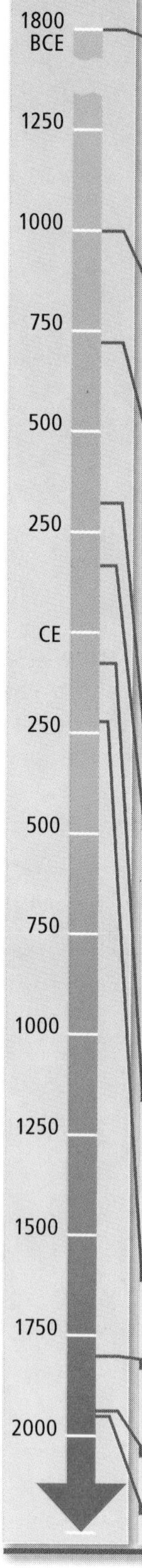

c. 1800–1280 BCE Abraham and Sarah travel to the Promised Land; Jacob and his 12 sons enter Egypt; the Hebrew people are enslaved in Egypt; Moses frees the people; Joshua leads them into the Promised Land

c. 1000–922 BCE David is anointed king over all of Israel; Solomon builds the Temple in Jerusalem; the kingdom is split into two parts: Judah and Israel

721–587 BCE Northern Israel is defeated by the Assyrian Empire (721 BCE); Southern Israel (Judah) is attacked by the Babylonians (587 BCE); they destroy the Temple (586 BCE) and exile the people to Babylon; after many years, the people are allowed to return to Judah and rebuild the Temple

331 BCE Alexander the Great conquers the region

164 BCE–100 CE The Maccabees (Judean rebels) recapture Jerusalem and reconsecrate the Temple (164 BCE); birth of several new religious movements in Judaism, including the Pharisees and the way of Jesus of Nazareth; birth of Rabbinic Judaism

70 The Romans lay siege to Jerusalem (in Judea) and destroy the Temple; Judaism and Christianity begin to part ways; Rabbinic Judaism takes hold

c. 220–600 The Babylonian Talmud and the Jerusalem Talmud are compiled

1800s Jews from Eastern Europe begin to emigrate to North America

1939–1945 The Holocaust

1948 Israel is declared a Jewish state

NEL

Mesopotamia and Canaan, 1800 BCE

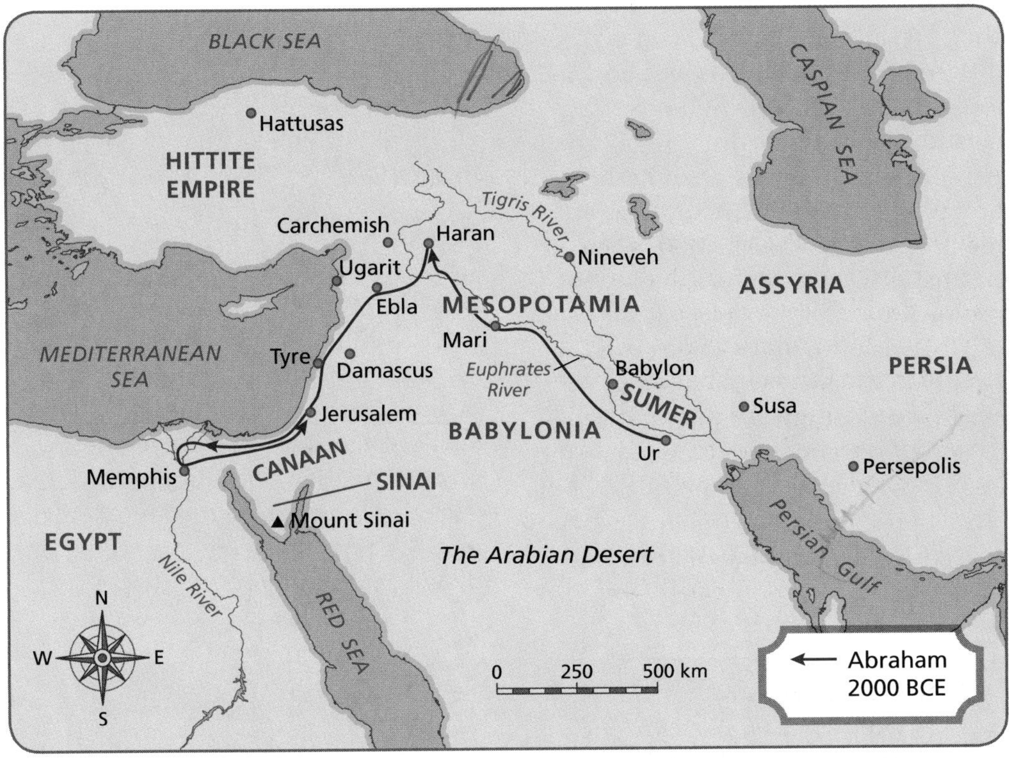

Mesopotamia and Canaan. In Chapter 12 of Genesis, God directed Abraham to leave Ur in Mesopotamia and go into the land of the Canaanites. This map shows Mesopotamia and Canaan around 1800 BCE. **Compare this map with a modern-day map of the same area. What differences and similarities do you see? Which peoples live in these areas today?**

Check Your Understanding

1. Explain the meaning of "covenant."

Think About It

2. Examine the timeline and draw out three or four important themes or ideas (for example, land) from the events described there. In your own words, explain the significance of each idea to an understanding of Judaism.

Making It Personal

3. Which of the themes in question 2 are important to you personally? Why?

The Birth of Modern Judaism

The Judaism practised in the time of King David and King Solomon was very different from Judaism as we know it today. Its current form and practices have changed greatly over the centuries. As well, a catastrophic event in the first century of the Common Era—the destruction of the Temple—had an enormous impact on Judaism as we now know it. The Temple was the centre of all Jewish worship and sacrifice.

In 66 CE, Judea was under the control of the Roman Empire. A group of Jewish revolutionaries known as the Zealots rose up against the rulers of the land. In response, the Romans laid siege to Jerusalem, destroying the city and the Temple. Three thousand people who had taken refuge in the Temple perished when the Temple fell in 70 CE.

Two religious movements, Christianity and Rabbinic Judaism, survived the terrible events of the year 70 CE, but they were also changed by it.

Christianity

The destruction of the Temple changed forever a Jewish movement that had begun with Jesus of Nazareth about 40 years earlier. This movement included both Jews and non-Jews who had accepted Jesus of Nazareth as the long-awaited Jewish **Messiah**, or Christ. Jesus had been crucified by the Romans in 30 CE. His followers came to be known as Christians.

Messiah

A word meaning "the anointed one"; the word "Christ" comes from the Greek word meaning the same thing

The Western Wall. The only part of the Temple of Jerusalem that remained standing after it was destroyed by the Romans was the Western Wall. For Jews today, this wall is Jerusalem's most sacred place. The wall is a reminder of the ancient Temple and of Jews' spiritual connection to the ancient land of Israel. Some believers pray and study at the wall and push prayers written on pieces of paper into the gaps of the historic Temple stones.

Christians presented Jesus as the fulfillment of God's covenant with Israel. As a result, a conflict developed between Christian Jews and Rabbinic Jews (known at the time as Pharisees). Toward the end of the first century and the start of the second century, the two groups parted ways.

The Resurrection of Christ. This painting is by Italian artist Raphael (1483–1520).

Rabbinic Judaism

The second movement, called Rabbinic (or Halakhic) Judaism, was begun by a group known as the Pharisees. With the Temple destroyed, the Pharisees found a new focus for Judaism in their sacred writings. They encouraged people to gather in synagogues or study houses to study the Torah—the "teaching" or guidance of God—found in their scriptures.

The Pharisees used the scripture translated into Aramaic, the language most people spoke in Israel. Studying and interpreting Torah became an important way of helping Jewish people follow the laws of the covenant wherever they lived. The interpreters of the Torah were known as scribes or rabbis. That is why this movement came to be called Rabbinic Judaism.

Catholic Connection

Jews believe that God will send a Messiah to save Israel. They believe that the Messiah has not yet come. Christians believe that Jesus is the Messiah promised by God.

Fast Fact

In the New Testament, the Pharisees are sometimes presented negatively. Even today, some people use the term to mean people who follow guidelines and teachings too strictly, or are hypocritical. This is not really fair. The Pharisees were sincere seekers of the will of God.

Check Your Understanding

1. In your own words, explain how Christianity started out as a Jewish movement.
2. Explain why Judaism today places such an emphasis on studying scripture to find guidance in life.

Think About It

3. Create a graphic (for example, a flow chart or mind map) to illustrate how the following groups were connected during the early history of Judaism: the Hebrew people; Israel; Judah; non-Jews; Christianity; Rabbinic Judaism.

Making It Personal

4. Where do you look for guidance in life?

Jews in Europe, 1400s and 1500s

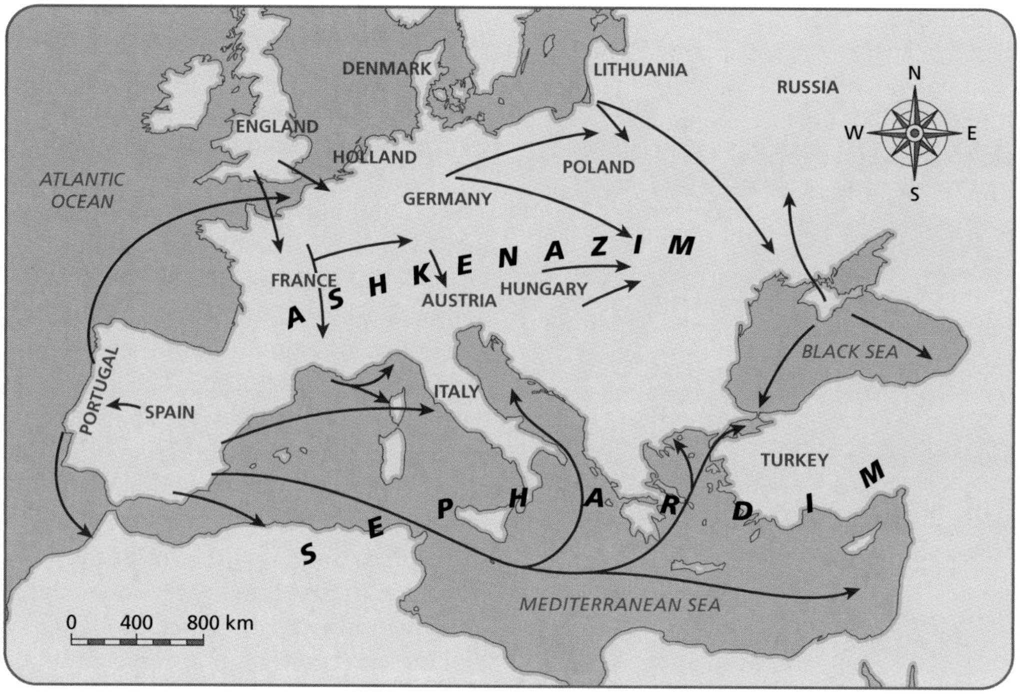

Jews without a Homeland. The map shows how, in the fifteenth and sixteenth centuries, Jews were constantly on the move in Europe.

Jews in the Diaspora

In 135 CE, the Romans expelled the Jews from Judea, forcing them to take refuge in other countries. Most Jews ended up living in foreign countries, in what became known as the **Diaspora** (meaning "dispersion" or "scattering"). This scattering among nations and the constant desire to return to the land of Israel and to Jerusalem is a key aspect of the history of the Jews and their faith.

Diaspora

The scattering of Jews outside of Israel in both ancient and modern times

Jews in Christian Europe

In the Diaspora, Jews became divided into two major groups: the **Ashkenazim**, in Northern, Central, and Eastern Europe, and the **Sephardim**, around the Mediterranean basin. Both groups had an immeasurable influence on the intellectual, economic, cultural, and spiritual life of every country in which they lived. And yet, in many cases, Jews remained set apart—they were "the other." In the largely Christian countries of Europe, Jews were often unjustly accused of being the killers of Jesus the Messiah and were treated as unbelievers.

Ashkenazim

Central and Eastern European Jews and their descendants

Sephardim

Primarily Spanish, Portuguese, and North African Jews and their descendants

The Kabbalah and Hasidism

Several Jewish mystical movements became popular in the Middle Ages. Mystics are people in search of God through a life of prayer, meditation, and reflection. The main Jewish mystical teachings are *Kabbalah* (twelfth century) and *Hasidism* (eighteenth century).

The Kabbalah

The teaching of the Kabbalah is found in many texts. One text, called *Zohar*, is best described as a journey into the self of each individual. The true nature of God, according to Kabbalah, is indescribable, except by saying what God is not. This true essence of God is known as *Ein Sof*, which means "without end." God has no boundaries in either time or space.

Hasidism

The founder of Hasidism was Israel ben Eliezer (1698–1759), also known as Ba'al Shem Tov. He taught that communion with God happened through prayer, good deeds, humility, and, especially, joy. He is best known for his humorous stories in which people encounter God as they do the simplest chores. Hasidic communities are led by charismatic leaders ("rebbes"), to whom followers come for guidance and sustenance.

Catholic Connection

There is a tradition of mysticism within Catholicism as well. St. Catherine of Siena, a mystic who lived in the fourteenth century, said, "My me is God."

Hasidic Jews. Most Hasidic communities in Canada are in Montréal (shown here) and Toronto. Hasidic Jews are easily identified by their dress. Most of the men wear dark suits and black hats, and many have long, uncut sideburns. Women dress modestly and cover their hair. Hasidic communities generally keep to themselves and maintain a strict observance of Jewish laws.

A Closer Look

The characters in Ba'al Shem Tov's stories are typically simple rural people without much education. They appealed to an audience who lived in small, mostly rural villages, and who were not able to follow the ascetic practices of other Jewish leaders of the time.

Check Your Understanding

1. What are some ways in which Jews have contributed to European culture?

Think About It

2. With a partner, look up the word "anti-Semitism" in a dictionary. Record the definition and give some examples from history. Why might it be especially important for Catholics to speak out against anti-Semitism whenever they encounter it?
3. Why do you think some religious communities, such as Hasidic communities, dress and eat in ways that set them apart?

Making It Personal

4. Jews and Christians have often been persecuted for their faith. How would you defend your faith if you were persecuted for it?

The Enlightenment, the Holocaust (Shoah), and Modern-Day Israel

Three events in particular have shaped Judaism in the past three centuries: the Enlightenment, the Holocaust *(Shoah)*, and the founding of the State of Israel. They still mark Judaism today.

The Enlightenment

During the seventeenth century, a new way of knowing began to dominate Western Europe: the way of reason. Until that time, mysticism and religion had been the ways of knowing and understanding life. This new movement came to be called the Enlightenment.

The Enlightenment emphasized intellectual freedom. Only what could be known by reason was considered acceptable. All else was superstition. People became very skeptical about traditional political, social, and religious beliefs.

A Jewish Day School. In Canadian cities with large Jewish populations such as Toronto and Montréal, many primary and elementary students attend Jewish day schools. In addition to the regular curriculum, students learn Hebrew. They celebrate Jewish holy days. This school, the Leo Baeck Day School in Thornhill, Ontario, is the only Reform day school in Canada.

The Enlightenment had an enormous impact on Judaism and Christianity. For one thing, as less emphasis was placed on religion, Jews in some parts of Europe became more accepted. At the same time, the Enlightenment caused divisions within Judaism, as Ashkenazi Jews split into three different traditions: Reform, Conservative, and Orthodox.

Reform Judaism

Reform Judaism attracted those Jews who had mixed more frequently with the rest of the population. They wanted to enjoy the same freedom as everyone else, to participate in intellectual life and work with non-Jews. Reform Jews began to interpret the scripture with modern methods. They also became less concerned with traditional purity laws and kosher food, and with the desire to return to Israel, the homeland.

Today, Reform Jews use a combination of Hebrew and English for religious services. Men and women sit together in the synagogue, and women are ordained as rabbis. Many, but not all, Reform Jews believe that as long as one parent is Jewish, the children are Jewish.

Individualism is encouraged in Reform Judaism, which stresses that each person must decide what beliefs and practices are key to his or her spiritual life. Reform Jews often accept secular moral values (the values of society in general), although they live by traditional values as well. Reform Jews also stress *tikkun olam*—repairing the world through social action.

Moses Mendelssohn. Moses Mendelssohn (1729–1786) laid the foundation for the Reform Judaism approach. He argued that reason and religion can live side by side.

Female Rabbis. Conservative Judaism has opened the position of rabbi to women. **Why do you think some Conservative Jews are reluctant for women to become rabbis?**

Conservative Judaism

As Reform Jews began to take part fully in every aspect of secular life, some Jews began to fear that they would lose their separate identity. In reaction, a Conservative movement arose.

Conservative Judaism follows many, but not all, of the 613 commandments of the Torah, as well as many of the earliest traditions, such as the order of prayers, the use of Hebrew, and some dietary laws. Although Conservative Judaism is open to using modern historical methods of study, it considers Reform Judaism too loose in its interpretation of the traditional authority of the scripture.

For Conservative Jews, the needs of the community and its Jewish identity always come before individual wants and needs. Active participation in the synagogue is very important. Like Reform Jews, Conservatives stress *tikkun olam*.

Men and women may sit together in the synagogue, and women are also ordained as rabbis in the Conservative tradition, although not every congregation agrees with this. Conservative Judaism is the largest branch of Judaism in Canada.

Orthodox Judaism

Orthodox Judaism continues to observe all the ancient rules and practices. Members of this tradition want to avoid "watering down" the Jewish faith. They believe that God gave the whole Torah—oral and written—to Moses at Mount Sinai.

While some Orthodox Jews accept some secular moral values, being Orthodox ("orthodox" means "correct teaching") means following the

Fast Fact

About 70 percent of Jews in Canada belong to one of the three main Jewish religious traditions. Four out of ten of these are Conservative, three out of ten are Reform, and another three out of ten are Orthodox. (The other 30 percent of Jews in Canada are **secular Jews** or belong to smaller Jewish sects.)

Secular Jew
An ethnic Jew who is not religious

Shabbat. Orthodox Jews leaving synagogue on Shabbat (Sabbath). By observing Shabbat, Jews enter into God's rest and God's appreciation of creation.

commandments of the Torah, strictly observing the Sabbath and other Jewish holy days, using Hebrew in the synagogue, dressing modestly, and following the dietary laws, among other things.

Men and women do not sit together in the synagogue. Orthodox Jews believe that being Jewish can only pass down through the mother. If the father is Jewish but the mother is not, the children are not considered Jews.

Check Your Understanding

1. Suggest ways in which the Enlightenment challenged religion. Compare your conclusions to those of others in the class.

Think About It

2. With a partner or in a small group, do some research on the distinctions between Orthodox, Conservative, and Reform Judaism. Then, create a three-column chart to show what you learned. Possible research topics include the role of the oral tradition, the Bible, women rabbis, traditional morality, and God's role in the Torah.

Making It Personal

3. Which form of Judaism appeals most to you? Explain your answer.

The Holocaust (Shoah)

How would it feel to know your own government wanted to eliminate you for no other reason than your ethnic origin or your religious beliefs? That is what happened to the Jewish people in Germany during World War II. Between 16 and 20 million people were killed in concentration and labour camps by German Nazis and their allies. About 6 million of these victims were Jews. The Nazis' attempt to exterminate the Jews became known as the Holocaust (***Shoah***).

Adolf Hitler was elected chancellor of Germany in 1933. Even though German Jews were among the most integrated into European society, Hitler considered them to be from an "inferior race" and declared them enemies of the state. He even blamed Jews for Germany's loss in World War I (1914–1918) and for Germany's economic problems during the Great Depression of the 1930s.

Many Jews, alarmed by Hitler's actions against them, tried to leave Germany. However, this was the period of the Great Depression, and many countries were severely limiting the number of immigrants they would allow in. Anti-Semitism was widespread at this time—not just in Germany but in other countries, including Canada—and this certainly contributed to the unwillingness to grant Jews asylum.

Shoah

From the Hebrew word for "catastrophe," "calamity," or, as it is usually translated, "holocaust"; it refers to Nazi Germany's deliberate attempt to exterminate the Jewish race between 1933 and 1945

Fast Fact

Other groups were also targeted by the Nazis. About 500 000 Roma (Gypsies), about 150 000 people with disabilities, 10 000 homosexuals, and 2000 Catholic priests and Protestant ministers were also killed.

MS *St. Louis*. In 1939, the MS *St. Louis* set out from Hamburg, Germany, carrying 907 Jewish refugees. One after another, six countries refused to allow the ship to dock at their ports. Canada was the ship's last hope of refuge. But, despite a desperate campaign by Canadian Jewish organizations, the government refused to allow the refugees into the country. The ship was forced to return to Germany, where many of its passengers later died in concentration camps. **With a partner, think of a fitting way to commemorate this event in Canada, as a reminder of our collective responsibility to care for those in need.**

Once in power, Hitler deliberately set out to eliminate all Jews in Europe. On his orders, Jews were imprisoned, starved, forced to do heavy manual labour, medically experimented on, tortured, and killed. The Jewish population of Europe was reduced from 9.5 million to 1.6 million in just 12 years.

Auschwitz Crematorium. In the crematorium at Auschwitz, a particularly brutal concentration camp in Poland, the bodies of Jews were burned after they died.

The Liberation of Auschwitz. In January 1945, the Nazi concentration camp in occupied Poland was liberated by Allied soldiers. Here, 15-year-old Ivan Dudnik, suffering from exhaustion and malnutrition, is carried out of the barracks.

Fast Fact

Of the 6 million Jews who perished in the death camps of Nazi Germany, 1.5 million were children or teenagers. Nobel Prize–winning novelist Elie Wiesel was a teenager when the Nazis deported his family and other Jews to Auschwitz from his town in Romania.

Profile: Irena Sendler

Irena Sendler was a Catholic social worker. At great risk to her own life, she helped smuggle 2500 children out of the Warsaw Ghetto, saving them from certain death in Nazi concentration camps. The children were carried out in boxes, suitcases, or trolleys, given new identities, and placed with convents and sympathetic Christian families.

On the night of October 20, 1943, Sendler was taken prisoner by the Nazis. Although they broke her legs and feet, and left her body permanently scarred, she refused to betray her network of helpers or the children she had helped save. She was sentenced to death but escaped when a guard was bribed to let her go. She immediately returned to her work using a new identity.

In her later years, Sendler was cared for in a Warsaw nursing home by a woman she had helped smuggle out of the Warsaw Ghetto; the woman had been six months old at the time of her rescue. Sendler died in 2008 at the age of 98. After her funeral, Poland's Orthodox chief rabbi offered prayers at her graveside.

Irena Sendler. In the 1940s, Irena Sendler was involved in the rescue of Jewish children from the Warsaw Ghetto. By 1942, the German army had crowded some 500 000 Polish Jews into a ghetto in Warsaw, the capital of Poland—an area of about one square kilometre. There, they awaited transportation to the extermination camps.

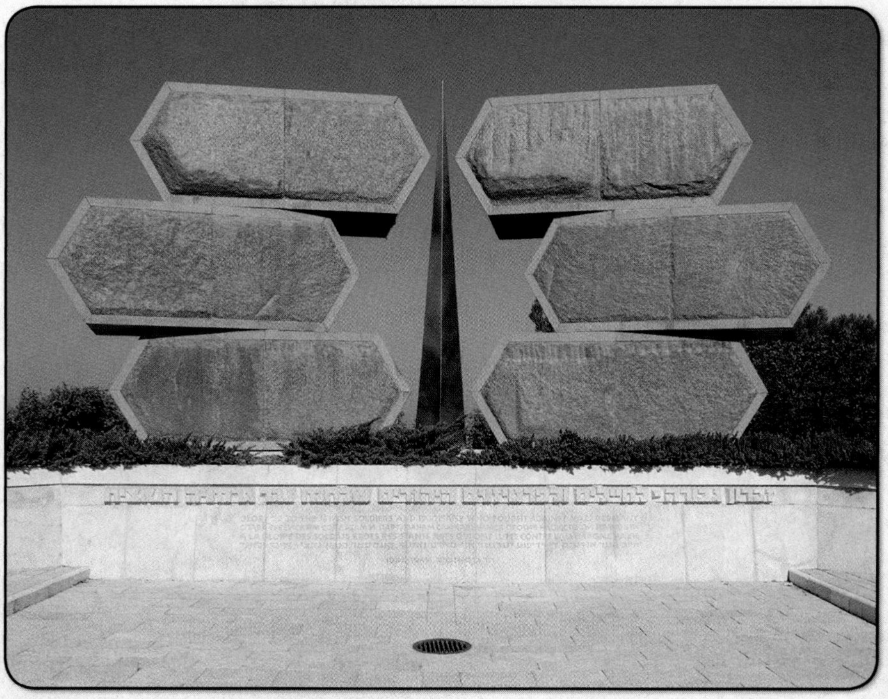

Holocaust Memorial at Yad Vashem. This sculpture stands outside The Hall of Remembrance at Yad Vashem in Jerusalem, a memorial to the 6 million Jews who died in the Holocaust. The names of the death camps are marked on the floor of the hall. In 1965, Irena Sendler became one of the first Righteous Gentiles to be honoured by Yad Vashem, the Holocaust Martyrs' and Heroes' Remembrance Authority in Jerusalem.

Emil Fackenheim. A Canadian Jewish philosopher and theologian and a survivor of the Holocaust, Emil Fackenheim (1916–2003) considered the Holocaust such a challenge to Jewish faith that he sought to add a 614th law to Jewish scripture. This new law would state: "The authentic Jew of today is forbidden to hand Hitler yet another, posthumous victory." To avoid giving Hitler another victory, Jews must carry on Jewish traditions and not give in to despair. **How can humans overcome tragedies such as the Holocaust?**

Effects of the Holocaust on the Jewish Community

After the horrors of the war, the faith of many Jews who survived was terribly shaken. How were they to make sense of this inhumanity? They wondered if God was punishing them for their lack of faithfulness and their indifference to the Torah. And yet, how could they stay faithful to the God of the covenant after all they had been through? This is the question still faced by many modern Jews. That Judaism lives on is a testimony, a witness to God, born out of this struggle to understand.

For others, however, the traditional Jewish belief that God is with us in good times and bad remains strong. They believe that goodness and love will prevail, and God's reign will triumph at the end of history. The central message of the Torah, in the words of Rabbi Hillel, is "What is hateful to you, do not do to others." This is the rallying cry for many Jews—Orthodox, Reform, and Conservative—in response to the Holocaust.

A greater emphasis on *tikkun olam* has become the response of religious Jews to the cruelty unleashed during World War II. As the group Rabbis for Human Rights stated in its Principles of Faith, "The Mishnah [oral Torah] teaches: 'Therefore was Adam created single, to teach you that the destruction of any person's life is tantamount to destroying a whole world and the preservation of a single life is tantamount to preserving a whole world'" *(Tractate Sanhedrin 4:5)*. For Jewish people, life is sacred because it is from God. Preserving life is, for many Jews, a key response to the Holocaust.

Check Your Understanding

1. Explain the effects the Holocaust has on the Jewish people today. How do Jews retain their faith in the God of the covenant in the face of such evil?

Think About It

2. Elie Wiesel—author, political activist, winner of the 1986 Nobel Peace Prize, and Holocaust survivor—said of the Holocaust: "While not all victims were Jews, all Jews were victims." What do you think Wiesel means by this statement?

Making It Personal

3. Create a short profile of someone you have read or heard about who survived the Holocaust. Explain how it affected or changed them.
4. The UN has designated January 21 as International Holocaust Remembrance Day. In the Jewish calendar, 27 *Nisan* is set aside for the same purpose. What do you think would be appropriate ways to mark these events? Discuss with a partner or small group.

NEL

Zionism and the State of Israel

Zionism

The persecution Jews experienced in Europe fuelled a desire to return to the land God had promised them. By the late 1800s, many Jews supported **Zionism**, a movement to establish a national Jewish state in Palestine. In the following decades, some of these Zionists began to emigrate to Palestine. Arabs who lived in the region objected to Jews coming to what they saw as *their* homeland, and fighting broke out several times.

After World War II, many Western countries began to support Jewish struggles for a homeland in Palestine. Finally, Britain, which held control of the region, submitted the issue to the United Nations. In 1947, the UN—pressured by Western nations—voted to divide Palestine into an Arab and a Jewish state, with Jerusalem under international control.

Arabs living in Palestine were shocked. They felt betrayed by the Western countries, whom they had supported during World War II. Palestinian Arabs felt particularly betrayed by the British, who in 1915 had promised them independence in Palestine. On May 14, 1948, Jews proclaimed the independent State of Israel. The very next day, neighbouring Arab nations invaded Israel in an attempt to destroy the new Jewish state.

Zionism

A movement that began in the nineteenth century for the purpose of creating a Jewish state in what is now modern Israel; today, "Zionism" refers to strong support for the State of Israel

Exodus. In 1947, the ship *Exodus* carried a large number of Jewish emigrants, mostly Holocaust survivors, to Palestine to settle there. However, they had no legal immigration certificates. The British navy seized the ship, and all the passengers were taken back to Europe.

The State of Israel, 1948

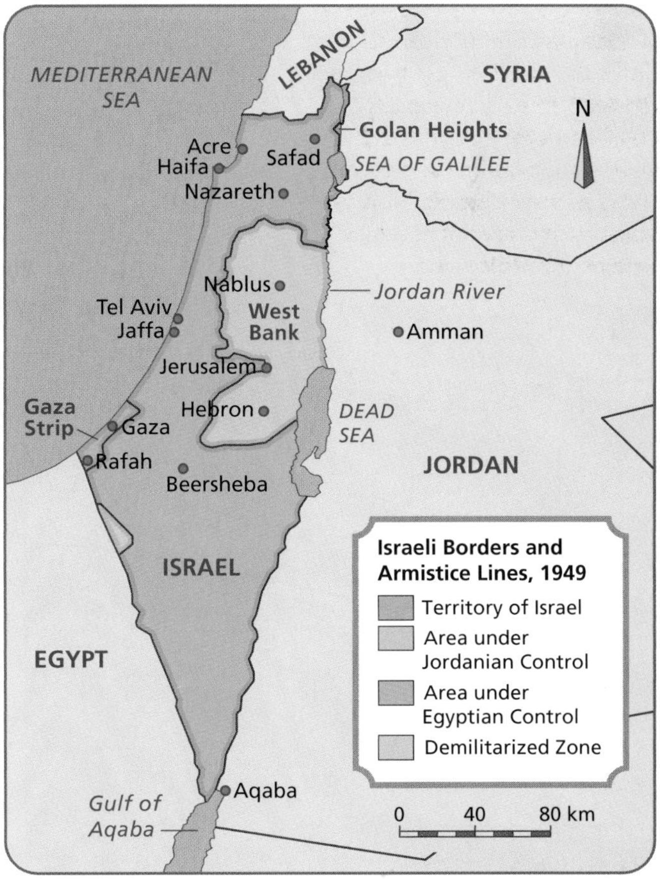

The State of Israel. Israel was immediately surrounded by nations opposed to its very existence. **With which nations has Israel come to peaceful terms?**

When the war ended about eight months later, Israel controlled not only its part, but also about half of the land that the UN had planned for the new Arab state. The rest was annexed by the Arab neighbours. Nearly a million of Palestine's Arab inhabitants left the country or were expelled by the Israelis. Most of them became refugees with no home and no country of their own, living in the Arab-controlled part of Palestine.

Displaced Refugees. Arab refugees are displaced by the establishment of the Jewish state. Since 1948, the conflict between Israel and the Palestinian people has become a major obstacle to Jewish–Muslim relations. Western support for Israel has also contributed to poor relations between Islam and the West. **What has happened to the Palestinian refugees since 1948?**

Israel, Tel Aviv. Israel now has a number of thriving urban centres. As well, Israelis have cultivated land that was once desert and transformed it into rich agricultural land.

Check Your Understanding

1. Explain how the focus of Zionism changed over time.

Think About It

2. Why did Western nations support the idea of a Jewish homeland after World War II?

Making It Personal

3. What can you do every day to include and welcome others, especially those whose beliefs are different from yours?

Rituals

As you saw in Chapter 2, rituals are the building blocks of a religion. Through rituals, people reflect on and practise their faith. Participating in religious rituals gives meaning to our lives.

Marking Time

The Jewish Calendar

The Jewish calendar is a lunar calendar, with each month beginning on the new moon. The chart on this page lists important Jewish holy days.

Important Jewish Holy Days

Holiday	Modern Calendar	Duration	Purpose/Commemorates
Pesach (Passover)	March/April	7–8 days	Liberation from Egyptian slavery
Shavuot	May/June	1–2 days	The giving of the Torah
Tisha b'Av	July/August	1 day	The destruction of the Temples/ Jewish tragedies
Rosh Hashanah	September/ October	2 days	Jewish New Year
Yom Kippur	September/ October	1 day	Day of Atonement
Succot	September/ October	1–8 days	The protection from the elements God provided during the wandering in the desert
Purim	February/ March	1 day	Queen Esther's part in ensuring the survival of the Jewish people
Hannukah	November/ December	8 days	The miracle of the Temple's rededication

Shabbat

Shabbat, or the Sabbath, the day the Lord rested "from all the work that he had done" (Genesis 2:2), is the most sacred day for Jews. Shabbat begins at sunset on Friday and ends at sundown on Saturday. Although it is celebrated in the synagogue, its focus is the family.

Shabbat celebrates that the heavens and Earth and everything on Earth are a gift of God. In the Ten Commandments, God says,

> *Remember the sabbath day, and keep it holy. Six days you shall labour and do all your work. But the seventh day is a sabbath of the Lord your God: you shall not do any work—you, your son or daughter, your male or female slave, or your cattle, or the stranger who is within your settlements. For in six days the Lord made heaven and earth and sea, and all that is in them, and He rested on the seventh day; therefore the Lord blessed the sabbath day and hallowed it.*
>
> (Exodus 20:8–11)

Shabbat
Hebrew word meaning "Sabbath"

A Family Observing Shabbat. This family is reading Torah outside for Shabbat.

One of the most important holy days of the Jewish year is *Pesach*, or the Passover. It is celebrated in the first month of the year, on the fifteenth day of Nisan. Like the Christian feast of Easter, this festival happens around the first full moon after the spring equinox.

The ritual of celebrating Passover is basic to Jewish identity. Passover celebrates an event that happened more than 3000 years ago—the freedom won by Jewish slaves when they escaped from the Egyptian Pharaoh.

Make It Your Own: Passover Seder Meal

The most important part of the festival is the Passover Seder, a ritual meal in which the participants recall how their ancestors were freed by God from slavery in Egypt. It includes readings from the *Haggadah*. The book explains the rituals involved in celebrating the *Seder*. Seder means "order." All the rituals are performed in a set order. The Seder takes place in the home on the first night of Passover.

In celebrating the Seder meal, Jews celebrate their escape to freedom and their never-ending bond with God. Sharing the food of the Passover Seder also connects the Exodus story to modern times by reminding Jews of the Holocaust, and of oppressed Jews everywhere. In this way, it reminds Jews always to work for freedom for all people. As the Torah teaches, "When one person is not free, no person is free."

Passover Seder Meal

Symbol	Meaning
Passover lamb shank bone	First Passover lamb; a reminder of the Temple sacrifice
The Matzah or unleavened bread	The flight of the Israelites from Egypt; they left so quickly that the bread did not have time to rise
Maror or bitter herbs	Bitterness of slavery
Celery	Springtime and gratitude for God's goodness and bounty
Egg	New life
Salt water	Tears and bitterness of slavery
Charoset: mixture of chopped apples, cinnamon, nuts, wine, honey	The mortar for bricks used by the Hebrews when they were slaves
Four cups of wine	Four stages of the Exodus from Egypt: freedom, deliverance, redemption, and being God's chosen people
Elijah's cup	Prophetic hope in the coming of the Kingdom of God upon our world

Activities

1. Research the structure, prayers, and songs associated with a Passover Seder meal. Plan a Seder meal and invite another class to participate.
2. Read the story of Passover in Chapter 12 of Exodus.

Seder Plate. This is a typical Seder plate. It is placed in the centre of the table at the Passover Seder.

From Rosh Hashanah to Yom Kippur: The Days of Awe

For Jews, the new year begins around September, with the celebration of Rosh Hashanah. The main celebration is held in the synagogue, where the people declare God king again for the coming year and pray for God's protection and blessing.

A new year is about new beginnings, so Jews also take this time to recall how God created the heavens and the Earth: "This day, on which was the beginning of Your work, is a memorial of the first day." God is the Lord of the people and of the universe. Rosh Hashanah also asks God to remember the covenant and the faith of the ancestors.

Perhaps the most exciting ritual at Rosh Hashanah is the sounding of the ram's horn, or *shofar*, to herald the beginning of the new year. After prayers are said, the rabbi blows the *shofar*.

During the time period from Rosh Hashanah to Yom Kippur, called the "Days of Awe," Jews turn inward and remember that God will be their judge at the end of time. The 10 days of celebration end with Yom Kippur, or the Day of Atonement. On Yom Kippur, a solemn day of fasting, Jews seek reconciliation with God. Anyone who has sinned against another person must atone for it by reconciling with that person and with God.

Fast Fact

"Rosh Hashanah" means "Head of the Year." Even though Rosh Hashanah falls on the first day of the seventh month in the Jewish calendar, it is celebrated as the beginning of the Jewish year.

Shofar. A rabbi blows the *shofar*. The ram's horn is blown many times during the Rosh Hashanah synagogue service as a celebration of God's creation and a heralding of the Messiah.

Check Your Understanding

1. Explain why the Days of Awe are significant to the Jewish people. Describe highlights from the celebrations of Rosh Hashanah and Yom Kippur.

Think About It

2. Research the origin of the ram's horn (*shofar*) in Israel's history. What is its religious meaning? Listen to an audio or watch a video of the *shofar* being blown. What effect do you think this sound might have on listeners?

Making It Personal

3. Reflect on how you celebrate the new year. Does it have religious significance for you? Explain.

Catholic Connection

Catholics belong to the Catholic Church through baptism rather than because their parents are Catholics.

Life-Cycle Rituals

The covenant with God is central to the existence of Jewish people. It forms the foundation for the rituals and practices of Judaism. We have already seen how aspects of this covenant are celebrated during Passover, Rosh Hashanah, and Yom Kippur. Now, let us take a look at some of the rituals that mark important events in people's daily lives.

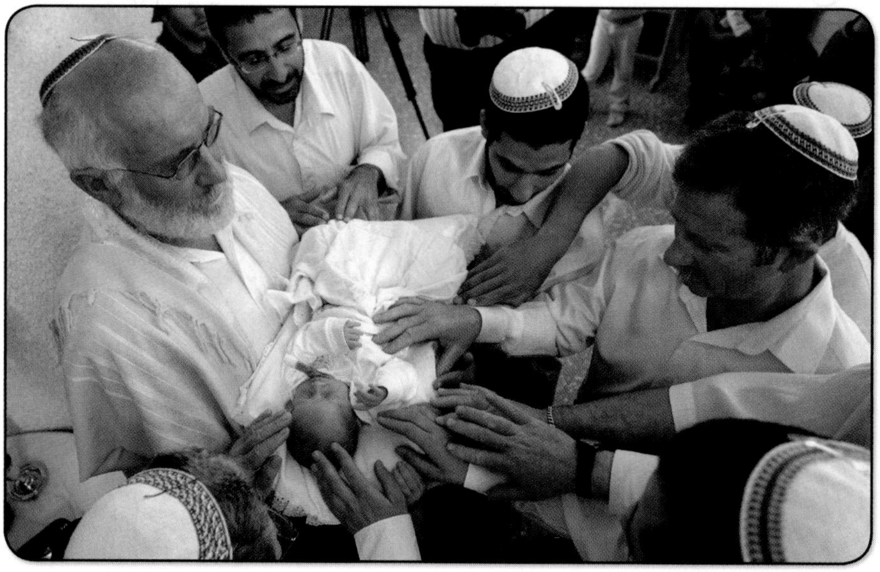

Brit Milah. Jewish men wear a sign of the covenant upon their bodies through circumcision.

Brit Milah or Bris

Eight days after the birth of a son, the rite of circumcision is performed. The *brit milah*, or *bris*, initiates the infant into the people of the covenant. The ceremony takes place in the presence of a *mohel* (usually a doctor, who performs the circumcision), the parents, the godparents, and other family members and friends, either in a synagogue or in the family home.

The *bris* is also the time when the baby is given a Hebrew name. The prayer that accompanies the name-giving emphasizes two things. First, Israel lives on through its bloodline. Second, God remembers the covenant made with Abraham forever. The circumcision is a bodily sign of this enduring covenant.

Betrothal and Marriage

In Judaism, people are strongly encouraged to marry. Getting married and having a family is the standard way of life for religiously observant Jews.

Before the wedding, a marriage contract is prepared. This tradition was developed over time as a way of ensuring that a husband treated his wife respectfully and met his obligations to her.

To celebrate its importance, the marriage ceremony is filled with rituals. A ring is given, symbolizing the marriage; then blessings are recited under a canopy, to symbolize the intimacy the couple is establishing. The ceremony ends with the recitation of the seven blessings for the marriage.

Simchat Bat. A baby girl receives her name on the Sabbath or at a Torah reading. Some parents choose also to hold a welcoming ceremony for girls, similar to the *brit milah*. It is called the *simchat bat*.

A Jewish Wedding. A Jewish couple gets married. The canopy represents the new home the couple will make together. It is open on all sides to show that their home will be open to guests, and even to strangers. The groom is shown here stomping on a glass, which has symbolic importance. **What are some important symbols or rituals of a Catholic wedding?**

Death

Faith also plays a role when a family member dies. When a parent dies, a son (and, in some communities, a daughter) recites the *kaddish*, a special **prayer of sanctification** in the synagogue each morning and each evening for 11 months after the death.

Traditionally, mourners gather at one home and receive visitors at certain times during the day. Neighbours often bring food for the family during this period. This frees the family from ordinary activities and helps them focus on what is more important: grieving their loss.

Prayer of Sanctification

A prayer to make something sacred

Sitting Shiva. For seven days after burial, the family of the deceased follows a practice known as "sitting **shiva**." During this time of intense mourning, the mourners wear sombre clothing and a torn garment to express their grief. **What similar practices have you heard of in your own faith for times of grieving?**

Shiva

A seven-day period of mourning

Check Your Understanding

1. Read the description of the Jewish marriage ceremony. Why do you think the covenant between God and the Jewish people is sometimes compared to a marriage?
2. Explain the significance of the *brit milah.*

Think About It

3. Find out about Jewish beliefs about the afterlife. Create a chart to show how they are similar to and different from Catholic beliefs.
4. How does each life-cycle ritual express a commitment to the covenant?

Making It Personal

5. What relationships in your life are more than simple arrangements or contracts and better understood as covenants? Explain.

Make It Your Own: Symbols and Sacred Objects

The Star of David. This is the six-pointed Star of David.

Menorah. This is the Jewish seven-branched menorah.

Torah Scroll. This is the Torah scroll, the most sacred ritual object of Judaism.

The Star of David is a six-pointed star that is formed from two overlapping triangles. It has seven spaces, the six points plus the centre. The number seven is important in Judaism, for example, the six days of creation plus the seventh day of rest.

A menorah is a seven-branched candelabra, created in the wilderness (in Exodus) and later transferred to Solomon's Temple in Jerusalem. The seven branches of the menorah symbolize the seven days of creation. Because its shape suggests a tree, the menorah is sometimes referred to as a "tree of life."

The most sacred Jewish ritual object is the Torah scroll. The Torah ("teaching") is the centre of Jewish life. The Five Books of Moses are inscribed by hand on parchment made from the

Make It Your Own *(cont'd)*

specially prepared skin of a kosher animal with a quill and ink. It takes six months to a year to write a Torah scroll.

A *mezuzah* is a container inside of which is a parchment with "Hear O Israel, the Lord our God, the Lord is one"—the Shema (Deuteronomy 6:4–9). The mezuzah is attached diagonally to the right-hand doorpost as one enters a room. As they enter and leave, some people touch the mezuzah with their fingertips, then bring their fingers to their lips to remind them of God.

Activities

1. Using Bristol board, create a large Star of David. In the centre of the star, place a Jewish symbol with a brief description.
2. Research additional Jewish symbols, such as the *tallith*, the *yarmulke*, or *kippa*, and *tefillin*.

Mezuzah. This mezuzah is mounted on a door frame at the entrance of a house.

The Jewish Community

The rituals outlined above shape the way the Jewish community marks time. Rituals also shape Jewish people as a community. How is the Jewish community formed?

With the Temple destroyed, there was no longer any centre of worship and no role for the high priest. There is no longer one person who can give a final interpretation of the Jewish tradition. Most Jewish people who want to observe their religion choose a rabbi or join a more structured community to help them discover how to live their lives faithfully.

The Synagogue

When Jews were exiled to Babylon, the people were dispersed among the nations. Synagogues were set up so that people would not have to depend on the Temple in Jerusalem. When the Temple was finally destroyed once and for all in 70 CE, even more synagogues were built.

Synagogues have two purposes. First, they are houses where Torah is taught to all Jews. Second, they provide places of worship outside Jerusalem. Through synagogues, Jewish people maintain their identity and their worship no matter where they live.

Fast Fact

Almost half of all Jews around the world do not belong to a synagogue. The others belong to synagogues with a broad range of practices, from very strict Orthodox to more liberal Reform.

Catholic Connection

The Gospels often speak of Jesus being in the synagogue. In one of his first visits to the synagogue of Nazareth after his baptism by John, Jesus presented himself as the Messiah. The people were so angry at what he said that they threatened to throw him off a cliff. (Luke 4:16–30)

Interior of a Synagogue. This is the interior of a modern synagogue.

The interior of the synagogue contains an ark, or cabinet, where the Torah scrolls are kept. The ark is usually positioned on the eastern wall so that members of the congregation face Jerusalem when they face the ark. The ark reminds worshippers of the Ark of the Covenant, which contained the tablets of the Ten Commandments. This is the holiest space in a synagogue. Services are conducted and the Torah scroll is read from a raised platform. The rabbi speaks from a pulpit to explain the Torah. A lamp is kept burning at all times as a reminder that God is present.

Torah. A young boy holds the Torah during his bar mitzvah ceremony. Before the service begins, the Torah scroll is carried around the synagogue to remind everyone of their duty to study and apply its teachings. As the congregation welcomes the Torah, the members turn so that they never have their backs to the Torah. **How does the Catholic Church show respect for the Bible?**

Check Your Understanding

1. Describe how the Jewish community is organized. How does this structure differ from the structure of Catholicism?

Think About It

2. Create a diagram of the layout of a synagogue. Label the diagram with brief explanations of the important features.

Making It Personal

3. As a class, visit a local synagogue. Describe your experience in an oral or written presentation.
4. Is the Bible important to the way you live? If so, how do you show your respect for the Bible?

Central Beliefs

On the first page of this chapter, you read the Shema: "Hear, O Israel, the Lord is our God, the Lord is one" (Deuteronomy 6:4). The Shema is the most important confession of faith in Judaism. The Jewish morning and evening prayers are built around this prayer. It sums up the Jewish scriptures, or **Tanakh**.

The Tanakh

The Tanakh presents the core teachings of Jewish faith in the form of a story. The basic story is found in the Torah, the first five books of the scriptures. Although the narrative is developed in later writings, such as the Books of the Prophets and the Books of Wisdom, the Torah remains the heart of Jewish faith. It tells of God making a covenant with a people.

Tanakh

Hebrew word for the sacred writings of Judaism; the word is formed from the first Hebrew letter of the three parts of the Jewish scriptures (what Christians call the Old Testament): **T**orah, **N**eviim, **K**etuvim

Parts of the Tanakh

The Torah or Teaching

Genesis *(Bereshith)*

The stories of Creation; Adam and Eve; Noah; Abraham and Sarah and their offspring

Exodus *(Shemot)*

The stories of Moses; the liberation from slavery in Egypt; the Ten Commandments

Leviticus *(Va yikra)*

The detailing of the laws of sacrifice and other laws pertaining to the priests

Numbers *(Bemidbar)*

The wandering of the twelve tribes of Israel in the wilderness for 40 years

Deuteronomy *(Devarim)*

A series of talks by Moses before the people entered the Promised Land; it is a "Repetition of the Law," a reminder that the gift of the land depended on obedience to the law

continues...

Parts of the Tanakh *(cont'd)*

The Prophets (Neviim)

Most of these books were written after 586 BCE, in a time when the Jewish people were in exile from their homeland. To keep the faith alive during this period, it was critical that the faithful be reminded of their covenant with God. The Prophets contains warnings to the Jewish people to stay faithful, to practise justice, and to be mindful of widows and orphans.

Joshua	2 Samuel	Isaiah
Judges	1 Kings	Jeremiah
1 Samuel	2 Kings	Ezekiel

12 Minor Prophets

Hosea	Jonah	Zephaniah
Joel	Micah	Haggai
Amos	Nahum	Zechariah
Obadiah	Habbakuk	Malachi

The Writings (Ketuvim)

These books were also written during the period of exile. The Writings are known as wisdom books, or the wisdom literature. They contain sayings or proverbs by wise people that reveal ways of living Jewish life.

Psalms	Ruth	Daniel
Proverbs	Lamentations	Ezra-Nehemiah
Job	Ecclesiastes	1 Chronicles
Song of Solomon	Esther	2 Chronicles

A Closer Look

If you are familiar with the Old Testament (which contains all the books of the Tanakh), you know that it tells an all-too-human story. It describes people of faith, hospitality, love, generosity, and forgiveness, but also people who kill, take revenge, cheat, revolt, and deceive.

On another level, though, this is God's story. It reveals that God has a purpose and plan for humankind. Despite our mistakes, sins, and wrongdoings, we see that God's plan for our salvation will be achieved. So, although the Tanakh contains historical events, the story itself is not history, but **revelation**. In and through the story, we learn about the God of Israel and how God interacts with Israel. Jews, Christians, and Muslims use the word "revelation" to express the way God reveals God's self to people. Sacred writings are a key source of this revelation. That is why sacred writings are understood as the word of God. All of the Tanakh is God's revelation to the Jewish people.

Revelation
The act of showing, or revealing, something that was hidden

Fast Fact

The 12 Minor Prophets are not called "minor" because they are less important, but because their writings are shorter.

Here is an example of wisdom from the book of Proverbs:

Lazybones, go to the ant;
Study its ways and learn.
Without leaders, officers, or rulers,
It lays up its store during the summer,
Gathers its food at the harvest.
How long will you lie there, lazybones;
When will you wake from your sleep?
A bit more sleep, a bit more slumber,
A bit more hugging yourself in bed,
And poverty will come calling upon you,
And want, like a man with a shield.

(Proverbs 6:6–11)

Catholic Connection

The Psalms are the centrepiece of the prayer practices of the Catholic Church, as they are in Jewish services as well. In the Liturgy of the Hours each day, the Church prays all 150 psalms in the course of a four-week cycle. In the Mass, a psalm is sung after the first reading. The prayer of Israel is also the prayer of the Church.

Check Your Understanding

1. Describe the Tanakh and explain its importance to the Jewish people.
2. Do some research to find out more about the prophets. Who were they, and what was their role in the Jewish tradition?

Think About It

3. Use the table of contents of a Catholic Bible to compare the Tanakh with the Old Testament. How similar are they? What might account for this similarity?

Making It Personal

4. Look through the book of Proverbs, and choose one proverb that appeals to you. In a small group, share your proverbs and explain why you chose them. What do these stories and sayings teach you about life?

Fast Fact

The Torah scroll is the most sacred object in Judaism. It is very carefully written by hand, in Hebrew, using sheets of parchment, special ink, and a goose quill. Because it contains God's words, a Torah scroll that has become too worn for further use is ceremonially buried in a service similar to the ceremony for human burial.

The Torah

The Torah, as we said, is the most important part of the Tanakh. It lays the groundwork of Israel's faith in God. From the Torah, we will explore three stories: (1) the story of creation, (2) the story of Abraham and Sarah, and (3) the story of Moses.

The Story of Creation (Genesis 1:1–3:24)

There are two different versions of creation in the book of Genesis. The first part tells of the six days when God created the world. On each of the days, God says, "Let there be ..." and light and darkness, night and day, the sky and the Earth, the seas and the land come to be. Then God creates life—first the plants, then the animals. Finally, on the sixth day, he creates humans. On the seventh day, God rests, making that day holy. Here is how it is described in Genesis:

1:3 God said, "Let there be light;" and there was light.

1:11 Then God said, "Let the earth sprout vegetation: seed-bearing plants, fruit trees of every kind on earth that bear fruit with the seed of it." And it was so.

1:12 The earth brought forth vegetation: seed-bearing plants of every kind, and trees of every kind bearing fruit with the seed in it. And God saw that this was good.

1:26 And God said, "Let us make man in our image, after our likeness. They shall rule the fish of the sea, the birds of the sky, the cattle, the whole earth and all the creeping things that creep on the ground."

1:27 And God created man in his image; in the image of God He created him; male and female He created them.

1:28 God blessed them, and God said to them: "Be fertile and increase; fill the earth and master it; and rule the fish of the sea, the birds of the sky, and all the living things that creep on earth."

2:3 And God blessed the seventh day [the Sabbath] and declared it holy.

Fast Fact

Catholics and both Reform and Conservative Jews understand that the creation stories are myths—stories that explain how things came to be. Myths describe what is "true" in narrative form. In doing so, they reveal a spiritual reality that is not accessible through historical studies, cultural studies, and scientific perspectives alone.

Fast Fact

The seventh day of creation is the Sabbath day. Just as God rested on the seventh day, all must rest.

The Second Story of Creation (Genesis 2:4–3:24)

The second story of creation tells of the first man and woman. God created Adam from clay of the earth, and Eve from Adam's side. They lived in God's garden (Eden). One day, they were tempted by a snake to eat fruit from a forbidden tree in the garden. As punishment, God banished them from paradise. Through their disobedience, evil and suffering came into the world.

This account tells us how sin and violence gained a foothold in God's good creation. It also tells how humans became moral beings, knowing good from evil, and why humans have to work, give birth in pain, and die. Evil and death became part of human reality, and people have had to struggle ever since to overcome the temptation of evil.

The Story of Abraham

The story of Abraham begins after God's good creation has been overwhelmed by sin and violence. God had already destroyed all creation once, with a flood, sparing only Noah's family and a pair of each animal. Genesis also

Adam and Eve in the Garden of Eden. This painting is by Flemish artist Jan Bruegel, the Elder (1568–1625). **Read the full story of the creation of Adam and Eve in the book of Genesis. What is your understanding of the creation story? What images or feelings does this story give you?**

tells the story of how humans tried—and failed—to take the place of God by building a tower up to heaven.

With Abraham, God wanted to start all over again. The story opens with the call of Abram—as he is first known—to leave the place of his ancestors and go to a land that God will show him. There, God will make him the father of a new people. Abram and his wife Sarai do what God asks.

Abram's trust or faith in God is tested time and again. The promised child does not come until his wife is in her nineties. When Isaac is born, Abram is tested again: God asks him to sacrifice his son. Abram's faith in God never wavers. In this way, Abram proves to be a **righteous** man.

God's covenant with Abram had promised him many descendants and a land for them to inherit. Abram, God said, would be a light and a blessing to all nations. To indicate his new calling, Abram's name was changed to Abraham: the father of nations. Sarai's name became Sarah.

The rest of Genesis tells the story of God's faithfulness to the covenant, through Abraham's son Isaac and Isaac's son Jacob. Jacob was renamed "Israel" after wrestling with someone whom he later identified as God (Genesis 32:22–32). The covenant with Israel's ancestors—the bond that connects God with Israel and Israel with God—is the heart of Jewish belief to this day.

Fast Fact

Several characters in scripture undergo a change of name that signifies a change in their relationship with God. For example, Jacob ("he supplants") became Israel ("he who wrestles with God").

Catholic Connection

Abraham is considered the patriarch (forefather) of Christians and Muslims, as well as Jews.

Righteous

Describes one who is just, or who is in a right relationship with God

Check Your Understanding

1. Read the two creation stories in Genesis. With a partner, discuss what each story reveals to us about God, and about human nature.
2. Explain why Abraham is a key figure for the Jewish people.

Think About It

3. What do you think it means that human beings are made in God's image? What privileges and responsibilities does this entail?
4. With a partner or in a small group, explore what Abraham's story tells us about how we can live rightly before God. Why does the Bible put so high a value on trusting God, or having faith?

Making It Personal

5. How would you depict the story of creation? Use words, music, or images to create your own representation of the seven days of creation.
6. What role does faith have in your own life? In whom or in what do you have faith? How do you express that faith?

A Closer Look

Jacob (Israel) had twelve sons, including Joseph. Ten of Jacob's sons and two of Joseph's sons became the ancestors of the "twelve tribes of Israel." The twelve tribes filled the land of Canaan, the land God promised to the people of Israel. Of these twelve, it was Jacob's son Levi who became the ancestor of the Jewish priesthood.

The Story of Moses

Exodus, the second book of the Torah, picks up the story when Jacob's descendants, the children of Israel, had become slaves to the Egyptians. Exodus tells how Moses freed the Jewish people from slavery and brought them to the Promised Land.

In Jewish tradition, Moses is honoured above all other humans. He was a leader, the founding father of the Israelites, a prophet, and a lawgiver. As the book of Deuteronomy says, "Never since has there arisen a prophet in Israel like Moses, whom the Lord knew face to face" (34:10).

Moses was born in Egypt into the priestly tribe of Levi. When the Egyptian Pharaoh decreed that all newborn Hebrew boys were to be killed, Moses's mother placed him in a basket and hid him in reeds along the Nile. Pharaoh's daughter found him and called him Moses.

Exodus tells of Moses having an older brother, Aaron, who became Israel's first priest, and a sister, Miriam, who became a prophetess.

Moses was raised in the luxury of Pharaoh's house. Yet, he identified strongly with the enslaved Israelites, whom he called his brothers. One day, when he saw an Egyptian beating a Hebrew slave, Moses was overcome with anger. He killed the Egyptian, then fled for his life. He ended up in Midian, between Egypt and Sinai, where he married and had two children.

The Call of Moses

In Midian, Moses had an encounter with God:

> *An angel of the Lord appeared to him in a blazing fire out of a bush. He gazed, and there was a bush all aflame, yet the bush was not consumed .... When the Lord saw that he had turned aside to look, God called to him out of the bush, "Moses, Moses!" He answered, "Here I am." And He said, "Come no closer! Remove your sandals from your feet, for the place on which you stand is holy ground. I am," He said, "the God of your father, the God of Abraham, the God of Isaac and the God of Jacob." And Moses hid his face, for he was afraid to look at God.*
>
> *(Exodus 3:2–6)*

In this encounter, Moses was told God's name in Hebrew, which translates as "I am who am," "I am who is," "I am who I shall be," or "I shall be who I am." Some see this answer as a mysterious refusal to give a name in the very act of giving a name. Others see it as a promise: "I will show you who I am in my being with you," or "I will be with you tomorrow as I have been up to now."

The Liberation of the Israelites

At the burning bush, the Lord gave Moses a mission. He was to go back to Egypt and lead God's people out of slavery. Moses and his brother, Aaron, tried appealing to Pharaoh, but Pharaoh refused to free the Israelites.

Moses showed the power of the Lord through a series of 10 plagues. The final plague, the death of all the firstborn in the land, finally convinced Pharaoh to let the people go.

The last meal of Israel in Egypt is called the Passover meal because the angel of death "passed over" the homes of the Israelites. Their firstborn sons were saved. Ever since that time, Jewish people celebrate Passover to commemorate that liberation from slavery. (Refer to page 118 to learn about how Passover is celebrated.)

Fast Fact

The name of God in the book of Exodus is given as four consonants: YHWH. In time, Jews stopped saying God's name. Instead, Jews say *Adonai*, or Lord. Translations of the Hebrew Bible have followed this Jewish tradition.

Fast Fact

A sacred status was attached to the firstborn male child, the first fruits of the harvest, and the first offspring of animals. These belong to God and must be dedicated or given back to God. Israel sees itself as God's firstborn. Egypt was punished for enslaving God's firstborn.

Pharaoh relented only long enough to allow the people of Israel to begin their journey to freedom, then sent his chariots after them. The book of Exodus recounts the miracle of the crossing of the Red Sea, when the waters parted to let God's people through, but drowned the men and horses of Pharaoh. As Moses and his people wandered through the wilderness, God fed them with manna, a sweet bread.

The Ten Commandments

At Mount Sinai, God made a covenant with Moses, and gave him the Ten Commandments and the rest of the Law. The revelation of God at Mount Sinai became the heart of the Torah. It is at Sinai that God taught the people how to live the covenant—and the most important instruction is found in the Ten Commandments.

During the Israelites' time in the desert, God travelled with them in a tent, called the Tabernacle. The Tabernacle held the central object of Israel's worship, the Ark of the Covenant. The Ark contained the stone tablets with the Ten Commandments, Aaron's staff, and some manna. This was the place of God's invisible presence among the Israelites.

The Ten Commandments

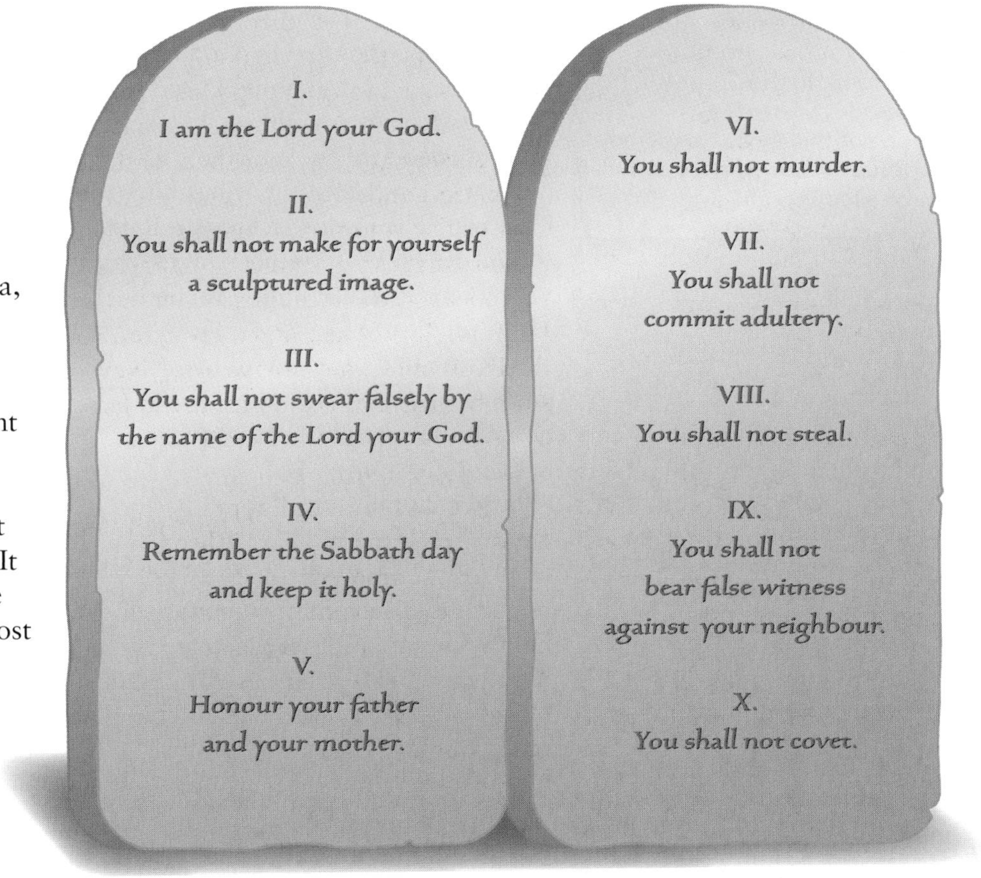

I.
I am the Lord your God.
II.
You shall not make for yourself a sculptured image.
III.
You shall not swear falsely by the name of the Lord your God.
IV.
Remember the Sabbath day and keep it holy.
V.
Honour your father and your mother.
VI.
You shall not murder.
VII.
You shall not commit adultery.
VIII.
You shall not steal.
IX.
You shall not bear false witness against your neighbour.
X.
You shall not covet.

The Ten Commandments. Explore the Ten Commandments. What must a person do to keep the covenant with God?

Check Your Understanding

1. Explain how Moses came to be a prophet of God.

Think About It

2. What does the name that God reveals to Moses tell us about God?

Making It Personal

3. How do the Ten Commandments guide your actions?
4. Reflect on a time in your life when you felt as if you were "wandering in the desert." What does this image mean to you?

Catholic Connection

Catholics and Lutherans number the 10 commandments differently, following Saint Augustine's example.

Catholic Connection

Catholics, like all Christians, see this covenant with David as being fulfilled in Jesus. In the Gospels, David is presented as one of the ancestors of Jesus. That is why Jesus is called Son of David.

The Story of David

The story of David is found in the Books of Kings. David was Israel's second king, anointed by God to replace Saul. God presents David as "a man after my own heart." David not only defeated the enemies of his people, he united all the tribes into one kingdom. The Books of Kings tell many stories of David's exploits. David was a model for all future kings, particularly for his dedication to God.

After he had defeated all his enemies and united all the tribes of Israel, David wanted to build a temple to honour God. God refused his offer, but in appreciation made a covenant with David:

> *When your days are done and you lie with your fathers, I will raise up your offspring after you, one of your own issue, and I will establish his kingship. He shall build a house for My name, and I will establish his royal throne forever. I will be a father to him, and he shall be a son to Me.*
>
> (2 Samuel 7:12–14)

David's son Solomon completed David's dream of building a temple in Jerusalem. The Ark of the Covenant containing the stone tablets of the commandments was placed there.

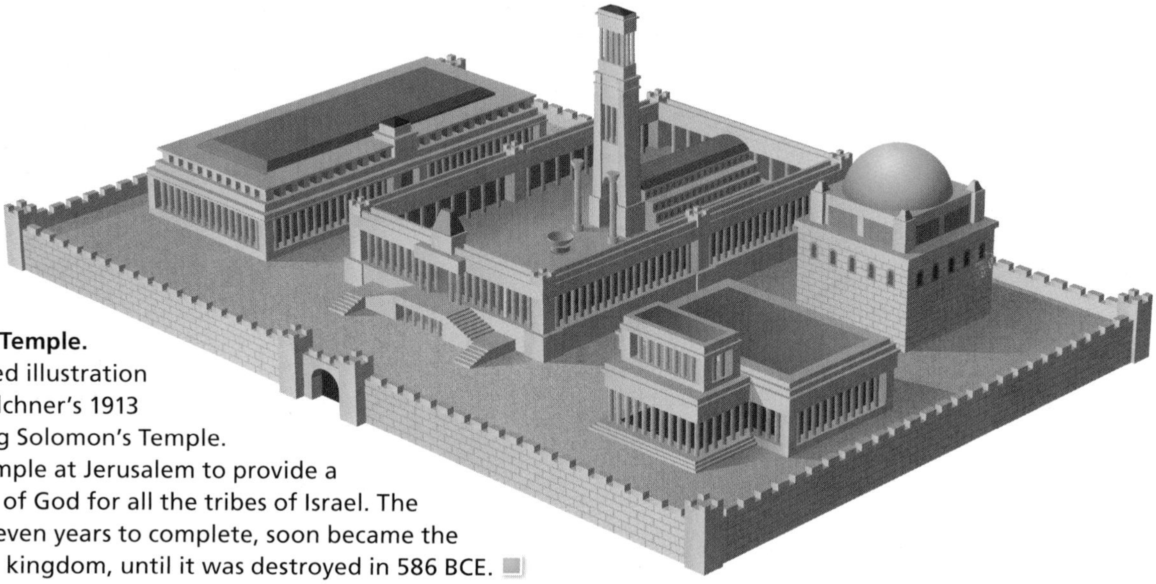

King Solomon's Temple. This is an undated illustration depicting John W. Kelchner's 1913 reconstruction of King Solomon's Temple. Solomon built the Temple at Jerusalem to provide a place for the worship of God for all the tribes of Israel. The Temple, which took seven years to complete, soon became the spiritual centre of the kingdom, until it was destroyed in 586 BCE.

Check Your Understanding

1. Explain the importance of the Temple.

Think About It

2. One of the most famous stories about David is the story of his battle with Goliath. Read the version of this story in Samuel 1:17. What does this incident reveal about David's character?

Making It Personal

3. How can temples and churches be places where God is present? What does it mean to you when it is said that God is present among us?

Talmud. The Talmud is a written record of the oral traditions, teachings, and laws of Judaism. In the centre of a page of the Talmud is the *Mishnah* text, the record of the oral tradition, debates, and opinions. The Mishnah is surrounded by interpretations and explanations of commentators through the centuries.

The Talmud

Second in importance to the Tanakh in Jewish sacred writings is the **Talmud**. The Talmud is an enormous book of Jewish civil and religious laws and ethical teachings. It consists of layer upon layer of interpretations of the Torah made by Jewish rabbis between the first and the fifth centuries.

To understand the Talmud, one must go back to the Pharisees and the beginning of Rabbinic Judaism in the first century CE.

The Halakhah (the Oral Torah)

As you read earlier in this chapter, the Pharisees believed that as well as the written Torah, Moses also received an "oral Torah" on Mount Sinai. This oral Torah consists of the ***Halakhah***, meaning "the path" of Jewish life. The *Halakhah* contains prescribed ways to apply the commandments found in the Torah.

The Pharisees were strict about following the laws of ritual purity of the *Halakhah*. To be holy, they believed, was to associate with holy things. One became impure when one touched what was seen as impure. Things considered to be impure included

- certain foods (meat from pigs, shellfish like lobster and shrimp)
- corpses
- women who were menstruating
- reptiles

It was also considered impure to mix certain foods, like meat and dairy, and to eat with sinners.

These laws were first kept by the priests who served at the Temple in Jerusalem. Later, the Pharisees also kept them. Through the rabbis, these ritual laws of purity became part of Jewish life, as they are today.

After the second defeat by the Romans in 135 CE, the rabbis began to write down and interpret this oral Torah. This process took place in different places and was done by different rabbis. As a result, two versions of the Talmud emerged. The Jerusalem Talmud was compiled in Israel between 170 and 400 CE.

Fast Fact

In Hebrew, "Talmud" means "teachings" or "tradition." There are two versions of the Talmud: the earlier Jerusalem Talmud and the later Babylonian Talmud.

Fast Fact

The printed editions of the Talmud today consist of 32 huge volumes containing about 5 million words.

Talmud

The compilation of written interpretations of the oral Torah (the *Halakhah*); after the second defeat of the Jews by the Romans in 135 CE, the rabbis began to write down and interpret this oral Torah

Halakhah

"Laws" or "the path"; the oral tradition of Judaism

Fast Fact

The Pharisees were Jews who, after the destruction of the Temple in 70 CE, saw Jewish faith continuing without temple worship. They saw Jewish faith as obedience to God's will as found in the oral and written Torah. To the Pharisees, keeping the Torah was paramount.

Another, more extensive version, the Babylonian Talmud, was compiled by Jews in exile. It is the most commonly used version of the Talmud today.

The tradition of commenting on the Talmud has continued for centuries. As a result, a single page of Talmud has many layers of interpretation, as you can see in the reproduction on the previous page.

Check Your Understanding

1. Explain what the "oral law" or "oral Torah" is. Why is it important to Judaism?

Think About It

2. The rules around impurity were one way that Jews set themselves apart. What ways can you think of that groups today use to differentiate themselves from others? Brainstorm a list in a small group.

Making It Personal

3. What do you do when you have a difficult moral decision to make? Who helps you to figure out the best course of action? In your experience, to what extent is it helpful to listen to the advice and experiences of others in these situations?

Morality

Responding to God's Covenant

In Biblical times, covenants had a special structure. Most started with God's reasons for making the covenant. The covenant with the Jewish people at Mount Sinai states: "You have seen what I did to the Egyptians, how I bore you on eagles' wings and brought you to Me" (Exodus 19:4). This loving act of freeing Israel is the foundation of the covenant. Next comes a request for the people to submit to God: "Now then, if you will obey Me faithfully and keep My covenant ...." Israel is told how it can keep the covenant. The covenant ends with a blessing: "You shall be My treasured possession among all the peoples" (Exodus 19:5).

Jews understand their moral life as a response to God's covenant. To keep the covenant means following God's ***mitzvot***. This word is often translated as "laws" or "commandments," but it is more accurate to use "guidance."

Mitzvah

Religious or moral path that Jews must follow; the plural form is "mitzvot"

Covenant Relationship. The covenant between God and God's people is like the relationship between spouses, which is rooted in faithfulness, trust, and mutual love. Moral life is what keeps the relationship healthy and beneficial for others. **Explain the ways in which a covenant relationship has a different effect on life than a contractual relationship.**

The *mitzvot* spell out how Jews can mirror in their lives the holiness of the God of the covenant. Following the *mitzvot* helps them to live in a right relationship with God. Those who live according to the *mitzvot* are said to follow the path, the *Halakhah.*

The Ten Commandments

The *mitzvot* are instructions on how to live, and at the heart of them are the Ten Commandments that God gave to Moses. The Ten Commandments are seen as God's laws or God's own instruction.

The Torah contains two versions of the commandments: one in Exodus (20:2–17), and one in Deuteronomy (5:6–21). The version found in the book of Exodus is shown below on this page.

In addition to the Ten Commandments, Rabbinic Jews follow as many of the other *mitzvot* as they can. These are found in the Torah, the oral law of the Pharisees, the Talmud, and Rabbinic law.

The *Halakhah* touches on all aspects of human life. The will of God is to penetrate all areas of life and be each person's guiding light. The *Halakhah* spells out what it means "to be holy as I, your God, am holy."

At times, the writers of the *Halakhah* had to adapt to new situations. For example, when the Temple was destroyed, all the rules dealing with the temple worship were no longer used.

God spoke all these words, saying:

I the Lord am your God who brought you out of the land of Egypt, the house of bondage: You shall have no other gods besides Me.

You shall not make for yourself a sculptured image, or any likeness of what is in the heavens above, or on the earth below, or in the waters under the earth. You shall not bow down to them or serve them. For I the Lord your God am an impassioned God, visiting the guilt of the parents upon the children, upon the third and upon the fourth generations of those who reject Me, but showing kindness to the thousandth generation of those who love Me and keep My commandments.

You shall not swear falsely by the name of the Lord your God; for the Lord will not clear one who swears falsely by His name.

Remember the Sabbath day and keep it holy. Six days you shall labour and do all your work, but the seventh day is a Sabbath of the Lord your God: you shall not do any work—you, your son or daughter, your male or female slave, or your cattle, or the stranger who is within your settlements. For in six days the Lord made heaven and earth and sea and all that is in them, and He rested on the seventh day; therefore the Lord blessed the Sabbath day and hallowed it.

Honour your father and your mother, that you may long endure on the land that the Lord your God is assigning to you.

You shall not murder.

You shall not commit adultery.

You shall not steal.

You shall not bear false witness against your neighbour.

You shall not covet your neighbour's house: you shall not covet your neighbour's wife, or his male or female slave, or his ox or his ass, or anything that is your neighbour's.

Moses Maimonides (1135–1204). Maimonides's interpretation of the Torah is still respected today.

Catholic Connection

The Acts of the Apostles in the New Testament seems to refer to the laws of Noah, too. The writings of Acts say that those who are non-Jews and who want to follow Jesus do not need to follow the *Halakhah*, but are bound by other laws that predate Judaism.

At other times, rabbis, such as Moses Maimonides (1135–1204) of Spain, had to clarify how to keep the Jewish moral life in the midst of huge cultural changes.

Sin

Failure to live the covenant—that is, to follow the *mitzvot*—is called sin. For Jews, sin involves not only deliberately going against moral laws, but also violating the ritual or purity laws. Sin is seen as the main obstacle to living the covenant. It is a break in the relationship with God, a breaking of the covenant.

In the days when Jews worshipped in the Temple, elaborate rituals and sacrifices were carried out to heal the breach and to restore the covenant relationship. Today, Jews celebrate a day of atonement and repentance at the fast of Yom Kippur.

At the beginning of the Yom Kippur evening service, the people pray, "May all the people of Israel be forgiven, including all the strangers who live in their midst, for all the people are in fault." Jews believe in a God of compassion, mercy, and forgiveness.

The Covenant with Noah

Judaism holds that non-Jews are also obligated to follow some of the *mitzvot*. These, they say, were pronounced before Abraham's time, in the time of Noah, and so they apply to all the descendants of Noah. These laws are found in the Talmud:

1. Do not commit idolatry.
2. Do not commit blasphemy.
3. Do not commit murder.
4. Do not commit theft.
5. Do not commit sexual immorality.
6. Do not remove and eat the limb of a living animal.
7. Establish a judicial system with courts of law to enforce the first six.

Sexuality

All forms of Judaism see human sexuality as a blessing from God and part of an essential pairing of male and female. How this blessing is to be enjoyed and how it is to be safeguarded differ somewhat among Jews.

The *Halakhah* states that human sexuality is to be celebrated and enjoyed only in marriage. This tradition forbids premarital sex, masturbation, and homosexual acts. Orthodox Jews emphasize modesty as a way to safeguard the value of human sexuality.

In Judaism, the child is protected even before birth. The Talmud permits abortion only in cases when the mother's life is in danger. Rules around abortion might be more broadly interpreted by some Jews, while others may not feel bound by the *Halakhah*. Jewish law permits breaking the rules of the Sabbath to save the life of an unborn child if the mother has died.

Usually, Reform Jews will share some of the sexual values of the culture they live in. Premarital sex is not always discouraged, abortion may be allowed, and homosexuality may be accepted.

Adultery, however, is not allowed in any form of Judaism.

In the Torah, a man is always permitted to divorce his wife, but the premarital agreement and the interpretation of the Talmud penalize husbands who seek divorce. A wife can initiate a divorce in Rabbinical court. Among Jews, either spouse has an equal right to divorce the other.

Catholic Connection

Pope John Paul II made this statement about sexuality in 1981:

> Sexuality, by means of which man and woman give themselves to one another through the acts which are proper and exclusive to spouses, is not something simply biological, but concerns the innermost being of the human person as such. It is realized in a truly human way only if it is an integral part of the love by which a man and woman commit themselves totally to one another until death (*On the Christian Family in the Modern World*, #12).

How does the teaching of Pope John Paul II relate to the Jewish understanding of sexuality?

Check Your Understanding

1. Draw a diagram or image to show the relationships among the following terms: *mitzvot, Halakhah*, sin.

Think About It

2. Explain the distinction between the Ten Commandments and Noah's laws.
3. Explain the Jewish attitude toward procreation. How is Reform Judaism's view of human sexuality similar to the traditional view? How is it different?

Making It Personal

4. With a partner, discuss whether you feel that some laws or rules of behaviour should be applicable to all people. If so, what might some of these laws be?

Family Life

Prayer and Ritual in the Home

The home is where a great deal of Jewish prayer is recited. Prayer and ritual in the home are especially important for educating children in the faith. For example, all meals begin and end with prayer. The most important meal and the most important family prayers are reserved for the Sabbath, or Shabbat, which takes place on Friday evenings.

Shabbat in the Home

As Shabbat begins at sunset, the mother lights at least two special candles. She offers a silent prayer for the well-being of her husband and her children while she waves her hands to and fro in front of the candles, welcoming the light of Shabbat.

Shabbat. A mother prepares candles at Shabbat. Keeping Shabbat is important to Jewish families. In our busy world, Shabbat brings the family together. It is an opportunity for meaning, a moment to connect with others and to belong. **Does your family celebrate something that resembles Shabbat in any way? Explain.**

Fast Fact

Because no food is to be cooked on Shabbat (Saturday), many Jews prepare food for Shabbat before sundown on Friday.

A Closer Look

Basing many of the prayers and rituals in the family has helped Judaism endure. It allowed religious practice to continue even when Jews lost their homeland and lived in societies around the world that were sometimes hostile to them.

Fast Fact

"Kosher" comes from the Hebrew word *kasher*, meaning "fit and right." For many Jews, following the kosher dietary laws is an important discipline and a way of expressing Jewish identity.

Before the Shabbat meal, the father or mother takes a special cup of wine and recites the *kiddush*—a declaration sanctifying and welcoming Shabbat with thanksgiving to God. This declaration is repeated on Shabbat morning.

Three meals are required on Shabbat. They are usually accompanied by songs of joy. At the end of Shabbat, the people recite a blessing thanking God for the division between Shabbat and the rest of the week.

A number of rules are to be followed on Shabbat. These are listed below. However, the three branches of Judaism interpret and apply these rules differently. Orthodox Jews see these requirements as an opportunity to do God's will and to lift Shabbat above the ordinary course of life. Observing the rules helps a person be constantly mindful of the purpose of Shabbat.

Conservative Jews interpret them more loosely. For example, they will switch on lights and drive to synagogue. Reform Jews do not feel obligated by these rules, but many still observe Shabbat.

All members of the three branches of Judaism follow *Halakhah* requirements. Where they differ is in how they interpret and carry out the *Halakhah* requirements.

Keeping Kosher

What does it mean to "keep kosher"? You may already know that it involves not eating pork products, but eating kosher has many other rules as well. For example, observant Jews do not eat shellfish and do not eat dairy products and beef in the same meal.

If you were to visit a Jewish home where kosher laws are observed, the kitchen might look a little unusual. For instance, some people keep separate sets of plates, pots, and utensils for dairy and meat dishes. They may even have two sinks to wash the dishes separately, and two sets of cupboards to store them. Jewish dietary laws are complex, but they are second nature to Jews who have grown up with them.

Orthodox Halakhah Requirements for Shabbat

No work is to be done.

No discussion of work or one's job is allowed.

No money is to be handled.

Nothing is to be carried in public.

No motor vehicle (that is, no car, taxi, bus, streetcar, or subway) is to be ridden, even if driven by a non-Jew.

No lights are to be switched on or electrical appliances operated.

No food is to be cooked.

Jewish Home Life, Montreal. This painting by Canadian artist William Kurelek (1927–1977) shows an Orthodox Jewish home in the 1920s. **What roles are represented in this painting? What sacred symbols do you see?**

Check Your Understanding

1. Describe what it might be like to spend a day following the rules for Shabbat outlined above. If you observed all these rules, what difference might it make to your usual Saturday activities?

Think About It

2. Create a menu for a kosher meal, based on what you know about the kosher laws. Why are these laws important to many Jews?
3. Compare some of the signs of faith you might find in a Jewish home with those in a Catholic home.

Making It Personal

4. What challenges and benefits can you see to keeping the commandment to observe Shabbat in modern society? What would you find most challenging and most appealing about this practice?

The Jewish Family and Community: Welcome and Outreach

Fast Fact

"Shalom" is the Hebrew word for peace. The Jewish emphasis on peacemaking is often expressed in liturgy and prayer. It is also reflected in Hebrew greetings, such as *"shalom aleikhem"* (peace be with you).

Hospitality is a key feature of Judaism. For Jews, it is an honour to welcome guests into their home. The guest is welcomed into a community and shares in the family meals and celebrations.

Jews also practise hospitality by reaching out to others. This includes meeting the needs of people who are elderly, sick, and poor in their own community and being active in causes that benefit the whole human family.

Another notion, similar to the Catholic teaching on social justice, is that of *tikkun olam* (repairing the world). *Tikkun olam* can range from political action to tree planting to preparing food in a soup kitchen. Jews say that all human beings are partners with God in creation. Humans must complete God's creation by reaching out to help others.

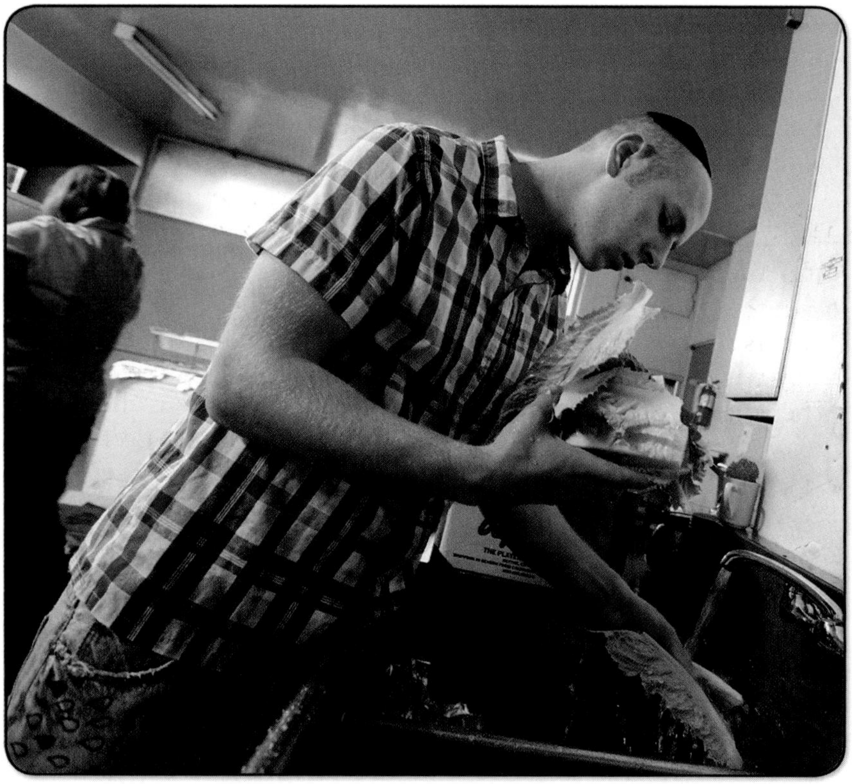

Volunteers. Jewish young people prepare Shabbat dinner at a shelter for recovering addicts.

***Tzedakah* Box.** Jews are to give charity every day, so people collect money for good causes in a *tzedakah* box like this one. *"Tzedakah"* means "righteousness." **What does the Catholic tradition teach about helping those who are in need?**

Check Your Understanding

1. Explain the importance of hospitality in Judaism.
2. How is the term *tikkun olam* usually translated? What significance does this term have for Jews today?

Think About It

3. Make a list of some ways that you can help those in need in your community or in other parts of the world. Compare your list with that of others in the class.

Making It Personal

4. If you could "repair the world" in some way, what would be the first thing you would fix? Explain.
5. What connection can you see between the Jewish emphasis on hospitality to guests and the notion of *tikkun olam*? Explain in words or pictures.

Skill Focus: Gathering, Organizing, and Synthesizing Information

Gather Your Information

1. Choose a topic with your teacher, group, or class. Think about the topic. What is your opinion or point of view about it? If you had to take a position for or against the topic, what would your position be?
2. Once you have a few ideas about your topic, start your research. Use sources such as this textbook, the Internet, library research, and interviews. As you do the research, jot down important points. Are there any questions that occur to you as you research? Make a note of these. Looking for answers to your questions will help you plan your research.

Organize Your Information

3. Make a category sheet for your topic. For example, if your topic is about history, examples of categories could be based on the W5 questions (who, what, when, where, why).
   - Who are the key historical figures?
   - What is the topic? What is my position on it?
   - When did the events take place? When did the key figures live?
   - Where did the events I am researching take place? Where did the key figures live?
   - Why am I taking this position? What are my arguments for or against it?

   For each of these W5 questions, ask yourself, "What information do I need to convey about this category (who, what, when, where, why) to my audience?"

Synthesize Your Information

4. Now you are ready to synthesize, or connect, all your information together into a pattern that will make sense to your audience. Analyze the information you have categorized during the organizing stage. If you had to explain it in one minute to someone who knew nothing about it, what would you want to say? Can you identify one key point from each of the categories that you identified during the organizing stage? Jot down your key points.
5. Find the connections between the key points. For example, to explain your topic, do you need to describe historical setting and place first before you introduce the key figures?

Interreligious Dialogue

Judaism and the Catholic Church

In the *General Directory for Catechesis*, an important church document on teaching the faith, Catholics are encouraged to give special attention to the Jewish religion. The *Directory* says that when the Church seeks to understand itself, it cannot help but discover its own roots in the Jewish people.

Christianity understands itself as coming out of Judaism. The New Testament, the message of Jesus, and even his death and resurrection make sense only when interpreted in light of the Old Testament. As Pope Pius XI once said, "Spiritually, we are all Semites." In other words, our origins are found in Judaism. People who study Christian traditions find links with Judaism everywhere.

Common Links

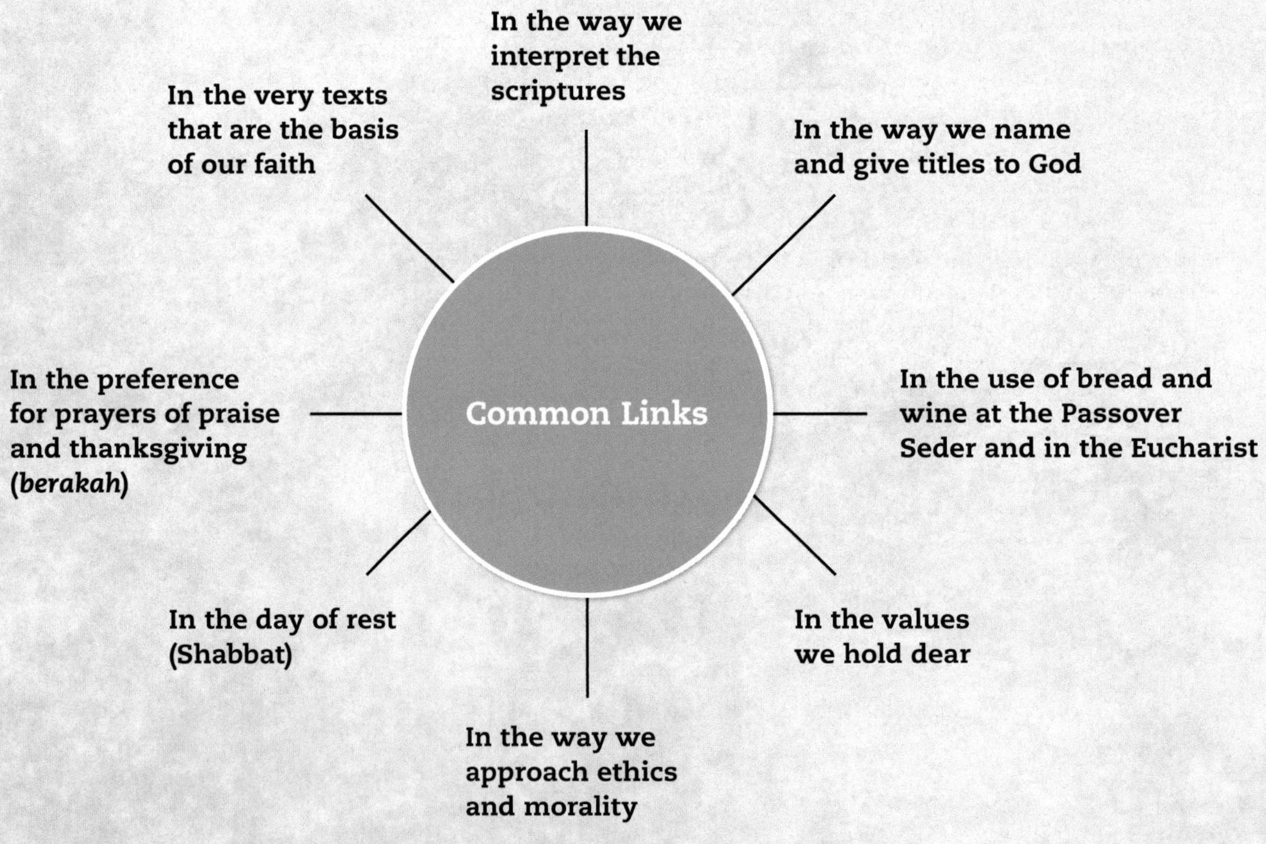

Common Links
In the way we interpret the scriptures
In the way we name and give titles to God
In the use of bread and wine at the Passover Seder and in the Eucharist
In the values we hold dear
In the way we approach ethics and morality
In the day of rest (Shabbat)
In the preference for prayers of praise and thanksgiving (*berakah*)
In the very texts that are the basis of our faith

Common LInks between Judaism and Christianity. Christianity is linked to Judaism through scripture, rituals, values, ethics, and morality.

NEL

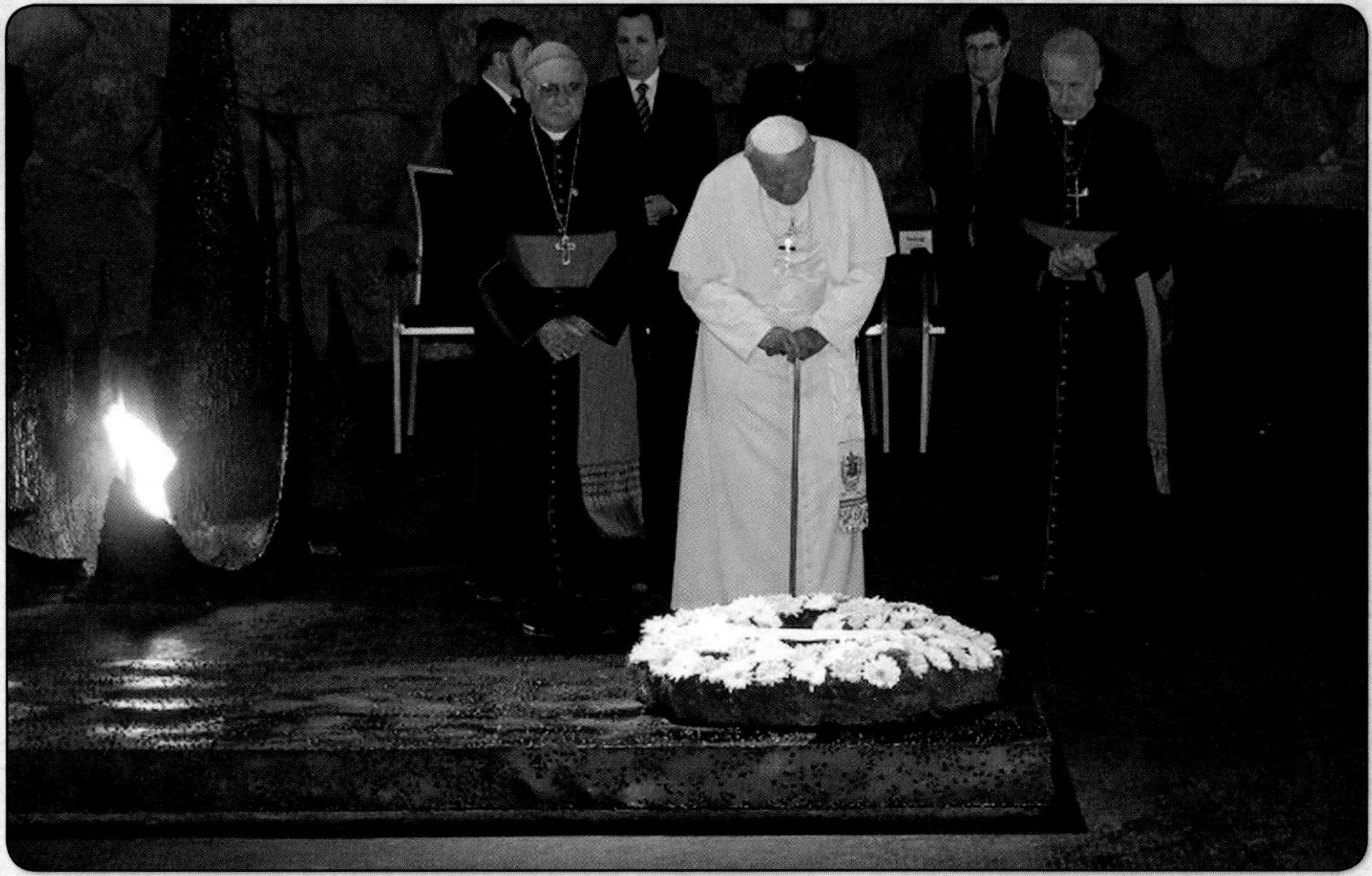

Pope John Paul II at Yad Vashem. On March 23, 2000, Pope John Paul II visited the Yad Vashem Museum in Jerusalem. There he spoke about the bond between Christians and Jews, and described his hopes for a peaceful world.

"Jews and Christians share an immense spiritual patrimony (heritage), flowing from God's self-revelation. Our religious teachings and our spiritual experience demand that we overcome evil with good. We remember, but not with any desire for vengeance or as an incentive to hatred. For us, to remember is to pray for peace and justice, and to commit ourselves to their cause. Only a world at peace, with justice for all, can avoid repeating the mistakes and terrible crimes of the past."

When Pope John Paul II visited the Synagogue of Rome in 1986, he said:

> With Judaism … we have a relationship which we do not have with any other religion. You are our dearly beloved brothers and, in a certain way, it could be said that you are our elder brothers … [we need] to remove all forms of prejudice, even subtle ones, to readjust every manner of self-expression and therefore to present always and everywhere, to ourselves and others, the true face of Jews and Judaism, as likewise of Christians and Christianity.

continues...

Interreligious Dialogue (cont'd)

Because we have these basic things in common, Judaism must be Christianity's first partner in dialogue.

As the two traditions of Judaism and Christianity went their separate ways between the first and the fourth centuries, they developed their own worship, structures, leadership, and spiritualities. Where they differed, right from the beginning, was in how they saw the person of Jesus of Nazareth.

It is a tragedy that relations between Judaism and Catholicism have so often violated the sacred bond that ties these two traditions together. How can we overlook the persecution of Jews by Christians and the fact of the Holocaust?

On the 2000th anniversary of the birth of Jesus, Pope John Paul II asked the Jewish people for forgiveness. This apology could not heal all actions of the past, but it shows that a new start has been made to appreciate each other's spiritual traditions.

For Christians, there is a new-found joy in rediscovering Judaism, our older relative.

What I Have Learned

In this chapter, I learned about

- Abraham, the patriarch or father of Judaism, Christianity, and Islam
- Moses receiving the Ten Commandments from God and leading the people toward the Promised Land
- symbols, prayers, beliefs, and practices of Jewish life
- some key events in ancient Jewish history
- some key events in modern Jewish history (the Holocaust, the founding of Israel)
- the three branches of Judaism
- Shabbat celebrations and requirements
- the kosher laws that outline for Jews how to prepare food
- the importance of the Torah, Tanakh, and Talmud
- *brit milah* (circumcision), bar mitzvah, bat mitzvah, marriage, and the reciting of special prayers at the death of a family member
- Jewish homes as places of hospitality

NEL

Amidah: Eighteen Blessings

(An excerpt from the Eighteen Blessings)

We acknowledge to You, O Lord, that You are our God,
as You were the God of our ancestors, forever and ever.
Rock of our life, Shield of our help,
You are immutable from age to age.
We thank You and utter Your praise,
for our lives that are delivered into Your hands,
and for our souls that are entrusted to You;
and for Your miracles that are with us every day
and for your marvellously kind deeds that are of every time;
evening and morning and noon-tide.
Thou art good, for Thy mercies are endless:
Thou art merciful, for Thy kindnesses never are complete:
from everlasting we have hoped in You.
And for all these things may Thy name be blessed
and exalted always and forevermore.
And all the living will give thanks unto Thee
and praise Thy great name in truth,
God, our salvation and help. Selah.
Blessed be Thou, O Lord, Thy name is good,
and to Thee it is meet to give thanks.

Chapter 5 The Story of Christianity

Christ Pantokrator. This mosaic of Christ Pantokrator (Christ, Ruler of All) is in the Hagia Sophia, in Istanbul, Turkey. The Hagia Sophia was built as a Christian church in the sixth century, in Constantinople, the government centre of the Byzantine Empire, and then made into a mosque in the fifteenth century, when the empire was conquered by Muslims. In 1935, the Republic of Turkey made it a museum. Christ Pantokrator is a common and important icon in the Eastern Churches.

This passage from the Gospel of John expresses in just a few words the mystery of salvation through Jesus Christ. Evangelical Christians often quote the passage to spread the Gospel, and the reference "John 3:16" is sometimes displayed in public places, such as on street corners or at hockey arenas. **What are your thoughts about displaying "John 3:16" or the passage in public places?**

"For God so loved the world that he gave his only Son, so that everyone who believes in him may not perish but may have eternal life."

(John 3:16)

What You Will Learn

In this chapter, you will learn about

- Christians in Canada
- the history of Christianity, including key moments, people, developments, and movements of the religion
- the relationship between Judaism and Christianity's origins
- the symbols and languages of early Christianity
- using primary and secondary sources to learn about religions
- the foundation stones of Christianity
- how the Christian Church became separated into East and West
- the experience of the Middle Ages in Western Christianity
- the Protestant Reformation in the sixteenth century and recent reform movements
- the diverse practices within Christianity
- the ecumenical movement

Personal Recollection

Gary Mak. Gary Mak is a university student in Alberta who is preparing for baptism in an Evangelical church. **As you read his words, think about your own experiences, and how they are similar and different, and any questions you would like to ask Gary.**

Growing up as an introvert, I had a deep longing to express myself and would ask myself, "Where is my purpose in life?" I would devour fantasy books and imagine myself a humble hero called from a mundane life to a path of deep hardship and triumphant victory. After reading the Narnia series and *The Lord of the Rings*, I would often wonder if other people thirsted to be part of adventures like these.

Years later, a friend and mentor from university would knock on my door, host me for meals, and invite me to Bible studies. At first, these scripture passages seemed to be only stories with morals and virtues, but they soon became places of life and excitement. I felt pulled away from the everyday "blah" of life, but couldn't help wondering whether what was portrayed in God's word was real, practical, or possible.

And then, I began to feel more and more that God was reaching out to me, trying to tell me that I was someone special to him. The people I was with were not perfect, but they were also supporting me. By Christmas of that year, I decided to call myself a Christian. I don't think I even knew what it meant, but it was good.

Even years later, I have no idea how to rationalize why I believe in Christ. He has tested me and blessed me immensely. I'm more confident, which is saying a lot, but the Lord's purpose also seems beyond me sometimes. I have strayed away at times, but when you think of life as an adventure alongside Christ, there is unshakeable joy. I am preparing for baptism. I want to pronounce my faithfulness to Christ. I can only say that I want to see what the next leg of our adventure together will be.

— **Gary Mak**

Christianity in Canada

Orthodox
Word meaning "those who believe correctly" or "those who glorify God correctly"; Orthodox Christians' origins coincide with the origin of Christianity

As of the beginning of the twenty-first century, Christians from around the world—from every church and tradition—have made their homes in Canada. Today, Christians who are recent newcomers to Canada have joined Christians who have a longer history in this country (Catholics, Protestants, and **Orthodox**). Truly, the French words of our national anthem are correct when they say that Canada is "de foi trempée" (strengthened in faith).

Political Map of Canada

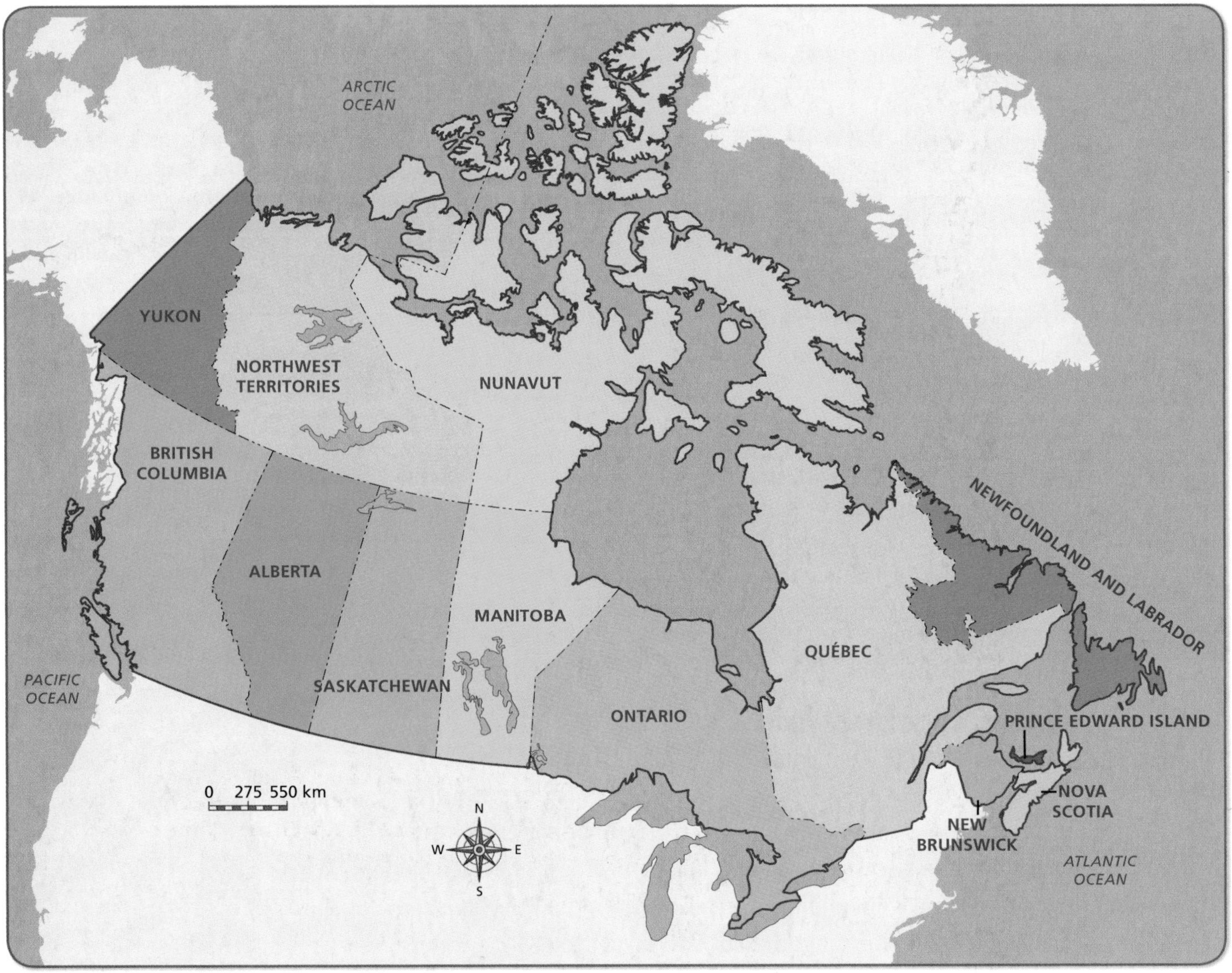

Christians in Canada. In Canada, Christians extend "from sea to sea." **What communities of Christians do you know of in your region? How could you get to know more about neighbouring Christian communities?**

Notre-Dame Basilica. Notre-Dame Basilica of Montréal was completed in 1829, replacing the original church, which dated from the seventeenth century. In 1982, Pope John Paul II raised Notre-Dame from church to basilica.

Christians in Canada—Percentage of the Canadian Population

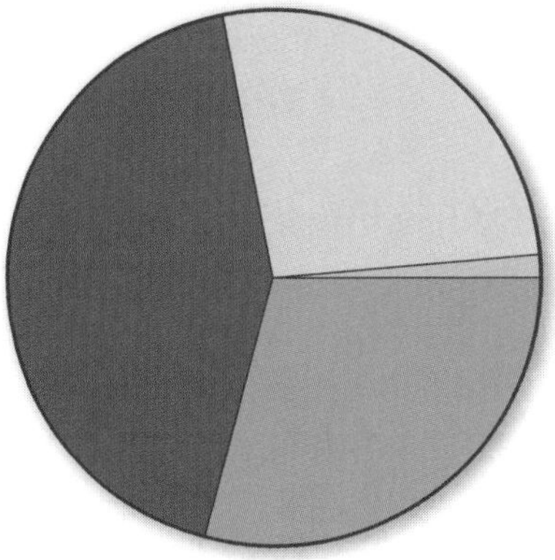

Percentage of Christians in Canada. As of 2002, the majority of Canadians were Christians.

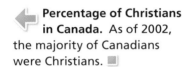

> **Fast Fact**
>
> Almost half of Canadian Roman Catholics live in the province of Québec.

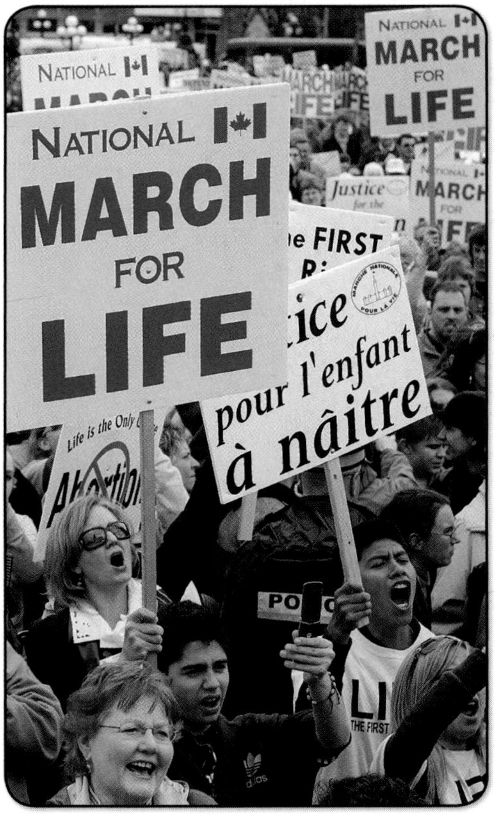

March for Life. These young people were among approximately 7800 people participating in the National March for Life in Ottawa in May 2008. **What do you think are some moral issues on which Christian churches in Canada could take a stand together?**

Check Your Understanding

1. Imagine that a Catholic student in another country asks you about Christians in Canada. How would you describe the Christian population of Canada in an e-mail of two or three sentences?

Think About It

2. Create a chart or web diagram to record what you learn about Christianity as you read this chapter. Also record questions you have about this topic. Of the questions you have now, which two would you like to focus on? Why?

Making It Personal

3. Do you know anyone from a church different from your own? If so, describe this person—the church he or she belongs to, any faith issues you have discussed, and so on. If not, what questions would you like to ask someone from another church?

The History of Christianity

The Following of Jesus

This chapter fills out the story of Christianity begun in Chapter 2. Christians in Canada are part of a long and varied tradition. The tradition reaches back in history to Jesus of Nazareth, in the first century CE. His life, death, and resurrection are for Christians the story of the living God in the flesh. For Christians, Jesus is true God and true man, like us in all things but sin. All Christian churches, in all their wide variety, turn to this historical person for their inspiration and the meaning of life: Jesus of Nazareth. It is his name that Christians bear.

As you read about the history of Christianity in this chapter, you will learn about key moments, people, developments, and movements. Many of these are noted on the timeline opposite.

Christianity's Roots in Judaism

In Chapter 4, we saw that Christianity is rooted deeply in the same covenant faith as Judaism. Christianity cannot be understood outside of the Jewish heritage. Christians tell the story of Abraham, Moses, David, and the exile as their own. To Christians, the new covenant of Jesus is the fulfillment of God's covenant with Israel. For Christians, Jesus is the Messiah (in Greek, *Christos*, Christ) promised by God.

In the early years of Christianity, those who knew Jesus and saw what he did asked, "Was he the Messiah,

Christ Is Risen! These Ethiopian Orthodox Christians are celebrating Easter in Deires Sultan, in 2007. The Acts of the Apostles in the New Testament very early on tells the story of an Ethiopian treasury official being baptized by Philip. Orthodox Christians use the Easter greeting "He is Risen!" The response is "Truly, He is Risen!" **How does this Easter celebration compare with Easter celebrations you know?**

or not?" In the previous chapter, we learned how toward the end of the first century there was a parting of the ways between Rabbinic Judaism and Christianity. The exact date of this separation is not known, but at some point Christians were excluded from synagogue services.

The Syriac Orthodox Church. The separation between Christianity and Rabbinic Judaism did not mean that there were no Jews who followed Jesus. Even today there are Aramaic-speaking Christians, remnants of these early Jewish Christians, living in Syria and Iraq. The Deyrulzafaran Monastery (shown here), built in the fifth century CE, represents the Syriacs in Mardin, Turkey.

Check Your Understanding

1. Why do Christians turn to Jesus to discover the meaning of life?
2. How is Christianity related to Judaism? With a partner, decide how you would explain this relationship to a child.

Think About It

3. When you look at the timeline on this page, consider
   - what on the timeline you already know
   - what you think about the details of the timeline
   - what is unfamiliar to you
   - what questions you have

   Keep a record to return to and update throughout this chapter.

Making It Personal

4. What does Christianity mean to you? In a journal entry, note your thoughts and memories.

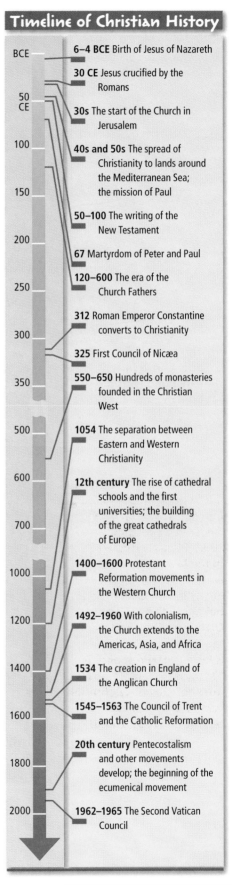

Timeline of Christian History

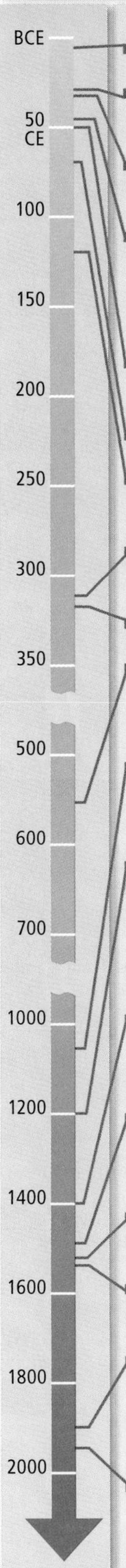

6–4 BCE Birth of Jesus of Nazareth

30 CE Jesus crucified by the Romans

30s The start of the Church in Jerusalem

40s and 50s The spread of Christianity to lands around the Mediterranean Sea; the mission of Paul

50–100 The writing of the New Testament

67 Martyrdom of Peter and Paul

120–600 The era of the Church Fathers

312 Roman Emperor Constantine converts to Christianity

325 First Council of Nicæa

550–650 Hundreds of monasteries founded in the Christian West

1054 The separation between Eastern and Western Christianity

12th century The rise of cathedral schools and the first universities; the building of the great cathedrals of Europe

1400–1600 Protestant Reformation movements in the Western Church

1492–1960 With colonialism, the Church extends to the Americas, Asia, and Africa

1534 The creation in England of the Anglican Church

1545–1563 The Council of Trent and the Catholic Reformation

20th century Pentecostalism and other movements develop; the beginning of the ecumenical movement

1962–1965 The Second Vatican Council

Expansion of Christianity

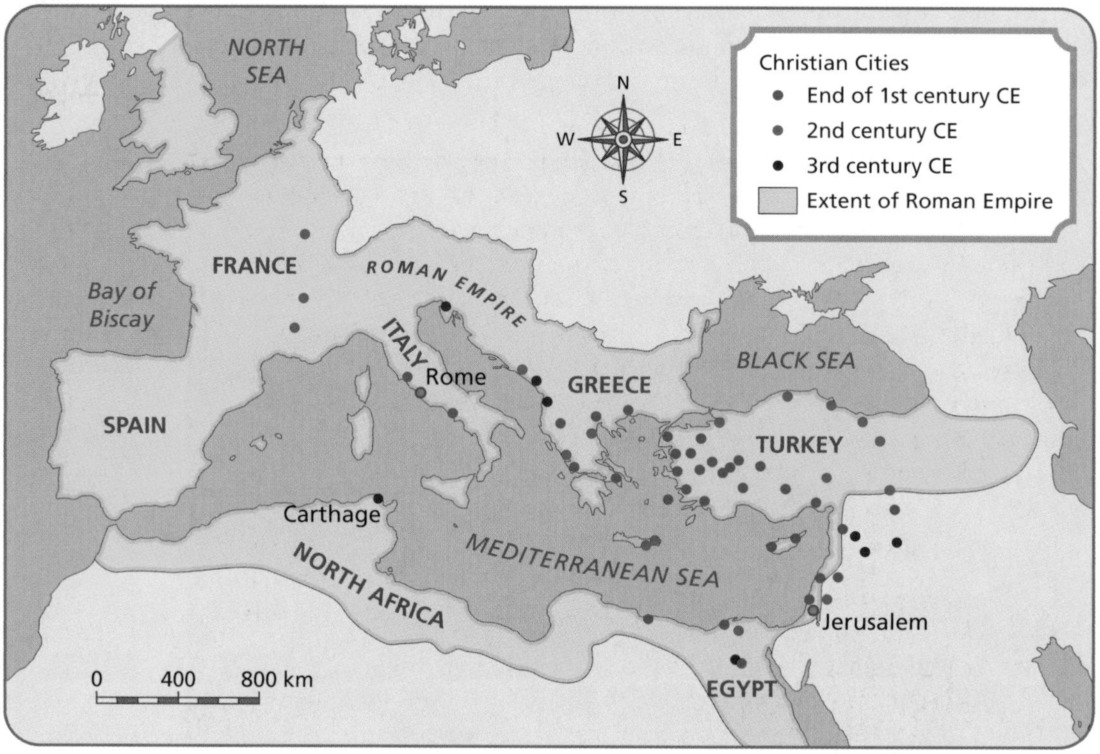

Expansion of Christianity. This map shows how Christianity expanded with the Roman Empire.

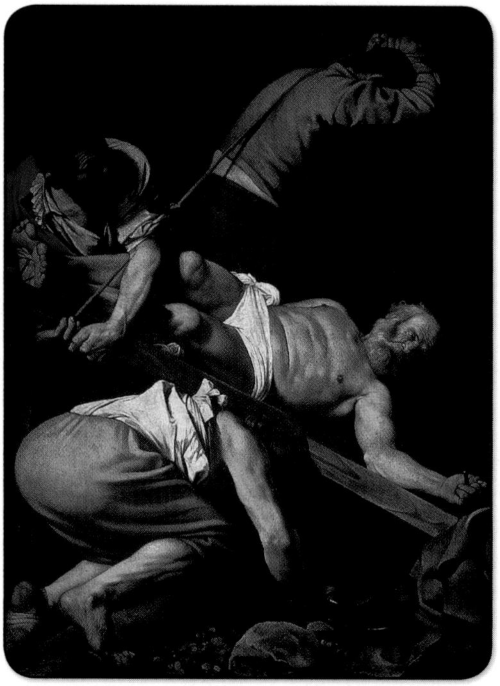

The Crucifixion of St. Peter (Caravaggio). Many Christians in the first three centuries were put to death, like Saints Peter and Paul, for following the way of Jesus.

Christianity Spreads around the Mediterranean

From the lands where Jesus lived and died, Christianity spread to lands around the Mediterranean Sea, taking root in Greek cities and in the Roman Empire. St. Peter and St. Paul, sometimes called the two founders of Christianity, came from Jerusalem to Rome to build up the early Christian community and establish the Church in Rome. From that point on, Rome became a central place for Christianity. St. Peter and St. Paul were put to death as martyrs for refusing to renounce faith in Jesus Christ. Martyrs for Christ can be found throughout Christian history. Their witness (*martyros* means "witness" in Greek) is an important influence in the spread of Christianity.

Make It Your Own: Ichthus

Many people in the ancient world spoke and wrote in Greek. Just as English is considered a key language for commerce and global communication today, the Greek language was a common language in the world of the early Christians. The New Testament was originally written in Greek, and two of the oldest symbols in Christianity are rooted in the Greek language.

Christ in Greek. In Greek, the Christ is called *Christos*. In the Greek alphabet, the first two letters of Christ's name are chi (X) and rho (R), and these came to be a symbol of Jesus.

Because Christianity was an illegal religion in the Roman Empire until the time of Emperor Constantine, early Christians developed a secret symbol. The Greek word for "fish" is *ichthus* or ΙΧΘΥΣ. The early Christians used that Greek word as an acronym to mean "Jesus Christ, the Son of God, the Saviour."

Ι	=	Iota	=	Iēsous	=	Jesus
Χ	=	Chi	=	Christos	=	Christ
Θ	=	Theta	=	Theou	=	God's
Υ	=	Upsilon	=	Huios	=	Son
Σ	=	Sigma	=	Sōtēr	=	Saviour

Activity

1. Create an acronym that represents the letters of your name and reveals your positive qualities. Alternatively, create an acronym that represents the letters in the name of someone you know and reveals that person's positive qualities. For example: MIKE: M = Mindful; I = Intelligent; K = Kind; E = Engaging.

A Closer Look

In the first centuries of Christianity, to be convicted of following Christianity resulted in execution. To avoid discovery, Christians used the *ichthus* symbol to identify themselves to other Christians. If a Christian wanted to know if someone else was also Christian, he or she would draw the fish symbol. If the other person recognized the secret symbol, then both recognized each other as Christians.

The symbol was also used to locate meeting places of Christians. If a Christian saw this symbol in the sand or drawn on a wall, he or she knew it pointed to where Christians could secretly gather, pray, and celebrate Eucharist.

Skill Focus: Using Primary and Secondary Sources

In studying history, students look at both primary and secondary sources. In religious studies also, learning about your own and other religions involves using both types of sources. The following describes some characteristics of primary and secondary sources.

Primary and Secondary Sources

Primary Source	Secondary Source
Primary sources are *of* the time. They • come from the time period • can include first-hand accounts, told by someone who was there • give a picture of the historical setting during which the events took place • are based on the attitudes and biases of people living at the time period when the events took place • sometimes omit information that modern readers need but that readers of the writer's time period would have taken for granted	Secondary sources *reflect* on the time. They • are created after primary sources, and often long after the time period of the events described in the primary sources • interpret and analyze the events and people of the primary sources • are based on the attitudes and biases of people living in a time period after the events of the primary sources took place • might attempt to fill in the missing details and historical context that the readers of the primary sources took for granted

As you read this chapter, think about the documents you are reading, and decide if each one is a primary source document or a secondary source document. What does each document describe or comment upon? What does it leave out? What is the perspective of the writer? What can you learn from the document? What other documents would you like to read?

Check Your Understanding

1. Where and under what circumstances did Christianity spread?
2. What languages and symbols did the early Christians use?

Think About It

3. Look for and document ways in which people in your community show their beliefs—for example, with religious buildings, jewellery, tattoos, or bumper stickers.
4. In a group, discuss your findings and how life today compares with life for early Christians.

Making It Personal

5. Consider how you could create a symbol for yourself. Develop and present your plan for a personal symbol that expresses who you are and what you believe.

The Spread of Christianity up to 600 CE

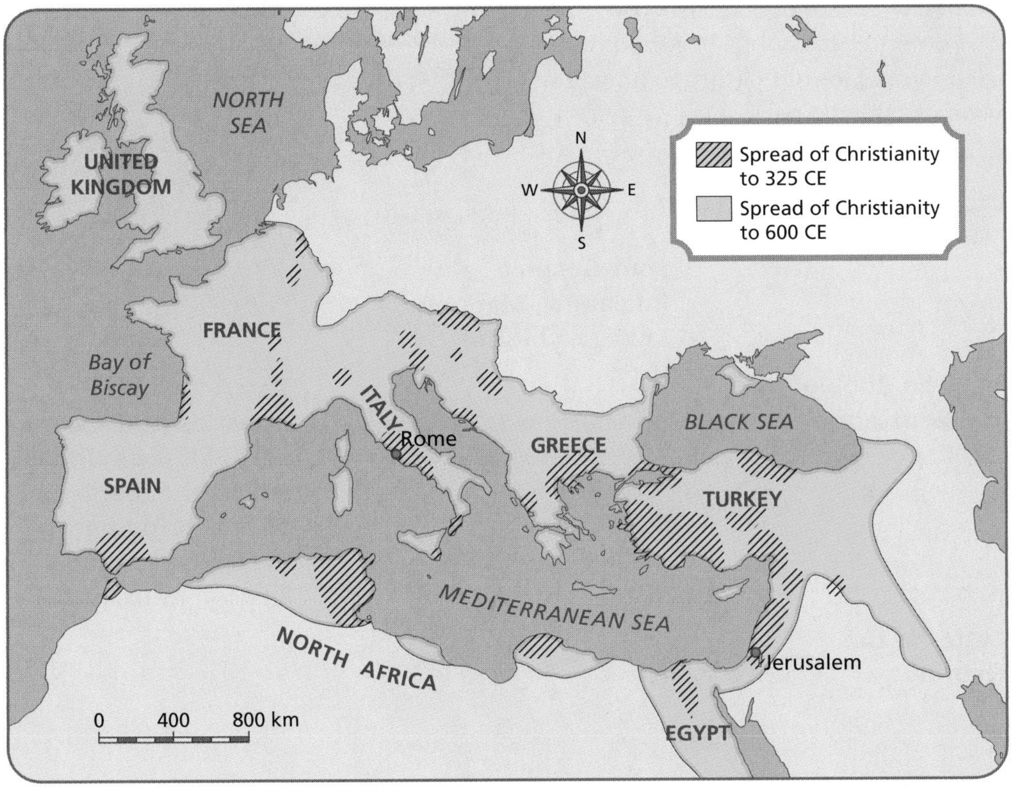

Spread of Christianity to 600 CE. Between the first and the sixth centuries, Christianity spread throughout the Roman Empire. Although the Roman Empire had an extensive road system, travel and communication were still very slow compared with today. Humans might travel up to 56 kilometres a day on foot. By sea, a trip from Rome's seaport to Gibraltar might take seven days.

The Foundation Stones of Christianity

From its roots in the Mediterranean, Christianity has spread to all regions of the world, to almost all countries. The early Christian Church was built on four major foundation stones:

1. keeping alive the memory of Jesus: the **disciples**, the Gospels, and Letters of Paul
2. professing the one faith: the creeds
3. the ministers of the Church: the role of bishops
4. Ecumenical Councils

These foundations have enabled the Church to develop and spread while remaining faithful to the teachings of Jesus.

Foundation Stone 1: Keeping Alive the Memory of Jesus

Jesus did not write down his teachings. However, he made a lasting impression on his disciples, and they told the story of Jesus to the peoples of the Roman Empire, based on their memories of him. Sometime during the first century, the Apostles wrote down these memories, which became the New Testament.

St. John the Evangelist. The image on this Victorian stained glass window shows St. John the **Evangelist** with a pen in hand, to emphasize his role as a Gospel writer. His writings provide the most intimate images of Jesus. Jesus is presented as the Good Shepherd, Living Water, Bread of Life, and Light and Word.

Disciple

Literally, a student; here it means a follower of Jesus

Evangelist

A writer of a Gospel of the New Testament

The New Testament

The New Testament consists of 27 books. These books began to be used in the Church's liturgy and were soon considered part of the sacred scriptures. The 27 books were added to the books accepted by Judaism (now known as the Old Testament) to become the Christian Bible.

The Organization of the New Testament

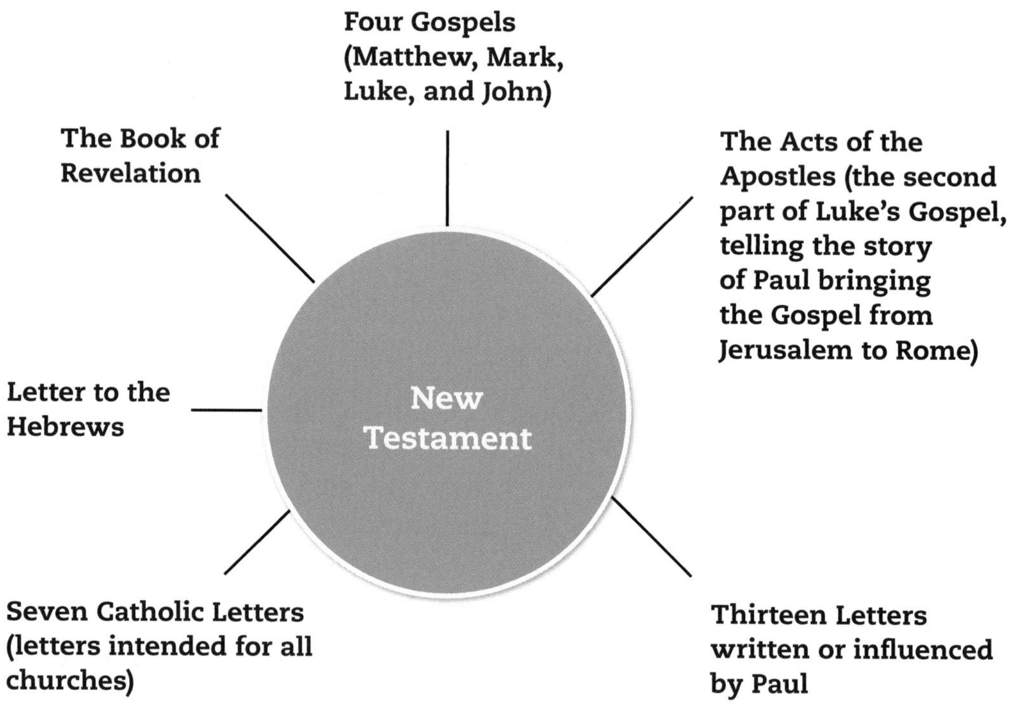
New Testament
Four Gospels (Matthew, Mark, Luke, and John)
The Acts of the Apostles (the second part of Luke's Gospel, telling the story of Paul bringing the Gospel from Jerusalem to Rome)
Thirteen Letters written or influenced by Paul
Seven Catholic Letters (letters intended for all churches)
Letter to the Hebrews
The Book of Revelation

The New Testament. This diagram shows how the New Testament is organized.

St. Peter. The Church in Rome counts St. Peter and St. Paul as its two founders.

The Gospels

Although the Gospels are history-like, they are not a history or a biography of Jesus. They are faith stories. The disciples wrote these accounts to pass on their faith in Jesus to others.

Each of the Gospel writers wrote about Jesus from a different perspective. The Church has accepted four Gospels as being authentic accounts of Jesus, even though each tells the story differently.

A Closer Look

Each Gospel in its own way tells the story of Jesus and the impact he made on different people. Each raises the question, "Who is this man?" During Jesus's life, no one seemed able to answer that question. It became a critical question when Jesus was crucified. His death so devastated the disciples that they lost faith in him. They could not imagine God's Messiah undergoing such a death.

The disciples credit their experience of Jesus as the Risen Christ as the turning point in their faith. It convinced them that Jesus was the Messiah. It is with this faith that they wrote the Gospels.

The Four Gospels

Writer	Date Written	Perspective and Story
Matthew	around 85 CE	• wrote of Jesus as a Jew and as the new Moses • here we find Jesus's Sermon on the Mount (Matthew 5–7), which is presented as the fulfillment of the Ten Commandments given to Moses
Mark	around 65 CE	• wrote for those who had difficulty accepting that God's Messiah had to suffer and die a shameful death on a cross • addresses this question: How could Jesus be the Messiah if he was crucified?
Luke	around 85 CE	• wrote for Christians who spoke Greek, in a style that citizens of the Roman Empire could understand • presents Jesus as the Great Example; portrays Mary, the Mother of Jesus, as a disciple of Christ who "magnifies the Lord"
John	toward the end of the first century	• wrote like a theologian who sought to enter into the mystery of Jesus as the Word of God • presents Jesus as the light of the world, God's Word

Check Your Understanding

1. a) With a partner, recall the four foundation stones of Christianity.

b) Join with another pair to discuss how the Gospels are part of the first foundation stone.

Think About It

2. Research the background of one of the traditional symbols for the Gospel writers: Matthew as a human, Mark as a lion, Luke as an ox, and John as an eagle. In a group, present your findings.

Making It Personal

3. From the Gospels, choose one passage that you consider personally significant. Copy and post this passage to a class bulletin board or website for others to reflect on.

Copies of the Bible. Throughout the centuries, Christians continued to copy the Bible so that they could use it in their liturgies. The earliest versions we have date back to the fourth century. These Bibles were often adorned with art. This version dates back to about 800 CE.

The Letters of Paul

Paul's 13 Letters were written mostly in the 50s CE, before the Gospels.

Paul was born Saul of Tarsus in Asia Minor (modern-day Turkey) around the time of Jesus. He never knew Jesus personally. Saul came to Jerusalem to study Torah because as a Pharisee (see Chapter 4) he was interested in the Jewish law. In Jerusalem, he heard about the Jesus movement. As a Pharisee, he was offended by the Christian proclamation of the crucified Jesus as the Messiah.

One day, the high priest in Jerusalem instructed Saul to arrest the followers of Jesus in Damascus. On his way there, he was surrounded by light. He fell to the ground and a voice said to him, "Saul, Saul, why do you persecute me?" He asked: "Who are you, Lord?" The reply came, "I am Jesus, whom you are persecuting" (Acts 9:3–5). Saul realized suddenly that the crucified Jesus was the Lord. This encounter with the risen Jesus radically changed Saul's life. Blinded by the light, he was brought to Damascus, where he was baptized and regained his sight.

Several years later, Saul (who had come to be known as Paul) visited Peter and James and began a life of preaching the Gospel to non-Jews. On his journeys throughout the Mediterranean region, Paul wrote letters to the various churches he visited, and these letters became part of the New Testament. The letters document Paul's life, his faith in Jesus Christ, and his concern for the churches he had founded.

Paul was martyred around 64 CE.

Fast Fact

Nicaea is a town (now called Iznik, in modern-day Turkey) where the first Church council was held.

St. Paul Preaching in Athens. This sixteenth-century painting by Raphael shows St. Paul preaching in Athens. His missionary life was hard: "Five times I have received from the Jews the forty lashes minus one. Three times I was beaten with rods. Once I received a stoning. Three times I was shipwrecked; for a night and a day I was adrift at sea; on frequent journeys, in danger from rivers, danger from bandits, danger from my own people, danger from Gentiles, danger in the city, danger in the wilderness, danger at sea, danger from false brothers and sisters" (1 Corinthians 11:24–26).

Foundation Stone 2: Professing the One Faith: The Creeds

The second foundation stone for Christians consists of the creeds. (See also Chapter 2.) They are brief statements, almost like summaries of the Gospels, that early Christians developed to use in baptism and Eucharist. They are professions of faith—usually introduced by "I believe in God," or as a question, "Do you believe in God?" Using the same formula in all the churches—"I believe in God the Father ... and in Jesus Christ ... and in the Holy Spirit"—ensured that wherever Christians went, they professed the same faith.

Foundation Stone 3: The Ministers of the Church

The third foundation stone was the structure of the Church. Each Church was governed in the same way. Within 30 years of the death of Jesus, churches had been established in Jerusalem, Syria, Turkey, Greece, Italy, and Spain. Each one had an

NEL

St. Polycarp. Polycarp, a disciple of John the Evangelist, was martyred in Smyrna (in Turkey) around 155 CE, when he was 86. Here is a segment from his trial: "The Romans urged him, saying, 'Reject Christ, under oath, and I will set you at liberty'; Polycarp declared, 'Eighty and six years have I served Him, and He never did me any injury: how then can I blaspheme my King and my Saviour?'"

Irenaeus of Lyons. In *Against the Heresies*, Bishop Irenaeus of Lyons wrote in 180 CE about his concern that the Church and all followers remain faithful to the teaching of Jesus:

> The Church, having received this preaching and this faith, although scattered throughout the whole world, yet, as if occupying but one house, carefully preserves it.... For the churches which have been planted in Germany do not believe or hand down anything different, nor do those in Spain, nor those in Gaul, nor those in the East, nor those in Egypt, nor those in Libya, nor those which have been established in the central regions of the world.

episcopos, an overseer, or a bishop at its head. Bishops were seen as the successors of the **Apostles**. They were responsible for preaching the Gospel and keeping people faithful to the creeds. This structure still exists today.

One example was St. Justin (100–165 CE). Before his conversion, Justin had trained as a philosopher, so had studied the contemporary understanding of wisdom. Once he discovered Christ, he tried to explain how wisdom had become flesh in Jesus Christ.

A number of bishops and famous teachers gradually won over many people to Christian faith and led many to abandon the Roman state religion. These saintly bishops and theologians are known as the Church Fathers. One of these is Irenaeus of Lyons.

Apostles

Followers of Jesus who were sent forth to bring the Gospel to others; the 12 especially chosen from among the disciples by Jesus

"Now a bishop must be above reproach, married only once, temperate, sensible, respectable, hospitable, an apt teacher, not a drunkard, not violent but gentle, not quarrelsome, and not a lover of money. He must manage his own household well, keeping his children submissive and respectful in every way—for if someone does not know how to manage his own household, how can he take care of God's church?"

(1 Timothy 3:2–7)

A Closer Look

There are many examples of bishops who played an important role in the first centuries of the Church. They became known as the Church Fathers.

Check Your Understanding

1. Summarize in a brief biography who Saul of Tarsus was and his contribution to the growth of Christianity.
2. The creeds and bishops were considered basic elements to keep the Church faithful to Jesus. In a small group, explain why.

Think About It

3. Review the quotations on pages 158 and 159. Reflect on how reading primary-source information adds to your understanding of the subject.

Making It Personal

4. Which one of the foundation stones is most meaningful to you and why?

The First Council of Nicaea. In this woodcut, Emperor Constantine is shown meeting with the bishops to discuss the wording of the creed that is now known as the Nicene Creed, after the city where the council was held. The Creed of Nicaea was one of the first creeds. It was the first instance of the Church using philosophical language to make sure the same faith was taught everywhere.

Foundation Stone 4: Ecumenical Councils

In the history of Christianity, there have been occasional disagreements and conflicts. For example, in the early fourth century, a man named Arius proclaimed that Jesus was not God, but only the first and highest creature of God. The conflict over this issue became so intense that the Roman Emperor Constantine feared for the unity of his empire.

The controversy led to the establishment of Ecumenical Councils. The first one took place in 325 CE to deal with Arius. Emperor Constantine called the bishops together in Nicaea so they could decide on wording that would clarify the divinity of Jesus. From this council came the Nicene Creed, which is still prayed today.

These gatherings of bishops have become known as Ecumenical Councils ("ecumenical" because they bring together bishops of all churches). In the history of the Church, Catholics hold that there have been 21 Ecumenical Councils. Each one is named after the place where it was held.

Check Your Understanding

1. Work with a small group to do the following:
   a) Demonstrate on a globe how Christianity spread to the Roman Empire.
   b) List at least three ways in which the early Church was different from now.
   c) Discuss the importance of Ecumenical Councils.

Think About It

2. Research one Ecumenical Council to identify when and where it took place, who called for it, and the issue to be considered. If possible, refer to both primary and secondary sources about the council. Present your findings in a written, oral, or visual presentation.

Making It Personal

3. Think of a group you belong to. How does the group remain clear about core beliefs, why it is together, and the roles of members? What happens when there are disagreements? What methods of communication do you find work best among group members?

NEL

The Development of the Western Church in the Middle Ages

In 312 CE, the Roman Emperor Constantine embraced Christianity. In 313 CE, he issued the Edict of Milan, declaring that Christians were free to worship without interference. Christianity soon became the official religion of the Roman Empire.

However, the Roman Empire itself was changing:

- By 330 CE, the capital had moved from Rome to Constantinople, in the East. Constantinople was the centre of the eastern empire and the centre of Eastern Christianity.
- In the West, the empire declined. In 410 CE, the Visigoths (a Germanic tribe) invaded and destroyed Rome. Rome's population decreased from 500 000 to 50 000.
- Islam developed (see Chapter 6). When the lands on the southern shore of the Mediterranean came under Islamic control in the seventh century, there was no longer a central power to guarantee the circulation of goods.

The West's economy, which depended on the trade routes of the Mediterranean, declined sharply. Europe had no clear political and economic centre, and so began a period of great hardship and poverty. Every region was on its own and had to fend for itself.

Although Western Europe lacked a political and economic focal point, the regions did still share one common bond: Christianity. This bond prevented a total breakdown in the region and helped Europe to survive.

Christianity Outlasts the Roman Empire. By the year 1200, most of Europe had become Christian. This church in Asturias, Spain, dates back to 848 CE. Since 1985, it has been a UNESCO World Heritage Site.

1. The Structure of the Church

Before the Roman Empire collapsed, the Church had already adopted an organizational structure. Each bishop was the head of a local church. The bishop of Rome, who was a successor to Saint Peter, the leader of the Apostles, was recognized as leader of all bishops. To him was given the title "Pope." This structure was already well established when the Roman Empire collapsed. Although the structure lost its centre when Rome fell, the local churches with their bishops remained. In the chaos that followed upon the destruction of Rome, these local churches, led by the pope who remained in Rome, became a source of continuity and stability.

2. The Role of the Scriptures

The Bible was another feature of Christianity that helped Europeans cope during these difficult times. Over time, Christians made many copies of the Bible. These, along with commentaries on the Bible by theologian bishops, circulated extensively. The copies of the Bible

Fast Fact

In the early years of Christianity, the Bible in the form of a book—or *codex*—became extremely popular. In contrast, the Jewish scriptures were in the form of a scroll, as they are today.

A Scriptorium. A scriptorium is a place where people made copies of the Bible. The main scriptoria were in monasteries.

St. Benedict of Nursia. The founder of Western monasticism was St. Benedict of Nursia (Italy) (480–546 CE). Benedict was from a noble Roman family; he went to live in a cave when he was 20. Under the guidance of another monk, he began his search for God. Benedict developed his Rule of Life, which describes how to live in community. Because of its balanced and moderate approach, Benedict's Rule was followed by monasteries all over Europe.

helped to unify the communities of Europe, bridging long distances and differences. In this way, a unity of teaching and doctrine based on books and texts developed in the Church.

3. The Theology of St. Augustine

A third factor in the Church that became a stabilizing force in Europe was the teaching of St. Augustine. Born into a wealthy North African family, Augustine (354–430 CE) embraced Christian life and became one of the most prolific writers in the history of the Church. His famous book, *Confessions*, tells the story of his life. It is the first full-length autobiography in Western civilization.

Augustine created a vision of Christian life that helped people to endure the destruction of the Western Roman Empire and look with confidence to the future. In his writings, he set forth his vision of God and the Church and addressed the controversies of his day. In his book *The City of God*, Augustine

- outlined how Christianity could continue without the protection and customs of the Roman Empire
- explained how Catholic teachings could form the basis for a way of life for all believers

4. Monasteries in the West

Perhaps the greatest influence upon Christianity in the West were its monasteries. A monastery is a place where a community of monks or nuns live in prayer and work. In both East and West, monasteries developed a form of Christian life that has greatly influenced how Christians see holiness and spirituality.

The monasteries Christian monks and nuns founded became important centres of prayer, work, and learning. The monks spent many hours each day tending the fields and caring for the animals they raised. Many monasteries became wealthy because monks shared labour and possessions. In times when Christianity was weak and in need of reform, monasteries were often islands of stability and dedication to the Gospel. They were the places where a rigorous form of Christianity flourished.

Check Your Understanding

1. Create a two-column chart. On one side, show factors related to the decline of the Roman Empire. On the other side, show factors related to the development of the Western Church.

Think About It

2. Research and summarize St. Benedict's Rule of Life. Why do you think it was followed in so many religious communities in medieval Europe?

Making It Personal

3. Jot down your ideas about what groups need to stay unified, what you want as an individual, and about leadership. Then, in a group, contribute ideas to a contemporary Rule of Life.
4. In times of crisis, what are the sources of stability and continuity in your life or your community?

Schism: The Church East and West

The vast former Roman Empire was changing. Christianity in the West and the East developed differences over key issues about how they lived their faith and how they interacted.

Difference between Christianity in the West and East

In the West	In the East
Europe was facing tremendous change and instability.	The Byzantine Empire (the eastern branch of the Roman Empire) continued, with Constantinople as its capital, until the fifteenth century.
The West was developing its own form of Christianity.	Eastern Christianity (the Eastern Churches) lived in isolation from the West and continued to flourish.
As Islam emerged in the seventh century, the results included a change in Western trade (refer to page 161).	As Islam emerged in the seventh century, the empire became smaller and was threatened by Muslim armies.

Icons

The use of images, or **icons**, has sometimes been a controversial issue in religion. This may seem strange to us today. Very early on, Christians had decorated their worship spaces with paintings or mosaics of Jesus, angels, and saints. In the East, the people began to give greater devotion to the images, sometimes using them in processions and praying to them for protection. But, Judaism and Islam do not permit images of God or humans. Some Christians agreed with this position. In the eighth and ninth centuries, this belief led to **iconoclasm**: the destruction of icons. The controversy was finally settled in favour of icons and confirmed by the Second Council of Nicaea in 787 CE, which accepted icons because, after all, God had become visible in Jesus. However, some in the Western Church disagreed with this position and felt that the East had gone too far in "worshipping" icons.

Icon

A sacred image (in a painting or carving, for example) of Christ and the saints used in devotion and other religious rituals

Iconoclasm

Breaking icons (images used in religious worship)

"You shall not make for yourself an idol."
(Exodus 20:4)

Icons and Eastern Christianity. The role of icons and iconography in Eastern Christianity is central. In this picture, Russian Orthodox clergy march carrying icons in Moscow, Russia, in 2007.

Creed

The second controversy developed when the Western Church added a short phrase to the Creed. In the profession of faith, where it said that the Holy Spirit proceeded from the Father, the West added "and the Son." The East found this addition unacceptable for theological reasons and felt that the pope had exceeded his authority.

In 1054, these and other conflicts led to a **schism** or break between the Eastern and Western Churches that has not healed to this day. From that time on, the Eastern Churches became known as the Orthodox Churches.

Schism

A separation, but not a full break, of two churches on the basis of a dispute over beliefs or practices

Conflict

Christians in the East faced different conflicts from those in the West, including the following:

- Christians of the East themselves felt the threat of Muslim armies around Constantinople.
- East and West did meet during the Crusades (1095–1274). However, in the Fourth Crusade, against the will of the pope, the Christian armies attacked Constantinople—the home of the very Christians they were trying to help.
- In 1453, the last remnant of the Byzantine Empire fell to the Muslim empire of the Ottoman Turks. With Constantinople in the hands of Muslims, Christianity in the area went into decline. Christians were permitted to retain their religion, but they often faced persecution and oppression. Taxation penalties, conscription to the army, and forced conversions to Islam weakened the vitality of Orthodoxy.

A Closer Look

In 1596, some Ukrainian bishops established unity with the Roman Catholic Church and with the pope while retaining their Eastern liturgy and customs, including married priests. The result today is that some Ukrainian churches are Catholic and some are Orthodox. Many Ukrainians settled in Canada, especially in the Western provinces. In the former Soviet Union (now Russia), all religions faced persecution, but after 1945 the Ukrainian Catholic Church was outlawed. It has undergone a revival since the collapse of the Soviet Union in 1991 and the independence of Ukraine.

The Conquest of Constantinople. The Crusades were an attempt to ward off the Muslim armies who were constantly threatening the Christian Byzantine Empire and to allow Christians to make a pilgrimage to Jerusalem. However, the Western Christians' attack on Constantinople in the Fourth Crusade, as depicted in this 1499 painting, made it difficult for Eastern Orthodox Christians to see Western Christians as allies.

Orthodox Christianity

Through centuries of separation and cultural differences, Eastern Christianity developed its own structure of churches along with rich liturgical traditions and other customs. These customs of Eastern Christianity—such as referring to themselves as Greek Orthodox, Serbian Orthodox, and Russian Orthodox—are not seen as affecting the unity within the Eastern Church. Their theology and beliefs are the same.

The Eastern Church does not have a leader in a position similar to that of the pope in the Catholic Church. The Eastern Church consists of a number of self-governing churches. For the Orthodox Church, Jesus Christ is the head of the Church, and the Church is the body of Christ.

A Closer Look

Eastern Orthodox Churches are in communion with each other and recognize the Patriarch of Constantinople as "first among equals."

Check Your Understanding

1. Give some of the reasons for the separation between the Eastern and Western Churches.
2. Describe Eastern Orthodox Christians using the following headings:
   - Who
   - When
   - Where
   - Central Beliefs

Think About It

3. Why are Eastern and Western Christianity so different from one another? In a small group, find one key difference to research, consider, and explain in a presentation to the class. How could understanding this difference be a means to find unity?

Making It Personal

4. Do you (or does someone you know) use images or icons in prayer? How do these help people focus their prayer?

Traditions of Western Christianity: Catholic and Protestant

During the Middle Ages, Christianity united Europe and pervaded all aspects of life—food, work, politics, education, culture, and so on. For example, the Cathedral of Chartres was not only a church—it also housed a marketplace and was a meeting place for skilled workers and a source of work for artists. Attached to it was a cathedral school.

In the fifteenth century, the unity in Europe began to break apart. The following three factors contributed to the break-up:

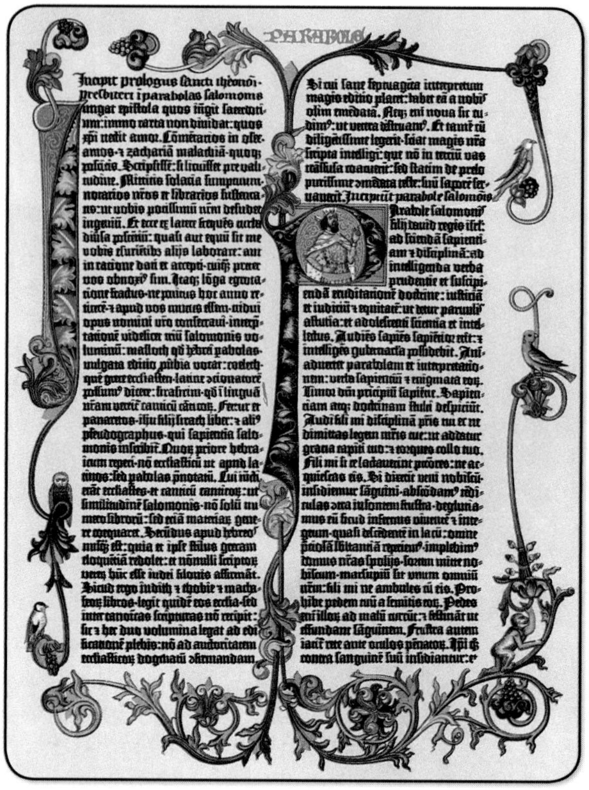

The Gutenberg Bible. The Gutenberg Bible is the first Bible ever printed. Not long after, the Bible was translated from Latin into other European languages. **Why was the invention of the printing press so important for Christianity? What was the impact of translating the Bible from Latin into local languages for peoples of the time?**

Cathedral of Chartres. During the Middle Ages in Europe, many magnificent buildings were created as people attempted to reproduce the beauty of God on Earth. At the Cathedral of Chartres in France, artists did not sign their work with their names. **Why do you think they did not sign their work? What do you know about—and want to know about—the Middle Ages?**

A Closer Look

Indulgences are concerned with the process of healing from sin and its effects. This healing cannot be bought with money. It was to this apparent abuse of indulgences that Luther objected.

- Trade was increasing and new towns formed. A new class, tradespeople, emerged in these towns.
- Johannes Gutenberg invented the printing press. The Bible was the first book printed. As a result of Gutenberg's invention, a growing number of people could own books and read the scriptures and other texts without the influence of the Church. People who were literate and therefore able to read the Bible began to question—and criticize— the power and authority previously held by the nobility and the leaders of the Church.
- The sad state of the Church. There were plenty of reasons for criticizing the Church at the time. A number of popes sought too much power and luxury. The clergy were poorly trained. The monasteries had become too powerful and wealthy. It was time for reform. However, the reform, when it came, broke apart the unity of the Western Church.

Martin Luther and Lutheranism

In 1517, a Dominican friar named John Tetzel began to sell indulgences in Germany to raise money for the Archbishop of Mainz, and for the pope's construction projects. An Augustinian monk named Martin Luther took notice. Luther, a 34-year-old teacher of the New Testament, had long been uncomfortable with the way indulgences seemed to be sold. Luther presented his criticisms in the form of 95 Theses. This conflict could easily have been settled peaceably. Both sides dug in their heels, and soon the criticism became a church-breaking event.

Luther did not originally set out to leave the Catholic Church nor to start a new movement. However, the more he felt backed into a corner by the arguments of those who opposed him, the more he expressed his opinion that Church authority was going against the authority of scripture. The conflict escalated:

- In 1517, Luther posted his 95 Theses.
- By 1520, Luther's writings recommended a rejection of the Catholic Church—not only the pope's authority, but Church authority generally.
- In response, the pope condemned 41 propositions from Luther's writings, insisting that he recant (take back and renounce) them.
- In December 1520, Luther publicly burned the papal document.
- At a tribunal in the spring of 1521, Luther was asked again to recant. He refused, and was declared an outlaw.
- Protected by Prince Frederick of Saxony, Luther began work on translating the Bible into German. He continued his writing and his work in reforming the churches of Germany.
- In 1526, some German princes who sided with Luther secured religious freedoms for their territories.
- In 1529, Catholic princes attempted to reverse this situation; the princes on Luther's side protested.

When Luther died in 1546, one of his legacies was his notion of freedom. Gradually, his notion of individual freedom from the authority of the Church became freedom from the authority of tyrannical rulers and freedom from laws over which people had no say. This notion of freedom became a dominant theme of modern times.

Martin Luther. This painting by Lucas Cranach the Elder shows Martin Luther (1483–1546). Luther posted his 95 Theses on the church door in Wittenberg, Germany, in 1517.

Fast Fact

The name "Protestant" refers to the protests made by the princes who sided with Luther.

A Closer Look

As a monk, Luther had agonized over his salvation. He had tried hard to overcome his sins, but without much success. By the age of 30, he had found the answer he had been looking for in St. Paul's Letter to the Romans, when the Apostle quotes the Old Testament prophet Habakkuk: "The just shall live by faith" (Romans 1:17). Luther determined that it is not by efforts to overcome sin that humans are saved, but by their faith, their unshakeable trust in God. We are saved not by what *we* do, but by what *God* does. Christian life, according to Luther, meant trusting in God. To emphasize this point, Luther said it was by "faith alone" *(sola fide)* that humans are saved. This became known as the doctrine of justification by faith.

Check Your Understanding

1. a) What were three factors leading to the break in the unity of Christian Europe?
   b) What prompted Luther to post his 95 Theses?
2. Summarize the following:
   a) how the conflict between Luther and the Church escalated
   b) what "salvation by faith alone" means

Think About It

3. Research Luther's 95 Theses. What were his main concerns and what did he hope to accomplish?

Making It Personal

4. Recall a time when you or someone you know protested something. Explain the circumstances and the outcome.

Fast Fact

Lutheranism spread beyond Germany and became the state church of the Scandinavian countries; it spread to the Americas and to Africa. There are approximately 60 million Lutherans in the world today. Lutherans make up 2 percent of Canada's population, or about 600 000 Canadians.

Other Reform Movements

Luther was not the only reformer. Others came before and after him. Here are some examples. As you learn about them, think about the different beliefs put forth and the actions taken.

A Closer Look

John Calvin (1509–1564) was born in Noyon, France. He later studied in Paris and was influenced there by Protestant ideas. In 1533, he fled Paris for Switzerland. In 1536, he published the first version of his main work, the *Institutes of the Christian Religion*. In Geneva, Calvin tried to govern the city as a theocracy, using his religious authority to punish offenders against morality and to ensure proper religious conduct. In some cases, his opponents were executed.

Calvinism

Another reformer was John Calvin. His key beliefs—and the main teachings of the Reformed tradition—are summarized in the table below. As you read them, think about how they compare with your own beliefs and others you know. What words and ideas are striking to you?

Calvin's Impact

Calvin's beliefs have had an impact through Calvinism or Reformed theology in Holland, Scotland, and in parts of France and Northern Ireland. Then, as a result of colonialism and emigration from these countries, the influence of Calvinism has spread much farther afield, to the United States and Canada, South Africa, and Indonesia.

John Calvin. Calvin died in Geneva, where he is honoured with this statue. Calvin is in the middle. One noteworthy Calvinist, Henry Dunant, was the founder of the Geneva-based International Red Cross.

Calvinism's Five Points

1. Total depravity of humans	Human beings cannot perform any acts that contribute to their salvation.
2. Unconditional election	Those who will be saved have been chosen before the creation of the world—not because of what good or evil they had done in life, but only out of God's mercy.
3. Limited atonement	Christ died in place of sinners. Only those who are elected by God are saved. Others are damned.
4. Irresistible grace	The power of the Holy Spirit cannot be withstood. It will overcome whatever obstacles the elect put in the way of God's purposes.
5. Perseverance of the saints	God's saving will cannot be opposed definitively. Those whom God has elected will be saved despite what they do.

Anabaptists

Another group of reformers who did not identify with Luther or Calvin were Anabaptists. These included several sixteenth-century dissident groups in Germany and Moravia (present-day Czech Republic). Anabaptists include Mennonites, who have had a great impact on Canada.

The Mennonite faith was founded by a priest named Menno Simons (1496–1551). He rejected Catholicism in favour of adult baptism only. He also rejected the militancy of some

NEL

Mennonite Community Cohesion. Mennonite communities are known for a high level of social cohesion. To complete large-scale tasks, the whole community will come together to help other members. In this photo, a Mennonite community is building a church together.

Anabaptists and promoted pacifism (literally, a belief in peace, but often meaning opposition to war). Mennonites have faced persecution for their separate ways. They are noted for their devotion to the Bible and their dedication to social justice through the Mennonite Central Committee. Approximately 200 000 Mennonites live in Canada.

Anglicanism

During the early years of the Protestant Reformation in Europe, the ideas of the Reformers did not take a firm hold among people in England. It was under the rule of Henry VIII that England first broke away from Rome and went from being a Catholic nation under the authority of the pope to a Protestant nation with the king as the head of the Church of England.

In 1530, King Henry VIII wanted his marriage to Catherine of Aragon declared invalid so that he could marry Anne Boleyn. When the pope denied his request, Henry declared himself the head of the Church of England and dismantled the connections between Rome and England. From that point, the religious climate in England under Henry VIII and his successors, Edward VI, Mary I, and Elizabeth I, was volatile. Catholics were often persecuted and there were many English martyrs. But, Christians on both sides suffered or were killed in the conflict.

Henry VIII. A portrait by Hans Holbein of Henry VIII, king of England from 1509 to 1547.

A Closer Look

In Canada, the Reformed tradition and its offshoots have about 6.9 million members. The largest denomination is the United Church of Canada, with 2.8 million members. However, while its worship service retains the traditional Reformation format, the United Church today reflects much more the social gospel movement in its outreach to the people at the margins of society. The Presbyterians, Christian Reformed, and some Baptists also trace their roots to John Calvin.

Fast Fact

The 2001 census reports that just over 2 million people in Canada identify themselves as Anglicans. According to the Anglican Church's own tally, there are 800 000 active members in 30 dioceses. The Anglican Church of Canada has played an important role in Canadian history, especially in the founding of universities and schools. Anglicanism spread with the influence of the British Empire. Around 70 million Anglicans are found in all countries where there has been British influence.

Fast Fact

Thomas More was a lawyer, author, and scholar, and was one of Henry VIII's chief advisors. More was a devout Catholic who became conflicted as Henry broke from Rome. As a Catholic, he refused to sign the *Act of Supremacy* that made Henry the Supreme Head of the Church of England, and he was executed for treason in 1535. Thomas More was canonized as a saint by Pope Pius XI in 1935.

Henry VIII—Family Tree

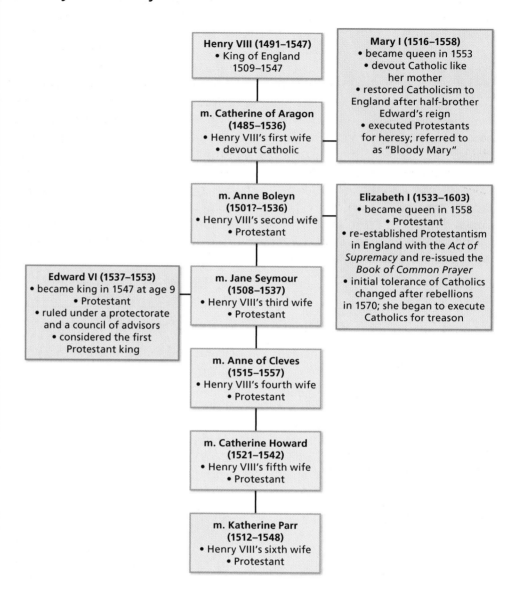

Henry VIII (1491–1547)
- King of England 1509–1547

m. Catherine of Aragon (1485–1536)
- Henry VIII's first wife
- devout Catholic

Mary I (1516–1558)
- became queen in 1553
- devout Catholic like her mother
- restored Catholicism to England after half-brother Edward's reign
- executed Protestants for heresy; referred to as "Bloody Mary"

m. Anne Boleyn (1501?–1536)
- Henry VIII's second wife
- Protestant

Elizabeth I (1533–1603)
- became queen in 1558
- Protestant
- re-established Protestantism in England with the *Act of Supremacy* and re-issued the *Book of Common Prayer*
- initial tolerance of Catholics changed after rebellions in 1570; she began to execute Catholics for treason

m. Jane Seymour (1508–1537)
- Henry VIII's third wife
- Protestant

Edward VI (1537–1553)
- became king in 1547 at age 9
- Protestant
- ruled under a protectorate and a council of advisors
- considered the first Protestant king

m. Anne of Cleves (1515–1557)
- Henry VIII's fourth wife
- Protestant

m. Catherine Howard (1521–1542)
- Henry VIII's fifth wife
- Protestant

m. Katherine Parr (1512–1548)
- Henry VIII's sixth wife
- Protestant

Timeline of the Church of England

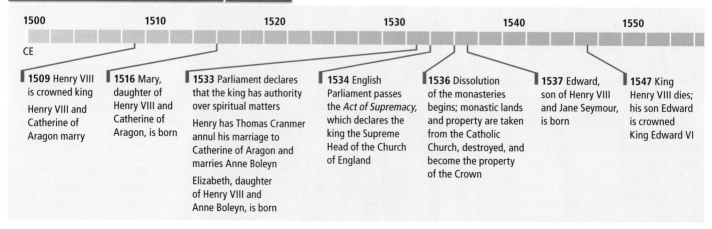

1500 CE — 1510 — 1520 — 1530 — 1540 — 1550

1509 Henry VIII is crowned king

Henry VIII and Catherine of Aragon marry

1516 Mary, daughter of Henry VIII and Catherine of Aragon, is born

1533 Parliament declares that the king has authority over spiritual matters

Henry has Thomas Cranmer annul his marriage to Catherine of Aragon and marries Anne Boleyn

Elizabeth, daughter of Henry VIII and Anne Boleyn, is born

1534 English Parliament passes the *Act of Supremacy*, which declares the king the Supreme Head of the Church of England

1536 Dissolution of the monasteries begins; monastic lands and property are taken from the Catholic Church, destroyed, and become the property of the Crown

1537 Edward, son of Henry VIII and Jane Seymour, is born

1547 King Henry VIII dies; his son Edward is crowned King Edward VI

Henry's motivations for breaking from Rome were more political than religious. On the political side, he no longer recognized the authority of the pope and he supported the destruction of the monasteries. But, the Catholic doctrine and the Mass remained essentially the same as they had been before. Henry VIII may not have been ideologically Protestant, but many of his advisors were more radical. These advisors would continue to influence the development of the Church of England under Edward VI.

Under Edward, Protestantism became more firmly established. The traditional Latin Catholic Mass was replaced with an English service structured by the *Book of Common Prayer*. The outward appearance of the church also began to change; church images were dismantled, vestments were forbidden, and stone altars were replaced with wooden communion tables. Edward was king for only a short time; after a brief illness, he died, and the throne went to his Catholic half-sister Mary.

Once Mary, a devout Catholic, became queen, she went to work dismantling Edward's reforms, once again establishing England as a Catholic nation. But, like her brother, Mary had a short reign and died just five years after becoming queen.

After Mary's death, Elizabeth became queen of England. Elizabeth's reign lasted 45 years. It was under her reign that Protestant control of the Church of England became permanent. Elizabeth re-established many of Edward's reforms, including the *Book of Common Prayer*. Elizabeth also kept many ancient traditions of the Church. Anglicanism since Elizabeth's time has seen itself as a middle way between Catholicism and Reformed Protestantism. High Anglicans remained closest to Catholicism, while Low Anglicans resembled the Reformed tradition.

A Closer Look

First written in 1549 by Thomas Cranmer, the Archbishop of Canterbury under Henry VIII and Edward VI, the *Book of Common Prayer* is the primary liturgical prayer book of the Church of England. Under the *Book of Common Prayer*, scripture became the basis of the service, now delivered in English instead of Latin. Over the years, it has undergone a number of revisions, but continues to be the foundational prayer book of Anglicanism and the Church of England.

The *Book of Common Prayer*. The *Book of Common Prayer* is the name of the prayer book used by the Church of England.

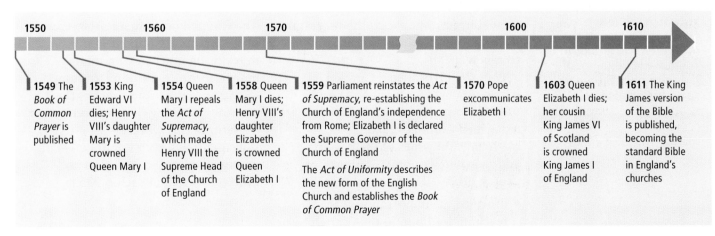

1550 — 1560 — 1570 — 1600 — 1610

- **1549** The *Book of Common Prayer* is published
- **1553** King Edward VI dies; Henry VIII's daughter Mary is crowned Queen Mary I
- **1554** Queen Mary I repeals the *Act of Supremacy*, which made Henry VIII the Supreme Head of the Church of England
- **1558** Queen Mary I dies; Henry VIII's daughter Elizabeth is crowned Queen Elizabeth I
- **1559** Parliament reinstates the *Act of Supremacy*, re-establishing the Church of England's independence from Rome; Elizabeth I is declared the Supreme Governor of the Church of England

  The *Act of Uniformity* describes the new form of the English Church and establishes the *Book of Common Prayer*
- **1570** Pope excommunicates Elizabeth I
- **1603** Queen Elizabeth I dies; her cousin King James VI of Scotland is crowned King James I of England
- **1611** The King James version of the Bible is published, becoming the standard Bible in England's churches

Check Your Understanding

1. On a chart like the one below, make jot notes about what you have learned. Then, in a group, discuss, compare, and refine your charts.

Movement	Time/Events	People	Beliefs	Legacy/Outcomes

Think About It

2. With a partner or in a small group, discuss the five points of Calvinism. What does each mean? For each point, answer the following:
   - What is the implication of the belief?
   - What could it mean in an example from contemporary daily life?
3. Choose one primary source document described in this chapter that is associated with a Protestant Church, and present an excerpt to the class.

Making It Personal

4. Research a Calvinist, Anabaptist, or Anglican church in your community. Make notes of the facts you find about the church (number of members, main theological teachings, rituals, and so on), and share your findings in a small group. Discuss how the church compares with your own religion. How is it familiar, and how is it different?

A Closer Look

The sixteenth and seventeenth centuries saw a great number of reform movements in the Church. One of the most dynamic groups was founded by Ignatius of Loyola in 1540 in Spain. The group became known as the Jesuits. They became one of the most effective groups to counter the influence of the reformers. Jesuits first came to Canada in 1611.

The Catholic Reformation

As the Church's unity was broken by the Reformation, there were a variety of reactions in the Catholic world. Some Catholics sympathized with the concerns of the Reformers, but most rejected their use of separation as a way to deal with concerns. Instead, they wanted change from within.

The calls for reform in the Church had begun long before Luther, but working toward this reform did not always result in renewal. However, in response to the Protestant Reformation, Catholicism began to renew itself.

Pope Paul III called a Council, which was held between 1545 and 1563. Known as the Council of Trent, it clarified Catholic teaching on the important issues of the day and addressed how to prevent abuses of church offices. The Council

- affirmed the importance of the teaching tradition in the Church as a necessary interpretation of the scriptures
- affirmed the importance of the seven sacraments
- responded to Luther's insistence that people need faith for salvation; but the Council rejected Luther's idea that faith "alone," without good works (page 167), was all that was needed
- insisted that priests needed improved education so that they would be better equipped to instruct and serve the people

The Council of Trent and the reform of the Catholic Church did not succeed in restoring unity in Christianity. The main effort of the Church became to convince the Protestants of their error and to bring them to conversion. Sometimes this worked—as it did in Bohemia (the Czech Republic)—but, in many countries, Catholics and Protestants fought each other.

From Intolerance and War to Tolerance

Catholic–Protestant conflicts in England during the sixteenth century were sometimes bloody. During the Thirty Years' War (1618–1648), nearly one-third of the population of the German states died.

Religious Tolerance Begins

Only with the Enlightenment, the major intellectual movement of the eighteenth century, did the idea of religious tolerance begin to become popular. This tolerance was twofold:

- tolerance between religions
- tolerance by governments for the different religions practised in their countries

However, the Enlightenment also led to a great opposition or hostility toward religion in general.

Catholic and Protestant conflict subsided somewhat in the nineteenth century as more and more European nations began to develop laws of religious tolerance. In Britain and Ireland, for example, Catholics were officially permitted to practise their religion as of 1829, without fear of penalties or discrimination. While there were always examples of charity and tolerance between Catholics and Protestants, it was not until the Second Vatican Council (1962–1965) that, for Catholics, official dialogue and openness between Catholics and Protestants became a reality.

St. Charles Borromeo. St. Charles Borromeo (1538–1584) put into effect the reforms of the Council of Trent in Milan, Italy, despite much opposition. **Why, in your opinion, does it seem so difficult to reform in these areas: in a religion, in schools, or in politics?**

Fast Fact

The Thirty Years' War took place mainly in Germany but extended into many countries in Europe. To establish peace, an agreement was reached that each nation's official religion would be determined by the religion of the nation's ruler. Citizens who did not practise the national religion could be charged with treason as well as heresy and punished accordingly. This situation of intolerance continued for centuries.

Check Your Understanding

1. Plot on a timeline from the Middle Ages to the French Revolution what you have learned about movements within Christianity.
2. Briefly summarize the following:
   a) the Council of Trent and its objectives
   b) the agreement ending the Thirty Years' War and its objectives
   c) the conversion of the Cathedral of Notre Dame to the Temple of Reason

Think About It

3. In a small group, brainstorm a list of people in the history of Christianity since the Middle Ages that you could research. Which seem the most interesting? Why? What resources could you use to learn more about one person and the context of his or her time?

Making It Personal

4. In your opinion, how should people facing religious persecution stand up for their beliefs?

A Closer Look

The French Revolution (1789–1799) at first tried to eliminate the Catholic Church in France. For a short while, the Cathedral of Notre Dame was converted into the Temple of Reason. Revolutionaries believed that human reason would supplant religion and overcome all divisions.

A Closer Look

During modern times, religious groups in the West have had to deal with a greater social emphasis on reason as opposed to faith. After the Council of Trent, the Catholic Church defined itself more and more as being united around the pope and holding correct doctrine. The churches of the Protestant Reformation, meanwhile, were facing two opposing trends, one that sought to adapt to the modern emphasis on reason, and another that reacted to it.

Recent Movements

As happens in all movements, after an initial period of deep religious enthusiasm, the churches of the Protestant Reformation lost their early energy. As settled institutions, they had to deal with day-to-day issues. At the same time, they also needed to address the changing times.

Evangelicalism

By the eighteenth century, the need for reform among Protestants was deeply felt. So, for instance, in England, John and Charles Wesley tried to revive the personal enthusiasm and evangelical fervour of early Protestant Reformation spirituality. This movement led to their breaking away from the Anglican Church and establishing the Methodist Church.

Similar movements occurred in the Lutheran and Reformed traditions. In the United States, this movement was known as the Great Awakening. It gave rise to periodic revivals (Revivalism), which have lasted to this day. The movement became known as Evangelicalism.

Evangelicalism involves a call to personal conversion as a conscious experience; it is called "being born again." Here are some typical characteristics of Evangelicalism:

- renewed emphasis on the authority of the Bible
- emphasis on uprightness of life—righteous or honourable behaviour
- baptism for adults only—a "Believer's Baptism"
- often, de-emphasizes official church membership and formal creeds
- spreading the Gospel through missionary activity

Fundamentalism

Some churches have tried to return to the basics, or fundamentals, of the Christian faith. Their approach is known as Fundamentalism. The Protestant Fundamentalist churches have been most insistent on teaching that the Bible is without error, that Christ is God, and that Jesus died on the cross for our sake. They have also rejected Darwin's theory of evolution in favour of the biblical story of creation.

Liberalism

Some churches have tried to adapt to the culture of the time. Liberalism within the context of Christianity means finding some common ground with modernity and its search for reason, with scientific and technological advances, and with modern political structures. However, not everyone within the various churches has agreed with what many called an unholy marriage of Christianity and the modern world. One of the most widespread movements against this liberal Christianity has been Pentecostalism.

Billy Graham. Born in 1918, the American preacher Billy Graham was one of the first Evangelical preachers to use television and large gatherings to modernize Revivalism.

NEL

Pentecostalism

The Pentecostal movement, often incorrectly identified with Fundamentalism, accepts the Bible as the Word of God without error. Pentecostals believe that the Holy Spirit guides them in how they should live, encourages them, and brings peace. The Holy Spirit also strengthens them to help them share their faith and serve others. This movement

- preaches God's judgment of the world and states that the message of Christ and the modern world are on a collision course
- anticipates the Second Coming of Christ at the end of history
- holds that believers can seek to be baptized in the Holy Spirit
- believes in what are seen as signs of the Holy Spirit's presence—for example, **speaking in tongues**, slaying in the Spirit

William J. Seymour. William J. Seymour was born in Louisiana, the son of freed slaves. His revivalist preaching on Azusa Street in Los Angeles in 1906 sparked the Pentecostal movement. People began to speak in tongues, and new worship services were started at which different races came together to worship, which was almost unheard of at the time.

Speaking in tongues
Vocalizing a string of syllables in religious practice; in Greek, the term is *glossolalia*, which means literally "gift of tongues"; it is believed to be the gift of holy language from the Holy Spirit

Pentecostalism. In Pentecostal worship, another sign of the presence of the Holy Spirit is slaying in the Spirit. During services, believers might fall to the floor in a faint, which is understood as a personal encounter with God's spirit.

Fast Fact

Pentecostalism is an important movement spreading rapidly throughout the world. With over 100 million members, it is the largest form of Protestantism today. There are about 370 000 members of Pentecostal congregations in Canada.

Fast Fact

Within the Catholic Church, the Pentecostal movement is expressed in the charismatic movement, in which we find the same manifestations of the Spirit.

Check Your Understanding

1. Describe the emphasis of modern times and specific religions' responses to it.
2. With a partner, create glossary entries (definitions plus examples) for the following terms:
   - Evangelicalism
   - Fundamentalism
   - Liberalism
   - Pentecostalism

Think About It

3. What comes to mind when you hear someone described as a Fundamentalist, Liberal, Evangelical, or Pentecostal? After you answer, check your associations with what you have learned about these movements. What questions do you have about any of these terms? Discuss your associations, knowledge, and questions in small groups.

Making It Personal

4. On one subject or issue, how do you think your beliefs would compare with those of a Christian who is described as a Fundamentalist, Liberal, Evangelical, or Pentecostal? Write your ideas in a short paragraph or on a Venn diagram.

Christianity Today

The various Christian churches have many things in common. However, they also differ in a number of ways. It would be easy just to accept these different practices. Our culture tells us to accept differences and be tolerant, but Christians recognize that these differences contain contradictions. Contradictions among Christians can lead to ambiguity and confusion about the way that Jesus Christ's mission can unfold in the world.

Most Christians today see the need for greater unity among Christians. Christians seek unity amid diversity. The intent is not to do away with all differences, but to do away with contradictions and conflicts. Before we look at the pursuit of unity, let us look at the range of ritual practices to see some similarities and differences.

Pentecostal Rock Band. Pentecostal churches often make use of contemporary music for worship. Gospel music of the kind used in Pentecostal churches is now so popular that there are professional groups. The rock group Audio Adrenaline pose with their Grammy Award for Best Rock Gospel Album. **What sort of music lifts your spirits and leads you to prayer?**

Tapestry of Christian Practices

	Catholic	Eastern Churches	Protestant Movements
Ritual	• baptism—retained in all Christian churches as an essential ritual of initiation, but practices vary		
	• baptismal water often only sprinkled or poured on forehead	• baptismal candidate is plunged or immersed in a large baptismal font	• infant baptism—some churches • Anabaptists and Evangelicals—only adults are baptized • Baptists—can range from sprinkling water over forehead, to pouring water, to full immersion
	• Eucharist considered "the source and summit of Christian life"	• similar to Catholic focus on Eucharist	• in many Lutheran and Anglican churches—similar to Catholic focus on Eucharist
	• Catholics, Orthodox Christians, and Anglicans celebrate both the Liturgy of the Word and the Liturgy of the Eucharist; must also be a ritual action, for example, with bread and wine		• in others—main emphasis is on the Liturgy of the Word • sermons may last 30 to 40 minutes or longer • Evangelicals—centre faith on the Bible as the Word of God, so focus on hymn singing, Bible study, and preaching
	• differences in the use of – bread (unleavened or leavened) – wine (wine or grape juice) – language (local, Latin, Greek, and so on)		
Who presides	• this varies: – in some churches—ordained person wearing special liturgical vestments – in others—man or woman, ordained or lay person, with or without a liturgical robe		
Physical church	• may be richly decorated with art or left bare • may emphasize music and singing (for example, may have an organ and choir loft), or may have minimal or no place for music		

Make It Your Own: Features of a Church

Churches have changed over the history of Christianity:

- from secret rooms in houses so that worshippers could meet privately to practise their faith, which society considered illegal
- to larger spaces with windows and artwork
- to churches set into monasteries
- to grand cathedrals
- to simple pioneer churches and places that combine worship space and community halls

A church often includes the following elements:

- an altar and lectern (pulpit) where the priest/minister stands
- an area where the congregation gathers
- space for the choir
- chapels or small areas for private prayer
- space for social gatherings
- windows, art, decorations, and so on

Catholic Church Interior. The interior of a Catholic church during a service. **How many elements from the list in the first column can you find?**

Activities

1. Think about the features in a church that you know. Would you add any features to this list?
2. Design a church building that you think would meet the needs of a modern community. Consider the following: What would it look like? What features would it have? Where would you build it?
3. Draw a floor plan or make a model of your church and describe it to your class.

Ecumenical movement

(Also called "ecumenism") the movement toward unity among the Christian churches; "ecumenism" comes from the Greek word meaning "the whole inhabited world" and reflects Jesus's desire that his word be spread to the whole of the human race

The Ecumenical Movement

Recently, many Christians have come to believe that what unites them is much greater than what divides them. This new awareness came about through what has become known as the ecumenical movement.

In the twentieth century, churches of the Protestant Reformation became more and more conscious that the divisions within Christianity were hurting the mission of the Church. Many mark the World Missionary Conference held in Edinburgh, Scotland, in 1910 as the start of the modern **ecumenical movement**. Then, in 1948, the World Council of Churches (WCC) was formed with the purpose of working toward Christian unity. By the mid-twentieth century, almost all Christian churches agreed that divisions went against the desire of Jesus for unity among his followers.

NEL

Check Your Understanding

1. Recall three areas in which Christian practices can vary. Give examples of practices that are the same as in Catholicism and those that differ from Catholicism.
2. What is the ecumenical movement and when did it start?

Think About It

3. If you want to know what a community or church believes, observe how members pray and what their prayers say. How would observing these practices help to explain some of the differences among Christians?

Making It Personal

4. Do you or someone you know have close family members from different Christian denominations? If so, how does the family deal with religious differences at home? If not, what ideas do you have about dealing with religious differences among Christians? In a small group, create a list of suggestions.

The Goal of Ecumenism

At first, the Catholic Church refused to participate in the World Council of Churches. It believed this movement would lead to relativism, a sort of indifference to the differences among Christians. However, during the Second Vatican Council, in 1965, the Church passed a Decree on Ecumenism and committed the Catholic Church to dialogue. Now the Catholic Church participates in all the WCC's commissions, although it is not a full member of the WCC. In Canada, the Catholic Church is a member of the Canadian Council of Churches.

Communion

The goal of ecumenism is unity, but what this unity would look like is hard to predict. One way of looking at unity is through the term "communion." Communion is the goal of ecumenism, and dialogue is the means of ecumenism.

What binds all the different Christian churches together is their confession of Jesus Christ and baptism. Catholics hold that, to the extent that churches confess Jesus Christ and practise baptism, they are already in partial communion or fellowship with these churches. That is why what unites the churches is greater than what divides them. The question, then, is "What divisions remain to block full communion?" In most cases, it involves how churches confess Jesus Christ and how they view Eucharist, baptism, and leadership in the Church. Dialogue most frequently begins on these issues.

Dialogue

The dialogue is intended to clarify what it means to be the Church of Jesus Christ. The Catholic Church and the World Council of Churches have committed themselves to resolve divisions through dialogue. This dialogue is based on two understandings:

- Dialogue is more than just talking with other churches. It means living, praying, studying, and working together in solidarity, overcoming the divisions that separate churches.
- A universal church of Christ will not be identical to any of the churches as they exist now. The one universal church of Christ must include all those who confess Jesus Christ and are baptized.

Fast Fact

The World Council of Churches is an international organization that has brought together the majority of Christian communities, totalling about 560 million Christians —21 families of Christian churches in approximately 350 churches, denominations, and fellowships. **How many different Christian churches do you know in your community?**

"The unity of all divided humanity is the will of God."

(Pope John Paul II in his 1995 letter on Ecumenism)

A Closer Look

"Communion" is a term used by the World Council of Churches and the Catholic Church as a trademark of the Church. The Church is a communion or fellowship first of all with God and with one another. Full communion is understood as a final gift of God. The Church today is only a foretaste of this final communion.

Fast Fact

According to the Catholic Church, full communion will be achieved when all can fully participate in the Eucharist.

Pope Benedict XVI, Leader of the Catholic Church. Catholics consider the role of the ministry of bishops, especially the pope, as crucial for the unity of the Church. The Church is not only a spiritual communion through Baptism and Eucharist, but also an institutional communion that unites its members in a visible institution under the leadership of the bishops.

The Catholic Church believes that in it, the fullness of the Church of Christ continues to exist. However, the Catholic Church believes that this is a wounded fullness as long as there is division among Christian churches. By entering into ecumenical dialogue, the Catholic Church acknowledges that it is wounded by the division.

The Church acknowledges that important elements of being church are present in the other churches. However, the Catholic Church does not find in the other churches the fullness of the Church of Christ that it sees in the Catholic Church. Therefore, the Catholic Church sees the need for dialogue.

For Catholics, the following elements must be present before there can be full communion—a common celebration of the Eucharist:

- unity of faith: a consensus on the core doctrines as found in the scriptures and the Creed
- acknowledgement of the importance of the sacraments, especially the Eucharist, for salvation
- the service and ministry of priests, bishops, and pope

Not all other churches see what it means to be church in the same way Catholics do. Nor do these churches, at present, want to be church in the same way. Ecumenical dialogue has the goal of clarifying what it means to be the church of Jesus Christ. This is why dialogue is so important. It helps churches understand each other better and arrive at a higher level of truth and unity.

Check Your Understanding

1. Explain what ecumenism seeks to achieve and how.
2. What, according to the Catholic Church, is needed to arrive at unity? When will all Christians be able to celebrate Eucharist together?

Think About It

3. a) In a small group, define what it means "to be church." In your discussion, make sure that all opinions are heard and that differences are discussed. Try to reach consensus.

   b) Present your definition to the class and comment on the process of trying to reach consensus.

Making It Personal

4. Have you experienced divisions in your family, with friends, or at school? What did you do about these divisions?

NEL

Dialogue of the Churches East and West

One of the great moments of the Second Vatican Council occurred when the Catholic Church (West) and Orthodox Church (East) began to call each other "sister churches." After 1000 years of separation, the churches broke the barriers of suspicion and isolation. They began to see themselves as members of one household, sisters to be treated the same, each bringing its own riches to the universal Church.

There are differences between the churches:

- different liturgies and Church orders
- different theological opinions regarding the role of the pope as being first among equals

However, these churches base themselves on Eucharistic communion, and they have accepted each other's Eucharist. The differences are seen not only as obstacles, but also as a source of enrichment. For example, through them, the Western Church has gained a new awareness that unity can co-exist with great diversity. It is permitted, therefore, to say that an almost perfect unity exists between Orthodox (Eastern) and Catholic (Western) Churches.

Patriarch Athenagoras I. In 1964, Patriarch Athenagoras I of Constantinople (left) and Pope Paul VI met for the first of many meetings between East and West. The most important part of the meetings of churches in dialogue has always been spending time together, getting to know each other, eating together, and praying together. **Why do you think spending time together is so important for dialogue?**

Dialogue among the Churches of the West

Dialogue between the Catholic Church and the churches of the Protestant Reformation is different from that between East and West. Because of the great differences among churches, the dialogues with the churches of the Protestant Reformation are usually conducted with each church individually. Many such dialogues have been established in the past 50 years—some including more than two churches, some including the Catholic Church, and some only among churches of the Protestant Reformation. In some cases, such dialogues have led to different churches uniting with one another.

As a result of the ecumenical dialogue, three Canadian denominations—Methodists, Congregationalists, and 70 percent of Presbyterians—joined in 1925 to become the United Church of Canada. After the Catholic Church, the United Church is the largest Christian denomination in Canada.

Overall, the Catholic Church has more in common with the Anglican and Lutheran churches than with others. At times, Catholics have taken the lead in working and praying together with Anglicans and with the other churches of the Protestant Reformation.

As in all the ecumenical dialogues, agreements were to be made on the basis of the Gospels and the earliest traditions of the Church. All differences were studied keeping this principle in mind.

- There is general agreement on how the Eucharist is understood.

Fast Fact

In a joint declaration in 1999, Catholics and Lutherans stated that both churches have overcome their main differences regarding the teaching on justification.

A Closer Look

In 1964, a statement from the Second Vatican Council said that Anglicanism has "a special place" among the Protestant churches because in it "Catholic traditions and institutions in part continue to exist." After the Council, a flurry of dialogues between the two churches began.

Catholic and Anglican Dialogue. In 2006, Pope Benedict XVI and the Archbishop of Canterbury, Dr. Rowan Williams, met to discuss issues concerning ordination to the priesthood and their churches' relations with Muslims.

- Catholics and Anglicans have reached a high level of agreement on most questions centred on the Church. These questions include the following:
  - What role does the Church have in our salvation?
  - What is the role of bishops in human salvation? What is the role of the pope? How necessary are the bishops and the pope? If they are necessary, what is the Church and what is its mission?
- A major issue is the stand on ordaining women and homosexuals. Some Anglican dioceses began ordaining women in the 1970s. For the Catholic Church and the Orthodox Churches, ordaining women is contrary to the earliest traditions of the Church.
- There are serious disagreements on a number of ethical issues. Catholics and Anglicans diverge on questions of divorce and remarriage, artificial birth control, abortion, and in vitro fertilization.

Because there are still major issues to resolve, dialogue has not yet led to a shared Eucharist. The most significant result of dialogue between the two churches is the ecumenism practised in parishes, homes, schools, colleges, hospitals, prisons, and in other places served by chaplaincies. People have begun to pray together, to meet each other, to use each other's parish churches, and to engage in social action together.

Check Your Understanding

1. Why are the Eastern and Western Churches called "sister churches"?
2. Create a diagram to indicate where Catholics and Anglicans are in their dialogue with each other.

Think About It

3. The idea of dialogue is based on the belief that the two sides are partners, not opponents. Create a poster about dialogue by starting to brainstorm a list titled "Dialogue Is ... /Dialogue Isn't ...."

Making It Personal

4. Have you ever prayed together with members of other churches or for other churches? If so, describe the event. If not, reflect on what opportunities and challenges you might face in those circumstances.

Ecumenism: A Difficult Task

Christianity understands itself to be a people with and through whom God enters into history and brings salvation to the world. The Holy Spirit is the breath of Christianity and the energy that keeps the Church faithful to God's work. In other words, Christianity does not see itself as merely a social movement. For Christians, Christianity is God's work into which they are taken up.

Because Christianity sees itself as engaged in God's desire to gather all humanity, it cannot ignore the fragmentation of Christianity. The divisions and wounds in Christianity must be healed. Fortunately, many Christians in the last century have found the courage and enthusiasm to work toward unity.

However, the work of healing and reconciling differences is extremely difficult. Lifelong convictions are not only a matter of the head but also of the heart. Convictions touch people's identity. It is hard to let go, hard to listen to another's convictions, when people are convinced of the truth of their own. This is especially true when, in the past, people gave witness to their convictions with their lives. Can we now ignore those witnesses and their sacrifices?

Christian Unity. Christian youths pray for the gift of unity.

A Renewed Ecumenism

A sustained spirituality is needed to feed the ecumenical movement. As with all movements, however, the movement toward unity has been hard to sustain because the initial enthusiasm and energy has dimmed. Sustaining the ecumenical movement has become more difficult for various reasons.

- Most Christians seem unable to understand why Christian churches separated in the first place. For example, outside of the experts, hardly anyone today understands Luther's teaching on justification by faith alone. Hardly anyone today would do battle as the Eastern Church did over a short addition to the Creed.
- Many Christians feel as if these battles are not theirs or these issues no longer matter.
- Christians today are focused on other issues. The issues of war and peace, world poverty, economic justice, and the health of our planet seem so much more urgent.
- It is easy for the young to be impatient with the slow pace of arriving at agreements.

Despite these difficulties, Christians who are not part of the theological dialogue can still make a contribution to the ecumenical movement. Here are some suggestions:

1. **Study the scriptures.** The scriptures are the foundation of Christian life and of the Christian churches. Prayerful reading of the Bible is food for life, growth, and mutual understanding. Christians can also read the Bible with those who have studied it and who can help them to understand it.

"Jesus longed that 'all may be one.'"
(John 17:21)

A Closer Look

Interchurch marriages (between Catholics and other baptized persons) challenge couples to live authentically within their own Christian traditions. The Church sees value in these marriages because of the contribution they can make to the ecumenical movement.

Both Catholic and non-Catholic clergy should be involved in preparing engaged couples for marriage. Elements of both traditions can be used in the ceremony.

Kairos Canada. Kairos is a Canadian ecumenical organization dedicated to social justice concerns such as HIV/AIDS, Aboriginal rights and other human rights issues, and environmental and economic issues. It responds to the call to "do justice, and to love kindness and to walk humbly with your God" (Micah 6:8). **On what specific issues in the news do you think Christians could work together?**

2. **Pray always.** Especially pray the Lord's Prayer. It contains the heart of prayer. By praying "Your kingdom come, Your will be done on Earth as it is in heaven," Christians pray for what Jesus prayed for: the unity of those who follow him. Another way to pray for unity is to take part in the Week of Prayer for Christian Unity, celebrated around the world from January 18 to 25 every year.
3. **Bring people together.** Always be hospitable. Never exclude anyone. Always be in solidarity with the poor and the oppressed. Be a friend to all.
4. **Take part in local ecumenical activities.** Activities involving Catholics and other Christian groups (for example, ecumenical meetings, retreats, or volunteering for causes) can enrich dialogue and help build understanding.
5. **Visit churches.** Talk to people who belong, find out what they believe, how they worship, and how they live.

Check Your Understanding

1. Why is ecumenical dialogue challenging?
2. Write a "to do" list summarizing what Christians can do to promote Christian unity.

Think About It

3. Imagine that Joe and Jen have decided to get married. Their families are happy to see them marry and start a family. There is only one concern: Jen belongs to a Pentecostal community, and Joe is Catholic. Both families want the wedding to be held in their own church. Jen's father is threatening not to walk her down the aisle if the wedding is in a Catholic church. In a small group, discuss the situation and what advice you would give the families.

Making It Personal

4. Describe a time in which you have seen two people reconcile with each other.

NEL

What I Have Learned

In this chapter, I learned about

- Christians in Canada
- key moments, people, and developments in the history of Christianity
- the relationship between Judaism and Christianity's origins
- symbols and languages of early Christianity
- primary sources and secondary sources as ways to learn about religions
- the foundation stones of Christianity—the work of the Apostles and the creation of the New Testament, the creeds, the ministers of the Church, and Church councils
- the schism between East and West
- the experience of the Middle Ages in Western Christianity
- Protestant movements—including Lutheranism, Calvinism, Anabaptism, Anglicanism, Evangelicalism, Liberalism, Fundamentalism, and Pentecostalism
- the diversity of Christianity, including how it is expressed in the physical churches
- the ecumenical movement today and the challenges of working toward unity

The Maasai Creed

We believe in the one High God, who out of love created the beautiful world and everything good in it. He created Man and wanted Man to be happy in the world. God loves the world and every nation and tribe on the Earth. We have known this High God in darkness, and now we know Him in the light. God promised in the book of His word, the Bible, that He would save the world and all the nations and tribes.

We believe that God made good His promise by sending His Son, Jesus Christ, a man in the flesh, a Jew by tribe, born poor in a little village, who left His home and was always on safari doing good, curing people by the power of God, teaching about God and Man, showing the meaning of religion is love. He was rejected by His people, tortured and nailed hands and feet to a cross, and died. He lay buried in the grave, but the hyenas did not touch Him, and on the third day, He rose from the grave. He ascended to the skies. He is the Lord.

We believe that all our sins are forgiven through Him. All who have faith in Him must be sorry for their sins, be baptized in the Holy Spirit of God, live the rules of love and share the bread together in love, to announce the Good News to others until Jesus comes again. We are waiting for Him. He is alive. He lives. This we believe. Amen.

Chapter 6 The Story of Islam

The Shahadah. This image of the Shahadah was carved into a mosque built in Granada, Spain. The Shahadah is the two-sentence creed for Muslims. It emphasizes the unity of Allah (God) and the importance of the prophet Muhammad. It is translated as "I bear witness that there is no God but Allah. And I bear witness that Muhammad is the Messenger of Allah." **If you could sum up your beliefs about God into a one- or two-sentence statement, what would the statement be?**

"In the name of Allah, the Compassionate, the Merciful.
Praise be to Allah, the Lord of the Worlds.
The Compassionate, the Merciful, Master of the Day of Judgment.
Only You do we worship, and only You do we implore for help.
Lead us to the right path,
The path of those You have favoured
Not those who have incurred Your wrath or who have gone astray."

(Qur'an, Sura 1, Al-Fatiha)

What You Will Learn

In this chapter, you will learn about

- Islam in the world and in Canada
- Muhammad and the history of Islam
- the ritual life of Muslims based on the Five Pillars
- the Muslim marking of time through the Five Pillars
- the Muslim community
- Muslim beliefs as found in the Qur'an
- Muslim morality, particularly shariah law
- Muslim family life
- Catholic–Muslim encounters

Personal Recollection

My earliest memory of being a **Muslim** was the Eid ul-Adha. On this feast, Ibrahim's dedication to God is celebrated by sacrificing an animal, usually a lamb, a cow, or a camel. This story of Ibrahim is one of the first stories I remember from childhood, and is often told on Eid. We dressed in our finest clothes and had a wonderful party.

Another memory of mine is fasting, which I started by choice when I was nine. My first fast was a huge day for me, because I felt that I was truly involved in something that only "grown-up" Muslims do. The party thrown for me because I started fasting was also a huge reward.

— **Alya Ahsan**

Muslim
A believer in Islam

Fast Fact

"Ibrahim" is the Arabic form of the Hebrew name Abraham. Abraham is an important figure in Judaism, Christianity, and Islam.

Women and Girls Praying at a Mosque Service. Daily prayer is an important spiritual ritual for Muslims around the world.

Islam in Canada

Muslim Men and Boys at Friday Prayer. Muslims do not separate their religion from the rest of their lives. **Islam is central to every facet of daily life. How central is your faith to your daily life?**

Muslims are becoming an increasingly important part of Canadian culture. They are among the fastest-growing religious groups in Canada. Much of this growth comes from new immigrants. Fewer than half of the 650 000 Muslims living in Canada were born here. Canadian Muslims come from all over the world—from India and Pakistan, from Arab and Middle Eastern countries, and from more than 30 other nations.

According to 2001 census data, most Canadian Muslims live in urban centres, such as the Greater Toronto Area. Sixty-one percent of Canadian Muslims live in Ontario. In the 1990s, the number of Muslims in Canada doubled. Rapid growth was expected to continue into the first part of the twenty-first century.

Being Muslim in Canada has its challenges. Many Muslims feel that the media has portrayed them and their faith in a negative light, especially since the attacks on the World Trade Center in New York City on September 11, 2001. They feel that the richness, goodness, and wisdom within their tradition have benefited the world in the past and can contribute to Canadian and global culture in the future.

The History of Islam

Islam around the World

There are about 1.5 billion Muslims in the world, making Islam the second-largest religion worldwide. Only Christianity, with about 2.1 billion members, has more followers.

Muslims come from different parts of the world and have diverse cultural practices. As is the case for Judaism, Christianity, and other world religions, we cannot speak of a single Muslim culture. Islam is sometimes associated with Arab culture. This view is misleading. Many countries with large Muslim populations also have distinct non-Arabic cultures. Islam is a religion that includes Africans from Nigeria, Europeans from Albania, Arabs from Iraq, and southern Asians from Pakistan and Indonesia, as well as many more ethnic and cultural groups.

NEL

Muslims around the World

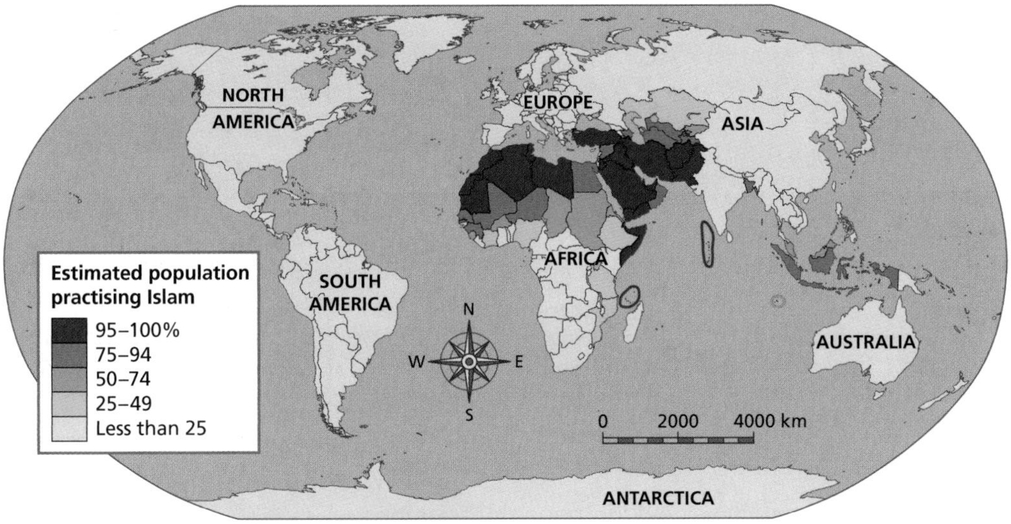

Muslims around the World. This map shows where Muslims live around the globe. Although Islam is centred in the Middle East, it extends into North Africa and Southeast Asia. The largest Muslim population lives in Indonesia. Today, Muslims live in every major urban area in the world. In Europe and North America they are a minority, but their numbers are growing faster than those of most other faiths.

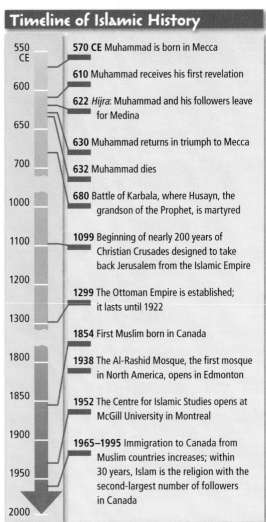

Timeline of Islamic History

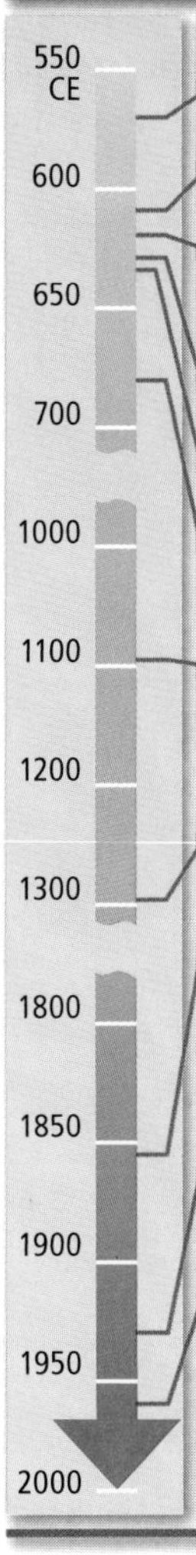

570 CE Muhammad is born in Mecca

610 Muhammad receives his first revelation

622 *Hijra*: Muhammad and his followers leave for Medina

630 Muhammad returns in triumph to Mecca

632 Muhammad dies

680 Battle of Karbala, where Husayn, the grandson of the Prophet, is martyred

1099 Beginning of nearly 200 years of Christian Crusades designed to take back Jerusalem from the Islamic Empire

1299 The Ottoman Empire is established; it lasts until 1922

1854 First Muslim born in Canada

1938 The Al-Rashid Mosque, the first mosque in North America, opens in Edmonton

1952 The Centre for Islamic Studies opens at McGill University in Montreal

1965–1995 Immigration to Canada from Muslim countries increases; within 30 years, Islam is the religion with the second-largest number of followers in Canada

Check Your Understanding

1. List some countries in which large numbers of Muslims can be found.

Think About It

2. Why is it important to study Islam? What ideas can you draw from the information in this section?

Making It Personal

3. What are the benefits and challenges of living in a multicultural country such as Canada?
4. If a Muslim family were to move next door to you, what questions would you have about their faith? What questions might a Muslim neighbour have about your faith?

A Closer Look

Although people in Europe and the countries of the Western hemisphere often describe Muhammad as the founder of Islam, Muslim scholars disagree. They claim that Islam was the original religion and that there was no human founder.

These scholars believe that Islam was the earliest religion and that it was incompletely revealed to these other religions. Muslims consider Muhammad to be the last, or the Seal, of all the prophets God sent to all humanity. He is the final Messenger who received the definitive and fully completed religion: Islam.

Muhammad and the Origins of Islam

Muhammad was born more than five centuries after Jesus in what is now Saudi Arabia. Muhammad has had a great influence on our world. To understand his impact, we must begin by exploring the culture into which Muhammad was born.

Mecca at the Time of Muhammad's Birth

In the seventh century, the Arabian Peninsula was an overlooked zone in the battle between the Roman and Persian empires. Its harsh desert, with only a few settlements around oases, was largely ignored. The people who lived there included Jews, Christians, and nomadic tribes, ruled by clans, who were **polytheists**.

Mecca became one of the desert settlements because it had a spring. At the time of Muhammad's birth, Mecca was the site of an annual pilgrimage to the *Kaaba*: a cube-shaped structure that held 360 deities. Islamic tradition holds the Kaaba to be the house of **Allah**. According to this tradition, the Kaaba is the centre of Earth—the point at which God's creation began, directly below God's throne in heaven.

Arabian Peninsula

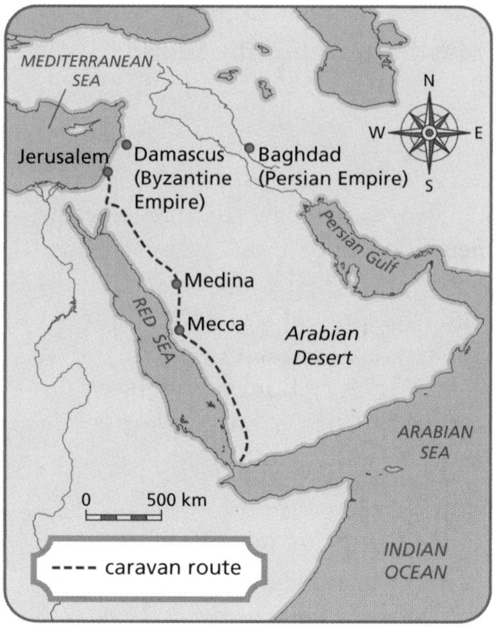

The Arabian Peninsula at the Time of Muhammad. How does this map compare with a current map of the area?

The Kaaba was sent down from heaven and rebuilt by the prophet Abraham and his son Ishmael. Later, the Kaaba was taken over by polytheists, who established the 360 deities there. In 630 CE, Muhammad restored the Kaaba by cleansing it of the deities, leaving only the house.

Polytheist

A believer in more than one god

Allah

Arabic word for God; Muslims worship the same God as Christians and Jews, but some of the revelations are interpreted differently. The word "Allah" is a unique word because it is genderless. It is neither masculine nor feminine.

The Kaaba. The Kaaba in Mecca is the destination of an annual Muslim pilgrimage called the hajj. Set in the southeast corner of the Kaaba is a black stone that is said to have been sent from heaven. Pilgrims touch or kiss the stone as an act of respect as they walk around the Kaaba seven times.

Muhammad's Early Life

Muhammad was born in the city of Mecca in 570 CE. His parents died while he was still very young, and he grew up under the protection of his clan, particularly his uncle, Abu Talib. Muslim tradition says that Muhammad had a harsh life and came to understand the fierce allegiance that **Bedouin** nomads had to their clans. Abu Talib was a trader and Muhammad travelled with him throughout Arabia and neighbouring countries. As a trader, Muhammad earned the title "the trustworthy one" and "the righteous one."

Mount Hira. Mount Hira, near Mecca, is the site of Muhammad's first revelation.

Bedouin

A nomadic or wandering tribesperson of the Arabian, Syrian, or North African deserts

Muhammad Receives the Qur'an

Because of his reputation as an honest trader, Muhammad was hired as a caravan manager by a wealthy widow, Khadijah, who proposed marriage to him. Their happy marriage produced six children.

Muhammad was deeply troubled by the inequalities in Meccan society, where many people were exploited by clans' richer members. He never accepted the multitude of gods worshipped at the Kaaba. For him, there was only one God. When he worshipped at the Kaaba, Muhammad devoted his prayers to Allah.

Muhammad would often retreat to a mountain cave on nearby Mount Hira to meditate. There, in 610 CE, he received a revelation. There are several versions of the story of Muhammad's first revelation. According to the best-known version, the Angel Gabriel visited him and commanded him to begin reciting.

The Angel Gabriel uttered the direct words of Allah to Muhammad while he was in a state of ecstasy so that he would later be able to recall the exact words. Until his death in 632 CE, Muhammad continued to receive these revelations. The sayings of Muhammad were recorded and collected in the Qur'an after his death.

Qur'an Calligraphy. This photograph shows an Arabic passage from the Qur'an.

Fast Fact

"Qur'an" means "recitation" or "reading" in Arabic. The Qur'an is the book in which Allah's revelations to Muhammad are recorded.

Check Your Understanding

1. Describe the culture into which Muhammad was born.
2. What were the key events in Muhammad's early life?

Think About It

3. Why might someone become known as a righteous or trustworthy person during Muhammad's time?

Making It Personal

4. What are some of the challenges you face in your search for your path in life?
5. What are three injustices in your community that you would like to correct?

A Closer Look

One of the early converts to Islam was Abu Bakr, a close friend and confidant of Muhammad. After Muhammad's death, Abu Bakr became the first *caliph*, or leader, of the Muslim community. His two-year rule as caliph included the conquest of the lands that are now Syria and Iraq.

Hijra

Arabic word meaning "migration"

Struggles in Mecca

Muhammad's first convert to Islam was his first wife, Khadijah. Few people converted to Islam in those early years between 610 CE and 622 CE. Revelations became less frequent, and Muhammad's novel ideas caused resentment among Meccans.

For example, Muhammad preached that "God is One," that all must surrender to Allah alone, and that he, Muhammad, was the Messenger of Allah. This teaching was not welcome news to the merchants of Mecca. Their business relied on the pilgrims who travelled to Mecca to honour the gods of the Kaaba. Even Muhammad's own tribe, the Quraysh, the protectors of the Kaaba, turned against him, until he had no protectors left in Mecca and his life was in danger.

Hijra

In 622 CE, something happened that was so important for Islam that it marks the beginning of the Muslim calendar. The people of Medina offered Muhammad a place to settle and protection from persecution. Life had become more difficult for Muslims in Mecca, so Muhammad led the people of Islam north. This migration from Mecca to the community of Medina became known as the ***hijra***.

Medina would be Muhammad's home for the rest of his life. There he set up his first community. It was governed by the things he was told in his revelations. Like Mecca, Medina was an oasis town with a large Jewish population.

Because his revelations were similar to the prophetic vision of the Jews, Muhammad tried to create bonds with the Jewish people. When the Jews in Medina opposed his views, he changed the direction of prayer from Jerusalem to Mecca. During this time, the revelations continued and Muhammad's spiritual understanding grew deeper.

Return to Mecca

Many Meccans had joined Muhammad in Medina. The Meccans who remained in the city fought back, but were defeated. This led to further battles,

The Dome of the Rock. The Dome of the Rock is an Islamic monument built in Jerusalem between 685 and 691 CE, half a century after the death of Muhammad. It is the oldest existing Islamic building in the world. Here, the Dome of the Rock gleams in the Jerusalem sunshine. According to Muslim tradition, the Dome marks the place where Muhammad is thought to have risen into heaven on a winged horse. Nearby is the Western Wall of the Temple, a sacred site for Jews (shown at the bottom of this photo). Within a kilometre of these holy places are Christian places of worship marking the sites of the crucifixion and resurrection of Jesus.

but eventually Muhammad negotiated a truce with the Meccans in 628 CE. When the Meccans later broke the truce, Muhammad marched on Mecca with a large force. The Meccans, outnumbered, surrendered without a fight in 630 CE. Mecca accepted Islam and Muhammad gave amnesty (pardon) to all. With the conflict resolved, Muhammad returned to Medina.

Muhammad decided in 632 CE to perform one final pilgrimage to Mecca. By doing so, he transformed this ritual into a Muslim celebration known as the ***hajj***. In his final sermon on this hajj, Muhammad spoke a message of justice and equality. He said, "There is no superiority for an Arab over a non-Arab nor for a non-Arab over an Arab, neither for a white man over a black man nor a black man over a white man except the superiority gained through consciousness of God ..."

Hajj

Arabic word meaning "pilgrimage"; the pilgrimage to Mecca that Muslims are asked to make at least once in their lifetime, if they are healthy and can afford it

The Plain of Arafat. The Plain of Arafat is the site of Muhammad's last sermon on justice and equality. Passing through the plain is part of the hajj. **How is Muhammad's last sermon similar to Jesus's Sermon on the Mount?**

Check Your Understanding

1. Why did Muhammad leave Mecca?
2. What message did Muhammad give at his final sermon?
3. How did Muhammad establish Islam as the dominant religion in Arabia?

Think About It

4. What policies would you recommend be put in place to ensure that followers of Judaism, Christianity, and Islam can worship at the shared sites of their shrines in peace?

Making It Personal

5. Is violence in pursuit of justice ever justified? Explain.
6. What values of Muhammad's do you admire? Why?

Islam after Muhammad

The Expansion of Islam

When Muhammad died, Abu Bakr became the Muslim leader or caliph. Islam spread rapidly through Arabia. Further expansion brought Muslims into conflict with two empires: the Persian Sassanid Empire to the east and the Christian Byzantine Empire to the north. Both empires were in decline. They were unable to resist many of the Muslim advances into their territory. By 637 CE, Muslims occupied Jerusalem. They held it until 1967, except for a short time during the Christian Crusades.

Muslim expansion was fuelled by the conviction that they were spreading the message of Islam. Yet Muslim rulers generally did not force conquered people to convert to Islam. They allowed Christian and Jewish communities to exist. Within 150 years of Muhammad's death, Islam had spread westward across northern Africa to Spain, and as far east as central Asia.

Shi'ite and Sunni

Because people could not agree on who should succeed Muhammad, very early on Islam split into two groups: **Shi'ite** Muslims and **Sunni** Muslims. Some Muslims did not want Abu Bakr to be the new leader. Ali, a cousin of Muhammad's, thought that he should have succeeded Muhammad because he was directly related. When Ali finally succeeded, he reigned as caliph for only five years. He was killed by an assassin in Iraq in 661 CE.

After Ali's death, his followers accepted his son Hussein as his successor. Ali's followers chose their leaders based on their blood relationship to Muhammad. Muslims who follow this branch of Islam are called Shi'ite.

Many other Muslims disagreed with the idea that their leaders had to be directly descended from Muhammad. They thought that the person best suited to the position should lead the Muslim community. Muslims who follow this branch of Islam are called Sunni.

Besides disagreeing about who should lead the Muslim world, Sunnis and Shi'ites differ in some beliefs and practices. Sunnis emphasize individuals' direct relationship with Allah, without any human mediator. Shi'ites place greater emphasis on the role of individual leaders and the authority of religious leaders. Today, about 90 percent of Muslims are Sunni, and about 10 percent are Shi'ite. Some other Muslim groups exist, but they are very few in number.

Shi'ite

Muslims who believe that leadership of the Muslim community should be passed down through the direct descendants of the Prophet; Shi'ites form the majority of the population in Iraq and Iran

Sunni

Muslims who believe that community leaders do not have to be descended from the Prophet. The name Sunni comes from Sunna, which is a collection of the words, actions, and practices of Muhammad, as taken down and transmitted by his inner circle of family and friends. Sunnis make up the majority of the world's Muslim population.

The Expansion of Islam

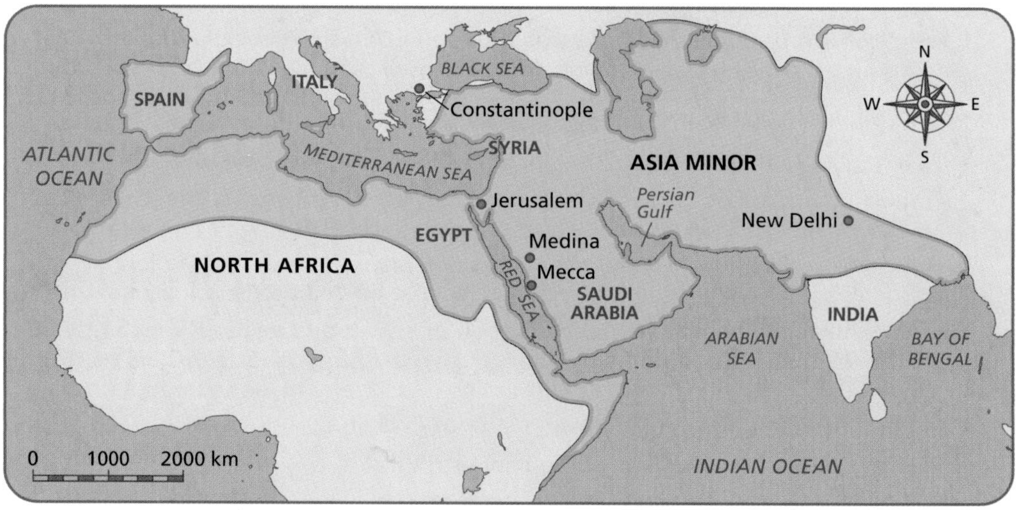

Map of the Expansion of Islam. What modern-day countries were part of the Islamic Empire as it expanded after Muhammad's death, from 632 CE to the early eighth century?

Make It Your Own: Important Muslim Sites

Throughout the world there are many important Muslim sites.

Important Muslim Sites

Site	Location	Description
The Kaaba and other important hajj sites	Mecca, Saudi Arabia	Muslims face the Kaaba in Mecca when praying. The Kaaba is also the focal point of the hajj, the fifth pillar of Islam.
Mosque of the Prophet	Medina, Saudi Arabia	Muhammad lived the last few years of his life on the site where this mosque was later built. He is also buried here.
Dome of the Rock and the al-Aqsa Mosque	Jerusalem	From this site, according to the Qur'an, Muhammad travelled to heaven during a mystical experience.
Shrine of Hussein (Ali's son)	Karbala, Iraq	This is the site on which Hussein, grandson of Muhammad, died in battle. For many Shi'ite Muslims, this event represents a turning point in their history.
Meshed Ali	Najaf, Iraq	This shrine marks the grave of Ali, who is the true heir of Muhammad, according to Shi'ite tradition.
Blue Mosque	Istanbul, Turkey	With its cascading domes, this seventeenth-century mosque is regarded by many as one of the world's most beautiful buildings.
Taj Mahal	Agra, India	Shah Jahan, a Muslim emperor of India, built this as an elaborate memorial (mausoleum) to his wife, Mumtaz Muhal.

Activity

1. Locate these sites on a map. Find photos of the sites and draw or paste them onto the map. What architectural features do they share?

Check Your Understanding

1. What are the origins of the differences between Sunni and Shi'ite Muslims?

Think About It

2. What were some significant events in Muslim history after Muhammad's death? Explain your choice of events.

Making It Personal

3. How do you deal with differences among members of your religion?

Rituals

The Five Pillars of Islam

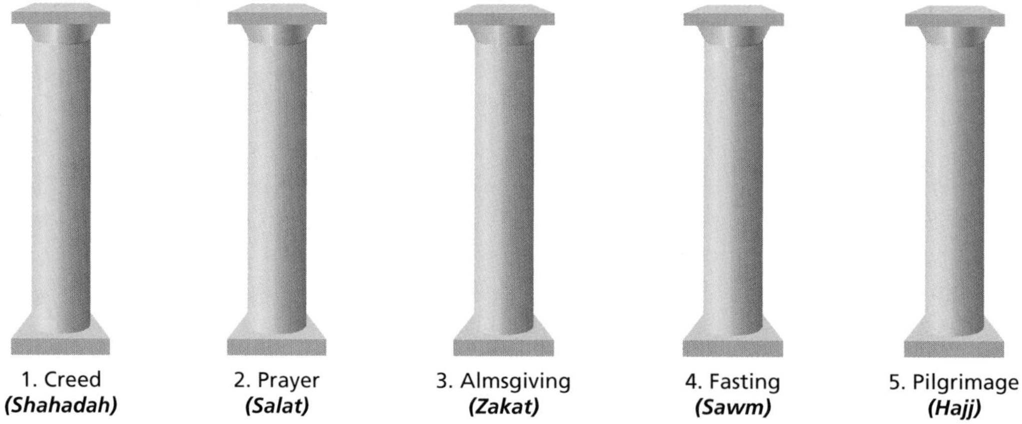

The Five Pillars. The Five Pillars are the duties that all Muslims are expected to observe.

Catholic Connection

In Catholicism, the main ritual is the celebration of the Eucharist. This is the Church's central service of thanksgiving for God's saving actions in human history, especially in the life, death, and resurrection of Jesus. The Eucharist is the source and summit of the Church's life and mission.

Fast Fact

The Shahadah ("There is no God but Allah") echoes the first part of the Shema in Deuteronomy 6:4: "Hear, O Israel! The Lord is our God, the Lord is one!"

The Flag of Saudi Arabia. The flag of Saudi Arabia features the Shahadah written on a green background. Green is the traditional colour of Islam. **Can you think of any other flags that include symbols of the country's main religion?**

The Five Pillars of Islam

As Islam spread to other nations, Muslim theologians wanted to ensure that new converts understood how to perform the rituals by which Muslims express their faith and identify themselves as Muslim. These rituals are known as the Five Pillars of Islam and are the main ritual acts of the Muslim faith.

The Five Pillars describe in practical terms how Muslims are to worship, or what it means to be a Muslim. They aim to help believers to state in word and in action that they are members of the Muslim community.

The First Pillar: Creed

The *Shahadah* is the Muslim profession of faith: "There is no God but Allah, and Muhammad is the Messenger of Allah." This is the underlying belief of Islam. There is only one God. No one and nothing should be worshipped but Allah. For Muslims, Muhammad is the final Messenger of God. The Shahadah is the sign of belonging to the Muslim community. A person need only say it aloud before two witnesses to be legally considered a Muslim.

The Second Pillar: Prayer

The second pillar of Islam is *salat*, the ritual prayer of praise and adoration of God that Muslims are required to say five times a day. *Salat* involves both quiet verbal prayer and gestures, such as standing with the hands either folded on the chest or stomach, or hanging loose on each side, bowing with the hands on the knees, sitting upright and kneeling with the hands and forehead on the ground.

Whenever possible, Muslims try to attend a place of worship for their prayers. But, prayer can take place at home, at work, or anywhere, as long as the place is clean. Many Muslim travellers and workers carry a prayer mat for such purposes. On Fridays, Muslims attend mosque for prayer.

As well as praying five times daily at specified times and with others at the mosque, Muslims can also pray privately throughout the day. These prayers are called *du'a*.

NEL

Worshipping at the Mosque

I am a Christian. When I was living in Palestine, a friend invited me to join him in worship at the **mosque**. The little mosque we went to is truly a centre of community worship. The local barber is also the ***imam***.

The men warmly welcomed me into their community. They showed me how to perform the prayer gestures. But, one of the men warned me, "You can't be a Muslim one day and a Christian the next." Another suggested that when I prayed, in the words of the Qur'an, "Guide us into the straight path," I was asking to be guided into the way of Islam.

When it came time to say the Shahadah, the Muslim creed—"I bear witness that there is no God but Allah. And I bear witness that Muhammad is the Messenger of Allah."—I was faced with a dilemma. I needed to be clear about where I stood. After all, reciting the Shahadah is how a person converts to Islam.

I know that God is one, but I also believe that God was in Christ. I suddenly realized that I could not say the Shahadah and remain true to myself.—*Les Miller*

Salat

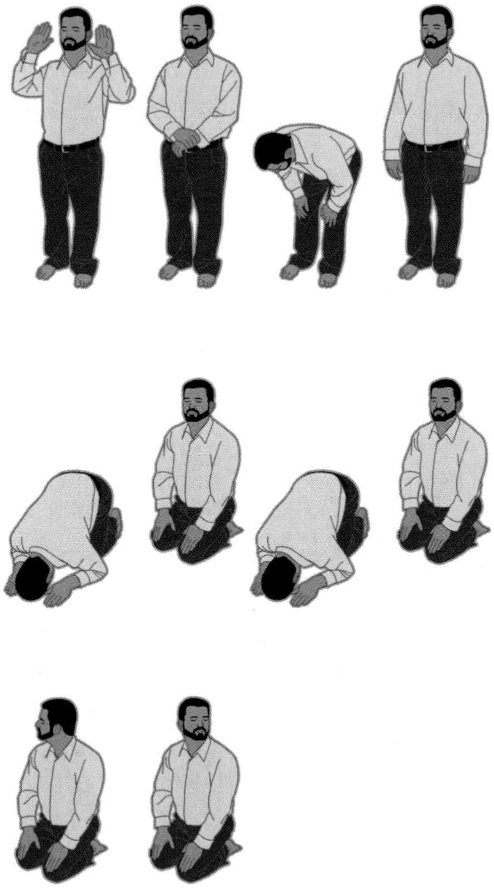

Salat. *Salat* involves moving through various prayer positions while saying quiet prayers. **What gestures do you use when you pray?**

Muslim Prayer. A young Muslim girl recites prayers. Catholics, too, often pray using words. **How else can they communicate with God?**

Mosque

A place where Muslims gather for group worship

Imam

A Muslim leader of prayer and giver of sermons in the mosque

Fast Fact

Prayer is always said facing the holy city of Mecca. Mosques are built or altered so that believers can easily find the correct direction.

Catholic Connection

Catholics, too, are urged to pray when alone. During the Sermon on the Mount, Jesus said, "But when you pray, go into your room and shut the door and pray to your Father who is in secret: and your Father who sees in secret will reward you" (Matthew 6:6).

Catholic Connection

Catholics also practise almsgiving: "Among all these [Works of Mercy], giving alms to the poor is one of the chief witnesses to fraternal charity: it is also a work of justice pleasing to God" (*Catechism of the Catholic Church*, #2447).

Orphanage in Kabul. Children at an orphanage in Kabul, Afghanistan, have their lunch. Orphanages such as this one are supported by *zakat*.

Zakat

The Muslim obligation to pay 2.5 percent of one's wealth to the needy

The Third Pillar: Almsgiving

Zakat, the third pillar of Islam, asks believers to give to those in need. Each year, Muslims who have more than a certain amount of money or goods are required to donate a portion of their savings, after debt, to the needy, to help build mosques, or to similar causes. This pillar helps to share wealth in a Muslim society more fairly.

The Fourth Pillar: Fasting

The fourth pillar is fasting (*sawm*), which takes place during the month of Ramadan, the month in which Muhammad first received the divine message of Allah. Since it also marks the beginning of the Qur'an, people are encouraged to spend more time reading the Qur'an and praying.

During the daylight hours of Ramadan, Muslims are expected to abstain from food, water, evil thoughts, drinking, smoking, and sex. (The sick, the elderly, pregnant women, and children may be excused from fasting.) On the evenings of Ramadan, families and friends gather to break the day's fast with a light meal and some merriment.

Ramadan ends with the three-day Feast of Eid al-Fitr, often called the Festival of the Breaking of the Fast. The festival is marked by special family meals and gift giving.

Eid al-Fitr. A family prepares for the Eid al-Fitr festival by weaving palm leaves. A special delicacy will be placed on the palm leaves for the celebrations.

Catholic Connection

Catholics are asked to observe the days of fasting and abstinence set by the Church (for example, Ash Wednesday and Good Friday). Fasting is the practice of eating less food than usual. Abstinence means avoiding certain foods: specifically, meat. This time of denial and penance helps prepare Catholics for the liturgical feasts and helps them to acquire mastery over their instincts and freedom of heart (*Catechism of the Catholic Church*, #2043). In Canada, Catholics are called to treat every Friday as a day of abstinence, or to replace it with another form of penance (for example, prayer or almsgiving).

NEL

The Fifth Pillar: Pilgrimage

The fifth ritual act of Islam is required only once in a lifetime: a pilgrimage—called hajj— to the Kaaba in Mecca. Only those Muslims who can afford to make the pilgrimage without causing hardship to their dependants or whose health allows are expected to do so.

Hajj is the supreme experience for Muslims. Those who have made the pilgrimage may add *"haji"* to their names. Hajj is the largest annual pilgrimage in the world. The hajj is filled with symbolic rituals that recall events from the time of Abraham and Muhammad. Hajj is seen as a time when Muslims should particularly strive to live honest and holy lives and to focus their minds on Allah. Through the hajj, Muslims strengthen their sense of unity with God, with their religious heritage, and with other Muslims.

Faithfulness to the Five Pillars reveals a Muslim's devotion to God. Each pillar is a form of worship. Each pillar reminds believers what it means to surrender to God.

Pilgrimage Clothing

On their way to Mecca, pilgrims must put on special clothing called *ihram.* Men are expected to wear two seamless garments made from white cloth. Women wear clothes that conceal their bodies and hair, leaving their faces and hands uncovered. *Ihram* has two aims: to emphasize equality and to remind pilgrims that in death they will leave behind all material things.

***Haji* Painting.** Many Muslims celebrate making the hajj by painting images, especially of Kaaba, on their homes. This painting by a *haji*, or pilgrim to Mecca, appears on the outside wall of an Egyptian man's home. **How do you or your family mark your special religious observances? Do you display religious images?**

Catholic Connection

Pilgrimage is a part of almost every world religion. Catholics, like Muslims and Jews, visit certain places (called shrines, such as the Martyrs' Shrine in Midland, Ontario; Lac Ste. Anne in Alberta; and Ste-Anne-de-Beaupré in Québec) thought to have been touched in a special way by God, Mary, or the saints.

***Ihram*.** Pilgrims on the hajj are dressing in *ihram.*

The Kaaba

At the heart of hajj is the Kaaba, the cube-shaped shrine in the centre of the Great Mosque in Mecca. The Kaaba is the holiest place for Muslims. On entering the Great Mosque, pilgrims circle the Kaaba seven times, to symbolize the seven times that Ibrahim circled it.

Pilgrims at the Great Mosque in Mecca. Pilgrims at the Masjid al-Haram Mosque, the initial focal point of the hajj. The Kaaba is in the centre of the mosque. About 3 million pilgrims will pass through here during the annual hajj.

Check Your Understanding

1. Imagine that you must explain the importance of the Five Pillars to a friend who knows very little about Islam. What key points would you like your friend to understand?

Think About It

2. What challenges does living as a practising Muslim pose for someone living in our world?

Making It Personal

3. If you were to go on pilgrimage, where would you go? Why?

NEL

Marking Time

The Five Pillars and Festivals

Besides providing guidelines for worship, the Five Pillars also guide Muslims on how to order their time. Although each day is determined by the rising and setting of the Sun, the month is measured by the Moon.

1. The profession of faith (Shahadah). All of daily life is permeated with this profession of faith in God as One.
2. The *salat* ritual prayer creates the rhythm of daily life. It occurs five times daily.
3. The fast of Ramadan is held in the lunar month named after the fast. Because Ramadan is measured in lunar time, each year it is celebrated 10 days earlier than the previous year. The completion of the fast is marked with a major festival, called the Festival of the Breaking of the Fast (Eid al-Fitr or the Minor Eid).
4. The hajj pilgrimage to the Kaaba in Mecca is done in a particular lunar month—the first 15 days of *Dhu'l-Hijja*, the month of pilgrimages. During the hajj, the Festival of Sacrifice (Eid ul-Adha or Major Eid) is celebrated.

On Eid ul-Adha, the sacrifice of Ibrahim (Abraham) is commemorated. Ibrahim was commanded to sacrifice his son as a test of faith. However, the Qur'an does not say which one of his sons, Isaac or Ishmael, was to be sacrificed. In the Muslim tradition, the son is understood to be Ishmael, not Isaac.

The Crescent Moon and the Eid. The sighting of the crescent new Moon signals the beginning of the feast of Eid al-Fitr. During the morning of Eid, Muslim families perform a special prayer in the early hours of the morning just after sunrise, then share a small meal to symbolize the end of Ramadan.

Eid al-Fitr Prayers. These Muslim women are offering Eid al-Fitr prayers. They have removed their shoes and are performing *salat* on a prayer mat. They use a mat to ensure that they are praying in a clean space.

Make It Your Own: The Star and Crescent Moon

The Star and Crescent Moon. The star and the crescent moon make up the unofficial symbol of Muslims. This symbol is found on flags of many Muslim countries, such as on this Turkish flag.

The most widely recognized symbol of Islam is the star and the crescent moon. It is found on the flags of important Muslim countries such as Turkey and Pakistan. It is also seen on the walls of mosques and other Muslim buildings. The star and the crescent moon had been used for centuries as religious symbols in ancient religious traditions from the Middle East. It was not until the Ottomans gained influence over much of Islam over 500 years ago that the symbol became known as a symbol of Islam.

Several reasons have been proposed to explain why the star and the crescent moon have become a symbol for Islam:

- The Moon and stars give light and can help people see their way in the dark at night. Like the Moon and the stars, Islam gives guidance to people in a dark and confusing world.
- The Moon and the stars are heavenly bodies, and so are associated with the dwelling place of Allah.
- Muslims use a lunar calendar, that is, a calendar based on the phases of the Moon. (The Western world uses a solar calendar based on the rotation of Earth around the Sun.)

Activities

1. Draw a large star and crescent moon symbol on a poster. On the symbol, place images of actions that guide us in our lives. Outside the symbol, write words in graffiti form of things that distract people from finding the sacred.
2. Create a collage of images that can be used as symbols to guide people in their lives. For example, you might choose a stop sign to symbolize stopping bad habits that prevent you from making the best of your life. You could also choose a person (for example, your school's patron) or object (a ring) that symbolizes a positive value for you.

Life-Cycle Rituals

Birth

When a child is born, two rituals welcome the baby into the Muslim world. The first sound that the newborn hears is the *adhan*, or call to prayer, spoken into the baby's right ear.

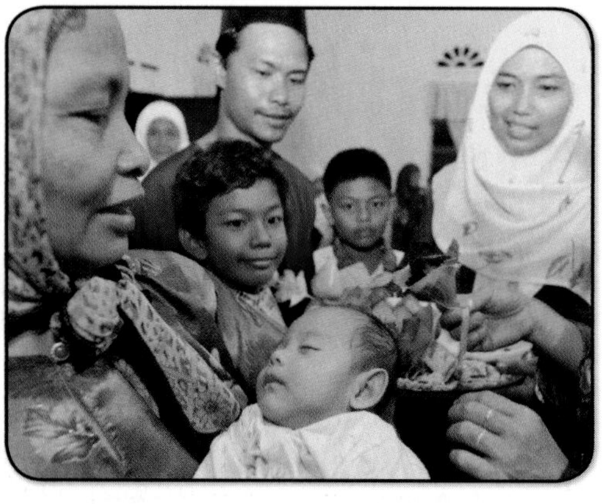

Naming Ceremony. Muslim families give the baby a name and cut some of his or her hair. The event is marked by joyous celebration and acts of charity. **When are Catholics called by name in their rituals?**

A naming ceremony is held in the presence of family and friends, often seven days after birth. Often, as part of this ritual, hair is cut from the baby's head or the head is shaved. The hair is weighed and the equivalent amount in silver is given to the poor.

The naming ceremony (*aqiqa*) is also used as an entrance rite for adults who convert to Islam. Sometimes converts receive an Islamic name in Arabic, but this is not a requirement. For example, the American boxer Cassius Clay took the name "Muhammad Ali" when he converted to Islam in 1964. Muslims believe that males should be circumcised. Often this takes place soon after birth.

Muhammad Ali Praying. Muhammad Ali, boxing heavyweight champion of the world in the 1960s and 1970s, is seen as one of the greatest athletes of the twentieth century.

A Muslim Marriage Ceremony. A cleric reads from the Qur'an to bind the bride and groom in this Muslim marriage ceremony in Indonesia.

Marriage

While some marriage practices can be traced to the actions and sayings of Muhammad, many traditions are a product of the local culture. While the Qur'an allows males to practise polygamy (marriage to more than one wife at a time), most Muslim males in the world today do not. Muhammad, who was himself married, saw polygamy as a way of forming political alliances and protecting widows who would otherwise have no money or support.

In Islam, marriage establishes a deep bond between the families of the bride and groom, as well as between the spouses. For this reason, many marriages are arranged. Islamic law sets the rights and responsibilities not only between the husband and the wife, but also between their families. Although divorce is permitted, it is strongly discouraged.

The wedding (*nikah*) is a simple ceremony. Usually, the wedding consists of reading from the Qur'an and the exchange of vows in front of witnesses for both partners. Often the leader of the mosque performs the ceremony.

Catholic Connection

The Islamic viewpoint on divorce, which discourages divorce but still allows it, differs from the Catholic view, which sees marriage as permanent. This view applies the words of Jesus: "What God has joined together, let no one separate" (Matthew 19:6).

Henna. Many Muslims from the Indian subcontinent decorate their hands and feet with henna in preparation for feasts such as Eid al-Fitr or for marriage celebrations.

Death

Just as the first thing a newborn baby hears is the call to prayer, the last words on the lips of a dying Muslim should be the Shahadah, the proclamation of faith. After the person dies, the corpse is washed, covered, and buried as soon as possible. The body is buried with the face toward Mecca, imitating the direction of prayer. Ritual prayers and memorials are observed at burial and at various times after, as in many other cultures.

Check Your Understanding

1. What are the important features of the Eid al-Fitr?

Think About It

2. How do Muslim life-cycle rituals link Muslims with Muhammad and the Qur'an?

Making It Personal

3. When you were born, what rituals took place?

The Muslim Community (Umma) and the Rituals of the Five Pillars

The Worldwide Community of Islam

The rituals of the Five Pillars help Muslim believers express their membership in the Muslim community, or ***umma***. Unlike Catholicism, Islam does not have a central authority or hierarchy. It has no supreme leader to keep Muslims around the world united. It has no priests. The *imam* is not a priest. Yet Islam knows itself to be a community inspired by God.

As a community, however, Islam is similar to the Catholic Church. Through the community, salvation is achieved. The community is kept alive by the common practice of all believers (for Muslims, the rituals of the Five Pillars). Wherever they live, their faith rituals bind them together. In this way, the community transcends all national, ethnic, racial, and sexual differences.

Umma
The Muslim community

The Mosque

Muslims gather to pray in a mosque. History has it that Muhammad built the first mosque. At the end of his migration (*hijra*) from Mecca to Medina, some villagers in Medina urged him to live under their protection. Muhammad refused their offer. He asked them to let go of the reins of his camel. The freed camel circled an old cemetery, then knelt down, prompting Muhammad to dismount. On that ancient cemetery, tradition says, Muhammad built a house, which also included a mosque. Following the example of Medina, Muslims have built mosques wherever there is a Muslim community that gathers for worship.

NEL

Islamic Centres in Canada. Many Islamic centres in Canada, such as the Islamic Foundation of Toronto in Scarborough, Ontario (shown here), contain a mosque, common spaces, and a community centre. **Why do you think these three functions are combined in one building?**

The Mosque of the Prophet. The second-holiest site in Islam is the Masjid-al-Nabawi (Mosque of the Prophet) in Medina. It is built on the site of the home Muhammad built after he arrived from Mecca in the *hijra* in 622 CE.

Friday Prayer

At Friday prayer (*jumu'ah*), the community gathers soon after midday to worship together. Men perform the Friday prayer together at a mosque. Women may join them or pray at home. After the call to prayer, the *imam* leads the congregation in prayers and gives a sermon that shows how the Qur'an can be applied to everyday life.

Wherever possible, Muslim communities close their businesses and other activities during Friday prayer. In countries such as Canada, where Muslims are a minority, many employers grant Muslim workers' requests for time on Friday to perform these prayers. Many Muslims return to work or school after Friday prayer.

Features of the Mosque

Mosques vary in appearance, size, and building materials, but they all have some common features and routines.

- Five times a day, from the top of a tower beside or in a mosque, Muslims are called to prayer by a prayer caller.
- Worshippers gather and perform ritual washing in an open courtyard before entering the prayer area. There is a place for storing footwear, because shoes are not allowed in the prayer hall. These actions are a sign that outer cleanliness can lead to inner purity.
- The prayer hall's simplicity is striking. There are no benches or chairs, just a large open area, which is usually carpeted. The only decorations are verses from the Qur'an or other sacred phrases written in calligraphy. Sometimes the hall will be divided, with one section for men and one for women. *Salat* involves a lot of movement. It was thought that mixing men and women in these actions could lead to distractions or impure thoughts.
- When praying, Muslims must face the direction of Mecca. This direction is shown by an alcove or recessed area.
- At Friday prayer, an *imam* gives a sermon from the pulpit.

Parts of a Mosque

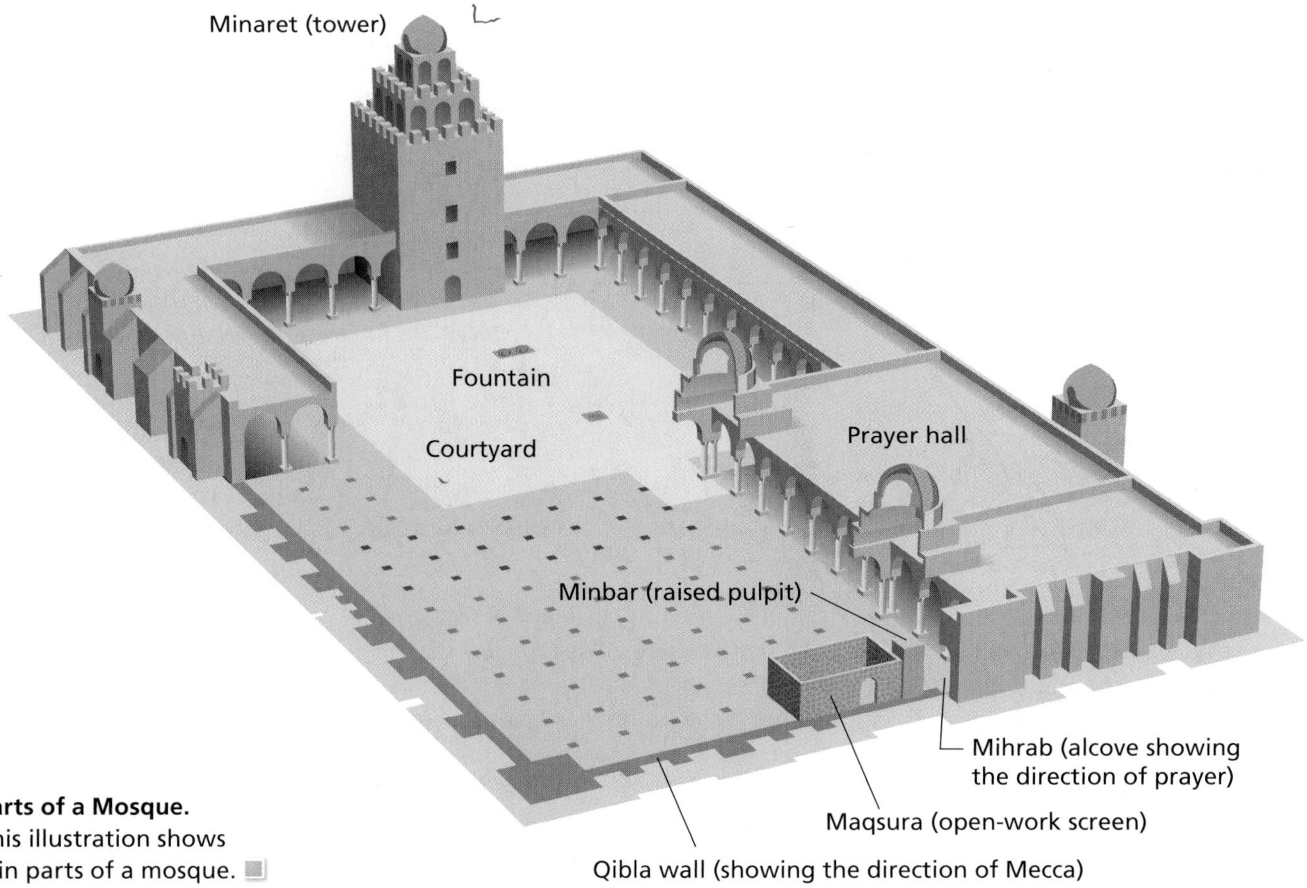

Parts of a Mosque. This illustration shows the main parts of a mosque.

NEL

Check Your Understanding

1. How is a mosque different from a church?
2. Describe the Friday prayer.
3. What is the role of the *imam*?

Think About It

4. Compare and contrast a religious service in the Muslim community and one in the Catholic community.

Making It Personal

5. What makes a place of worship an inviting space for prayer and ritual?
6. Muslims hold prayers on Friday. Jewish people observe the Sabbath on Saturday. Christians worship on Sunday. What are the benefits of setting aside time for spiritual activities?

Central Beliefs

The Qur'an

In the Muslim rituals of the Five Pillars, the first pillar is the Shahadah: "I bear witness that there is no God but Allah. And I bear witness that Muhammad is the messenger of Allah." The Shahadah sums up the Muslim scripture, the Qur'an. For Muslims, this book is the voice of Allah spoken to the Prophet Muhammad by the Angel Gabriel. The Qur'an gives guidance on how to worship, behave, and see the world.

In most Muslim homes, the Qur'an is carefully wrapped to keep it clean. It is placed on the highest piece of furniture in the room and nothing is ever put on top of it. Children start learning prayers and teachings from the Qur'an at a very early age. Most also learn Arabic early so they can read the Qur'an in its original language. Anyone who memorizes the whole of the Qur'an by heart is given the special title of *hafiz*, or "memorizer."

The Qur'an. Because Muslims believe the Qur'an is the direct speech of God in Arabic, translation of the work is seen to weaken the original message. When the Qur'an is recited in prayer and in the mosque, classical Arabic is used.

The Qur'an—A Work of Art. This eighteenth-century copy of the Qur'an has beautiful calligraphy and gold ornamentation but no images. **Why do you think Muslims pay such attention to creating a work of art when they transcribe the Qur'an?**

A Closer Look

Islam recognizes three sets of scriptures as containing partial revelations of Allah's will:

1. The Torah of Moses (the first five books of what Christians call the Old Testament)
2. The Psalms (also in the Old Testament)
3. The Gospels of the New Testament

These are known as the Inspired Books. However, for Muslims, the Suras of the Qur'an represent the final and complete revelation of God.

Organization of the Qur'an

The Qur'an is divided into 114 *Suras*. The Suras are more like chapters than books. The first (The Opening Chapter, Al-Fatiha) is found at the beginning of this chapter. It is very short. Starting with Sura 2, the Suras are generally organized from longest to shortest. Each Sura has a name as well as a number (for example, The Star, The Cow, and The Resurrection), and is divided into verses. Most Suras begin like this: "In the name of Allah, the Compassionate, the Merciful."

The Qur'an is not written in a sequential pattern, where one idea builds on another, like this textbook or like a modern work that tells a story. It is organized more like a piece of classical music, which has repetitive themes and dramatic movements.

The Interpretation of the Qur'an: Sunna and Hadith

The Qur'an, it was originally believed, did not need interpretation. But, after Muhammad's death, as Islam spread rapidly to new countries with different cultures and languages, many Muslims needed help understanding the Qur'an's teachings.

Two sources that complement the Qur'an are the *Sunna* and the *Hadith*. The Sunna is a collection of Muhammad's own words and actions, as recorded by his inner circle of family and friends. For example, if Muhammad taught a prayer or explained a religious practice, his followers memorized and carefully recorded what he said and did. The word "Sunna" means "beaten path"; in other words, it is the customary path that all Muslims should follow.

Like the Sunna, the Hadith is a record of Muhammad's words, actions, and his statements about current religious practices by others (and whether or not he approved of those practices). The Hadith also gives stories about what Muhammad was like in person. However, unlike the Sunna, the Hadith is not based on first-person accounts by Muhammad's inner circle of followers. Some Hadith texts are debated by Islamic scholars to this day.

A Muslim with a problem will look first in the Qur'an and then in the Sunna or Hadith to find what Muhammad said or did in a similar situation. Although the traditions in the Hadith are not as authoritative as the Qur'an, together the three books form the law (called *shariah* in Arabic) for Muslims. There are also other sources for shariah.

Themes in the Qur'an

Recurring themes are woven throughout the Qur'an:

- People need to submit to the will of Allah. The word "Islam" means "to surrender." "Muslim" means "one who surrenders." For Muslims, life is a struggle (*jihad*) to submit to Allah's will. Polytheistic practices (worshipping more than one god) are condemned.

The Qur'an in a Canadian Classroom. A student at the Our Children Our Hope ISNA Elementary School in Mississauga, Ontario, looks through the Qur'an during an Arabic class.

Fast Fact

Here are a few of the 99 names of Allah.

Al-Ghaffar: The Ever-Forgiving

Al-Hakam: The Judge

Al-Wadud: The Loving One

Al-Muhyi: The Giver of Life

Al-Mumit: The Bringer of Death, the Destroyer

Al-Hadi: The Guide

- Allah requires that people pray.
- Allah is beyond easy definition and has many dimensions. Allah is compassionate and merciful. Allah is also a stern judge but is not remote or distant. A deeper understanding of the many dimensions of Allah is revealed in the 99 names of Allah.

Tawhid: The Unity of God

Tawhid is an Islamic term that describes the unity of God. To Muslims, Allah the Almighty is one. Anything that distracts one from this unity, such as money, possessions, nationalism, or reputation, is to be avoided.

The Qur'an describes the nature of God:

> *... He is Allah, the only One,*
> *Allah, the Everlasting.*
> *He did not beget and is not begotten,*
> *And none is his equal.*
>
> (112:1–4)

Allah in Calligraphy. No physical representations of Allah are permitted in Islam, but this calligraphy on a mosque wall in Turkey hints at the reverence Muslims have for Allah. Allah literally means "the God," and is the same God that Christians and Jews believe in.

Catholic Connection

Muslims often recite the 99 names of Allah. Allah's names are his attributes. Catholics know similar practices in litanies. In the Litany of the Saints, they pray to God, Jesus, Mary, and the Catholic saints, asking each to "Pray for us."

Catholic Connection

The *Catechism of the Catholic Church* says that "The mystery of the Most Holy Trinity is the central mystery of Christian faith and life. It is the mystery of God in himself. It is therefore the source of all the other mysteries of faith, the light that enlightens them" (*Catechism of the Catholic Church*, #234).

Catholic Connection

In a meeting with Muslim leaders in Kenya in 1980, Pope John Paul II said, "The Catholic Church realizes that the element of worship given to the one, living, subsistent, merciful and almighty Creator of heaven and earth is common to Islam and herself, and that it is a great link uniting all Christians and Muslims."

Creation and the Qur'an

Many of the Quranic verses portray a view of creation similar to Christian and Jewish ones:

- Since Allah is the Creator of all things, the creation has dignity:

  > *The seven heavens and the earth and what is in them praise Him, and there is nothing which does not celebrate His praise ...*
  >
  > *(17:44)*

  When we violate the dignity of creation, we are harming Allah's work.
- From the beginning, Allah has sent prophets to warn the people to return to paths of justice and mercy. Muslims show their devotion to God by observing Allah's moral commands, by striving personally and publicly to follow God's will, and by doing rituals, including prayer and *zakat.*
- A final judgment and resurrection of the faithful will take place at the end of time.

> *Permission is given to those who fight because they are wronged. Surely Allah is capable of giving them victory.*
>
> *Those who were driven out of their homes unjustly, merely for their saying, "Our Lord is Allah."*
>
> *(22:39–40)*

> *And fight for the cause of Allah those who fight you, but do not be aggressive. Surely Allah does not like the aggressors. (2:189)*

A Closer Look

The Qur'an mentions 25 prophets and indicates that there are more. Most of the prophets are familiar figures from the Hebrew and Christian scriptures, such as Adam, Nuh (Noah), Ibrahim (Abraham), Ya'qub (Jacob), Musa (Moses), Dawud (David), Yahva (John), and 'Isa (Jesus).

Muslim UN Peacekeepers. Muslim United Nations peacekeepers from Indonesia donate blood to the Lebanese Red Crescent organization. Many Muslim countries are involved in peacekeeping around the world. Indonesian peacekeepers have been deployed in Bosnia, Lebanon, and the Sudan. This is one way that jihad can be followed non-violently.

Check Your Understanding

1. In your own words, describe the main themes and messages of the Qur'an.

Think About It

2. How is the Muslim concept of Allah similar to the Christian concept of God? How is it different?
3. How is the Qur'an similar to scriptures from other faiths, for example, the Torah and the Bible? How is it different?

Making It Personal

4. Of the Quranic themes presented above, which one do you agree with most strongly?

A Closer Look

When non-Muslims hear the term "jihad" these days, they may think of a holy war. But jihad literally means "struggle" or "strive," as in "And strive for Allah as you ought to strive" (22:78). A jihad is the struggle to do what is right. It is both an internal struggle toward good, away from evil, and an external struggle striving to correct injustices, using armed force only if necessary.

Despite these restrictions, early Islamic history did involve military conquest. Today, some extremists have carried this aspect of Quranic teachings (permission to fight) to justify aggressive acts against people they see as infidels (non-believers). Many Muslim leaders have spoken out against such violent actions.

The Role of Jesus in Islam

For Muslims, Jesus ('Isa) is a revered prophet who plays a special role in what has happened and what is to come. They accept that Jesus was born of a virgin, Mary (Maryam). According to Muslim sources, after giving birth to Jesus, Mary rested under a palm tree. An angel then spoke to her, telling her to shake the tree to gather its fruits.

Jesus also soothed Mary's fears of a scandal surrounding his conception, saying, "Indeed, I am the servant of Allah, who gave me the Book and made me a Prophet. And He made me blessed wherever I am, and has commanded me to give the alms, so long as I live; and be devoted to my mother" (Qur'an 19:29–32).

The Qur'an speaks favourably of the Gospels, saying that they are a source of guidance and light:

> *... [W]e sent Jesus, the son of Mary, confirming what he had before him of the Torah, and We gave him the Gospel, wherein is guidance and light, confirming what he had before him of the Torah and a guidance and admonition to the God-fearing.* (5:46)

Maryam and 'Isa. This depiction of Maryam (Mary) and the newborn 'Isa (Jesus) illustrates the scene described in 19:23–26 of the Qur'an: "Then labour pangs drove her [Maryam] towards the trunk of a palm tree. She said: 'I wish I had died before this and had become completely forgotten.' Whereupon [a voice] called out to her from beneath her, 'Do not grieve! Your Lord has created below you a stream. Shake the trunk of the palm tree towards you and it will drop upon you fresh, ripe dates. Eat, drink and rejoice....'"

Muslims believe that the Gospels, however, were not transmitted correctly. One distortion has to do with the divinity of Jesus. Muslims believe that Jesus was an important prophet but not the Son of God. Catholics believe that Jesus was both fully human and fully divine.

> *... They neither killed nor crucified him; but it was made to appear so unto them. Indeed, those who differ about him are in doubt about it. Their knowledge does not go beyond conjecture, and they did not kill him for certain; rather, Allah raised him unto Him. Allah is Mighty, and Wise.*
>
> (4:157)

Sufi

A Muslim who uses mysticism to gain a special understanding of Allah that goes beyond rational thought; Sufis can be Sunni or Shi'ite

Muslims believe that another person was substituted for Jesus on the cross, and that Jesus was taken up into heaven, where he lives today. They expect Jesus to return on the Day of Judgment. Jesus will defeat the enemies of Islam: he will die after establishing the Kingdom of God on Earth and be buried in Medina beside Muhammad. At the Day of Judgment, Jesus will rise to bear witness for or against his community.

Sufism

Mystics are people who try to have a deep sense of communion with the divine. Most religious traditions have mystics: St. John of the Cross and St. Teresa of Avila are well-known Christian mystics. Many mystics use prayer and meditation to draw closer to God. They might also use physical self-discipline, such as fasting, to clear their minds.

In Islam, **Sufis** follow this mystical path. One group of Sufis is called whirling dervishes (*Mevlevis*). To create a state of consciousness where they can reach an ecstatic union with the sacred, the mystics gracefully spin around, accompanied by special music. Some conservative Muslims frown on this practice. They believe that released emotions belong to the less noble parts of the human condition.

Whirling Dervishes. Whirling dervishes in Istanbul, Turkey, demonstrate their prayer form. By gracefully turning in circles in rhythm to music, they often achieve a sense of mystical union with the sacred. Today, touring companies visit Canada and other countries to demonstrate this art.

Profile: Rab'ia

Rab'ia was born a century after Muhammad, across the Arabian Desert in what is now southern Iraq. She was a mystic who was devoted to loving Allah. She believed that a person should have the right motivation for devotion. Rab'ia criticized those who prayed to Allah out of fear of punishment or in search of personal spiritual rewards.

In a story told about her, Rab'ia was running through the streets carrying a bucket of water and a flaming torch. When asked what they were for, she said that the bucket was to quench the fires of hell and the torch was to burn down heaven. To explain, she turned to Allah and prayed:

> O Lord, if I worship you out of fear of hell, burn me in hell. If I worship you in the hope of paradise, forbid it to me. And if I worship you for your own sake, do not deprive me of your eternal beauty.

Rab'ia. Rab'ia was a Sufi mystic who lived in Basra, Iraq, in the eighth century CE. Her prayers and stories reflect a deep understanding of the love of Allah.

Check Your Understanding

1. How do Muslims see Jesus?

Think About It

2. What aspects of mysticism might make it attractive to people? Why?

Making It Personal

3. Muslims and Christians have different understandings of Jesus. If you could interview Jesus, what questions would you ask him? What answers would you expect?

4. What might stop you from exploring mystical prayer?

Morality

Shariah. The word "shariah" comes from the Arabic word meaning "a clear path to the oasis." If a person strays off the path in the desert, then his or her life could be in danger. Shariah is the path people follow to avoid moral dangers.

Shariah Law

Shariah, the set of moral rules that Muslims follow, was set out by Allah. This law is intended for individuals and society. It sets the path for Muslims to live a devout life. In a narrower sense, shariah also consists of legal rules that help govern Muslim society.

Catholic Connection

The Church is a community of saints and sinners. Moral laws are provided as guides for human behaviour so people will follow the Gospel message. Canon law is the set of rules that govern the organization and practice of the members of the Catholic Church. Catholic canon law does not touch as many areas as shariah law.

Origins of Shariah

There are three sources for determining shariah.

1. The Qur'an, which contains extensive passages on how a person should live a good life. Not all circumstances are covered, however.
2. The Sunna, which is a collection of Muhammad's sayings and actions, taken down and transmitted by his family and friends.
3. The Hadith, which is a collection of Muhammad's sayings, actions, and statements about Islam as it was practised in his time. The Hadith contains stories about Muhammad and the early Muslim community, and provides moral and legal interpretations of specific issues.

Fiqh

To adapt shariah to situations that were not covered in the Qur'an, Sunna, or Hadith, Muslim legal experts provided interpretations, called *fiqh*, for new situations. *Fiqh* are seen as having less authority than the Qur'an, Sunna, or Hadith.

Implementing Shariah

How shariah law is interpreted often reflects the customs and civil laws of each country or culture.

Islamic law or shariah divides human action into five categories:

NEL

Five Categories of Shariah Law

Action	Examples or comments
Obligatory actions or duties	Following the Five Pillars of Islam
Recommended actions	Making charitable contributions beyond *zakat* and doing volunteer work
Neutral actions	Neutral actions are not addressed by the Qur'an, Sunna, or Hadith
Discouraged actions	Divorce; however, no penalty is imposed in Islamic law
Forbidden actions	Murder, theft, adultery

Muslim Relief Agencies. During times of natural disasters, Muslim relief agencies join with other religious and secular agencies to bring comfort to the homeless and injured. Members of the Red Crescent team in Syria transport a man into an ambulance during an earthquake simulation exercise. (The Red Crescent is affiliated with the Red Cross.) **Under shariah law, what type of action would this be?**

Islam has been accused of imposing harsh penalties for crimes such as theft, where the penalty in Islamic shariah law is cutting off the hand. In fact, this punishment is rarely carried out, for two reasons. First, the Qur'an includes a saying about Allah who forgives the repentant sinner. Also, the judge considers the value of what was stolen, as well as the circumstances. If a man steals bread to feed his starving family, for example, the entire community is judged guilty of creating this unjust situation.

Shariah Law in Canada

In Canada, Muslims observe shariah in the non-legal moral aspects of their behaviour. Some people in the Muslim community wish to apply shariah to resolve certain types of legal disputes, such as family disputes, marriage, and divorce.

Some Canadians, both Muslim and non-Muslim, fear that the equality rights of women, which are part of the *Canadian Charter of Rights and Freedoms*, could be threatened in some cases if shariah replaces civil law on these matters.

Societies need to find a healthy balance between freedom of religious expression and existing legal codes in a multicultural nation. Canadian Muslims are guided by reasonable accommodation in the pursuit of shariah in their daily lives.

Shariah Law in Canada. Mubin Shaikh (far right) argues for the benefits of shariah law during a protest in Toronto in 2005.

Fatwas: Interpretations of Scripture for Today

A *fatwa* is a religious edict (a decree or order) on Islamic law delivered by a learned scholar versed in the Qur'an, Hadith, and other sources of jurisprudence. A fatwa can be issued on any matter, from a difficult legal problem to an everyday issue, says Dr. Jamal Badawi, a professor emeritus of religious studies at St. Mary's University in Halifax. "It could be fatwa on how to pray, what kind of charity that you should pay, how to fast," he says. Some fatwas are prompted by current events. "When there are events ... that affect a larger number of people, this sometimes is a good justification for an Islamic scholar or council of scholars to come forward in order to remove any misunderstanding and misconception," he says.

Check Your Understanding

1. What are the sources of shariah?
2. How is shariah put into practice?
3. What is a fatwa and when is it issued?

Think About It

4. How far should Canada go to accommodate the culture and traditions of immigrants? Should, for example, some elements of shariah law be allowed in Canada? Why or why not? Be prepared to argue your view in front of the class.

Making It Personal

5. What are the most important moral laws that you follow?
6. How does your relationship with God affect your moral actions?

Family Life

The Role of the Family

For Muslims, the family is the basic building block of a healthy society. Family bonds are nurtured. A stable family unit, where expectations and roles are clear, can help avoid many of the challenges of modern society.

The moral upbringing of children is important. Parents are seen as agents of Allah, providing all authority and guidance needed for mature development. They do this through teaching their children, but especially through example. If parents model the virtues of respect, modesty, and justice, then children are much more likely to do the same.

Patriarchal society

Society in which women are defined by their relationships to men (father, husband, uncle, brother, or son)

Gender Roles

From a modern Canadian perspective, Arabia at the time of Muhammad was a **patriarchal society**, and could even be considered harsh. Some modern Muslim interpreters of the Qur'an ask that people see the historical context of Muhammad's teaching. The Qur'an greatly improved the position of women in Arabia. In fact, women in Arabia were better treated than women in many other cultures. As Islam spread, Muslim attitudes to gender roles were formed mostly by the Qur'an, Sunna, and Hadith.

Muslim immigrants to Canada come from all over the world. These newcomers may share a common religious heritage, but they do not always share a common ethnic background, cultural history, or language. This is important to remember when we look at gender roles—the behaviour expected of males and females.

In Canada today, men's and women's roles are much more flexible than in the past. Most jobs are available to men and women. Husbands and wives tend to share in household chores, cooking, and child rearing. In other cultures, however, roles may be more clearly defined. Often, women's work involves the home, and men's work takes place outside the home. This arrangement is seen as natural. When people from these cultures arrive in Canada, assumptions about who does what and about how males and females ought to behave may be tested.

Encountering unfamiliar behaviours can test Canadians' attitudes about gender roles, too. Instead of judging or criticizing the behaviour and attitudes of new immigrants, we can learn about the cultural or religious worldviews that support and sustain them.

The challenge today for many Muslims in Canada is to find gender roles that respect Canadian laws, and that nurture individuals, families, and the common good, and still reflect the teachings of Islam. Many Canadian Muslim women and men have been able to find this balance.

Muslim Family. In this image from the film *The Peace Tree*, the children see the Eid Moon announcing the end of Ramadan and the beginning of Eid al-Fitr. In the background, the father prays in thanksgiving. **How does this picture show that the father is following principles of Muslim family life?**

Muslim Women and Head Scarves. Young Muslim women in North America often encounter very strong pressure to adapt to North American ways. **Why might it take courage for a 16-year-old girl to cover her hair?**

A Closer Look

In the Qur'an we read, "... Men have a share of what they earned, and women a share of what they earned. ..." (4:32) This point underlies the Muslim worldview in which males and females are not equal but are complementary.

"Muhammad granted women rights and privileges in the sphere of family life, marriage, education, and economic endeavours, rights that help improve women's status in society."

(From *Islam, Gender and Social Change,* Haddad, Esposito, 1998, p. 163.)

Hijab

Arabic word for "cover"; a scarf that covers most or all of a woman's hair

Asmahan Mansour. In 2007, Asmahan Mansour, an 11-year-old Ottawa Muslim girl, was ejected from a soccer tournament for wearing a hijab. A league spokesperson said the ban on hijabs is not racist or anti-religion but is aimed at preventing children from being accidentally strangled. To protest the ruling, Asmahan's team, along with four other teams, left the tournament.

Clothing

Islamic teaching on women's clothing is based on virtues of modesty and respect. Except when with immediate family, women are not to wear revealing clothing. This command has been interpreted in a range of ways in different times and places. Styles vary around the world. Some women wear a garment that covers their entire bodies when they are outside their homes; it may or may not cover their faces. These garments include the *abaya*, *burka*, and *chador*. Some wear Western clothing and a headscarf or veil such as the ***hijab***. Others dress modestly according to the customs of their particular country. The same is true in Canada.

Most Muslim scholars expect men to dress modestly and to be covered at least from the navel to the knees.

Abaya. A woman wears an abaya.

Hijab. A student wears a hijab.

Burka. Afghani women wearing burkas

Chador. Chador-clad Muslim women

Check Your Understanding

1. What is the role of the family for Muslims?
2. What are the traditional gender roles for Muslims?

Think About It

3. In the past, some Canadian schools have said that head coverings such as the hijab do not conform to the school's dress code and must not be worn in school. Suggest arguments in support of people being allowed to wear hijabs whenever and wherever they want. Suggest arguments opposing people wearing them in certain locations, such as in schools that have school uniforms, or while on police duty.

Making It Personal

4. What gender role differences do you experience in your culture?
5. Do you believe that Muslim women should be able to wear the hijab, abaya, chador, or burka in public in Canada? Why or why not?

A Closer Look

Katherine Bullock of York University interviewed women who wore the hijab, and reported the following:

"When asked to explain why they covered, the women I interviewed said they believed that in the Qur'an God commanded women to cover their hair, and that Prophetic statements backed that up. For them, Hijab symbolizes, not oppression or terrorism, as it does in mainstream Western discourse, but 'purity,' 'modesty,' a 'woman's Islamic identity,' and 'obedience, or submission to God and a testament that you're Muslim.' Halima, a convert to Islam, adds that Hijab symbolizes 'the woman's power to take back her own dignity and her own sexuality.'"

Education

For centuries, Muslim children have learned to read Arabic so they could eventually read the Qur'an in its original form. Children grow up surrounded by the Qur'an, reading the scriptures, and hearing recitations of the Suras. In Islamic schools, religious education and Arabic are part of the curriculum.

Muslim schools are called *madrasas*. Courses include Arabic, Quranic studies, shariah (Islamic law), Hadith, logic, and Muslim history, as well as other courses that are important for Muslim students in particular cultures. As you read earlier, students who memorize the entire Qur'an earn the title *hafiz*, or "memorizer."

Fast Fact

In Canada in 2008, there were 35 private Islamic schools. Students in these schools learn Arabic and do Islamic studies alongside the provincial curriculum.

Students Studying the Qur'an. Muslim students recite the Qur'an.

ISNA Logo. This logo from the Islamic Society of North America Canada indicates that the meat product is allowed.

Halal

Permissible; usually refers to foods that are allowed

Diet

For Muslims, certain foods are allowed (***halal***) and others are forbidden (*haram*). For example, milk is allowed and alcohol is forbidden. Muslim dietary laws are similar to Jewish dietary laws, except that shellfish are permitted for Muslims. For meat to be allowed, it has to be slaughtered in a prescribed ritual way. Permitted meat must be slaughtered while the name of Allah is being said. Muslims are allowed to eat kosher food when allowed foods are not available, because kosher standards are even stricter than the rules governing allowed foods.

Muslims observe these dietary laws as an act of obedience to the will of Allah. Allowing sacred rules to govern life reminds people that meaning in life is to be found outside of one's own desires.

Halal Food. This restaurant in Toronto serves halal food.

Sexuality

Catholics, Jews, and Muslims affirm the joy of the sexual relationship between husband and wife. Islam also encourages partners to fall in love with each other. They also agree on the two purposes of conjugal love:

- the good of the spouses themselves
- the transmission of life

Islam teaches that sexual relations cause ritual impurity, so a ritual purification needs to happen before people can engage in formal prayer after having sex.

Islam considers premarital sex, masturbation, homosexual acts, and pornography to be sins. Islam does not prohibit artificial birth control, but Muslims at the 1994 United Nations International Conference on Population and Development in Cairo joined with Catholics in condemning government-imposed birth control regulations.

Profile: Vancouver's Muslim Youth

Living in a pluralistic and increasingly secular (non-religious) Canada puts pressure on young Muslims to "fit into" Canadian society while still seeking to remain true to their faith tradition. Here, four Vancouver-area Muslim teens (Sana Siddiqui, Mustafa Abousaleh, Ammir Mushin, and Hanan Dumas) talk with reporter Douglas Todd about growing up Muslim in Canada.

Vancouver's Muslim Youth. Muslim teens (from left to right) Sana Siddiqui, Mustafa Abousaleh, and Ammir Mushin

Music—As the talk turns to erotically tinged popular music, it becomes clearer how Greater Vancouver's young Muslims are the same as other teens, but also different. But Siddiqui is appalled by the blatant sexuality in so many music videos. "If a woman wants to succeed in music, it seems they have to wear less and less clothes." The teens soon turn to how they all like Islamic music—or ***nasheeds***.

TV—When she grew curious about watching the Kiefer Sutherland TV series thriller *24*, Siddiqui soon grew annoyed at the way the plots so often relied on Muslim terrorists. "What's not bothersome about that?" she asks, rhetorically. "It pushes all Muslims out to the margins, suggesting they're all violent."

Politics—Before we explored things they found disturbing about the global conflict between the West and much of the Muslim world, Mushin talked about just how grateful he is for Canadian freedom of speech. "There would be no chance to have this discussion with a journalist in a lot of countries," said Mushin, who has lived in B.C. for 11 years. That's not to say these Muslim teenagers do not have their concerns about politics in Canada. Muslim doctrine tends to lead to support for both market capitalism and the redistribution of wealth, said Siddiqui. She cited how the Islamic tradition of the consumer bazaar complements Muslim values about egalitarianism and charitable giving. "Islam is neither totally socialist nor totally capitalist. But it does teach that the rich, because of their wealth, are more accountable, and need to have more personal responsibility," said Siddiqui.

Ecology—In line with the Quranic virtue of ***khalifa***, or stewardship, Abousaleh said Muslims believe in taking care of both their families

Nasheeds

Music that is traditionally sung a cappella, accompanied only by the beat of a large drum; *nasheeds* often consist of religious stories and recitations of the Qur'an in Arabic

Khalifa

The Muslim duty of stewardship that lies at the heart of Muslim ecological ethics; although *khalifa* refers to other areas of responsibility, it is used to make the point that certain destructive environmental actions, such as polluting water and wantonly killing animals, are forbidden

continues...

and the environment, in part since many come from desert regions where conservation is of ultimate importance, particularly of water. Echoing contemporary ecological ethics, Abousaleh said, "Islam teaches we're sent to take care of the Earth."

A Muslim Family Meal. A Muslim family enjoys a meal together. **What shows that this is a Muslim family?**

Sex and Marriage—The Muslim teens definitely do not believe in sex outside marriage, even though Mushin said non-Muslim male friends sometimes tease him for abstaining. The teenagers believe many non-Muslims carry around "stereotypical" beliefs that Muslim youngsters are forced into arranged marriages. Although there is an extensive network of Muslim family members who take on the role of introducing young men and women to each other for the purpose of marriage, Siddiqui said it's not true that a Canadian "Muslim girl does not get a choice of who she'll marry. She gets ultimate choice."

Social Life—When it comes to dating or partying, Dumas said her friends in Richmond don't "do drugs or alcohol or any of that stuff. I don't feel tempted at all by any of those things." If Siddiqui is invited to university parties where non-Muslims will likely be drinking alcohol, which is forbidden in Islam, she said she doesn't go "because that would sort of be endorsing it."

Prayer—These four teenage Muslims would not for the world give up their faith, despite the challenges, both outer and inner, that come with it. "The Qur'an teaches that you can satisfy your body and soul by giving them back to the Creator through prayer," said Siddiqui, acting as if her devotion to Allah was a no-brainer. "Prayer is sort of like to calm myself, or relieve stress," added Dumas, showing self-awareness beyond her 15 years. "Your day is so busy. And prayer gives you five minutes to slow down and connect with God."

(From "Growing Up Muslim" by Douglas Todd. *Vancouver Sun*, 8 September 2007.)

Check Your Understanding

1. What do students in Islamic schools study?
2. What is the purpose of Muslim dietary laws?

Think About It

3. How are Muslim teachings on sexuality similar to Catholic teachings? How are they different?

Making It Personal

4. Do you consume any food and drinks that have a symbolic meaning for you? What is the symbolism?
5. Do you share any of the views of the Muslim teens in the profile? Which views?

Islam and the Catholic Church

A Difficult Encounter

Catholics and Muslims are engaged today in a dialogue to learn more about each other and to overcome prejudices. This approach was not always the case. From the beginning, Muslims crossed paths with Christians and Jews. After all, the three religions began in the Middle East. Muslims see Islam as the correction, completion, or fulfillment of Judaism and Christianity. Muhammad is seen to be the final Messenger of God.

Yet, Muhammad did not reject the previous messengers of God who are at the heart of Judaism and Christianity: Noah, Abraham, Moses, and Jesus. Muhammad believed they were authentic messengers of God for all humanity.

As Islamic rule spread over most of the Middle East, North Africa, and Spain, Jews and Christians living in the conquered countries were allowed to keep practising their faiths. Christians and Jews had special status. Their properties were protected and they were free to worship God, although they did have to pay a special tax and they did not have equal rights with the majority of the population. Many of these Christians, for a number of reasons, later converted to Islam.

Islamic Tolerance

Catholicism's relationship with Islam has not been easy. In the Eastern Church, Muhammad was often presented as a deceiver and heretic, and Islam as a false religion. The Qur'an, so it was said, was a work of humans and not divine revelation. Islam was feared because much of the growth of Islam was accomplished by means of forceful territorial expansion. The Muslim Empire was vast and powerful.

Muslim capture of the Christian holy places and the constant threat to Constantinople led to nine Crusades

"There is no compulsion in religion; true guidance has become distinct from error. Thus he who disbelieves in the Devil and believes in Allah grasps the firmest handle that will never break. Allah is All-Hearing, All-Knowing. Allah is the Supporter of the believers. He brings them out of darkness into light. ..."
(Sura 2:258–259)

Assisi Interfaith Gathering. At the Assisi Interfaith global gatherings in 1986, members of Christian, Muslim, and other faiths were invited to gather in Assisi, Italy, to pray together for peace. Here, Pope John Paul II meets with a Muslim leader. **Do you think interfaith dialogue is important? Why or why not?**

continues...

Archbishop Faraj Rahho of Iraq (left) with Pope Benedict XVI in 2007. In March 2008, Paulos Faraj Rahho, Archbishop of Mosul in Iraq, was kidnapped by Muslim militants. He was found dead outside the city of Mosul a few days later. Three of his companions were also killed. Violence against Christians unfortunately occurs in several Islamic countries. Despite new efforts to understand each other, it is apparent that full mutual dialogue and trust are difficult to attain.

against Muslim rulers by Christians between 1095 and 1272. Mutual relations were also not helped when in 1492, the Catholic rulers of Spain, Ferdinand and Isabella, expelled all Muslims from the country by force.

There were some efforts, however, that used dialogue. Among them were those of St. Francis of Assisi (1181–1226), who visited the Sultan of Egypt to try to convert him; Peter the Venerable (1094–1156), who initiated the first translation of the Qur'an; and St. Thomas Aquinas (1225–1274), who wrote a long theological debate.

Despite these positive steps, the twenty-first century has already seen bloody clashes between Muslims and Christians in Nigeria, Sudan, Iraq, and Indonesia. Many Christians have left other Islamic countries for the West, as their religious freedom became limited. In some of these countries, Christianity may soon disappear.

Canadian Sitcom about Muslims Goes around the World. *Little Mosque on the Prairie*, a CBC-TV sitcom that first aired in 2007, is the story of a small Muslim community in the fictional prairie town of Mercy, Saskatchewan. In this widely distributed show, cast members (shown here) portray Muslims and non-Muslims interacting with and sometimes misunderstanding each other, often with hilarious results. The show's creator, Zarqa Nawaz, sees comedy as one of the best ways to break down barriers and promote dialogue and understanding between cultures. **How can humour help break down barriers?**

Make It Your Own: Love of Learning

One of the great contributions of Muslims to the world has been their love of learning. We see this in their preservation of many of the works of Greek thinkers such as Plato and Aristotle, as well as the development of mathematical ideas such as algebra. Cairo's Al-Azhar University predates the European universities of Bologna, Oxford, and Paris by several centuries. On several occasions, the Qur'an calls people to be rational and thinking beings. Some modern Muslims are calling for a renewed emphasis on questioning and thinking.

Activity

1. Create a list of questions that you have regarding Islam, Christianity, faith, nature, and relationships. Try to list five questions for each category. From your list, choose the top three questions that are most important to you. Explain how you could answer each of these questions.

The Catholic Church Re-examines Islam

A major turnabout in relations between Catholicism and Islam took place in the mid-twentieth century. During the Second Vatican Council, the Catholic bishops of the world accepted a declaration about the value of other religions, saying, "The Catholic Church rejects nothing of what is true and holy in these religions" (Vatican Council II, *Declaration on the Relation of the Church to Non-Christian Religions*, #2). The Council urged Catholics to "enter with prudence and charity in discussion and collaboration with members of other religions."

Of Muslims, the same document says,

> The Church regards with esteem also the Muslims. They adore the one God, living and subsisting in Himself; merciful and all-powerful, the Creator of heaven and earth, who has spoken to men; they take pains to submit wholeheartedly to even His inscrutable decrees, just as Abraham, with whom the faith of Islam takes pleasure in linking itself, submitted to God. Though they do not acknowledge Jesus as God, they revere Him as a prophet. They also honour Mary, His virgin Mother, and they pray to her for peace. In addition, they await the day of judgment when God will render their deserts to all those who have been raised up from the dead. Finally, they value the moral life and worship God especially through prayer, almsgiving and fasting.

Although both religions claim to possess universal truth and the final revelation, dialogue between Christianity and Islam does occur. Here are the points where the two religions agree:

- Along with Jews, Muslims and Christians believe there is only one God.
- They believe that God spoke with humans.
- They desire to submit wholeheartedly to God's demands.
- They believe in the resurrection of the dead, the last judgment, and reward for good deeds. They attach great value to a moral life of justice and peace, and worship of God through prayer, almsgiving, and fasting.

"We are brothers and sisters in the faith of Abraham"—Pope John Paul II

The Catholic Church recognizes Islam as a religion that expresses in its beliefs and rituals an authentic faith in a personal, almighty God.

But there are also some important issues separating the two religions. Respect for another religion means recognizing not only common beliefs and practices, but also our differences. Here are three such differences:

- Muslims believe in One God; Catholics believe in One God in Three Persons.
- The understanding of revelation: In Islam, the Qur'an in Arabic is directly the Word of God. For Catholics, Jesus is personally the Word of God. In Islam, the Word of God is in a book. In Catholicism, the Word of God is a person. Jesus is the very Word of God. For Islam, the Qur'an is the Word of God transmitted to Muhammad in a direct revelation. For Catholics, Jesus is the revelation of God.
- The roles of Jesus and Muhammad. Islam presents Muhammad as the final Messenger of God, surpassing and completing the message of the prophet Jesus. For Catholics, Jesus is more than a messenger. He is the Son of God and the fulfillment of all revelation. No other public revelation is needed nor expected.

Pope Benedict XVI Meets with Muslim Leaders. In 2007, Pope Benedict XVI met with Grand Mufti Mustafa Cagrici (right) and other Muslim leaders to discuss areas of mutual concern and interest. **What do you think they talked about?**

Skill Focus: Evaluating Different Perspectives

Many topics can be seen from more than one perspective. Sometimes these perspectives are opposing. How do you evaluate different perspectives?

1. Identify two or more different viewpoints on the same topic. How are they different? Create a chart like the one below with headings for the different positions.
2. Write a point-form statement that summarizes each position.
3. Find evidence to support or oppose each position statement. Even if you agree with only one side of the position, it is important to identify advantages and disadvantages for each side. Sometimes identifying and analyzing the argument for the other side can help you see its weaknesses. Sometimes it will help you determine how to make your own argument more convincing.

Analyzing the arguments for the opposing side can also help you understand another point of view and empathize with the people who hold it, even if you disagree with their point of view.

Position 1		**Position 2**		**Position 3**	
Summarize the position		Summarize the position		Summarize the position	
Supporting Evidence	**Opposing Evidence**	**Supporting Evidence**	**Opposing Evidence**	**Supporting Evidence**	**Opposing Evidence**

What I Have Learned

In this chapter, I learned about

- Muhammad's importance
- the Qur'an and the Islamic Holy Scriptures
- the development of Sunni and Shi'ite Islam
- the meaning of jihad
- obedience to the will of Allah
- the Five Pillars of Islam
  - reciting the creed (Shahadah)
  - praying five times a day (*salat*)
  - giving to charity (*zakat*)
  - fasting during Ramadan (*sawm*)
  - making a pilgrimage to Mecca (hajj)
- the rituals surrounding birth, marriage, and death
- shariah law
- the history of the relationships between Muslims and Catholics

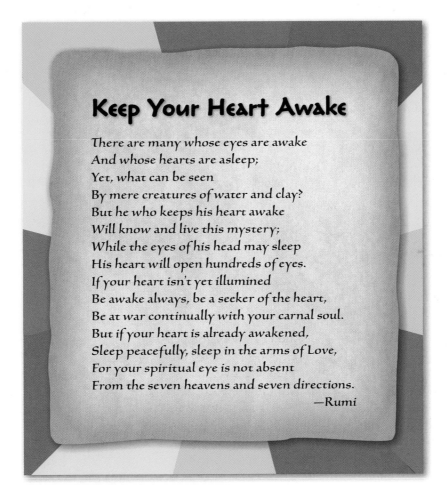

Keep Your Heart Awake

There are many whose eyes are awake
And whose hearts are asleep;
Yet, what can be seen
By mere creatures of water and clay?
But he who keeps his heart awake
Will know and live this mystery;
While the eyes of his head may sleep
His heart will open hundreds of eyes.
If your heart isn't yet illumined
Be awake always, be a seeker of the heart,
Be at war continually with your carnal soul.
But if your heart is already awakened,
Sleep peacefully, sleep in the arms of Love,
For your spiritual eye is not absent
From the seven heavens and seven directions.

—Rumi

Chapter 7 The Story of Hinduism

Swaminarayan Mandir in Toronto. The BAPS Swaminarayan Mandir in Toronto is a centre of worship and service to the needy. The *mandir* (temple) was built by 1800 skilled workers in India and 400 volunteers in Canada, who put it together from stone carved in India. **What Hindu temples do you know of in your community or region?**

Namaste. *Namaste* means "I bow respectfully to you." *Namaste* is both a word and a gesture—one you might know about from yoga. **What words or gestures do you use to show respect when you greet someone?**

"To those who are continually disciplined, who worship me full of joy, I grant the discipline of intelligence by which they can come to me."

(Bhagavad Gita 10.10)

What You Will Learn

In this chapter, you will learn about

- Hinduism in Canada
- where Hinduism is practised and its origins
- how Hinduism developed and its sacred books
- some rituals, symbols, and deities of Hinduism
- the key beliefs of Hinduism—including *samsara*, *moksha*, *dharma*, and *karma*
- structures and paths of the Hindu religion
- Hindu family life
- Catholic–Hindu encounters

Personal Recollection

My name is Harsha. My family are all practising Hindus.

For me, this means several things. Every day begins with prayer. Our home has a room that has been set aside as a shrine. We call it our ***puja*** room. There are probably 75 or more images of **deities** (pictures and statues of the God in many forms) in this room. Every morning, my mom performs her *puja*. She recites prayers and hymns and offers food, flowers, and fruit to the images. We're a Vaishnavite family, which means we are devoted to the divine in the form of the Lord Vishnu and his consort, Lakshmi. Most of the images in our room are of these two deities, but Shiva and Ganesha are there also. My father and I also do morning *puja*, but our version is a bit quicker. He has work and I have school. One of my mom's prayers is the recitation of the 1008 names of Vishnu. I do the shorter version. One of my morning prayers calls the deities down upon my hands. Each part of the prayer is accompanied by a hand gesture: "I call Lakshmi to my hands. I call Saraswati. I call Govind (Vishnu), and I open my hands to see all three." The idea is that if you invite the God into your hands, how can you sin? How can you commit crimes if God has blessed your hands? How can you do anything wrong if you've invited God to be with you throughout your day? It's also a prayer for the blessings that these deities have the power to grant: wealth, knowledge, and power, for example. In the evening, we thank Vishnu for the blessings of the day, ask him to bless our dreams, and so on. I also like to pray a prayer that helps me do well in school.

— **Harsha Kasi-Vishwanathan**

Harsha's Story. In what ways is Harsha's family life and daily routine similar to yours? Different from yours?

Puja

Hindu worship ceremony

Deities

Images of the God in many forms

Hinduism in Canada

Fast Fact

"Hindu" is a word that comes from the name of the Indus River, which also gives the name of the modern state of India. Most Hindu people of the world have roots in the region.

The world is home to over 900 million Hindus. Most of them live in India, a country with 1.166 billion people, of whom about 80 percent are Hindu. Large numbers of people who follow the Hindu religion are also found in Nepal, Bangladesh, Indonesia, Sri Lanka, Malaysia, and beyond. As it did with Harsha and her family (page 229), Hinduism has spread with immigration to Canada and other countries. Hinduism is the third-largest religion in the world, after Christianity and Islam. As you read through this chapter, think about the many ways in which Hinduism compares and contrasts with Christianity and other faiths you have learned about.

In Canada, according to the 2001 statistics from Statistics Canada, the figure for the Hindu population was 297 200, or just under 1 percent of the national population. This makes Hinduism Canada's fourth most followed religion, after Christianity (76 percent), Islam (2 percent), and Judaism (1.1 percent). Most Hindus in Canada—more than 70 percent—were born elsewhere, mainly in India but also in lands to which Hinduism and Hindus travelled, including Sri Lanka, Indonesia, Uganda, Guyana, and Trinidad and Tobago. Most Hindus in Canada live in Ontario, Québec, Manitoba, and Saskatchewan.

What does it mean to be a Hindu? Hinduism is a tradition that means many things and has many variations. It is not a single, unified, centralized religion the way Roman Catholicism is. It is very individualized and has no formal church and no single authority. It has no founder and no fixed doctrines. To a Canadian who is not Hindu, the religion may seem a kaleidoscope of different rituals, movements, and beliefs. Here are three snapshots of Hinduism.

Hindus around the World

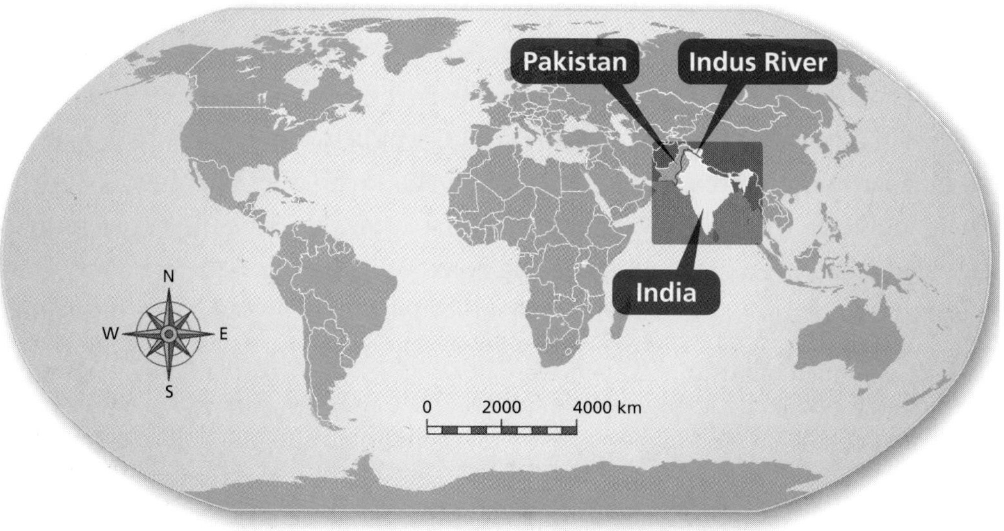

Hindus around the World. The Indus River flows from the Himalayas to the Arabian Sea through what is now Pakistan. Most Hindus live on the Indian subcontinent, but others are part of the Indian diaspora. "Diaspora" means "scattering of seeds." The Indian diaspora dates back to Britain's control within the region from 1858 until 1947. **What do you know about nineteenth-century history in this region and the creation of modern-day India and Pakistan?**

A Hindu Wedding. A Hindu bride and groom ride to their wedding ceremony on an elephant. The wedding was held at the BAPS Swaminarayan temple in Toronto.

The Swaminarayan Mandir in Toronto. The Swaminarayan Mandir was opened in 2007 by the Indian high commissioner to Canada, Rajamani Lakshmi Narayan, Prime Minister Stephen Harper, and Dalton McGuinty, premier of Ontario. Carvers were brought from India to help construct the temple following ancient Hindu rules. The building is also home to the Canadian Museum of Cultural Heritage of Indo-Canadians. The $40 million to build the temple was donated by Hindus from Canada and from around the world.

Ritual Bathing in the Ganges. Every 12 years, a sacred ritual takes place at Prayag, near Allahabad, on the Ganges in northern India. At each festival, millions of people bathe in the sacred Ganges River to come closer to the source of life, to wash away their sins, and to cleanse both their bodies and their spirits. For Hindus, however, a pilgrimage to the Ganges is not considered necessary, but highly desirable.

The History of Hinduism

Hinduism is one of the oldest religions in the world. For centuries, the native religion of ancient India was known as *sanatan dharma*, "the way of life." It was not until centuries later that the name "Hinduism" was first used.

Hinduism can be described as evolving over three historical periods. During each period, Hinduism adapted to new situations, but kept traces of the previous periods.

Pre-Vedic Period

An ancient civilization thrived in the fertile valley of the Indus River in the third and second millennium before the birth of Christ—about 2500 to 1500 BCE. Historians and archaeologists still have many questions about the Indus Valley Civilization. One reason is that the Indus Valley Civilization's language has not been deciphered. However, scholars do know that

- most of the people lived in cities—cities that were impressively complex, built with bricks, and that included sophisticated drainage and sewage systems
- it was a matriarchal society—one in which women, especially mothers, took a leading role

Hinduism in Asia

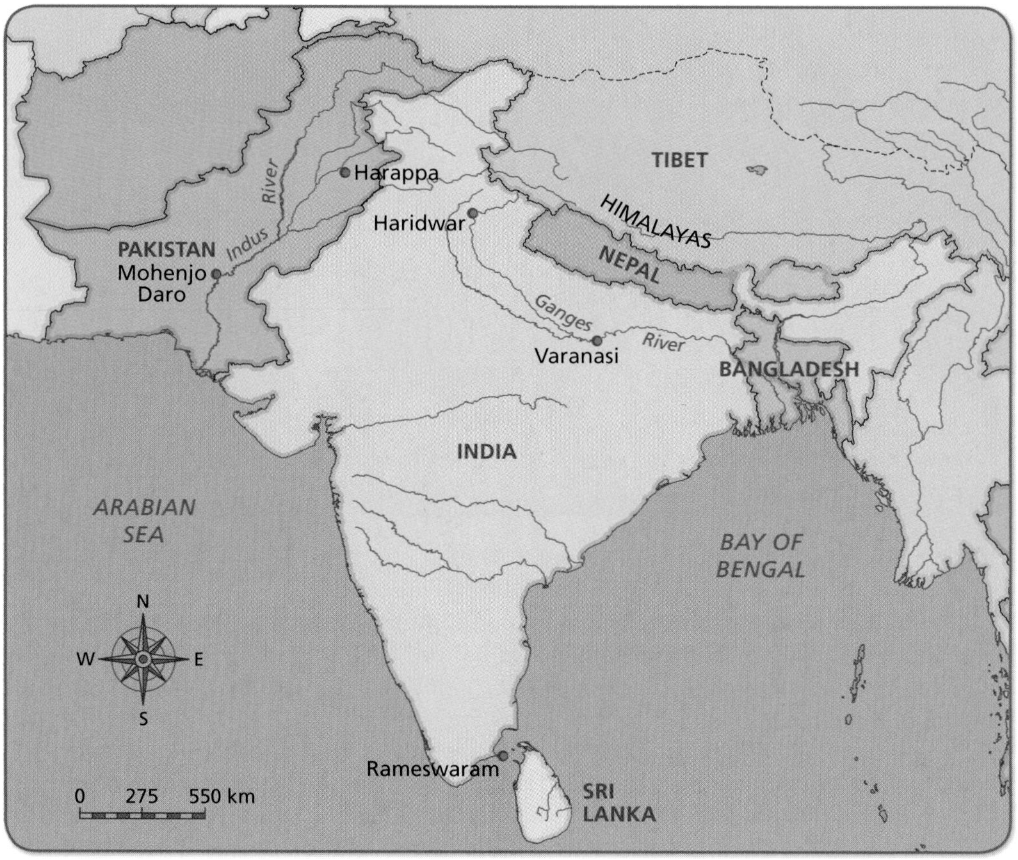

Hinduism in Asia. Hinduism began in the Indus River Valley in what is now Pakistan and northern India. Sacred sites and temples are now found throughout the subcontinent.

- people worshipped a mother goddess—whom some later Hindu deities resemble

Scholars believe that later Hindu deities evolved from goddess images of this period.

Vedic Period

The Vedic period, which began around 1500 BCE until 600 BCE, is named for the first sacred writings of Hinduism, the **Vedas**, because scholars think those writings were collected during this period. The language of the Vedas is **Sanskrit**, and "Veda" is the Sanskrit word for knowledge. Rituals during the period focused on prayers, the elements of nature, and animal sacrifices.

The Upanishadic Period

The third and final period in the history of Hinduism began around 600 BCE. From about 600 to 200 BCE,

- ancient India's culture was unified
- Hinduism both accepted the Vedas and added to them, with the Upanishads
- worship began in temples

The **Upanishads** are interpretations of the Vedas added to the end of each. With these powerful additions, Hinduism as we know it emerged. The Upanishads moved Hinduism from a focus on sacrificial practices to a philosophical and meditative way of life—a focus more on the inner self.

The Indus Valley Civilization. Images from the Indus Valley Civilization and archaeological ruins show large baths. These were most likely used for purifying rituals, which are still important among Hindus in India.

Vedas

Early sacred scriptures of Hinduism

Sanskrit

The language of ancient India

Upanishads

Sacred scriptures; the final dialogues ending the Vedas

Ritual Bathing in the Ganges River. These Hindu women are bathing in the Ganges River. The oldest of the Vedas, the *Rig Veda*, includes more than 1000 hymns addressing the elements of nature—earth, fire, air, and water. **What aspects of other religious rituals can you think of that involve earth, fire, air, or water?**

Timeline of Hinduism History

2500 BCE	**2500–1500 BCE** Pre-Vedic period; Indus Valley civilization
1500 BCE	**1500–600 BCE** Vedic Period; Vedas are written
600 BCE	**600–200 BCE** Upanishadic Period; India's culture is unified
500 BCE	**500 BCE** Buddhism and Jainism become offshoots of Hinduism
CE	**400–100 BCE** Other key sacred texts are compiled, including the Bhagavad Gita and the Ramayana
250 CE	**200 CE** Hindu influence starts to spread to what is now Cambodia, Thailand, Malaysia, and Indonesia
1250	**1175** The beginning of the first Muslim empire in India
1500	**1818** The beginning of British rule in India
1750	**1869–1948** The life of Mohandas Gandhi, political leader
2000	**1947** End of British rule. Creation of the modern states of India and Pakistan

Angkor Wat. Angkor Wat was built in Cambodia around 1200 CE as a Hindu temple. It is the world's largest religious structure. It is now a Buddhist temple and a national symbol for Cambodia.

Fast Fact

Buddhism and Jainism (see the timeline above) are both offshoots of Hinduism. (You will explore Buddhism in Chapter 8.) Jainism is a religion with about 4 million followers in India and about 2500 in Canada.

Check Your Understanding

1. Where does the word "Hindu" come from?

Think About It

2. For what you have learned so far about Hinduism, create a diagram on which you
   - summarize key points from the chapter so far in one colour
   - note your initial impressions in a second colour
   - write two or three questions you have in a third colour
3. Compare diagrams with a partner and discuss how you might find answers to your questions.

Making It Personal

4. Look back at Harsha's story on page 229. What questions would you ask her about what her religion means to her?

Rituals

Puja is the most common form of Hindu worship. It involves worshipping one or more Hindu deities. The image of a deity is called a ***murti***. It is believed to contain the particular aspect of the essence of the Supreme Being or of the one God. Hindus believe that there is only one God or Supreme Being, but that this Being has many different forms. The main place for offering *puja* is in the home. Whether at home or in a temple, the ritual involves sounds, light, washing, food, scent, and prayers.

Puja

Puja in a Hindu Home

Most Hindu families have a place of worship in their homes—a room, a corner, or an alcove set aside as a shrine. To start, worshippers remove their shoes, a bell is rung to summon the presence of the *murti*, a lamp is lit, and incense is burned. The *murti* is washed and decorated with garlands or flower petals. A special powder is mixed with water to make a red paste. A small amount of this paste is placed on the foreheads of the *murti* and the worshippers. The worshippers make an offering of fruit, light, flowers, or sweets to the *murti*. The lamp is moved around the *murti* in a clockwise direction to indicate the presence of God. The devotees then each place both hands above the lamp flame and touch their foreheads, showing that they are receiving the deity's blessing. Any food that has been part of the *puja* must be eaten by everyone present, to honour the deity and share in the deity's power. At the end of the ritual, some Hindus turn around three times to show that they remember God is all around them.

Hindu Home Shrines. A Hindu family home shrine. **Which types of objects from this Hindu home shrine might you find in a Catholic home shrine?**

Temple Worship

Hindus visit the ***mandir*** to offer prayers and devotion any time or day of the week, just as they might drop in on friends for a visit. A Hindu temple is a complex of shrines, each devoted to a different deity. The main deity is enshrined in the centre. Temples can be very large, and able to accommodate hundreds of thousands of devotees. As worshippers enter the temple, they remove their shoes and wash their hands. Then they approach the shrine to make an offering. As they approach, they ring a bell to announce their arrival to the *murti*.

When *puja* is performed in the temple, the ritual is similar to that done in Hindu homes, but a priest leads the ritual. A ritual service begins with the singing of ***mantras*** and traditional Indian music. Then the priest will perform *puja* while chanting verses from the scriptures. Worshippers sing and clap while the lamp is circled around the deities, and the priest may take the lamp among the worshippers so everyone can receive a blessing. The service ends with a sharing of the blessed food offering.

Catholic Connection

In contrast to some Catholic rituals you might know, *puja* can be offered by anyone (not only by priests) and is often conducted in the home.

Murti
An image of a Hindu deity

Mandir
A Hindu temple

Mantra
Sacred sounds, words, or phrases, repeated in ritual

A Closer Look

Hindus may focus their devotion on one or more deities and follow the teachings of a specific **guru**. For example, the BAPS Swaminarayan Mandir in Toronto is one of 700 mandirs and 3300 centres worldwide that recognize Bhagwan Swaminarayan as a guru.

Guru
Wise teacher

Another important ritual, which is called *havan*, involves offering fire. In this ritual, the priest lights the fire, then pours pure butterfat or oil into it while chanting from the Vedas. The priest offers prayers for purity, dips his finger into water, and then touches his ears, eyes, nose, mouth, arms, body, and legs. The other worshippers do the same to remind themselves that God lives within them. Prayers are then offered to all the supreme deities.

Check Your Understanding

1. What is *puja*? Describe how it is offered.
2. What is a *mandir*? Describe its main features.

Think About It

3. Imagine that you must explain how Hindus practise *puja* at home to an eight-year-old Catholic friend. How would you describe it? What comparisons and contrasts would you make?

Making It Personal

4. If you were to create a sacred place in your home, what would it look like? What objects would you put there? Why? How do you express devotion to God?

Skill Focus: Web Research and Evaluating Websites

The Internet is a vast and wonderful resource for doing research and finding information. When you use the Internet, keep in mind the following guidelines, which will help you use it more effectively.

1. Wherever possible, use more than one source to verify the accuracy of information. Material that appears on the Internet is not always reviewed and fact-checked by people who have expert knowledge of the content.
2. Is the website biased? Is the material presented in a fair and balanced way? If you are researching a controversial topic, it is helpful to ask yourself the following questions:
   - Who produced this website?
   - What is the viewpoint of this individual or this organization?
   - What is the purpose of this website?
3. Does the author on the website have expert credentials? For example, is the author a teacher or professor? Is the author a religious leader or member of a religious community with backing from that community? Is the author a spokesperson for a religious or cultural institution or group?
4. Is the information on the site appropriate for your topic? Is it current? (Check the date.)
5. If you find useful information, remember that you cannot cut and paste it into your own work. You must rewrite the information or quote the source. You must insert any quotation in quotation marks and give the source of the website (for example, the organization, the web address).

   Use quotations sparingly. Your project or essay should demonstrate that you have understood the information and synthesized it into something new. You may need to reorganize your research findings to suit your purposes. Keep in mind that you may not end up using all of the information you found—focus on using the information that is most relevant to your topic. Whether you rewrite the information or quote it directly, always remember to credit it by recording the details of your online source.

The Eternal Cycle of All Life

As a man leaves an old garment and puts on one that is new, the Spirit leaves his mortal body and then puts on one that is new.
(Bhagavad Gita 2.22)

All life, according to Hinduism, is governed by a law of birth, death, and rebirth: all life must return to the world after death. This law is called the Wheel of Life, or ***samsara***, and it applies to all living things—not just human life. All reality dissolves and is recreated in an unending flow. People may not end up being reborn as humans; they could be reborn, or reincarnated, as animals.

The goal of life for Hindus is, ultimately, to be freed from the wheel of life. This liberation from the cycle of rebirths is called ***moksha***. According to this belief, Hindus can be reborn in a higher state of life, moving gradually upward from lifetime to lifetime. How someone is reborn is determined by the law of ***karma***: that whatever one does in life affects what one will be in the next. The best way to ensure good *karma* (and so a favourable rebirth) is to perform good deeds and follow one's duty or ***dharma***. In contrast, ignoring *dharma* builds up bad *karma* and increases the chances of an unfavourable rebirth. For humans, *dharma* is a code of conduct. Every Hindu's *dharma* is related mainly to his or her family and place in society.

India's Flag. The flag of India shows a wheel at the centre. **What can you find out about the significance of the symbol on this flag?**

Samsara

The law of birth, death, and rebirth, or the process of reincarnation

Catholic Connection

Whereas Hindus believe in reincarnation, Catholics believe in resurrection. To believe in resurrection means to hold that people die only once, but that one day they will be raised from the dead with their own bodies by the power of God's Spirit, just like Jesus at Easter. Hindus believe that whatever they did in this life—the good and the bad—they bring with them into the next life. For Catholics, Jesus Christ is the judge of each person's life. Discuss how this is different from reincarnation.

Moksha

Freedom or liberation from *samsara*, or the cycle of rebirth

Karma

The law of cause and effect, of one's actions having an impact on one's future life

Dharma

One's personal code of conduct relating to family and society; one's duty

Check Your Understanding

1. For Hindus, what is the penalty for a harmful act? For Christianity, what is the penalty for sin?

Think About It

2. Based on the chapter so far and some brief Internet research, write a dictionary definition of the Hindu term "reincarnation" and illustrate it with an example.

Making It Personal

3. How would you describe your place in society and your duty in life? Share your ideas in a small group. Discuss them with the class.

The Divine: Brahman, Atman, and Maya

Brahman
The supreme cosmic force

"The fire which is the sun, the fire which is the earth, the fire that is in my own heart."
(The Vedas, Maitri Upanishads, VI.17)

"[What] is soundless, intangible, formless,

Undecaying, and likewise tasteless, eternal and odourless;

Having realized That which is without beginning and end,

Beyond the Great, and unchanging—one is freed from the jaws of death."
(Katha Upanishad I.iii.15)

Hindus believe in an underlying unity of all reality. In the early Vedic period of Hinduism's history, this unity was thought to be fire, and fire was the origin of all things. Later on, this transcendent unity of everything was called ***Brahman***. *Brahman* is the power that sustains the universe and is its deepest reality.

With the Upanishads, the great shift in Hindu belief was that consciousness—not fire—united all. The universe, all reality, is one great act of consciousness. Consciousness underlies everything, and is in everything. Because humans are conscious beings, Hinduism holds that "the self is *Brahman*." The self that people experience in their consciousness is one with *Brahman*, the reality of the universe. According to Hindu belief, *Brahman* cannot be named, and many forms of the deities are needed to express the various aspects of *Brahman*.

For Hindus, by going beyond their bodies, beyond their thoughts and feelings, they discover their true selves. Hindus call this true self ***atman***.

Hindus believe that each *atman* is a fragment of the divine *Brahman*. Everyone, therefore, is part of the divine. *Brahman*, it is said, is like the ocean. Living creatures, including humans and everything else of living nature, are like drops of ocean spray, momentarily hovering above the water.

Hindus believe that coming to a consciousness of themselves as *Brahman* is the surest way to defeat death. What keeps humans from this consciousness is their many distractions. Most humans live through their senses. What they see and sense is that things are different from one another. They see flowers, trees, birds, stones, animals, other humans. For Hindus, this is an illusion, called ***maya***. When people see things as separate from each other, they do not perceive the divine oneness (*Brahman*) that surges through all things. To live in *maya* is to be imprisoned in ignorance and distraction. Realizing that *Brahman* or *atman* is present in everyone and everything is to be set free.

Atman
The true self

Maya
Illusion

Catholic Connection

Christians have a belief of Christ pervading all things. As the Letter to the Colossians says, "In him [Christ] all things in heaven and on earth were created ... in him all things hold together." (Colossians 1:15–17)

An Ocean of Droplets. Each droplet of water is part of the ocean. The droplet may consider itself unique and beautiful as it catches the rays of the Sun, but its truth is the ocean from which it has come. For the droplet to see only its unique beauty is to live an illusion (*maya*). **What other images can help you understand the idea of *maya*?**

Check Your Understanding

1. Describe the Hindu version of salvation (the ultimate end).

Think About It

2. With a partner, make a list of the distractions in your life that could be considered *maya*. How do these distractions keep you from perceiving *Brahman*?

Making It Personal

3. Try to imagine the true nature of the soul. Create a description of yourself without referring to any physical qualities.

Sacred Cow. In Hinduism, ***ahimsa*** is the principle of doing no harm. Because everything is a manifestation of *Brahman*, to attack any living thing is to attack *Brahman*, and therefore to attack the self. For this reason, most Hindus are vegetarians. The cow, in particular, is sacred in India for its role in Indian society and what it symbolizes. **Search the Internet to learn more about Hinduism's sacred cow.**

The Caste System

In traditional Hindu society,

- each person had a certain social position in life
- all life was arranged as a hierarchy, from highest to lowest
- performing good deeds and following their assigned code of behaviour determined whether people had earned the right to be born at a higher level

These traditional beliefs were expressed in Hindu society's division into **castes**. Roles, jobs, social standing, and religious structures were organized according to the hierarchy of castes.

The caste system is said to have come to ancient India around 1500 BCE, with the Aryans. The caste system had four groups: priests, defenders of the realm, business people, and farmers. More recently, another caste developed: the **Untouchables** or outcastes. (The development of this caste, however, is not part of the philosophy of Hinduism. It is counter to the spirit of Hinduism.)

1. ***Brahmans:*** This is the priestly caste. Their role is to study and teach in matters of faith, especially the Vedas. They lead most key rituals.
2. **Kshatriyas:** This has been called the warrior caste. Their role is to protect the people and run a fair government.
3. **Vaishyas:** This caste consists of producers—traders, merchants, farmers, artists, and businesspeople. This group has traditionally taken care of the economic needs of the community.
4. **Sudras:** This is the lowest caste. Their main purpose is to serve the three higher castes. This group includes unskilled workers, servants, and anyone doing menial work.
5. **Untouchables:** Also called "outcastes," people in this group are considered outsiders: they may not interact in any way with members of the four castes. Traditionally, they do the dirtiest work in society and live apart, in small communities. However, this situation is changing. There are now quotas in place to ensure that members of this caste have access to better jobs.

According to traditional Hindu belief, following one's *dharma* means strictly following the rules of caste. The best way for a person to move to a higher caste in the next life is to act according to one's caste in this life. Acting above one's caste in this life is seen as ignoring *dharma* and generates bad *karma*, so

Ahimsa

The principle of non-violence

Caste

A traditional Hindu social level or class

Untouchables

In the traditional Hindu social levels, the lowest outsider class

Fast Fact

In June 2009, Meira Kumar, a member of the untouchable caste, became the first woman to hold the post of Speaker in the Indian parliament. There have been many other members of the untouchable caste who have held political positions in India.

Hymn of Purusha

1 The Man has a thousand heads,
A thousand eyes, a thousand feet.
He pervaded the Earth on all sides
and extended beyond it as far as ten fingers.

11 When they divided the Man,
Into how many parts did they apportion him?
What do they call his mouth, his two arms
and thighs and feet?

12 His mouth became the Brahman;
His arms were made into the Warrior,
His thighs the People,
And from his feet the Servants were born.

14 ... Thus they set the worlds in order.

(Rig Veda 10.90.1, 11, 12, 14)

Traditional Hindu Caste System

The Traditional Hindu Caste System

it hurts a person's chances of being promoted in the next life. The belief is that people are born into the lower castes based on the *karma* of their previous lives.

Today in India, discrimination based on caste or occupation is illegal. Many Hindu teachers now argue that the Hindu sacred writings never intended the social and occupational discrimination of the caste system. However, the traditional lines drawn between groups often persist. Here in Canada, caste is no longer important for many Hindu families. This shift away from tradition may bring about changes to Hinduism, in both India and in Western countries.

Check Your Understanding

1. Is it possible to move from one caste to another during a lifetime? Explain.

Think About It

2. What issues does the existence of a social category such as the Untouchables raise? Use Internet research and your understanding of both Canadian culture and Catholicism to consider the issues.

Making It Personal

3. Respond to the traditional Hindu caste system personally—for example, by comparing it with your present life, relating it to your family history, or imagining what it would mean if you lived now in a caste system. Present your response as a letter, scrapbook page, or another form of your choice.

Marking Time

Just like Christianity, Judaism, and Islam, Hinduism has many ritual celebrations that relate to the history of the religion. Hinduism has celebrations throughout the year, many of which mark special moments in life and relate to certain stages in life.

The Four Stages of Life

In Hinduism, what people need to enjoy a happy and fulfilling life is seen to change as they grow older. Life is divided into four main stages, each with its own focus and certain duties. These life stages have generally been followed only by males in the top three castes. However, the idea is that a Hindu man who moves through the stages performs his duty and comes to recognize that all life is ultimately illusion and that the ultimate goal is liberation (*moksha*).

Sanyasin. A sanyasin, or wandering ascetic, is the fourth and highest stage of life in Hinduism.

The Four Stages of Life

Stage of Life	Approximate Ages	Focus
Stage 1: Student	7 to 20	• religious education and a willingness to search for the truth
Stage 2: Householder	20 to 50	• duty to family, raising children, earning a living
Stage 3: Semi-retired	when family is self-supporting	• retreat from worldly life, focus on spiritual matters
Stage 4: Wandering **ascetic**	when ready	• holy, detached life, with no possessions or responsibilities

Life Milestones

Hinduism marks certain moments in life as especially important—conception, birth, the naming of a child, the first haircut, religious graduation, marriage, retirement, and death and cremation. Hindu scriptures note 16 of these moments. Some families observe all 16 with rituals.

Naming a Baby

Most Hindus mark the naming of a baby. For the first 10 days after birth, mothers and babies are kept apart from others for ritual purification. The naming ceremony often takes place on the twelfth day, usually in the home. Precise traditional rules relate to the number of syllables, caste, and deity of devotion. Modern Hindu naming practices are more flexible, especially outside of India.

Sacred Thread

Among Hindus of the upper castes, a boy between 7 and 12 might have an initiation ceremony called the sacred thread ceremony. This ceremony marks

Ascetic

Someone who practises severe self-discipline or abstains from physical pleasures for religious purposes

Fast Fact

Astrology plays an important part in the naming of the baby. The first syllable is often determined by the position of the Moon at the baby's birth.

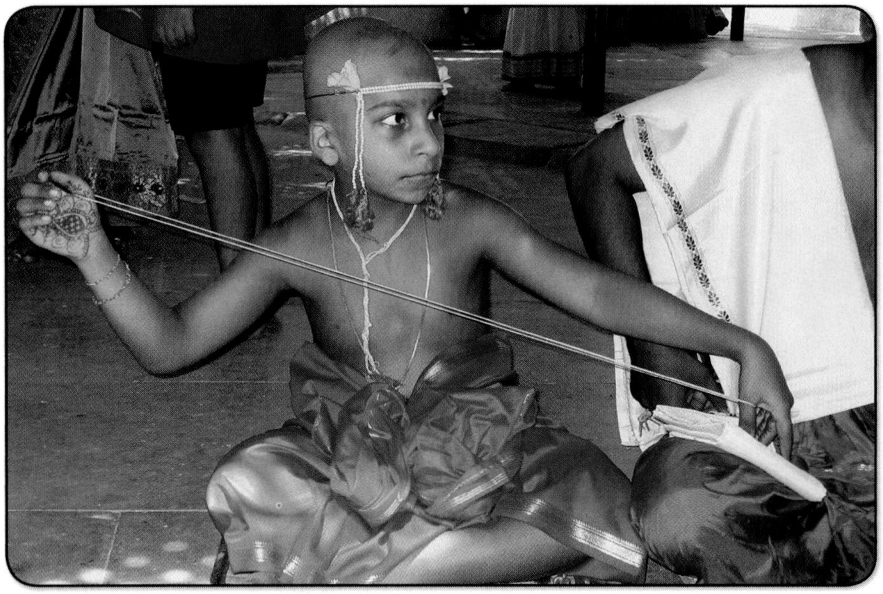

Sacred Thread Ceremony. A typical Hindu sacred thread ceremony. **Have you ever worn a symbol showing your commitment to your faith? What was it?**

his becoming a student—the first stage in life. In this ceremony, the boy is introduced to his guru, and a sacred thread is draped over his shoulder and chest. The boy is to wear this thread at all times as a sign of his responsibilities to his caste and to his study of the Vedas. This joyous family occasion marks the death of childhood and the birth of a responsible adult.

Death

According to tradition, Hindus mark death with families moving in a procession from the dead person's home, carrying the corpse on their shoulders, to the cremation grounds. The body is placed on the funeral pyre (fire). Mantras are recited and offerings are made to the deity of fire, who leads the dead to the eternal realm. The fire integrates the person with the cosmos as family and friends watch and pray. They later scatter the ashes on water, preferably a river.

In Canada, Hindus have had to adapt their funeral practices. Some Hindu communities have built their own crematoria to allow families to follow traditional practices as much as possible.

Check Your Understanding

1. Which of the four stages of life has an accompanying ritual? Which stages have no ritual? Why do you think that is the case?

Think About It

2. In a group, create a timeline showing Hinduism's life stages and some milestones. How do these stages and milestones reflect Hindu beliefs and values?

Making It Personal

3. What have been some key moments in your life so far? How do they compare with those marked in Hinduism?

Central Beliefs

Hindu Scriptures

Hinduism is possibly the world's oldest religion, and it has changed and grown over the centuries. For many years, Hindu teachings and stories were not written down, but were memorized and passed on by word of mouth. Eventually, the teachings were gathered into written collections. In general, these scriptures are categorized as

- "heard" or "revealed" scriptures, meaning that they have come from the deities through holy people

- "traditional scriptures" or "remembered scriptures," which are mostly popular stories about the deities

Revealed Scriptures

The oldest Hindu scriptures are the Vedas, named for the Sanskrit word for knowledge. The Vedas were written by and for the *Brahmans* (priestly caste), and divisions within the Vedas result from various *Brahman* families becoming specialists in different areas of ritual.

Over the years, the Vedas came to include

- verses or liturgical formulas
- prose that explains the meaning of the liturgy
- explanations meant only for the most learned practitioners
- Upanishads

"Upanishads" means literally "sit down near." Each of the Upanishads is like a conversation in which a person sits down beside a wise teacher to learn about the Vedas. The Upanishads were shared orally for more than 1000 years before they were written down. For Hindus, all of the Vedas are revelations, but the conversations in the Upanishads came to be seen as the heart of the Vedas and have had the strongest influence on Hinduism to this day.

Traditional Scriptures

The second type of Hindu scriptures are the traditional or "remembered" scriptures. Many of these are epic poems, including popular stories that give instructions and examples of how to behave. Most Hindus have not been especially concerned about whether these are historically accurate. Many of the remembered scriptures are stories of beloved Hindu characters who are role models of *dharma* living. The following are the best-known examples:

Hindu Gurus. The Hindu guru Bodhinatha (third from left) during a visit to Canada. **Do you have a mentor (male or female) who guides you?**

- **Ramayana** (Rama's Way), the story of Prince Rama and his wife Sita
- **Bhagavad Gita** (Song of the Blessed One, or Song of the Lord), a dialogue between a great prince, Arjuna, and his charioteer, Krishna

Ramayana

A Hindu epic about Prince Rama and Sita

Bhagavad Gita

A sacred Hindu story about Prince Arjuna and Krishna

Bollywood Films. Stories from the Ramayana have often been presented in popular Bollywood films. The term "Bollywood" is a combination of Bombay (Mumbai's former name) and Hollywood. **What are some popular movies, songs, and poems that you know that tell about heroes and (possibly) true events?**

Check Your Understanding

1. Describe "revealed" scriptures and "remembered" scriptures, and give at least one example of each.
2. What are the Upanishads? Why are they so important?

Think About It

3. From within this chapter or from Internet research, locate an example of Hindu scripture to read and examine carefully. Share your understanding of the scripture.

Making It Personal

4. In what ways have you learned valuable life lessons? Possibly you have learned through listening to a wise teacher, or by reading a story in which the character faced an important decision. Or perhaps you have learned and followed a particular set of rules. Describe a lesson you have learned and how you learned it.

Deities, Avatars, Epics

Hindus believe that there is only one God or Supreme Being, but that this Being is manifested in many different forms, which are called deities. Each deity is one of many different expressions of the divine; in other words, each deity represents a different facet of the supreme deity or eternal spirit, *Brahman*. Many Hindus devote themselves primarily to one personal deity, such as Vishnu or Shiva, as the highest and most perfect form of *Brahman*. However, almost all Hindus worship and honour other deities as well.

The Hindu Triad

Brahman is said to manifest in the form of many deities. According to some Hindu traditions, three of these deities together symbolize the cycle of existence.

Interplay of Brahma, Vishnu, and Shiva

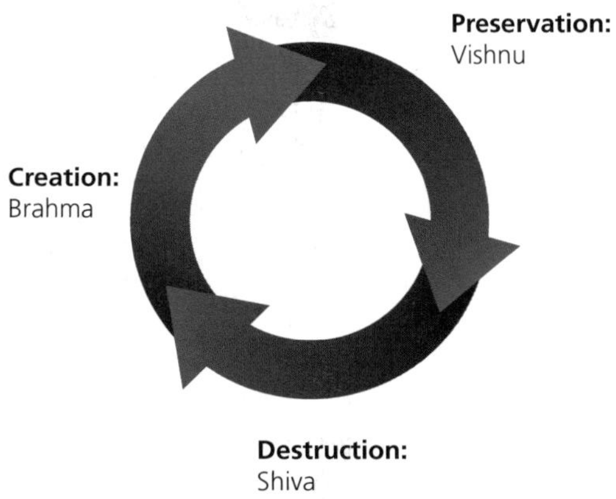

Creation, Preservation, and Destruction. This simple circular diagram shows the interplay of Creation (Brahma), Preservation (Vishnu), and Destruction (Shiva).

NEL

Brahma: The Creator

Brahma is the creator of the universe. He is most often shown with four faces, looking to the four compass points, showing that he is all-seeing and all-knowing. He is usually dressed in white and often shown riding on a swan or peacock, or seated on a lotus. He is considered above worship, so there are few temples to him.

Vishnu: The Preserver

Vishnu, the preserver, is most often shown dressed in yellow, with blue skin. He is often pictured with his partner, Lakshmi, riding on the back of a huge half-bird and half-man creature. Hindus believe that Vishnu descends to the world from time to time in human form to maintain order and save the world from danger. Incarnations of a deity are called **avatars**. So far, Vishnu has appeared in human form in nine different avatars. His seventh and eighth avatars are Rama and Krishna, heroes whose adventures are told in famous Indian epics. His ninth avatar is Gautama (the Buddha, the founder of Buddhism, which you will read about in Chapter 8). Hindus wait for the tenth avatar, the mighty warrior Kalkin, who will rid the world of oppression.

Shiva: The Destroyer/Redeemer

Shiva is both destroyer and redeemer. He is the deity of the cosmic dance. Shiva is dangerous, destructive, and lethal, yet he is joyful and a creative force. In his role as redeemer, he destroys the sins of believers in order to lead them to redemption. Shiva is often shown wearing a tiger-skin loincloth and a snake collar, and sometimes a necklace of skulls.

Shiva's dance has both a creative and destructive side. The joyful dance is associated with the creation of the cosmos. The violent dance is associated with the destruction of the cosmos, so that Brahma can recreate it. For Hindus, this ending may not be the worst fate, because the universe has to be destroyed in order to be recreated. Many people believe that ultimate truth is best experienced through Shiva because, they feel, they must look at the evil as well as the good—pain and suffering as well as life and growth.

A Closer Look

Hinduism has many deities, and its male deities often have female partners. Without the feminine side, these deities are seen as incomplete. All the female deities embody a strong, cosmic, feminine energy known as *shakti*. Many Hindu women offer devotion to this feminine force.

Avatar

A deity who has descended into the world in earthly form

Brahma. Brahma is the creator of the universe.

Vishnu. Vishnu, the preserver, often descends into the world in human form.

Shiva. Shiva, the destroyer and redeemer, is a complex deity.

A Gallery of Hindu Deities

Saraswati. Saraswati is the goddess of the arts.

Lakshmi. Lakshmi is the goddess of prosperity.

Ganesha. Ganesha is the remover of obstacles.

Parvati. Parvati is kind and gentle.

Durga. Durga is a warrior goddess.

Kali. Kali is the goddess of destruction and change.

Other Important Deities

The ultimate reality or *Brahman* is represented by three gods: Brahma, Vishnu, and Shiva. Each deity has other avatars with distinctive symbols that are associated with them. The term for symbols and associations used to describe and represent a deity is "iconography." Some of the best-known deities are listed in the table on the next page. The iconography of each deity is given under the heading "Principal Features" in the table.

Best-Known Deities of Hinduism

Name of Deity	Principal Features
Krishna	• has blue skin, wears yellow clothing and peacock feather headgear • often shown playing a flute • often depicted as a little boy or as a charioteer
Ganesha	• the son of Parvati • deity of wisdom, prudence, learning, and the remover of obstacles • has a potbelly, four hands, and an elephant head • often shown with a mouse or rat as a symbol of the obstacles Ganesha overcomes
Parvati	• one of the three female forms of Shiva's partner • the mother of Ganesha • kind and gentle
Durga	• one of the three female forms of Shiva's partner • shown with eight or ten hands and three eyes; carries weapons and a lotus • warrior goddess who slays demons
Kali	• one of the three female forms of Shiva's partner • symbolizes destruction, but also time and change • has four arms, black or blue skin, with tongue hanging out; wears a necklace of human heads • often shown standing on a demon's body
Lakshmi	• the goddess of wealth and prosperity • has four arms; in one hand she holds gold coins; sits or stands on a lotus, often surrounded by elephants
Saraswati	• female partner of Brahma and the goddess of wisdom, learning, the arts, and music • has white skin, with a crescent on her brow; often shown playing a musical instrument • shown sitting on a lotus, often with swans nearby

Make It Your Own: Iconography

"Iconography" is the word we use to describe how a god, deity, or saint is shown in art. In times and cultures where most people could not read, the symbols that were used to represent the religious figure helped worshippers immediately identify the figure. Often, the iconography is tied to a story from the life of the religious figure, or it ties in with some character element of the deity.

The above table of the Hindu deities describes the iconography used when the deities are illustrated or sculpted. For example, Ganesha's elephant head is an important feature of his iconography.

Activity

1. Search the Internet for images of a Hindu god such as those described in this table. Reproduce this image in the centre of the page. Find out the meaning of the symbols used to represent the deity in art. Search the name of the deity and the term "iconography." Label your representation of the deity by drawing a line from the symbol to a brief explanation in the margin.

Check Your Understanding

1. Choose one deity and describe the iconography of this deity to a partner. If you wish, do some research to discover why the deity is depicted with those characteristics.

Think About It

2. In a group, discuss Hindu beliefs about the Supreme Being, deities, and avatars. How do these differ from Catholic beliefs? What questions do these Hindu beliefs raise for you? Have one group member present a summary of your discussion for the class.
3. Why do you think destructive deities are popular in Hindu worship? Why might they be more popular than the gentler forms? Explain.

Making It Personal

4. Can you think of the iconography used to describe a Christian figure, for example, one of the Four Apostles?

Morality

Yoga. There are three yogas or paths to liberation. **Have you taken yoga lessons? How did they make you feel?**

Yoga

Hindu path (or discipline) to liberation

The Paths of Liberation: The Three Yogas

The ultimate goal of Hinduism is *moksha*—liberation from the eternal cycle of rebirths. But how can Hindus reach this goal? To answer this, Hindus turn to the Bhagavad Gita. In it, Krishna describes three **yogas** that lead to liberation. Many North Americans who are not Hindu think of yoga as a certain physical discipline, but in Hinduism, the three yogas are

- knowledge
- devotion
- action

The Path of Knowledge

The path of knowledge stresses the quest for spiritual knowledge and truth. Hindus who follow this path must study with a guru. One of the main goals of this type of yoga is to understand that *atman* and *Brahman* are one. Because the illusion (*maya*) of the material world is powerful and seductive, Hindus train their minds to see the world as it truly is. The best way to train the mind is through meditation.

Meditation means concentrating and focusing the mind to control one's thoughts. In Hinduism, it involves special positions and breathing exercises to help people clear their minds. For Hindus, repeated practice in meditation allows them to go beyond their egos (the conscious self) and detach from the world of illusions. Then they can see the true nature of *atman*.

Two techniques that help in meditation to focus the mind are

- using a mantra—a word, phrase, or sound that is repeated
- using a mandala—a symbolic circle diagram that may represent the universe or even the self

NEL

Make It Your Own: Breathing in Meditation

One of the most important disciplines in the practice of meditation is breathing. Although breathing is an automatic action, attentive and disciplined breathing can help meditators gain deeper concentration. Yoga breathing is centred in the lower abdomen, not in the chest muscles. Those who practise yoga say that deep, slow, smooth breathing is needed for concentration. Breath prayer has been part of the Christian tradition for centuries. In the Jesus Prayer, which consists of the short phrase "Lord Jesus, have mercy on me, a sinner," attention to breathing helps the person meditating enter more deeply into relation with the person of Jesus.

Activity

1. Choose a phrase to concentrate on as you pray. Find a quiet place where you will not be disturbed. Sit in a position that you can maintain for 10 minutes. First, concentrate on your breathing. Try to breathe deeply, slowly, and peacefully. After a few minutes, say or think about your phrase as you exhale your breath. Afterwards, describe your experience orally or in writing. How did you feel? How were you different? Was it difficult to focus on your breathing or on the phrase or word?

Make It Your Own: Aum

One of the most common symbols of Hinduism is *Aum* (or *Om*), the sacred sound or mantra that some Hindus use in meditation. Meditators pronounce every letter as a separate sound that flows together, A-U-M. For Hindus this is the most sacred and basic sound, so calling it a mere word is insufficient.

Aum can be seen as a way of saying the name of the ultimate reality, *Brahman*. Just as *Aum* has three letters, *Brahman* has three main representations that you have read about: Brahma the creator, Vishnu the sustainer, and Shiva the destroyer.

Aum could also be seen as all of time (past, present, and future) and all of space (heavens, ground, and underground). It includes all the creative forces of the universe as well as all the destructive forces.

Aum often forms the opening and closing of many Hindu prayers. It helps those praying to bring a sense of the sacred to their rituals. *Aum* is often found in Hindu art, in its writing and decoration. The symbol is often worn as a pendant around the neck in the same way that Catholics wear a crucifix. It is often prayed at the beginning of a journey. When a child is born, the baby is cleansed, and then honey is put on the baby's mouth in the shape of this symbol.

Aum

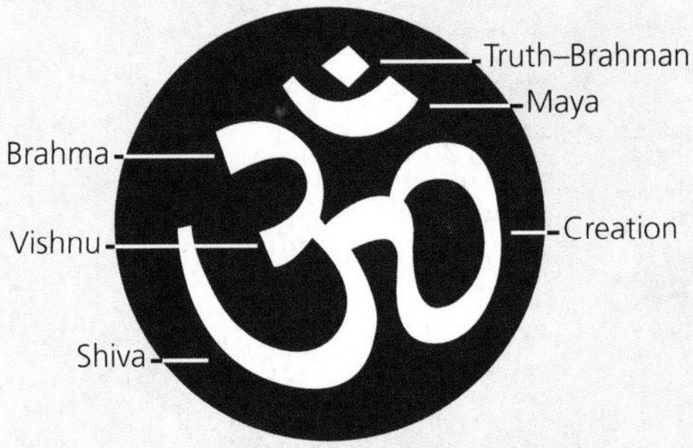

The *Aum* Symbol. *Aum* is both a visual symbol and a sound. It consists of three sounds—A-U-M. Each sound represents a different aspect of God.

Activities

1. Create a poster using the *Aum* symbol. In the centre of the poster, create a collage of pictures that represent the meaning of this symbol.

continues...

Make It Your Own *(cont'd)*

2. Create a diagram or mind map to show how *Aum* represents the Hindu concept of the sacred. This diagram will have a central symbol (*Aum*), and then three parts representing each of the three letters of *Aum*. In each of the three areas of the diagram, place words and symbols to explain the different realities that can make up *Aum*.

3. Create a list of 50 of the most sacred sounds in the world. These would be sounds that could tell us something about the sacred. From this list, identify the top 10 sounds. Explain why each of these sounds made your top 10 list.

Shri Yantra Mandala. The Shri Yantra Mandala is a visual help with meditation.

The Path of Devotion

A second yoga that leads to liberation is the path of devotion. In this path, Hindus choose a particular deity and spend their lives worshipping that deity. In the Bhagavad Gita, Krishna tells Prince Arjuna,

> *Fix your mind on me, and so devoted to me, sacrificing to me, reverencing me, having disciplined your self, with me as your final resort, you shall come to me.*
>
> (Bhagavad Gita 9.34: © Oxford University Press)

In giving his will completely over to the will of the deity Vishnu (in the form of Krishna), Prince Arjuna becomes a model of devotion. This yoga is important for many Hindus; they see their religious identity as tied to one preferred deity, but it does not exclude worshipping other deities.

The Path of Good Works

The final yoga is known as the path of good works, or *karma* yoga. This involves Hindus doing their *dharma*, or duty, to the best of their ability. This duty will be different for everyone—depending on caste, job, social status, stage of life, and so on. To correctly follow the path of good works, Hindus strive to act without passion or attachment. They are not to act in the hope of being rewarded with good *karma*. They simply try to act according to what is required by their *dharma*. This path stresses discipline, ritual action, and moral choices. The Bhagavad Gita instructs as follows:

> *Acting for the body alone, without expectation, having abandoned possessions, restrained in thought and self, he incurs no defilement ... Therefore, without attachment, always do whatever action has to be done; for it is through acting without attachment that a man attains the highest.*
>
> (Bhagavad Gita 4.21; 3.19)

The Laws of Manu

Another Hindu scripture, the Laws of Manu, governs actions and virtues. This book contains many important instructions for living according to caste and acting according to duty. The passage below describes some specific karmic consequences for future rebirths:

> *A man becomes a stationary object as a result of the faults that are the effects of past actions of the body, a bird or wild animal from those of speech, and a member of one of the lowest castes from those of mind-and-heart.*
>
> (Laws of Manu 12.9)

"Stationary" would mean life as a plant, for example. Other prominent themes in the Laws of Manu are the importance of patience, discipline, truthfulness, knowledge, and living according to the four stages of life.

Check Your Understanding

1. Identify and describe the three yogas practised by Hindus.

Think About It

2. With a partner, discuss what you have learned about yoga and meditation. How has learning about Hinduism added to your understanding of these practices and their purposes?

Making It Personal

3. In your life, what goals, possible paths, techniques, and teachers do you see? Write your thoughts or express them in a poster.

Family Life

Traditionally, men and women have very separate roles in Hindu society.

These gender divisions are seen sometimes in educational and work opportunities. For example, girls from poorer families in rural areas may not have the chance to attend high school, but girls from wealthier families tend to receive a good education and, in turn, find good jobs. In urban areas and in Western countries, gender roles outside the home are less structured.

One aspect of the traditional gender roles is the idea of a dowry. A dowry is money or other valuables that the bride brings to her marriage. In some cases, a bride's family must give the groom or his family the valuables before the wedding. Although the Indian government has made the practice illegal, many Hindu families in and outside of India pay or require dowries.

A Closer Look

A dowry leads some people to believe that female children will drain wealth from the family, while male children will bring in wealth.

Tradtional Roles in Hindu Society

Traditional Male Roles	Traditional Female Roles
The eldest male is head of the family.	Women make all decisions about running the household.
All property is passed down from father to son.	Women tend to take charge of the family's participation in religious rituals.
Only men may be *Brahman* priests and lead public worship.	

Mumbai, India. People of many cultures, faiths, and times have given dowries. In fact, Mumbai, or Bombay as it was once called, was given to the British royalty by the Portuguese in 1661, when King Charles II married Catherine, a princess of Portugal.

Marriage

Many North Americans think of meeting someone, falling in love, and then marrying. However, for some Hindus, this practice seems backward: according to one expression, "in the West, you marry who you love. In India, you love who you marry." Hindu society has a tradition of arranged marriages, and most marriages in India are arranged. Those Hindu marriages that are not arranged are called "love matches."

The process of matching potential husband and potential wife can be extensive. Sometimes friends or neighbours arrange marriages between their children. The search for a spouse can also involve newspaper ads, Internet sites, and paid matchmakers (or matrimonial agencies). Introducing the couple to each other is very formal, with no "dating" as we know it—for example, the couple is never left alone.

According to traditional Hindu beliefs, parents and others who arrange marriages

- are looking out for the best interests of the young people involved
- have greater wisdom and insight into what it takes to make a successful marriage

A Hindu Wedding Ceremony. Hindu weddings involve a sacred fire, which reminds everybody that God is present and witnessing the marriage. **Have you attended a Catholic wedding? What were some of the rituals you remember?**

- know their own children well; for example, if the son is easily attracted by physical beauty or other fleeting qualities, parents may look for enduring qualities of character
- consider qualities of character, education, caste, and tradition—and whether the two young people have similar or compatible backgrounds
- consider practical matters, such as whether the man can provide a stable home
- give the couple a say in what happens; if either person in the proposed match does not want to marry the other, then the process stops and the search starts again
- believe that love develops gradually *after* marriage, not before

Today, "love marriages" are becoming more common. As well, Hindus are marrying Hindus of other castes or non-Hindus. This shift undoubtedly is both a challenge to tradition and an opportunity for dialogue.

Check Your Understanding

1. How do the roles of males and females differ in traditional Hindu families?
2. Explain dowry and arranged marriages. What are three reasons given in support of arranged marriages?

Think About It

3. Think about dowries and the arguments that might be made in favour of them and against them. Then state your own opinion and reasons.

Making It Personal

4. Imagine that your parents were arranging a marriage for you. How would you feel? Why?

Interreligious Dialogue

Hinduism and the Catholic Church

A Closer Look

About non-Christian religions, the Second Vatican Council said, "The Catholic Church rejects nothing of what is true and holy in these religions." It specifically said the following about Hinduism:

> From ancient times down to the present, there is found among various peoples a certain perception of that hidden power which hovers over the course of things and over the events of human history.... This perception and recognition penetrates their lives with a profound religious sense. ... Thus in Hinduism, men contemplate the divine mystery and express it through an inexhaustible abundance of myths and through searching philosophical inquiry. They seek freedom from the anguish of our human condition either through ascetical practices or profound meditation or a flight to God with love and trust (Vatican Council II, *On the Relation of the Church to Non-Christian Religions*, #2).

"So, we can only pray, if we are Hindus, or if we are [Muslims] not that a Christian should become a [Muslim], not that a Hindu or a Christian should become a [Muslim]; nor should we even secretly pray that anyone should be converted; but our innermost prayer should be that a Hindu should be a better Hindu, a Muslim a better Muslim, and a Christian a better Christian. That is the fundamental truth of fellowship."

—Gandhi on other religions

Mohandas (Mahatma) Gandhi. Gandhi is often called the father of India for his role in the Indian independence movement. **What do you know about Gandhi from books, movies, and websites? How did Gandhi help people become more accepting of each other's faiths?**

Mohandas Gandhi was born in 1869 in a small village in western India, when the country was under British rule. His parents were of the Vaishya caste and they raised him as a Hindu with a special reverence for Vishnu. He favoured texts from the Bhagavad Gita, the Upanishads, and the Ramayana. Rama was a central figure in Gandhi's devotion throughout his life. When he was 13 years old, Gandhi was married in an arranged marriage.

Gandhi studied law in London, England, and was soon after sent to South Africa, where Indian immigrants faced discrimination and exploitation. To help improve their rights as workers and citizens, Gandhi developed such tactics as public protest, work stoppages, clever use of the media to promote his message, and non-violent resistance to unjust laws. In South Africa, and later in India, Gandhi was often jailed for his actions. By the time he left South Africa in 1914, the conditions for Indians there had greatly improved.

When Gandhi returned to India, he became involved in the struggle for Indian independence from Britain. He put into practice, on a massive scale, the principles of non-violent resistance that he had developed in South Africa. Many doubted that India could gain independence without military force, but Gandhi maintained his beliefs despite many setbacks. Indian citizens (both Hindu and Muslim) and the British rulers clashed violently. Whenever this happened, Gandhi would publicly stop eating as a protest until peace was restored.

During this time, Gandhi also began to see the treatment of women and Untouchables as discrimination. He also made the choice to simplify his life with plain clothing and few possessions, and he practised vegetarianism all his life—reflecting again the principle of doing no harm.

As India moved toward independence, violence continued between India's two dominant religious groups—the Hindu majority and the Muslim minority. As a result, India under British rule was divided into two parts: the modern state of India and the modern state of Pakistan. Many leaders, but not Gandhi, saw partition as a way to end the violence. However, the violence continued after partition. As the violence increased, Gandhi again responded by fasting. This time, he nearly died of starvation. In response, the riots on both sides stopped. In January 1948, a Hindu extremist who was outraged by Gandhi's position on religious tolerance, particularly toward Muslims, shot and killed Gandhi. The next day, nearly 3 million people took part in his funeral procession.

Early in his struggle for Indian independence, Gandhi was given the nickname "Mahatma," which means "great soul." He is considered a father of India and has inspired many movements for social justice worldwide.

Catholic Connection

Thomas Merton (1915–1968) was an American monk, writer, and social activist. To teach other Catholics about the important belief and practice of non-violence, Merton used the example of Mohandas Gandhi, Gandhi's belief in *ahimsa* (the principle of doing no harm), and his practices.

Based on what you have learned in this chapter, what do you think are the "rays of that truth" that the Catholic Church finds in Hinduism?

Vasco da Gama. In 1524, on his third visit to India, the explorer Vasco da Gama died in this church in Kochi.

Fast Fact

Christians are a small minority in India—about 2.3 percent. In India's large population, however, that means about 24 million people.

Christian Missionaries in India

Christianity came to India in the first century, when the Apostle Thomas travelled to Malabar (now the state of Kerala, on the southwestern tip of India). In the seventeenth century, other missionaries went to India, including Robert de Nobili and Francis Xavier. Because of their work, Goa (a small state on the western shore) and Kerala became major centres of Christianity in India.

Catholic Monks Learning from the East

In the late 1940s, the Benedictine monk Henri le Saux went to India, where he wanted to explore two traditions: Christian and Hindu spirituality. It is said that he travelled to the Himalayas where he stripped practically naked and then recited the Psalms and chanted *Aum*, the mystical sound of oneness, for three weeks. He became known as Swami Abhishiktananda. Le Saux spent the rest of his life seeking to understand the spirituality of *Brahman* and *atman* while remaining faithful to his own Catholic faith and spirituality. He knew that, like Hindus, Christians believe that God and the world are not two separate things. Like Hindus, Christians believe that at the core of the self, our human identity, there is God. However, Christians do not say that God *is* the self.

Another monk, the Benedictine monk Bede Griffiths, lived in India for many years and said the following about Hinduism:

> In Hinduism … there is a most profound sense of "mystery" and "sacrament." No people on earth has gone further towards the penetration of that ultimate mystery which lies beyond all human words and thoughts, transcending every name and form, and yet manifesting itself in all the forms of nature and human consciousness. Here we have perhaps the deepest expression which can be found of the primeval revelation of the presence of God in nature.

Many Western Christians have benefited from the teachings of these monks who were seeking the truth about God and themselves in other faith traditions.

Check Your Understanding

1. What are three examples of interreligious dialogue between Christianity and Hinduism?
2. What is the principle of *ahimsa* and how did Gandhi use it?

Think About It

3. Gandhi defined Hinduism as a search for truth through non-violent means. Based on this chapter, including the monks' reflections on Christianity and Hinduism, how would you define Christianity?

Making It Personal

4. Gandhi practised literally Jesus's command to "turn the other cheek" (Matthew 5:39). Respond to this personally. Do you believe that people can oppose violence with peace? Or do you believe that violence must be checked with violence? Explain.

What I Have Learned

In this chapter, I learned about

- the presence of Hinduism in Canada
- where Hinduism is practised, its origins, and how it developed
- the ritual life of Hindus
- the teaching of the presence of *Brahman* in reality
- Hindu ideas of the eternal rebirth of all things (*samsara*) and the linked notions of *moksha, karma,* and *dharma*
- the traditional caste system
- the key deities and scriptures in the Hindu tradition
- the goals of Hindu life and the paths to salvation
- family life for Hindus
- examples of interreligious dialogue
- the way Gandhi lived the teaching of non-violence

A Prayer: A Hindu Hymn of Creation

There was neither non-existence nor existence then;
There was neither the realm of space nor the sky which is beyond.
What stirred? Where? In whose protection?
Was there water, bottomlessly deep?
There was neither death nor immortality then.
There was no distinguishing sign of night nor of day.
That one breathed, windless, by its own impulse.
Other than that there was nothing beyond.
Darkness was hidden by darkness in the beginning;
With no distinguishing sign, all this was water.
The life force that was covered with emptiness,
That one arose through the power of heat.
Desire came upon that one in the beginning;
That was the first seed of mind.
Poets seeking in their heart with wisdom
Found the bond of existence in non-existence.
Their cord was extended across.
Was there below? Was there above?
There were seed-placers; there were powers.
There was impulse beneath; there was giving-forth above.
Who really knows? Who will here proclaim it?
Whence was it produced? Whence is this creation?
The gods came afterwards, with the creation of this universe.
Who then knows whence it has arisen?
Whence this creation has arisen—
perhaps it formed itself, or perhaps it did not—
The one who looks down on it, in the highest heaven,
only he knows—or perhaps he does not know.

(Rig Veda 10.129.1–7)

Chapter 8 The Story of Buddhism

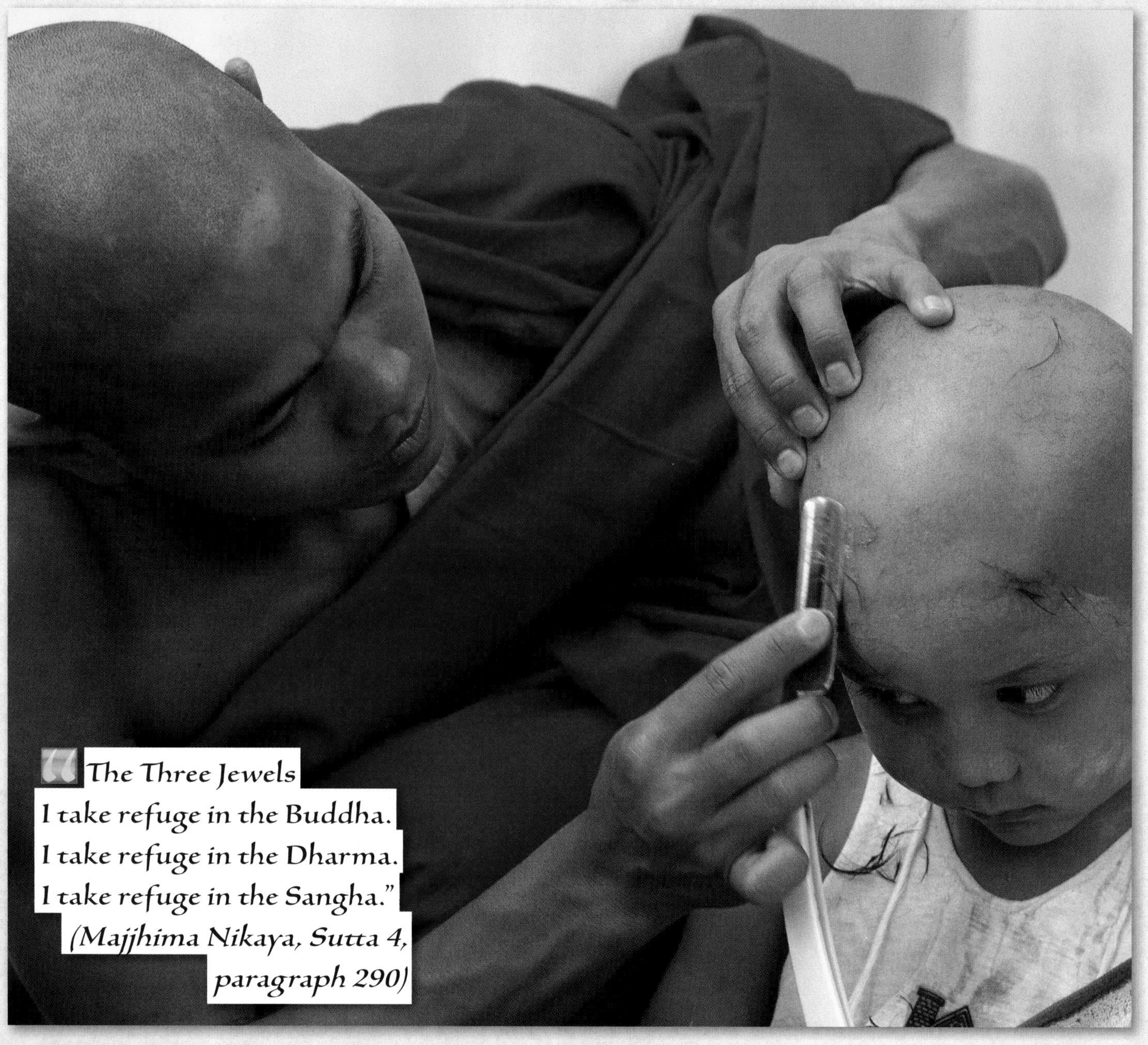

"The Three Jewels
I take refuge in the Buddha.
I take refuge in the Dharma.
I take refuge in the Sangha."
(Majjhima Nikaya, Sutta 4, paragraph 290)

The Three Jewels

The Three Jewels. This is the symbol for the "Three Jewels." The concept of the Three Jewels is central to Buddhists and refers to the founder of Buddhism, to the Buddha's teachings (*dharma*), and to the Buddhist community (*sangha*).

Head-Shaving Ceremony. When a monk is preparing for initiation into the community of Buddhist monks, his or her head and eyebrows are shaved as a sign of commitment to the many rules he or she must follow. Buddhists cannot become monks until they are 20, but younger boys and girls are allowed to become novices. This young boy in Myanmar (Burma) is a *samanera*, a novice monk. **With a partner, brainstorm ideas and questions about Buddhist rituals and their meanings so that you can reflect on and add to them throughout the chapter.**

What You Will Learn

In this chapter, you will learn about

- where Buddhism is practised, and Buddhism in Canada
- the founder of Buddhism, the history of the religion, and its development into different types of Buddhism
- Buddhist rituals (including meditation) and festivals
- central beliefs of Buddhism: the Three Jewels, the Four Noble Truths, the Eightfold Path
- Buddhist morality: the Five Precepts and Buddhist values
- family life and daily life for Buddhists
- the Catholic Church and Buddhism

Personal Recollection

I was born in the northeastern part of India near the Burmese border. My family wasn't particularly religious, but I remember when the monk came to our village. He came on the full moon day in July to teach. I was only seven years old.

He spoke the words of the Buddha: "Come and see for yourself." He also taught about suffering. We all suffer and have pain. I asked him how we can get rid of suffering. His answer: "Become a monk." But, I was not sure if I wanted to dedicate my life as a monk. It was a big step. I would have to leave my family and live a life of great simplicity and discipline.

My parents let me become a temple boy and accept the Five Precepts, the basic moral teaching that every Buddhist needs to follow. For five years I helped around the temple while going to school. Five years later, I became a novice monk. My head was shaved and I received the simple saffron-coloured robes and the alms bowl of the monk.

— **Gyanosri Sharaman**

Venerable Gyanosri Sharaman. The Venerable Gyanosri Sharaman today ministers to the Indian Buddhist community at the Ambedkar Mission in Toronto. He leads meditation and worship services, education, and community building. **If you could ask this monk about his life and decisions, what questions would you ask?**

Buddhism in Canada

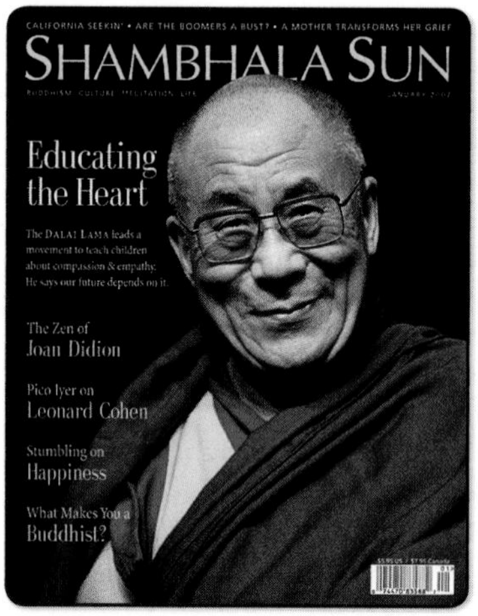

***Shambhala Sun* Magazine.** The Canadian magazine *Shambhala Sun*, published in Halifax, has introduced many North American readers to meditation, yoga, and Buddhism.

Today, Buddhism is the twelfth-largest religion in Canada. Thanks largely to immigration, Buddhism is one of the fastest-growing religions in Canada. According to census figures, the number of Canadians who identified themselves as Buddhists increased by 84 percent—to about 300 000 followers—between 1991 and 2001.

Many Canadian Buddhists trace their faith origins to family roots in Asian countries. Most Buddhists in Canada live in Ontario (43 percent) and British Columbia (29 percent). Since the 1980s, Halifax, Nova Scotia, has developed a substantial Buddhist community and become the centre of an international network of meditation centres founded by a Tibetan Buddhist leader, Chögyam Trungpa Rinpoche.

Buddhism has many faces in Canada and internationally. As you read this chapter, note how reading about different representations of Buddhism and followers of Buddhism adds to your understanding.

Aung San Suu Kyi. Aung San Suu Kyi is a Buddhist, a political leader in Myanmar (formerly known as Burma), and Nobel Peace Prize winner. Suu Kyi has been under house arrest since 1989 for criticizing the military, undemocratic Burmese government.

Buddhist Psychology Course. These students and professor are in a Buddhist psychology course at the University of Toronto.

The History of Buddhism

Buddhism has its roots in northern India and Hinduism. It began as a reform movement within Hinduism. The founder of Buddhism, Siddhartha Gautama, sought a new way of practising religion.

The Life of the Buddha

Around 400 BCE, Siddhartha Gautama was born as a prince of a small Hindu kingdom spanning northern India and Nepal. A wise man prophesied that the young prince would become either a great king or a great saviour (a great religious leader): if the child were exposed to suffering, he would follow the spiritual path. Siddhartha's father wanted him to become a great king, so tried to shield Siddhartha from all suffering. Siddhartha married at age 16 and was on his way to achieving political leadership. However, as a young man, Siddhartha took a journey that exposed him to suffering and led to the creation of Buddhism.

Catholic Connection

The title "the Buddha" is applied to Siddhartha Gautama in the same way as the title "the Christ" is applied to Jesus. The title means the "Enlightened One." Siddartha Gautama was never considered divine as Jesus is.

Birth of the Buddha. According to Buddhist tradition, the newborn Buddha walked immediately. Where his feet touched the earth, lotus flowers appeared. Buddhists see the lotus flower as a symbol of Buddhist thought: the flower's roots are in the mud but its face turns toward the Sun. This painting is from a temple in South Korea.

When he was approximately 35, **the Buddha** gave his first sermon, called the Dharmachakra, or the Wheel of Dharma, about the nature of human existence and what people must do to release themselves from suffering.

The Buddha continued to teach his message for 45 years, until his death at the age of 80. During that time, the Buddha taught largely through the use of stories. However, his teachings were not written down during his lifetime; in fact, they were first written down 400 years later by his followers.

Siddhartha first witnessed suffering when he saw a stiff and worn-out old man, an ill man in great pain, and a dead man whose family was weeping over him. Until then, Siddhartha had not known that old age, disease, or death existed. Finally, he saw a calm and peaceful holy man. Curious about the calmness of the holy man, he decided to leave his wife and newborn son to become a religious **ascetic** and look for answers to the suffering he had seen.

The Buddha

The founder of Buddhism, Siddhartha Gautama; teachers who fully understand the nature of mind and reality are also called Buddhas

Ascetic

Someone who practises severe self-discipline or abstains from physical pleasures for religious purposes

The Buddha's First Sermon. This temple, the Dhamekha Stupa, marks where the Buddha gave his first sermon near the Ganges River, in northeastern India.

Siddhartha Becomes the Buddha

Siddhartha travelled from teacher to teacher with five companions for six years, but failed to find **enlightenment** as to the cause and cure of suffering. He concluded that neither his old life of luxury nor the harsh existence of a religious ascetic was the right way to live. So he began to develop a middle way between luxury and asceticism, one that involved finding a thoughtful and balanced way to live, giving up greed and selfishness at one extreme and harsh denial of pleasure at the other.

Siddhartha resolved to sit in meditation until he attained enlightenment. For 49 days, he engaged in meditation that involved a spiritual struggle against the evil god Mara. Finally, he attained the Great Enlightenment and became known as the Buddha. The Buddha's enlightenment gave him a special understanding of human suffering and of how people might escape that suffering, attain complete peace, and enter **nirvana**. Rather than immediately entering into nirvana, the Buddha decided to remain on Earth to share his insights. He accepted disciples (male and female) and converted his five ascetic companions, who became the first monks.

Enlightenment

A state of perfect happiness and understanding; unconditional compassion for all beings

Nirvana

The end of personal suffering and the experience of unchanging peace

Where Buddhism Is Practised

Buddhism originated in the northern part of the Indian subcontinent and spread from there to other parts of Asia. Most Buddhists today live in Southeast Asia. In total, Buddhists make up about 6 percent of the world's population (around 383 million people). This makes Buddhism the fourth-largest religion in terms of number of followers.

Where Buddhists Live

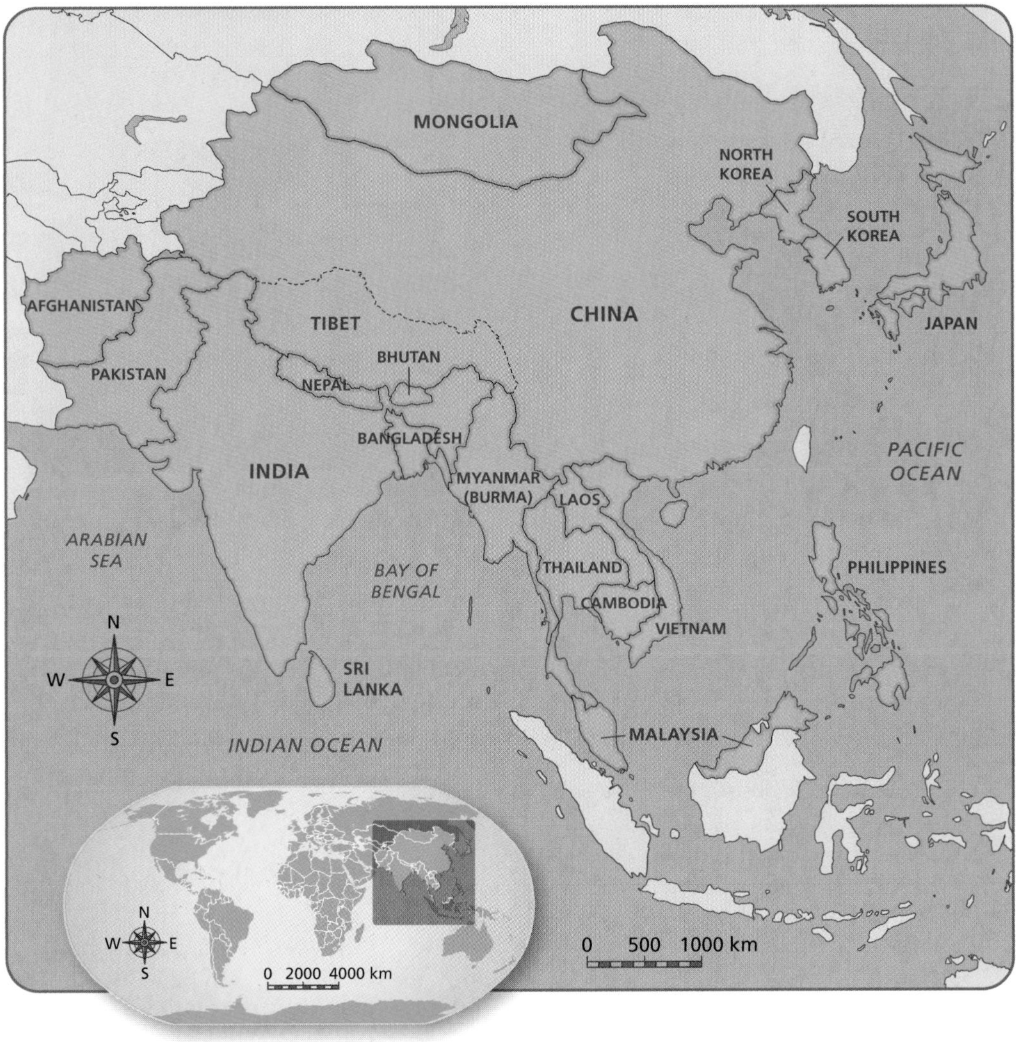

Where Buddhists Live. What do you know about the cultures and religious practices of people living in these countries? How have these countries been in the news lately?

Make It Your Own: The Life of the Buddha

It is hard to know the historical accuracy of accounts of the life of the Buddha:

- We know that he lived about 2500 years ago, and we also know that some parts of his story are more legendary than factual.
- Certain parts of his life provide lessons to his followers about the choices we make in life. Maybe that is why they were included in his biographies.
- Also, when we look at somebody who lived 2500 years ago, we look at his life through present-day eyes. It is not easy for us to understand what life was like in his time.

These conditions make it difficult to know the historical situation of the Buddha. Nevertheless, the story of the Buddha makes fascinating reading.

Activities

1. Create an illustrated timeline or a multimedia presentation of the life of the Buddha. Illustrate the dates and events with pictures or photographs or slides.
2. Find songs or video clips that represent key moments in the Buddha's life. Explain why you made these selections.

The Parinirvana of the Buddha. This statue from the Ajanta Caves in India dates back to the second century BCE. The Buddha's peaceful expression reflects the Buddhist teaching about calmness and fearlessness in the face of suffering and death.

Fast Fact

The Buddha's remains, such as his teeth, were divided among his followers. These remains (called relics) were placed in special stone burial mounds called *stupas*, which became centres of Buddhist devotion.

Fast Fact

Some groups within Buddhism are

- Theravada Buddhists
- Mahayana Buddhists
- Vajrayana (Tibetan) Buddhists
- Zen Buddhists

Buddhism Spreads through Asia

The ideas taught by the Buddha were spread by his disciples throughout India. By about 390 BCE, there were two distinct groups within Buddhism: Theravada and Mahayana Buddhists. (You will learn more about these later in this chapter.)

Buddhism became the state religion of a powerful empire in the Indian subcontinent ruled by Emperor Asoka. Not only did Asoka convert to Buddhism himself and send out missionaries, but he also called on a council to agree on the Buddhist scriptures. Under Asoka, Buddhist missionaries travelled in every direction: west as far as modern-day Afghanistan, north into Tibet and Mongolia, south into what is now Sri Lanka and Indonesia, and east through China as far as Korea and Japan.

Over time, the spread of Islam and a strengthening of Hinduism reduced the influence of Buddhism in India. However, Buddhism was growing and developing within other lands and cultures. Buddhism today is practised in many different ways in countries around Asia and the rest of the world.

Beyond Asia, followers have developed what some people call Western Buddhism. Today, the majority of Buddhists in Canada follow the Mahayana school of Buddhism.

A Martial Arts Class in Toronto, Ontario. Many of the martial arts practised now in Canada (such as kung fu, tae kwon do, tai chi, karate, jujitsu, and judo) are said to originate in ritual exercises developed by a fifth-century Buddhist monk called Bodhidharma. Buddhists are not allowed to provoke combat, but they may defend themselves. These two young Canadian women are practising a martial art, which originated in Thailand, called Muay Thai boxing.

Timeline of Buddhism History

750 BCE, 500 BCE, 250 BCE, CE, 250, 500, 750, 1000, 2000

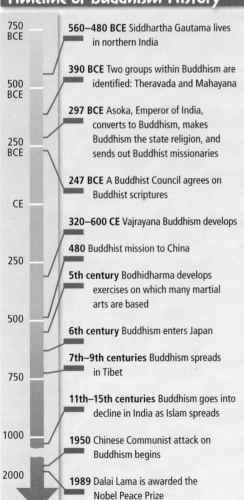

- **560–480 BCE** Siddhartha Gautama lives in northern India
- **390 BCE** Two groups within Buddhism are identified: Theravada and Mahayana
- **297 BCE** Asoka, Emperor of India, converts to Buddhism, makes Buddhism the state religion, and sends out Buddhist missionaries
- **247 BCE** A Buddhist Council agrees on Buddhist scriptures
- **320–600 CE** Vajrayana Buddhism develops
- **480** Buddhist mission to China
- **5th century** Bodhidharma develops exercises on which many martial arts are based
- **6th century** Buddhism enters Japan
- **7th–9th centuries** Buddhism spreads in Tibet
- **11th–15th centuries** Buddhism goes into decline in India as Islam spreads
- **1950** Chinese Communist attack on Buddhism begins
- **1989** Dalai Lama is awarded the Nobel Peace Prize

Check Your Understanding

1. On a world map, identify where most Buddhists live and the historical reasons for this.
2. Briefly summarize the life of Siddhartha Gautama and at least three developments in Buddhism after the Buddha's death.

Think About It

3. From what you have learned so far about Buddhism, summarize on a diagram or in writing the options available to Siddhartha Gautama at key moments in his life and the choices he made. Evaluate each choice.

Making It Personal

4. Buddhism is a faith that values simplicity, calmness, and detachment from material possessions. As a Canadian teenager, what challenges do you think Buddhist teenagers would face in Canadian culture? Share your ideas with a partner, then join with another pair to compare ideas.
5. Siddhartha Gautama sought the *middle way* between luxury and asceticism. In your life, what would be examples of luxury, asceticism, and the middle way? Have you ever tried to be an ascetic to strengthen your faith?

Rituals

Buddhists believe that their rituals help them to achieve enlightenment either in the present life or in the future. Rituals also allow them to bond with the Buddhist community (*sangha*). The main rituals of Buddhism are

- meditation
- worship—at home or at a temple or shrine
- rituals that mark milestones in life
- festivals marking the history of Buddhism

Meditation

The Buddha is often shown as a meditating figure with a calm expression. The Buddha used the Hindu techniques of meditation as a way of gaining enlightenment. As Buddhism spread, meditation techniques from other traditions were added to the Hindu methods practised by the earlier Buddhists.

The purpose of meditation is to quiet the mind so that the meditator can more fully enter into the spiritual world. The ritual of daily meditation practised by many Buddhists also connects them with the community of Buddhists (*sangha*) and helps them to identify with the founder of the faith.

Meditation is more than thinking deeply. It is a way of removing distractions so a person can be in touch with the present moment, free from memories of the past or anxieties about the future. Buddhists who meditate can bring about a state of mindfulness (awareness only of the present moment) by focusing on the act of breathing, following the passage of air into and out of the body. Meditators can also focus on a visual object, such as a flame, a sacred diagram, or a ***mandala***. They can also recite or chant continuously a single word or phrase, called a ***mantra***, such as the Mahayana *Om Mani Padme Hum* (Hail the jewel in the lotus).

Catholic Connection

The main purpose of meditation in the Christian tradition is to enter into the life of Jesus Christ so that the person meditating may become more like Jesus Christ.

Mandala

A visual object, usually in the form of a circle, that can be used as an aid for focusing in meditation

Mantra

A word or phrase that is chanted as an aid to meditation

Hand Gestures of the Buddha. The hand gestures seen in images of the Buddha can show the Buddha meditating, teaching, being generous, reassuring or protecting an approaching person, or touching the earth as witness to his worthiness for Buddhahood. **What gestures have you seen in images of the Buddha?**

Skill Focus: Meditation

Many people in the West have become interested in meditation as it is practised in religions such as Buddhism and Hinduism. Meditation has many benefits: it focuses the mind and helps one to remain calm under stress. Learning and adapting some of the techniques from Buddhist meditation can help you study for a test, prepare for an oral presentation, perform onstage before an audience, or compete in a sports event. Meditating is difficult, but there are some guidelines for beginners.

1. Make a habit of meditating at the same time each day. Start with small periods of time from 5 to 15 minutes.
2. Have a purpose for meditating. Choose a subject, mantra, or virtue to meditate on. If you are preparing for some stressful event (for example, a school or driving test, a performance, a job interview, a competition), you might wish to meditate on courage or on staying calm. If you are having trouble getting started on a difficult task (for example, studying, writing an essay, doing a chore), you may wish to meditate on the virtue of persevering.
3. Choose a place where you will be comfortable and where you will not be interrupted or distracted. Turn off your cellphone, the computer, and the TV.
4. You may wish to meditate with your eyes closed, but if that is too difficult, choose an object to look at. The object should be something that is meaningful and calming for you to contemplate (for example, a religious object, a photograph).
5. Pay attention to your breathing as you meditate. Take long, slow breaths in and exhale slowly. Slow breathing helps to slow down the heart rate and helps concentration.

The Big Buddha of the Buddha Beach Temple. The Big Buddha of the Buddha Beach Temple in Koh Samui, Thailand, shows the Buddha meditating in a typical pose called the Lotus. Although it may be uncomfortable to those who are new to meditation, this cross-legged posture gives great stability and allows practitioners to stay in a meditative state for a long time. **Have you ever meditated? Explain why you meditated and what position and other techniques you used. Why did you use these techniques? If you have not meditated before, what do you think would motivate you to try meditation?**

Check Your Understanding

1. Explain why Buddhists meditate, and describe three techniques that help them meditate.

Think About It

2. Why do you think a close bond has developed between some Catholic and Buddhist monks and nuns?

Making It Personal

3. Many religions include meditation. For example, Christians might use the Aramaic word *Maranatha*, from one of the earliest Christian prayers, in their meditations. *Maranatha* means "Come, Lord." Have you ever used a repeated word in prayer? Which one do you use and how does it help you pray?

Buddhist Worship. This Buddhist monk beats the drum during morning worship at Gampo Abbey in Pleasant Bay, Cape Breton, in Nova Scotia, as the other monks and nuns of the abbey chant.

A worshipper entering a monastery, temple, or *stupa* bows to show devotion and respect. A worshipper may bow three times: once for each of the Three Jewels—for the Buddha, the *dharma*, and the *sangha*. This bowing can range from simply lowering one's head with palms together to kneeling and touching the head to the floor.

Buddhists make offerings to the Three Jewels by burning incense, lighting a candle, and giving food (often fruit) and flowers. Offerings symbolize respect for the Three Jewels, can help a Buddhist get closer to enlightenment, and give material support so that the monks can live.

Worship practices vary between cultures and interpretations of Buddhism, but can include

- silent meditation
- chanting in deep, rhythmical voices
- sermons about applying some aspect of the *dharma* to daily life

Fast Fact

Puja is also the word for a form of worship in Hinduism. Because Buddhism has its roots in Hinduism, many terms and practices in Hinduism carried over to Buddhism.

Worship

Buddhist worship, called *puja* in some cultures, takes place at home or at a temple or shrine. It can include simple, individual acts of worship, such as venerating the Buddha by bowing at a home shrine, or a service at a local temple led by monks with a formal sequence of chants.

Buddhist temples and shrines are usually built to symbolize the five elements of the Buddhist faith: sky—vertical line; water—horizontal line; fire—circle; air—oval; and earth—square. All Buddhist holy buildings have a broad base to symbolize earth and a spire or point at the top to symbolize sky.

Temples or monasteries often have decorative arches, curving rooflines, bells, gongs, and gardens. Entranceways also usually include large cylinders with Buddhist teachings on them. As people pass the cylinders, they spin them, asking for guidance.

Catholic Connection

Buddhists venerate (regard with deep respect) the Buddha, but most do not worship him. Similarly, Catholics venerate, but do not worship, Mary and the saints.

The Five Elements of Buddhism. The five elements of Buddhism are sky, water, fire, air, and earth. These are often symbolized in the exterior of Buddhist shrines and temples. In the interior of the Cham Shan Temple in Niagara Falls, Ontario, shown here, there are also many Buddhist works of art and artifacts.

A Japanese Zen Buddhist ceremony, for example, would include longer periods of meditation and less preaching on the *dharma* than a Theravadin ritual would.

Fast Fact

Some Buddhists have a day like a Sabbath day, on Sunday. However, many celebrations are celebrated according to the lunar calendar.

Buddhist Prayer Flags. Some Buddhists also use prayer flags. For example, in Tibet, Buddhists string cloth flags in front of homes and from mountaintop to mountaintop. The flag colours represent the five elements of the faith, and the flags have Buddhist prayers, mantras, and symbols written on them so that the wind may spread goodwill and compassion everywhere. **How would you spread goodwill and compassion everywhere?**

Make It Your Own: The Wheel of Dharma

The Wheel of Dharma. The eight spokes of the Wheel of Dharma, or Dharmacakra, represent the eight central teachings of Buddhism.

The Wheel of Dharma is one of the most important symbols in Buddhism. The eight *spokes* of the wheel represent each of the steps of the eightfold path. These are eight important teachings of the Buddhist tradition:

- Right thinking or understanding
- Right thought or intention
- Right speech
- Right action or behaviour
- Right living or livelihood
- Right effort
- Right mindfulness
- Right meditation or contemplation

Wheels are meant to be turned. This means that the Buddhist teachings are not just to be memorized but to be put into motion. Buddhists are expected to live according to their beliefs. In fact, one of the names of the Buddha can be translated as "Wheel Turner." The Buddha's purpose was to set in motion a new set of laws to help people live their lives without suffering. The wheel could also represent the endless cycle of suffering that humans face, called ***samsara***.

The *hub*, or centre of the wheel, is a three-part design representing the Three Jewels of Buddhism: the Buddha, the *dharma* (teaching), and the *sangha* (community). This hub can also refer to the spiritual discipline of meditation that is required to put the teachings of Buddhism into practice.

The *circle*, or wheel, represents life as well as the Buddhist understanding of the perfection of the teaching. The Wheel of Dharma also resembles a ship's steering wheel. In this way, Buddhist teachings help people navigate the difficult waters of life.

Activity

1. A mandala is a circular object or diagram that is used to help meditation. It is often illustrated with symbols to represent life and the universe. Search for examples of mandalas on the Internet, and then create your own mandala to show your understanding of Buddhism. Your mandala could
   - show the Wheel of Dharma at the centre
   - use colours and symbols to represent other Buddhist teachings

   Provide a written explanation of what each colour and symbol represents.

Samsara

The law of birth, death, and rebirth, or the process of reincarnation

Marking Time

Buddhist Wedding Ceremony. This Tibetan Buddhist royal wedding ceremony took place in Halifax, Nova Scotia, on June 10, 2006.

Merit

The idea in Buddhism that a person can be reborn in a form closer to enlightenment if he or she accumulates merit; wholesome deeds and intentions can add to a person's merit

Catholic Connection

For an explanation of the difference between reincarnation and resurrection, see page 237 in Chapter 7.

Milestone Rituals

Buddhists mark some milestones in life, especially birth and death. In contrast to many other faiths, they do not mark a change in adolescence except for those becoming novice monks. They also consider marriage a civic practice, rather than a religious act or obligation, so Buddhist monks do not generally officiate at weddings, and marriage rituals vary from culture to culture. However, Buddhist teachings do address family life.

Birth

The birth of a child is a time for celebration for Buddhists. All living beings are considered precious and not to be harmed. The rituals to celebrate births vary in Buddhism. In the Theravadin tradition, a Buddhist family may take the newborn to a temple to be blessed. The closing ritual consists of melting candle wax into a bowl to symbolize the union of earth, air, fire, water, and sky. The Three Jewels are recited on behalf of the child.

Death

The rituals dealing with death and funerals are both important and distinctive. A dying Buddhist may be visited by monks, who will offer comfort by chanting verses from the scriptures that deal with death.

Buddhists believe in reincarnation: until someone achieves enlightenment and nirvana, death is the end of one life and the beginning of another. Death is also a time for passing on **merit** (positive impact of one's life) to the next rebirth. In some funeral rituals, a cup is filled until it overflows, meaning that the merit built up in this life spills into the next.

Festivals

For Buddhists, the full moon is a sign of power, and many festivals are celebrated when the moon is full. Festivals vary from culture to culture—and from tradition to tradition. Here are some of the most important annual rituals.

Vesak

Vesak celebrates the birth of Siddhartha Gautama and, in some countries, also the day of his enlightenment and death. People decorate statues of the Buddha, re-enact scenes from his life, and set off fireworks. Some people spend the day in meditation and reflection.

Vesak. Buddhists from the Zen Buddhist Temple in Toronto, Ontario, celebrate the birth, enlightenment, and death of the Buddha on Vesak Full Moon day, one of Buddhism's most hallowed days. In many countries, Vesak is celebrated on the full moon in May. Other events during the Zen Buddhist temple celebration include the blessing of children.

Esala Perahera Parade. Elephants wear golden costumes and lights during the Esala Perahera festival in Kandy, Sri Lanka.

Asalha Puja

Asalha Puja, or Dharma Day, marks the beginning of the Buddha's teaching. Buddhists show thanks that the Buddha and other enlightened teachers shared their knowledge. Dharma Day is held at the beginning of the rainy season in Southeast Asia, when travelling becomes difficult and monks and nuns stay in one place for three months, meditating and reading scriptures. Lay people may give up luxuries such as sweets, meat, or alcohol to reinvigorate their spiritual practices.

Esala Perahera

After the Buddha's death, one of his teeth was placed in a temple in Kandy, Sri Lanka. In August, a colourful procession carries the tooth through the city. Pilgrims from around the country journey to Kandy to celebrate Esala Perahera.

Catholic Connection

In Canada, some Buddhists refer to Vesak as Buddhist Christmas. Dharma Day is sometimes called Buddhist Lent. What similarities and differences can you see?

Check Your Understanding

1. With a partner, create a list or draw a diagram of what you would see in Buddhist worship. Display and discuss your recollections as a class.

Think About It

2. In small groups, discuss how Buddhist rituals are similar to Catholic ones. How are they different? Note your ideas on a Venn diagram and be prepared to summarize them.
3. Buddhist practices vary among traditions and from culture to culture. Compile a list of questions you would like to ask a Buddhist to understand the detail of his or her own ritual practices.

Making It Personal

4. Many Buddhists have home shrines. If you were to create a sacred space in your home, what would it look like? Sketch your space. Explain your choices of symbols.

The Community and Scriptures

Leonard Cohen and Buddhism. Some celebrities, such as Canadian poet and singer-songwriter Leonard Cohen, have made it known that they follow Buddhism. **What advantages and disadvantages do you think there might be to a public figure expressing his or her faith?**

Although Buddhists share central beliefs, there are differences among the three main groups of Buddhists and the scriptures they follow. The following are the three main groups: the smaller, more traditional Theravada Buddhism; the majority Mahayana Buddhism; and Vajrayana Buddhism, developed in Tibet and Mongolia. In addition to these main three, there is also Zen Buddhism, a Japanese adaptation of Mahayana Buddhism.

Catholic Connection

"Hurt not others in ways that you yourself would find hurtful." Some people call this quotation from the *Sutta Pitaka* (Udana 5:18) the Buddhist Golden Rule. What words of Jesus say the same thing?

Theravada

Theravadins believe that only monks make up the *sangha*, and only monks can achieve enlightenment, although others can gain merit by following the teachings of the Buddha. Theravadins' ideal figure is the monk who is so saintly that he is close to achieving enlightenment. However, they reject the idea of heavenly figures and others, such as the saintly monk, helping followers. Theravadins take seriously the Buddha's last words: "Work out your own salvation with diligence." Theravadins do not consider the Buddha to be divine. To them, he is an enlightened human being.

Theravada Buddhists believe in the *Tripitakas* (Three Baskets), which are often called the first Buddhist scriptures.

***Tripitakas* (Three Baskets)**

Vinaya Pitaka
Rules of conduct for monks and nuns

Sutta Pitaka
A large collection of the Buddha's teachings

Abhidhamma Pitaka
Explanations of the Buddhist view on laws of nature and the mind

Mahayana

Mahayana incorporated elements of religions and cultures it encountered. Here are some key distinguishing beliefs:

- All followers of the Buddha, not just monks and nuns, are members of the *sangha* and all can achieve enlightenment.
- The ideal is the *Bodhisattvas*—people who have achieved enlightenment but have chosen to stay on the human plane of existence, suffering, death, and rebirth. Their purpose is to teach and to heal others on their journeys.
- They will accept help from both *Bodhisattvas* and other forms of the Buddha besides the historical one.
- The *Tripitakas* are worthy scriptures, but there are others, such as the *Lotus Sutra*. Mahayana Buddhists also use teaching stories called *Jataka*, which can be humorous as well as instructional.

Vajrayana

A third and later form of Buddhism, called Vajrayana, developed in Tibet, Mongolia, Bhutan, and Nepal. Vajrayana Buddhists absorbed elements of the local religion into their own beliefs. The result was a unique set of spiritual disciplines—the style of meditation, chanting, and the use of objects in prayer.

Zen Buddhism

Zen Buddhism emphasizes enlightenment through meditation. To achieve this state, people do certain exercises and practices, such as meditating on riddles or puzzling questions—for example, "What is the sound of one hand clapping?"

The Dalai Lama. The Dalai Lama is the spiritual and political leader of exiled Tibetans—and revered as the incarnation of a *Bodhisattva*.

Zen Garden. How might a Zen garden such as this one in the Montréal Botanical Garden in Montréal, Québec, help in meditation?

Fast Fact

Many Mahayanans appeal to these other Buddhas, who can be deities or compassionate human beings, for help in their Earthly spiritual journeys.

Fast Fact

Many Chinese people draw upon Buddhism as well as Taoism and Confucianism. These Chinese philosophies date back to the fifth and sixth centuries BCE.

Check Your Understanding

1. In a small group, create a chart noting the main divisions of Buddhism and key details of beliefs. As a class, discuss your charts and create one central chart.

Think About It

2. Meditation is a practice common to all Buddhists despite their differences. Why do you think this is so? Express your ideas in a poster or brief essay or speech.

Making It Personal

3. The Buddha expressed his teachings in many ways to suit many people. What teachings of your faith have best suited you? What are your favourites? Why?

Central Beliefs

The Buddha grew up as a Hindu and accepted large parts of the Hindu worldview. This included the belief in *samsara*—the cycle of birth, death, and rebirth. Buddhists aim to break out of the cycle to achieve nirvana. Nirvana is the state of being freed from having desires: it involves letting go of personal attachments and the illusion of oneself, or individuality. When a person has achieved nirvana, there are no more goals to reach, possessions to hold, or suffering to feel. It is a state of complete peace and balance.

Buddhists, like Hindus, use the term ***karma*** related to *samsara* and reincarnation. Buddhism understands *karma* as being directly related to intentions and to the Buddhist concept of merit. For Buddhists, intention is central.

Karma

The law of cause and effect, of one's actions having an impact on one's future life

A Closer Look

In Buddhism, the ideas of "right," "good," "evil," and "wrong" are relative. The intention behind a deed and its effect on oneself and others are critical in determining whether it is right or wrong.

In contrast to Hindu understandings of God and deities, the Buddha taught that questions about the existence of God were for individuals to discern and address themselves. Theravada Buddhists believe it is no good focusing on the possibility of outside help when we have the means to save ourselves.

Catholic Connection

Catholics attach great importance to having a relationship with God. Catholics do not believe that they can save themselves; that is why they seek a relationship with God.

The main Buddhist beliefs about how a person should live are reflected in the *dharma*—the teachings the Buddha gave to his disciples in the years following his enlightenment. The teachings are arranged into numbered sets of teachings:

- the Three Jewels
- the Three Marks of Existence (Three Universal Truths)
- the Four Noble Truths
- the Noble Eightfold Path

Buddhist morality and values are also reflected in

- the Five Precepts
- five Buddhist values to live by

As you read summaries of these central beliefs, think about how they relate to each other—and how they compare with the central beliefs you know.

The Three Jewels

The Buddhist creed can be summed up as the Three Jewels. Where can meaning be found in our troubled world? A Buddhist would respond, "I take refuge in the Buddha, the *dharma*, and the *sangha*."

The Three Marks of Existence (or the Three Universal Truths)

The Buddhist view of the material world is based on three understandings, or marks, of existence:

1. ***Anicca* (Impermanence):** Buddhists believe that nothing is permanent. People, animals, plants, and even mountains are changing all the time. Our mental and physical processes are constantly changing. The Buddha taught that nothing remains the same for long and there is no rest except nirvana. Clinging to the notion of permanency adds to our dissatisfaction and suffering in life. We are to try to wake up to reality: life is ever changing, unpredictable, uncertain.
2. ***Dukkha* (Suffering):** All life involves suffering. Suffering includes physical pain and illness as well as things like being bored and being uncomfortable. It also includes the

desire to acquire pleasure and to maintain it. People may be happy for most of their lives, but in the end they must face physical decay and death.

3. *Anatta* (Not Self): *Anatta* means that there is no permanent identity or existence. The Buddha taught that there is nothing more to a person than can be seen or experienced, and that everybody is made up of five parts: the body, feeling, perception, mental actions, and awareness. Nothing in ourselves is actually "self." All of these parts are impermanent and ultimately an illusion. For Buddhists, the aim is to get beyond the egotism of "me" and "mine." Wise or enlightened Buddhists are detached from material goods and images of themselves. (Some Buddhists have taught that energy is created by all people. It is this force that carries on into the next life.)

Thich Nhat Hanh. Thich Nhat Hanh was born in Vietnam in 1926 and entered a Zen monastery when he was 16. In the 1960s, during the Vietnam War, he created an organization to help rebuild bombed villages and schools, set up medical centres, and resettle homeless families. His style of Buddhism is known as Engaged Buddhism, which reaches out to those who are suffering.

Tibetan Monks Creating a Mandala. These Tibetan monks are creating a mandala with sand. It takes weeks to complete, then it will be swept away. **What do you think are the lessons of this spiritual exercise?**

Fast Fact

The term "right" was not used by the Buddha to indicate a religious or moral duty. "Right" means skillful. The Buddha did not command Buddhists to follow the Noble Eightfold Path for his sake. Rather, he encouraged them to examine the path for themselves.

The Four Noble Truths

1. People suffer (*dukkha*). From the cradle to the grave, we hurt physically and emotionally. Even when we are fit and healthy, we can feel inadequate or lonely. We suffer from physical or emotional pain and longing.
2. This suffering is caused by desire, greed, ignorance, and attachment. We can adapt to physical pain, but unfulfilled longings and cravings make our suffering deep.
3. To remove suffering, we must remove desire, greed, ignorance, and attachment. If we can stop the things that cause us to desire, then suffering will stop. Taming our desires requires great discipline.
4. To end suffering and achieve enlightenment, unending peace, and freedom from all desire, people should follow the Noble Eightfold Path.

The Noble Eightfold Path

The Buddha had experienced the harshness of disappointment and sorrow in his life. The source of these, he believed, was our human expectations and desires. To deal with these expectations and desires, the Buddha proposed a way, which Buddhists call the Noble Eightfold Path.

The Noble Eightfold Path

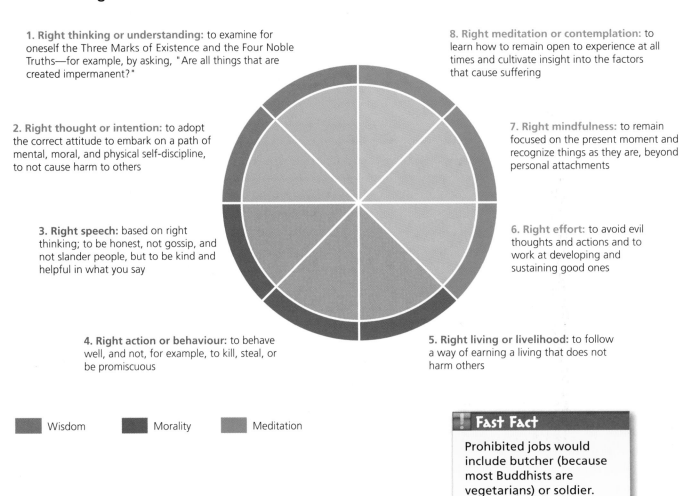

1. Right thinking or understanding: to examine for oneself the Three Marks of Existence and the Four Noble Truths—for example, by asking, "Are all things that are created impermanent?"

2. Right thought or intention: to adopt the correct attitude to embark on a path of mental, moral, and physical self-discipline, to not cause harm to others

3. Right speech: based on right thinking; to be honest, not gossip, and not slander people, but to be kind and helpful in what you say

4. Right action or behaviour: to behave well, and not, for example, to kill, steal, or be promiscuous

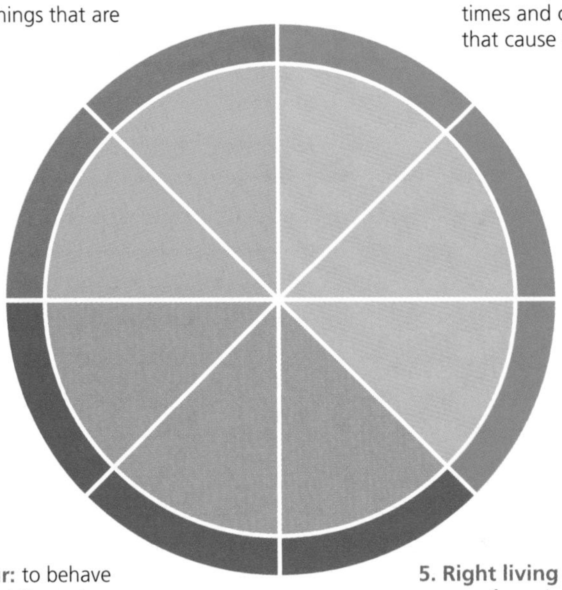

5. Right living or livelihood: to follow a way of earning a living that does not harm others

6. Right effort: to avoid evil thoughts and actions and to work at developing and sustaining good ones

7. Right mindfulness: to remain focused on the present moment and recognize things as they are, beyond personal attachments

8. Right meditation or contemplation: to learn how to remain open to experience at all times and cultivate insight into the factors that cause suffering

Wisdom   Morality   Meditation

Fast Fact

Prohibited jobs would include butcher (because most Buddhists are vegetarians) or soldier.

Morality

The Five Precepts

The Five Precepts are the ethical guidelines that Buddhists follow.

1. I undertake the precept to refrain from destroying living creatures.
2. I undertake the precept to refrain from taking that which is not given.
3. I undertake the precept to refrain from sexual misconduct.
4. I undertake the precept to refrain from incorrect speech.
5. I undertake the precept to refrain from intoxicating drinks and drugs, which lead to carelessness.

Buddhist Values

In addition to the explicit teachings that Buddhists follow, they also share common values:

1. **Self-determination** Each person is responsible for following the Noble Eightfold Path alone, not relying on outside help.
2. **Mindfulness** The *dharma* asks Buddhists to be aware of the present moment, and not to daydream or become distracted by the past or future.
3. **Compassion** Compassion is the ability to see and feel things from another's point of view; compassion must lead to action to help someone who suffers.
4. **Loving-kindness** Loving-kindness (*metta*) is extending goodwill, caring, and warmth to others without expecting any reward.
5. **Detachment** Detachment means not clinging to guilt or pride from past events, and not approaching future events with anxiety and expectation, but looking at all events without bias and emotion.

Catholic Connection

"And what is right speech? Abstaining from lying, abstaining from divisive speech, abstaining from abusive speech, abstaining from idle chatter: This, monks, is called right speech" (*Magga-vibhanga Sutta* of the *Sutta Pitaka*).

How does this compare with the ninth commandment of the Bible: you shall not bear false witness against your neighbour?

Make It Your Own: Buddhism by the Numbers

In studying Buddhism, you will notice that numbers are very important. There are

- Three Jewels
- Four Noble Truths
- Five Precepts
- the Noble Eightfold Path

One of the reasons for grouping these teachings by numbers is to make them easier to remember. If I know that there are Three Jewels and I can remember only two, then I know that I have to find out the third.

Activity

1. Numbers can be put into geometric forms. For example, the Three Jewels can be shown as a triangle. Create a diagram that combines all of the teachings listed above. You can use lines, shapes, or any other type of symbol. Make sure to label the names of the teachings.

Check Your Understanding

1. In small groups, explain these key teachings of Buddhism: the Three Jewels, the Three Marks of Existence, and the Eightfold Path.

Think About It

2. Explain why, according to Buddhists, people suffer. Do you think that desire causes human suffering? Why or why not?
3. Explain why Buddhists try to focus on the present rather than the past or future.

Making It Personal

4. Create two lists: your top five values and your top five rules for living a good moral and spiritual life. Is it easy or hard to live these values and rules every day? Explain.
5. In small groups, discuss how following the Five Precepts might be difficult for Buddhist teens living in Canada today. How might following the Five Precepts help them?
6. Create your own eightfold path for removing suffering from your life.

Family Life

Fast Fact

Buddhism's main contribution to family life is the Five Precepts, which guide individual morality. The precepts help everyone by outlining life-affirming attitudes and actions toward each other.

"Supporting one's father and mother, cherishing wife and children and a peaceful occupation; this is the greatest blessing."
(Sutta Nipata 261)

Although the Buddha left no specific instructions about family life, and Buddhism does not favour any particular form of family organization, Buddhist teachings address daily life and morality extensively. Buddhists see the family as the foundation of the community.

- Husbands and wives are expected to honour, respect, and be faithful to each other.
- Parents are expected to raise their children as Buddhists.
- Children are expected to obey their parents and to preserve family traditions.

Divorce is not forbidden in Buddhism, but it seldom occurs. Similarly, no teachings or doctrines specifically forbid abortion. However, because life is sacred to Buddhists and because they consider life to begin at conception, abortion is generally condemned as the taking of life.

***Dharma* in Daily Life.** In the daily life of family and work, everything a Buddhist does relates to the *dharma*. When a Buddhist brings mindfulness to everyday actions, then the *dharma* is being applied. For example, Thich Nhat Hanh teaches about bringing mindfulness to washing dishes. Similarly, University of Toronto professor Jack Miller, who follows Buddhist teachings, says, "When I cut celery, I cut celery." **In your own words, explain what Miller means.**

One of the more challenging values of Buddhism is non-attachment. Buddhism teaches that attachment to desires and cravings ultimately brings suffering. Buddhism also teaches a focus on the present. How and why might these teachings be a challenge to family members? to you?

The Buddha himself left behind his wife and son. Theravada tradition expects only monks, who leave their families when they take their vows, to achieve enlightenment because of the challenges involved. Others see the family as a spiritual environment where a deep understanding of attachment can be explored. Living in a family involves necessary material and emotional attachments. Buddhism asks followers to let go of the negative bonds that tie us to others, such as lust, prejudice, jealousy, fear, and hate.

The *dharma* offers this teaching story:

> Two monks are walking through a forest when they come to a shallow river. At the bank of the river, a beautiful young woman asks the monks to help her cross to the other side. The elder monk immediately picks her up and carries her across the river and puts her down. Then the monks go on their way and the young woman goes on hers.
>
> After two hours of silent walking, the younger monk can no longer contain his disapproval. He scolds the elder monk, saying, "How could you touch a woman? It is against our vow!" The elder monk smiles and replies, "I left her at the riverbank. Are you still carrying her with you?"

***Dharma* Teaching Story. In this *dharma* teaching story, what do you think the younger monk was "still carrying"?**

The Buddha on Friendship

The Buddha encouraged Buddhists to treat their friends with generosity, kind words, helpfulness, impartiality, and integrity. Being attentive and present in our encounters with our friends brings a sense of respect. Buddhism also teaches that Buddhists should choose friends who will help them to follow the teachings of the Buddha, not lead them away from the values of Buddhism.

Catholic Connection

Compare the story of the two monks to the attitude of the elder son in the story of the Forgiving Father (Luke 15:11–32).

Check Your Understanding

1. Explain what *dharma* says about how Buddhists should live their family lives.
2. What makes for a good friend, according to the Buddha?

Think About It

3. Which of the central beliefs of Buddhism do you think apply most directly to family life for Buddhist teens in Canada? Explain your choices.
4. Read the teaching story from the *dharma* and discuss the accompanying question with a partner or in a group.

Making It Personal

5. Make a table in which you list ways friends and peers influence your life and your worldview, and ways your family and your faith influence you. Are some of these influences in conflict? If so, how can you bring them together?

Buddhism and the Catholic Church

Catholic Connection

A close bond has developed between some Buddhist and Catholic monks and nuns. They have welcomed each other into their monasteries and convents, joining together in silence, meditation, and reflection. Some communities co-operate on social projects and, in a world marked by violence, are working together for the cause of peace.

With the Second Vatican Council (1962–1965), the Church expressed its desire to learn how the Spirit may be at work in Buddhism. Both faiths have since learned from each other in a genuine dialogue between theologians on both sides.

> Buddhism, in its various forms, realizes the radical insufficiency of this changeable world; it teaches a way by which men, in a devout and confident spirit, may be able either to acquire the state of perfect liberation, or attain, by their own efforts or through higher help, supreme illumination (Vatican Council II, *On the Relation of the Church to Non-Christian Religions*, #2).

Buddhism is a very practical religion. The Buddha rejected discussion of God because he wanted his followers to focus on something they could understand and do something about: suffering. For Catholics, suffering is not the main evil to be overcome. Suffering can in some cases be redemptive. For Catholics, God suffered and died on a cross. This suffering for others is seen as an act of liberating people to love. Love is what Christians seek. God, for them, is the greatest example and source of love. Not surprisingly, the question of suffering is at the heart of Catholic–Buddhist theological dialogue.

One way in which Catholics have considered how Buddhists look at suffering is by examining the concept of *metta*:

> Through our dialogue we have come to appreciate the importance that you Buddhists give to love for one's fellow human beings which is expressed in the concept of *metta*, a love without any desire to possess but only to help others. It is understood as a love which is willing to sacrifice self-interest for the benefit of humanity. So *metta*, according to Buddhist teaching, is not confined to benevolent thought, but extends to the performance of charitable deeds, to the service of one and all (Pontifical Council for Interreligious Dialogue, *Message to Buddhists for the Feast of Vesakh,* 2006).

How do the actions of Thich Nhat Hanh and Engaged Buddhism, described on page 275, help you understand the term *metta*?

Most Catholic–Buddhist dialogue has been about spiritual experience. Both faiths have an intense and long spiritual tradition. Some areas that both faiths have examined are meditation (which you explored earlier in this chapter), monasticism, and ecology.

Monastic Traditions

Because both Catholicism and Buddhism have long-standing monastic traditions, the Church turned to one of its monastic communities, the Benedictines, to initiate the dialogue. Since then, Buddhist monks and nuns have lived with Catholic monks and nuns to learn the other's spiritual traditions and meditation techniques. Because of the dialogue, Buddhist monks, such as the Dalai Lama and Thich Nhat Hanh, have encouraged

Christians to enter more deeply into their own tradition in order to bring peace and compassion to the world.

Catholic monks have likewise spent time in Zen and Tibetan monasteries. They have learned from each other "the universal value of self-discipline, silence and contemplation" in the development of the human person, as Pope John Paul II said in 1991.

Profile: Thomas Merton

Thomas Merton's early life showed little sign of the direction he would take. He was born in France, baptized as an Anglican, and raised largely in the United States and England. During his university days in New York City, he would have identified himself mainly as a communist and atheist. However, a sequence of events, including moments of revelation in a church in Rome, led to his joining the Catholic Church in 1938. While teaching at St. Bonaventure University in New York state, he attended a retreat at a Trappist monastery in Kentucky. Soon after, he joined the Trappist order.

Merton became a strong supporter of interreligious understanding. By the early 1950s, he was exchanging ideas with writers around the world on issues of prayer, justice, and the contemplative life. In 1968, Merton met with Buddhists, Hindus, and Christians in India and Southeast Asia, exchanging ideas and insights. Meetings with the Dalai Lama and Thich Nhat Hanh greatly influenced his ideas.

Thomas Merton and the Dalai Lama. Thomas Merton (1915–1968) was a Catholic Trappist monk who practised Christian meditation, was a leader in interreligious dialogue, and was increasingly influenced by Buddhist practice. In his search to deepen the dialogue with Buddhist monks, Thomas Merton (left) met with the Dalai Lama in 1968.

Ecology

Catholics and Buddhists also share a common concern for the health of the Earth. Both faiths believe that

- there is a spiritual dimension to the ecological crisis of today, which is related to greed, the human desire for large amounts of material goods
- dealing with this greed is part of the contribution that religions can make to these issues

For Buddhists, greed is an aspect of the desire that causes suffering. From a Buddhist perspective, these desires for material possessions can bring only sorrow and ecological peril for our planet. Similarly, Catholics also see greed as spiritually destructive. It is one of the seven deadly sins. The tenth commandment forbids greed and the desire to amass Earthly goods without limit.

Today, Catholics and Buddhists are applying their beliefs by taking a more active part in trying to solve environmental problems. For example, in some countries, Buddhists have formed a Green Buddhist Movement. In one project, in parts of northern Thailand, monks have organized local villagers to replant trees, build dams, and irrigate the land.

Buddhism and Vegetarianism. Many Buddhists are vegetarians, and the fifth precept of Buddhism is about working to have good health by practising mindful eating, drinking, and consuming. **In what practices among Buddhists and Catholics do you see an ecological effort?**

Check Your Understanding

1. In your own words, explain Buddhist and Catholic perspectives on suffering.

Think About It

2. Research the life of one prominent Catholic or Buddhist mentioned in this chapter (for example, Thomas Merton, Thich Nhat Hanh). Write a short biography of this person and his or her accomplishments that would be suitable for posting on a website about Buddhism.

Making It Personal

3. How can you bring a faith perspective to concerns about the environment? List three actions you can take to become more involved in this issue.

What I Have Learned

In this chapter, I learned about

- where Buddhism is practised, and Buddhism in Canada
- the origins of Buddhism as an offshoot of Hinduism, the history of Siddhartha Gautama and the religion, and its development into different schools of Buddhism
- Buddhist rituals (including meditation), symbols, and festivals
- the concepts of *samsara*, nirvana, enlightenment, *karma*, merit, *dukkha*, *metta*
- central beliefs of Buddhism—the Three Jewels, the Four Noble Truths, the Eightfold Path
- Buddhist morality: the Five Precepts and Buddhist values (self-determination, compassion, loving-kindness, and detachment)
- similarities, differences, and interreligious dialogue between Catholics and Buddhists

A Buddhist Prayer

May I be a guard for those who are protectorless,
A guide for those who journey on the road.
For those who wish to cross the water,
May I be a boat, a raft, a bridge.
May I be an isle for those who yearn for land,
A lamp for those who long for light;
For all who need a resting place, a bed;
For those who need a servant, may I be their slave.
Just like the Earth and space itself
And all the other mighty elements,
For boundless multitudes of beings
May I always be the ground of life, the source of varied sustenance.

—The Way of the Bodhisattva

Chapter 9

The Story of Sikhism

The Golden Temple. The city of Amritsar in the Punjab province of India is the centre of Sikh devotional life. Standing proudly in the middle of the city is the Sikhs' holiest shrine, the first *gurdwara*, the temple where Sikhs meet and worship—the Golden Temple, or Harmandir. The temple has four doors that open to the north, south, east, and west, symbolizing the Sikh philosophy that all are welcome. It houses the original Guru Granth Sahib (Sikh holy book). In the early 1800s, it was rebuilt in marble and copper overlaid with gold foil, creating the distinctive golden appearance that the temple displays today.

"Infinite His goodness,
and the ways of exaltation;
Infinite His creation
and His benefaction;
Infinite the sights and sounds,
infinite His great design;
Infinite its execution,
infinite without confine."

This prayer was composed by the founder of Sikhism, Guru Nanak. It is one of the many hymns that Sikhs recite during worship.

What You Will Learn

In this chapter, you will learn about

- Sikhism in Canada
- the historical development of Sikh sacred texts and traditions of Sikhism
- the rituals, prayers, worship, and festivals through which Sikhs express their faith
- the concept of God and the importance of scripture in Sikhism
- the goals of Sikh life and the way Sikhs view the world and all of reality
- Sikh teachings of morality
- the role of the family
- Sikhism's relations with the Catholic Church

Personal Recollection

Bikram Gill. Bikram Gill is a student at Ascension of Our Lord Secondary School in Mississauga, Ontario, and a practising Sikh.

My name is Bikram Gill. Although I go to a Catholic school, I am a practising Sikh.

My family are Sikh, but we're not really all that strict about it—maybe a 6 or 7 out of 10. As you can see, I don't wear a **turban** or any of the other traditional Sikh items like a ***kirpan***. That's because I haven't taken the Sikh baptism. I'd like to when I get a bit older.

A few years ago, I visited my grandparents who live in Amritsar, in the Punjab. My visit really got me interested in my religion. Since then, I've taken a few classes in Punjabi so I can read the Guru Granth Sahib [Sikh holy book] in its original language, but it's tough. You have to learn a whole different alphabet.

Our family goes to the local ***gurdwara*** pretty often, and always for special occasions like New Year's Eve or the birthday of a **guru**. One event I really enjoyed was when our friends got a new house. The celebration lasted for two and a half days. The people read the whole of the Granth from beginning to end. They took turns and read during the whole celebration.

On my own, I try to pray every morning. I go to my room and cover my head. Then I usually pray the *Mul Mantra*. I usually use a black iron rosary with 28 beads that helps me count how many times I say the mantra.

I never really worried about what being Sikh would mean in a Catholic school. My brother had come here before me, and he told me I didn't have to worry about that. I suppose there are other Sikh kids here, but we don't really stick together. Everybody sort of blends in together.

I guess the first time I had to go to a school Mass, it was kind of strange. I didn't really know what to do or say. But, now I'm pretty good at following along. In religion class, it was obviously Catholic, but that wasn't too bad. Nobody tries to force you into believing anything you don't want.

— **Bikram Gill**

Turban
Head covering worn by male Sikhs

Kirpan
Small sword or dagger

Gurdwara
Sikh place of worship

Guru
A prophet and teacher

Sikhism in Canada

In world religion textbooks written before 1980, Sikhism tended to be overlooked. If Sikhism was mentioned at all, it was at the end of a chapter on Hinduism, under the heading "Sects within Hinduism." At that time, Sikhism was often mistakenly assumed to be an offshoot of Hinduism. Things have changed over the past few decades. Sikhism is now recognized as a separate religion with its own proud tradition of scripture, art, architecture, ethical living, and military service. It includes more than 20 million members worldwide. Appreciation and understanding of Sikhism have grown greatly in recent years, especially in Canada. This recognition is due in large part to growing Sikh immigration to Canada in the last several decades. Sikhs first came to Canada, mainly to British Columbia, in the early twentieth century.

Canadian census figures tell us that there were 278 410 Sikhs in Canada in 2001 (almost double the 1991 population estimate of 145 000). Sikhs accounted for approximately 5 percent of the 1.8 million new immigrants who came to Canada during the 1990s.

Sikhs were not always accepted as immigrants. When they first began to come to Canada in the early twentieth century, they frequently met with discrimination in the workplace and at school, and when looking for housing.

Sikh Schools in Canada. Religion and education are combined for these Grade 4 students at Mississauga's Khalsa Community School. Here, students study the Ontario curriculum as well as Sikh teachings, tradition, and music. **Why do you think Sikhs establish their own schools?**

G.K. Singh and Fred Taylor. G.K. Singh and Fred Taylor first met in 1914. In that year, Singh was one of 350 people from the Indian subcontinent who were refused entry into Canada. Taylor was the immigration officer who enforced the ban. They met again in 1976, the year Singh was finally allowed to immigrate to Canada. When he arrived, the two men shook hands. In the early twentieth century, Sikhs were not welcome in Canada. **What had changed between 1914 and 1976?**

Herb Dhaliwal. Herb (Harbans) Dhaliwal was the first Sikh Canadian federal cabinet minister.

Today, there is much less discrimination, although it has not completely disappeared.

Despite discrimination, Sikhs have contributed much to Canadian society. Canadian Sikhs have become elected politicians, judges, businesspeople, athletes, artists, scientists, and journalists.

Check Your Understanding

1. Explain how attitudes toward Sikhism as a separate religion have changed since 1980.
2. In which provinces do most Sikhs in Canada live?
3. What are some of the contributions made by the Sikh community to Canadian life?

Think About It

4. Sikhs generally are very tolerant of other people's ways of life, and fight against discrimination. Yet many Sikhs in Canada have experienced discrimination. In small groups, discuss what you can do as an individual and what members of the Catholic Church can do to defeat such discrimination.

Making It Personal

5. What could you do to make Sikhs in your school or community feel at home?

The History of Sikhism

Guru Nanak. Guru Nanak is the founder of Sikhism.

Guru Nanak

Sikhism's origins can be traced to one man: Guru Nanak. Nanak was born into a Hindu warrior-caste family in northern India in 1469. Both Hindus and Muslims lived in the Punjab area where Nanak grew up. He was greatly influenced by the teachings of both religions. He married at the age of 16 and had two sons.

When he was about 30 years old, Nanak left his family to follow a path of religious exploration. A key moment in the development of Sikhism came when Nanak had a life-changing vision. In this vision, God is said to have appeared to Nanak and told him to be the prophet of a new religion—one that proclaimed there to be "no Hindu and no Muslim, but only one human being who is a disciple of God." Nanak's mission from this point on became to bridge these two faiths.

He travelled throughout India, preaching that Hindus and Muslims had to move toward a more united and socially responsible faith. His ministry took him to Iraq, Tibet, Sri Lanka, and to the heart of Islam—Mecca, in Saudi Arabia. Many people converted to the new religion.

The Ten Divinely Directed Gurus

Nanak's new way of looking at religion included limiting formal religious

A Closer Look

When Nanak left to travel throughout India preaching his new religion, he gave his wife Sulakhani the task of being the spiritual and moral support of his growing congregation. As well, out of the 146 people he chose to help him spread the message of Sikhism, Guru Amar Das appointed 52 women missionaries.

Guru Nanak and the gurus who followed him worked for the equality of women and encouraged them to take part in social, religious, and political affairs as equals. This new approach, which turned the traditions of Indian society upside down, met with much opposition.

Modern Punjab in India

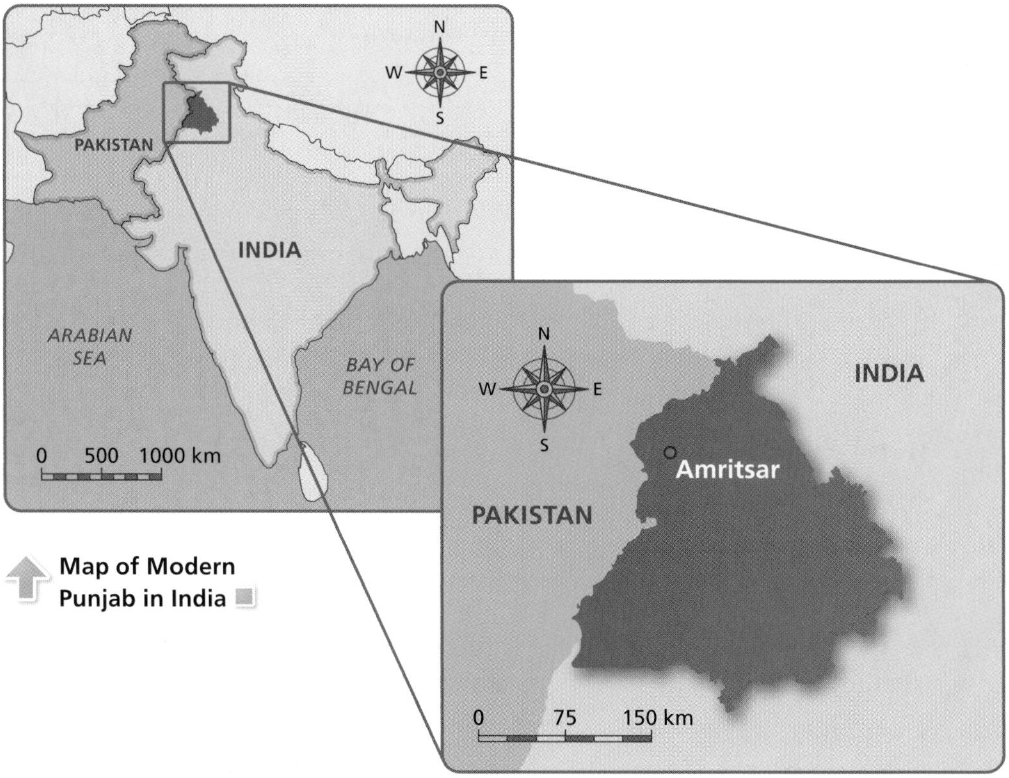

Map of Modern Punjab in India

NEL

practices and ceremonies. Rituals were replaced with obedience to a divinely directed guru. In all, ten gurus led the faith. Unlike Hindu gurus, who interpreted ancient Hindu scriptures and taught God's wisdom as found in those scriptures to the people, the ten Sikh gurus revealed truth directly from their own experience. Their revelations became the basis of Sikhism. Sikhs believe that the gurus were ordinary human beings, but were blessed with divine grace.

The Granth Sahib and the Golden Temple

The first four of the ten gurus of Sikhism followed Guru Nanak's teachings and ideals very closely. The fifth guru, Arjun Dev, collected sacred hymns, poems, and Sikh wisdom and compiled them into the Adi Granth, the Sikh scripture. Arjun Dev believed that there should be a central temple worthy of housing such a book, a gathering place for members of this new religion. He is credited with building the Golden Temple. From the time of the sixth guru on, Sikhs were often persecuted by Muslim rulers. In response, the gurus led Sikhism in a more military direction.

The Living Guru

On October 3, 1708, three days before he died, the tenth guru, Gobind Singh, declared that there would be no more human gurus. From that point on, the Sikhs' sacred writings would be their spiritual guru. As of that day, the holy book, which for Sikhs contains the word of God, was called Guru Granth Sahib, or Adi Granth. It is known as "the Holy Book that is the living guru."

The Creation of Pakistan

In August 1947, India became independent from Britain. In an effort to calm divisions between the majority Hindus and minority Muslims within India, the country of Pakistan was created from northern India to make a home country for Indian Muslims. About 1.5 million Muslims, Hindus, and Sikhs moved away from their homes due to fears that they would otherwise be part of a powerless religious minority. As a result, Sikhs were forced to abandon many of their holy places (such as the birthplace of Guru Nanak) because the places were on the Pakistani side of the Punjab.

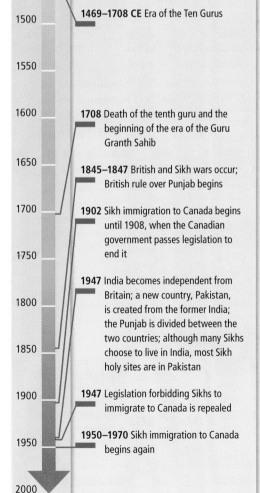

Timeline of Sikhism History

1450 CE, 1500, 1550, 1600, 1650, 1700, 1750, 1800, 1850, 1900, 1950, 2000

- **1469 CE** Birth of Guru Nanak, the founder of Sikhism
- **1469–1708 CE** Era of the Ten Gurus
- **1708** Death of the tenth guru and the beginning of the era of the Guru Granth Sahib
- **1845–1847** British and Sikh wars occur; British rule over Punjab begins
- **1902** Sikh immigration to Canada begins until 1908, when the Canadian government passes legislation to end it
- **1947** India becomes independent from Britain; a new country, Pakistan, is created from the former India; the Punjab is divided between the two countries; although many Sikhs choose to live in India, most Sikh holy sites are in Pakistan
- **1947** Legislation forbidding Sikhs to immigrate to Canada is repealed
- **1950–1970** Sikh immigration to Canada begins again

Fast Fact

The word "sikh" means "disciple" or "learner of truth," in Punjabi.

Ten Gurus. Sikhism rejects any form of idol worship, including worship of pictures of the gurus. Artists' portrayals of the ten Sikh gurus are for inspirational purposes only. **Discuss how the Sikh approach to the gurus is similar to or different from the Catholic approach to Mary and the saints.**

Check Your Understanding

1. What does "guru" mean? How were Sikh gurus different from Hindu gurus?

Think About It

2. In small groups, debate the practice of replacing human gurus with the word of God enshrined in a sacred book of writings. Name at least three implications for the Sikh religion that resulted from this move. Summarize your group's findings and compare them with those of other groups.

3. Brainstorm reasons why the tenth guru may have decided that there would be no more human gurus. Which reason(s) do you think are the most plausible?

Making It Personal

4. What do you think it would be like to be a part of a religion with limited formal religious practices and ceremonies?

Rituals

Prayer

The essence of the Sikh scriptures is contained in the first few pages of the Guru Granth Sahib, which are called the *Japji Sahib*. Sikh morning prayer begins with the *Mul Mantra*. In the *Japji Sahib*, Guru Nanak talks about truth and how to gain knowledge of God. Sikhs are expected to recite five formal prayers throughout the day.

Gurdwara. This Sikh temple, or gurdwara, is located in Vancouver, British Columbia.

Ardas, or prayer, is an important part of Sikh ritual. This prayer is always offered before or after significant Sikh religious gatherings and ceremonies. The prayer consists of the following elements:

- a call for the blessings of God and the ten gurus
- a recitation of the key events in the life of the ten gurus and a concise history of the Sikhs
- a worshipful recitation of the name of God
- a call for peace, well-being, and prosperity for all humanity

Prayers for specific functions or reasons include a supplication to God for the success of the function, gathering, or project.

Worship

For Sikhs, the primary method of worship is meditation on God.

Guru Granth Sahib. Inside the gurdwara, the Guru Granth Sahib is the focal point. Because it is the Sikhs' living guru, it must be treated with great respect and reverence. It is covered with richly embroidered cloths and rests on cushions on a specially made platform with a canopy over it. The canopy is a symbol of sovereignty and shows the importance of the Guru Granth Sahib. All Sikh ceremonies are conducted in the presence of the Granth. At home, some families keep a copy of the Guru Granth Sahib in a special room where they can go for prayer and meditation or to worship with their friends on ceremonial occasions. **What does the way people treat their holy book reveal about their beliefs?**

The Gurdwara

Although Guru Nanak worked hard to take the emphasis away from ritual worship and practice, he encouraged Sikhs to gather for shared worship at the gurdwara.

Gurdwaras are the main centres of prayer and religious observance for Sikh communities. The main hall of the gurdwara hosts the primary religious ceremonies. These halls are plainly decorated, with no statues or images. The central object of attention is the sacred scripture itself.

Like Hindus and Buddhists, Sikhs visit their place of worship whenever they wish, alone or with family and friends. Sikhs do not regard any particular day of the week as a holy day. In Canada, they often go to a gurdwara on Sundays, as this practice aligns with the pattern of Canadians who attend church worship services.

A Closer Look

Sikh Meditation

Although Sikhs emphasize doing good works over spending time in prayer and ritual, they see value in certain prayer experiences. Sikhs believe that the presence of God is within all individuals. This indwelling of God is known as *Nam*. It is of central importance for Sikhs to remember the presence of *Nam* within them, often through meditative prayer. One technique is to pray or recite the mantra *Waheguru* ("God, the wondrous teacher"). This practice calls forth the *Nam* so that God within may be revealed and known.

Another technique is to train the mind on the sacred mantra. Paying attention to one's breathing, one focuses on *Wah* while breathing in, and on *Guru* while breathing out. Sikhs believe that meditating on the name drives away evil, gives knowledge of truth, and brings the person into closer relationship with God.

Hymn-singing. Sikh women sing hymns in a gurdwara. **How does this presentation of music compare with music that is led at Catholic churches?**

Sikhism does not have a formal priestly structure. Worship can be led by any member of the congregation who has studied the Sikh scriptures and who has a good working knowledge of Sikh religion and history. The person who performs the daily prayer service is known as the *granthi*. The main part of the service is the singing of hymns. Professional hymn singers, called *ragis*, normally play the music and lead the singing. The congregation listens to them and from time to time joins them in their singing. The service also includes short readings from the Guru Granth Sahib. Formal Sikh services last three to four hours, and people come and go as they please.

The service ends with a distribution of *parshad*, a sweet, pudding-like dessert made of flour, water, butter, and sugar. The *parshad* is considered to have been blessed by the Guru, and is eaten in the worship space. Receiving it is a key part of the hospitality practices within the gurdwara. After worship, the people share a meal that is prepared in the gurdwara's community kitchen known as the *langar*. This meal is a symbol of the unity and equality of all people. No matter what their religion, age, gender, education, or status, all people generally sit in rows on floor mats.

Fast Fact

Langar literally means "eating together." *Langar* refers to both the kitchen and the meal. It is open to everyone. Food is usually served three times a day.

Worship in the Gurdwara

Before entering a gurdwara, all visitors remove their shoes and cover their heads as a sign of respect. On entering the main hall, visitors bow before the Guru Granth Sahib. After they place their offering and say a prayer, they back away respectfully and find a place to sit. Although men and women sit on either side of the hall, there is no strict rule to do so. Congregational worship involves prayer, hymns, and reciting poems or other religious compositions.

Check Your Understanding

1. Define *Nam* and *Waheguru*. Describe a typical Sikh meditation.
2. Explain the importance of the *langar* to Sikhs.

Think About It

3. What do you think about a religion without a leader, where worship can be directed by any informed member of the community? Explain.
4. Compare and contrast how Sikhism, a religion without a leader, is different from Catholicism.

Making It Personal

5. Have you ever meditated? If so, what did you focus on?

Marking Time

The fourth guru, Guru Ram Das, laid down the following routine for Sikhs to follow:

- Sikhs are to wake up every morning before dawn and bathe.
- Morning prayer begins with meditation on the name of God, followed by the rest of the *Japji Sahib.*
- Sikhs are then to go out into the world to earn their living. The work Sikhs do should keep them away from dishonesty and unfairness.
- Sikhs are to recall the name of God at every opportunity during the day, whether working or walking.
- Sikhs are to offer prayer again at evening and before going to bed.

Life-Cycle Ceremonies

The passage through the stages of life is accompanied by rites of passage. Most common are the rituals around the naming ceremony, baptism, marriage, and death.

Birth and Naming

The naming ceremony takes place after the mother and child have recovered from the birth. The parents host the event at the local gurdwara. The ceremony begins with the *granthi* (service leader) bringing out a bowl of water and placing it nearby. He or she then makes the ***amrit***, the ceremonial water that is also used in adult baptism, by adding sugar to water and stirring it with a kirpan, a small sword or dagger. Then prayers are recited and hymns are sung to bless the newborn child.

A random reading from the Guru Granth follows the hymn. The first letter of the first word of the reading becomes the initial letter of the child's name. For example, if the first letter of the reading is an "S," and the baby is a boy, then he could be called Surjit Singh or Surinder Singh, or any other traditional Sikh name beginning with S. If the baby is a girl, the name might be Sunita Kaur or Savinder Kaur.

Baptism

Despite their general opposition to ceremony, one ritual is central to the lives of many Sikhs: *amrit*, the Baptism of the Sword. When he initiated the Baptism of the Sword ceremony in 1699, Guru Gobind Singh created a community within the larger Sikh community. These initiated Sikhs were known as the *Khalsa Panth* ("commonwealth" or "brotherhood"). Baptized Sikhs are easily identifiable because of the visible symbols of their baptism. Members of the *Khalsa* are expected to wear the 5 Ks at all times. Each of the 5 Ks has both practical and symbolic significance:

1. **Kesh** Uncut hair and beard (symbolizes saintliness and respect for the body; hair must be kept clean)
2. **Kangha** Wooden comb with which to care for the hair (symbolizes personal cleanliness)
3. **Kachha** Short pants worn by the soldiers of the time (symbolize restraint and discipline; they ensure ease of movement in battle; *Khalsa* Sikhs are warriors, always ready to defend their faith)
4. **Kara** Steel bracelet worn on the right wrist (symbolizes God, who is without beginning or end, and also the strength and fearlessness of the Sikh *Khalsa*)

Fast Fact

Today, the name "Singh" is given as a surname to every male Sikh child, reinforcing the Sikh ideal of equality. (Singh is also a common name for warrior-caste Hindus, so not all Singhs are Sikhs.) All female children are given the name "Kaur," which means "princess."

Catholic Connection

Some Sikh rituals involve the random reading of the Guru Granth Sahib. Catholics do not incorporate such a practice of randomly choosing texts in their own liturgy because it could be seen as a testing of the Holy Spirit.

Amrit

Ceremonial water used in Sikh rituals

A Closer Look

The Turban

Although not spelled out as one of the 5 Ks, another visible symbol of the Sikh faith is the turban. Men who are part of the *Khalsa* must wear a turban, as the gurus did, and some Sikh women who have been baptized wear them. Many Sikhs who are not members of the *Khalsa* also wear turbans. The turban is a symbol of equality, humility, dignity, and devotion to the teachings of the Guru Granth Sahib.

If the turban is seen to be inappropriate for certain activities, such as swimming or sports, it can be replaced by a small scarf called a *patka*. *Patkas*, which are knotted at the top to keep the hair neat, are worn by many young Sikhs before they begin wearing the turban. Many Sikh men put their hair into a *patka* before putting on their turbans.

5. **Kirpan** A small sword or dagger to be used only for self-defence or to uphold justice (symbolizes power, self-reliance, and dignity; Sikhs are "slaves to no person")

Guru Gobind Singh blessed the new members of the *Khalsa* and bound them to a very strict moral code. He charged them to uphold right; to help the poor and protect the weak; to avoid evil at every opportunity; not to use alcohol, tobacco, or any other stimulant; and to use force only if necessary. True to the Sikh beliefs about equality, Sikhs allow any man or woman, regardless of race, status, or prior faith tradition, to be baptized.

Baptism may take place at any age, but people are encouraged to wait until they have reached maturity. The ceremony takes place in the gurdwara, in the presence of the Guru Granth Sahib. Five respected members of the *Khalsa* explain Sikh beliefs and the *Khalsa* obligations to the candidates, who then vow to live according to those beliefs and obligations. The *Ardas* (prayer) is recited, and a passage from the Granth is proclaimed. Anyone accepting Sikhism for the first time is given a new name. Finally, all baptized Sikhs share *parshad*.

The majority of Sikhs do not undergo the ritual of baptism, so they do not have to follow the military vows set out by Guru Gobind Singh for the *Khalsa*. Although these Sikhs are also not bound to wear the 5 Ks, many choose to wear some of the 5 Ks to varying degrees.

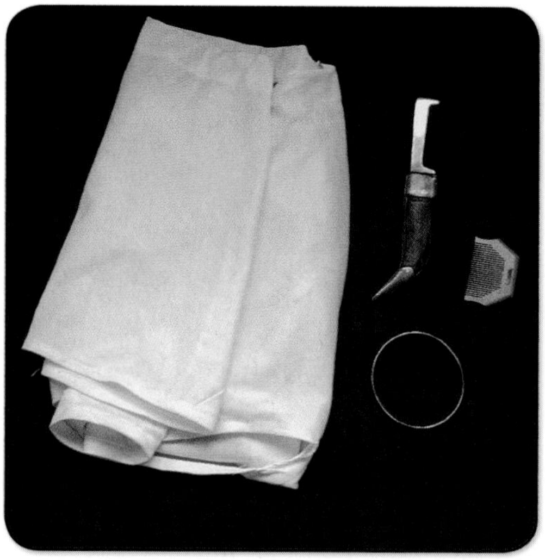

The 5 Ks. This photo shows the four objects that, along with unshorn hair (kesh), make up the 5 Ks of Sikhism (left to right, clockwise): the kachha, kirpan, kangha, kara.

Patka. A young Sikh boy with a *patka*. **What other religious traditions also have rituals involving cutting, covering, or shaving of hair? Why do you think these kinds of rituals involving the appearance of hair exist?**

Amrit. Respected members of the *Khalsa* prepare the *amrit*, the baptismal sweet water. At the end of the baptism, those to be baptized drink the *amrit* out of the bowl and are declared members of the *Khalsa*.

Make It Your Own: Understanding the Khanda

The *khanda* is one of the most important and recognizable symbols of Sikhism. It is found as a bumper sticker, an emblem on Sikh flags, and extensively in Sikh places of worship (gurdwaras). It is both a sign of identity for Sikhs and an illustration of their basic beliefs.

It also shows key points about their beliefs. It is really four symbols combined into one. The central object is a double-edged sword. The edges represent the virtues of truth and justice. This is a spiritual weapon that is used to represent the cutting away of false pride and vanity through discipline. The circle found around the central sword represents the one God who has neither beginning nor end. It also represents compassion and unity. The *khanda* is framed with two kirpans that represent the daily circumstances of living (right) and the spiritual dimension of life (left). Note that the worldly and the spiritual cross over each other.

Khanda. The *khanda* combines four symbols into one of the most recognizable Sikh symbols.

This symbol reveals the essence of Sikhism. It shows the values of unity, discipline, and compassion. Sikhs defend the use of a weapon in their symbol by stating that the kirpan does not mean aggressive conquest of other people but rather the inward removal of all that stops us from being holy.

Activities

1. Create a labelled diagram of the *khanda* with a brief description of the four elements.
2. Create a symbol for Christianity that blends three or four different symbols. Explain what the symbol represents.

Check Your Understanding

1. How would you describe the 5 Ks to someone who was unfamiliar with Sikhism?

Think About It

2. Use a chart to show how the Sikh day is similar to and different from a typical Catholic's day.

3. In small groups, debate whether Sikhs should be able to wear turbans instead of the required helmets when they are playing hockey or baseball, riding motorcycles, or working in construction, the armed forces, or other jobs requiring protective headwear.

Making It Personal

4. If you had to wear a visible symbol of the Catholic faith at all times, what would it be? Explain.

Fast Fact

Anand Karaj means "ceremony of bliss" or "blissful union."

Marriage

The marriage ceremony, called *Anand Karaj*, is more than a civil contract: it is a holy union. Guru Angad summed up Sikh marriage in this way: "A union of bodies is no union, however close it may be; it is only when souls meet, can we speak of a union true." For Sikhs, marriage is an ideal state of life, and family life has the highest honour.

Sikhs do not believe in celibacy (adults remaining single). Marriages are typically arranged with the help of parents and extended families, but not always, especially in Canada. The marriage can take place anywhere, as long as the place is free of alcohol and other intoxicants. There are no barriers due to race, caste, or status. However, Sikhs are encouraged to marry Sikhs.

The main ceremony consists of reciting the sacred wedding hymn. Each stanza of the wedding hymn gives important instruction for the couple on how to bring their marriage into true communion.

Funeral Rites

As friends and loved ones gather for a traditional Sikh funeral, the body is bathed, dressed in clean clothes, and placed on a wooden frame. If the person is *Khalsa*, the 5 Ks are displayed on the body. The mourners then form a procession and sing hymns as they carry the body to the cremation ground. In Canada, the procession may take the form of a motorcade that drives to the crematorium. At the site of cremation, a funeral hymn is sung or recited with the special intention of blessing the departed. During this journey, public displays of grief are discouraged, as Sikhs believe strongly in the immortality of the human spirit.

After cremation, the ashes are collected and disposed of in the sea or another body of water. Some families may take the ashes to the Sikh homeland in Punjab, India. Friends and relatives then return to the house of the deceased. There they may begin a ceremonial reading of the entire Guru Granth. This task is undertaken by friends, family, and occasionally a paid reader, and is to be completed within nine days. On the last day, the mourners reassemble for the singing of hymns, the reading of the final five pages of the Guru Granth, the *Ardas* (prayer), a random reading from the Granth, and the sharing of *parshad*.

Sikh Wedding. This wedding took place in Guelph, Ontario, at the Guelph Gurdwara. During the ceremony, the man and woman offer vows to each other and bow before the Granth to signify their consent. The groom wears a sash, and the bride's father hands one end of the sash to the bride. **What do you think is the significance of this action?**

Fast Fact

Sikhs believe that, in death, the soul or spirit of a person is reborn into another body. This process is called reincarnation. As the soul becomes more purified through good works over a number of lives, it eventually achieves the ultimate human goal, union with God.

Sikh Funeral Pyre. Sikhs in Punjab light the traditional funeral pyre. **What is the significance of burning the body? Why do you think more Catholics are choosing to be cremated today than in the past?**

Festivals and Holy Days

Several festivals are celebrated in most Sikh communities worldwide. These times of joy and celebration are occasions to revitalize faith and renew positive religious practice. Two of these festivals are discussed below.

Make It Your Own: Celebrating Nanak Jayanti

The birthday of the founder of Sikhism, Guru Nanak, is celebrated each year in November or December. The feast is celebrated with processions and continuous readings of the Guru Granth Sahib for three days before Nanak Jayanti. In Amritsar, the holiest city of Sikhism, the scripture, garlanded in flowers, is carried in procession, accompanied by drummers and religious leaders who carry the saffron-coloured flag of their faith. Afterward, followers go to the huge community dining hall to eat together. Up to 40 000 people can be fed per day on these holidays. People from different faith traditions are welcome to participate in this festival.

Guru Nanak's Birthday Celebrations. Children light candles outside the Golden Temple in Punjab, India, during the celebrations for the birthday of Guru Nanak.

Activity

1. Create a ritual to celebrate the patron of your school. Where would it take place? What symbols would be used? What actions would take place? What words would be spoken? Who would be involved? What would be gained by holding such a ritual?

Baisakhi

This day is celebrated both as the birthday of the *Khalsa* and as the Sikh New Year. It remembers the first Baptism of the Sword. In addition to the usual ritual elements, baptisms take place on this day, and new members are welcomed into the *Khalsa*. The Guru Granth is often carried through the streets in procession by five members of the *Khalsa*, followed by a great many Sikh believers. Baisakhi also celebrates the beginning of the spring harvesting of grain, especially in the Punjab.

Baisakhi Celebrations. Approximately 80 000 Sikhs parade in downtown Toronto. The celebrations commemorate Baisakhi, the anniversary of the creation of the *Khalsa* and the Sikh New Year.

Check Your Understanding

1. List festivals that Sikhs worldwide take part in and describe one important feature of each.

Think About It

2. Write a letter to a Sikh friend explaining some of the major Catholic festivals.

Making It Personal

3. What Catholic festivals do you, or friends of yours, participate in? Describe the purpose and activities involved in one of the festivals. Are any of them similar to Sikh festivals?

The Community

The Gurdwara

A gurdwara is not just a place of worship. It is a centre for community life and charitable outreach. Sikhs believe that service to humankind is service to God. Giving money to the needy and sharing meals together, including with strangers, are important acts of service. A *langar* (free kitchen) is always part of the structure. Gurdwara services offer blessing and support through most of life's important events. They also play an active role during important Sikh festivals.

Langar. On a visit to the Ontario Khalsa Darbar in Mississauga, students enjoy *parshad.* All the food is prepared by volunteers. At a traditional *langar*, everyone sits on the floor, but in a few gurdwaras, people sit on benches at tables. Cooking and serving at *langar* is a service in honour of God. **How does serving food to others honour God?**

Gurdwara. The inside of a Sikh gurdwara in Toronto. Typical gurdwaras include rooms for religious instruction, dining, accommodations for travellers, libraries, classrooms, and community meeting rooms.

Branches of Sikhism

Today there are three main branches of Sikhism.

- The first branch is the *Khalsa* or *Singhs*, the initiated commonwealth of baptized Sikhs.
- The second branch is the *Keshdhari* Sikhs. This term refers to Sikhs who keep their hair uncut and wear a turban, but have not undergone the Sikh baptism.
- The third branch is the *Sahajdharis* Sikhs. This term generally refers to those Sikhs who accept the beliefs and philosophies of Sikhism, but do not take the full baptismal vows of the *Khalsa*. They cut their hair and do not wear a turban.

Check Your Understanding

1. Describe some of the community functions of the gurdwara.
2. Explain the three main divisions within Sikhism.

Think About It

3. Why do you think Sikhism is divided into three main branches?
4. Compare and contrast Sikh and Catholic practices of giving aid to the poor and those in need.

Making It Personal

5. How is your place of worship the same as and different from a typical gurdwara? With a partner, suggest reasons for any differences.

Central Beliefs

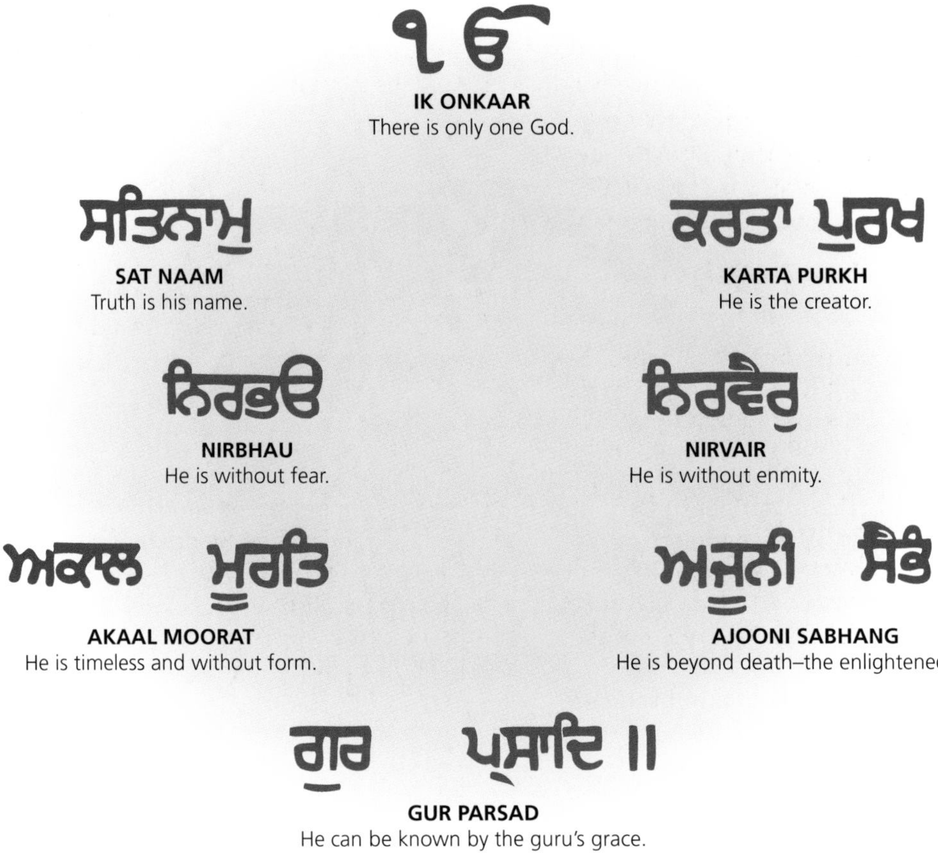

ੴ
IK ONKAAR
There is only one God.
ਸਤਿਨਾਮੁ
SAT NAAM
Truth is his name.
ਕਰਤਾ ਪੁਰਖ
KARTA PURKH
He is the creator.
ਨਿਰਭਉ
NIRBHAU
He is without fear.
ਨਿਰਵੈਰੁ
NIRVAIR
He is without enmity.
ਅਕਾਲ ਮੂਰਤਿ
AKAAL MOORAT
He is timeless and without form.
ਅਜੂਨੀ ਸੈਭੰ
AJOONI SABHANG
He is beyond death–the enlightened one.
ਗੁਰ ਪ੍ਰਸਾਦਿ ॥
GUR PARSAD
He can be known by the guru's grace.

The *Mul Mantra*. These words open the morning prayer of Sikhs, and as such are the first words spoken by Sikhs at the beginning of every day.

> **Fast Fact**
>
> At the beginning of each chapter of the Guru Granth Sahib, there is a sacred hymn or chant that sums up the most important aspects of Sikh beliefs in a few short words. The hymn is called the *Mul Mantra*. The *Mul Mantra* was the first hymn written by Guru Nanak.

Major Teachings

The ten gurus and the Guru Granth Sahib provide Sikhs with a well-developed system of beliefs to guide how they worship and live their lives. In general, Sikhs follow the beliefs described below.

1. Monotheism

There is only one God: Creator, Timeless, Unincarnated (without a physical body), Eternal.

2. The Reality of the World

The world is not illusion, nor is it a source of suffering. The world is good. It exists as a location for all to practise good and virtuous action. Human life is not an illusion, either. It is the beautiful opportunity to gain full spiritual achievement and become one with God.

3. Spiritual Achievement in This Life

The goal of life is to escape our self-will or self-interest and become one with God. For Sikhs, the highest achievement is to become a *Gurmukh* (a God-man), who is completely in touch with the will of God. The *Gurmukh* acts selflessly in all things, wishing to carry out God's will and to set all people free.

4. Union of Spiritual and Worldly Lives

Guru Nanak did not believe in asceticism or turning away from worldly responsibilities. He favoured the Householder stage of Hindu life, where the faithful work hard, support a family, and give generously to their community. Faithful Sikhs are required to involve themselves in community life, take care of the poor, and act against injustice. Consumerism and materialism are strongly discouraged.

5. Nam

God lives within each human heart. The word for this indwelling of God is *Nam*. One of the most important duties for Sikhs is to come to a better relationship with *Nam*. All Sikhs must strive to keep this "God-within" in mind at all times and in all things. By cultivating *Nam*, Sikhs become more loving, truthful, humble, and content.

6. Good Deeds, Not Rituals

Ritualism is condemned. It is through good deeds, not the performance of religious rituals, that Sikhs will be judged. Sikhs feel that at the end of their lives, they will be judged solely on the quality of their actions. The end of a just life brings reunion with the absolute.

7. Equality and Human Dignity

Sikhs profess that all human beings are equal. Nanak rejected the Hindu caste system entirely. His teachings apply to any aspect of race, culture, or religion. Similarly, Sikhs profess the equality of women and men.

8. A Just Society

Nanak was concerned with more than the salvation of individual souls. He wanted to establish a just and compassionate society here on Earth. In his ideal community, all would work together, pray together, eat together, and be treated equally.

Check Your Understanding

1. Describe at least three important features of the Guru Granth Sahib.

Think About It

2. Using a three-column chart, compare and contrast the major teachings of Sikhism with those of Catholicism and Buddhism. How are they similar? How are they different?

3. How does having a well-developed system of beliefs help to guide how people worship and live their lives?

Making It Personal

4. How often do you recite your beliefs? When do Catholics do this together?

Morality

Ramandeep Grewal. Lawyer Ramandeep Grewal is active in women's issues in the Sikh community in Canada.

Gurdwara Khalsa School. Sikh children at the Gurdwara Khalsa School in Toronto.

Social Responsibility

The Sikh code of moral conduct, the *Rahit* (or *Reht*) *Maryada*, provides specific guidelines for how to perform religious rites and how to live an ethical life. It is based on the teachings of the ten gurus and the Guru Granth Sahib. Sikhism teaches that God, who created everything, gave people free will. Only humans can see the difference between right and wrong, and make moral choices. Although evil exists in the world, it is not inflicted by God.

Sikhism requires that its followers live according to three principles:

- devotion to the Divine Name
- earning an honest living
- sharing earnings with those less fortunate

It is not against the Sikh religion to gain wealth in this world, as long as it is gained in an honest way, and help is always given to those in need.

Sikh Virtues and Vices

The Sikh Gurus encourage five principal virtues and discourage five vices.

In describing a moral life, the Sikh Code

- prohibits sexual intercourse outside marriage
- forbids adultery, pleading with men to see all women to whom they are not married as their sisters and daughters; the same restrictions apply to women
- urges that all people be treated as equals, regardless of skin colour, race or religion, sex, or caste
- encourages Sikhs to keep good company, and to act with modesty and humility
- requires Sikhs to contribute one-tenth of their earnings to charitable causes
- requires Sikhs to take part in the *langar* through financial charity or food donations, or by donating time to cook, clean, or distribute food

Although it is not mentioned specifically in the Code, most Sikhs regard homosexuality as inconsistent with nature. The Code also provides guidelines about food and drink:

- Do not take intoxicants (alcohol or any non-medicinal drug).
- Do not smoke.
- Do not eat kosher or halal meat (meat prepared ritually for Jews or Muslims). (As well, Sikhs believe that animals should be killed humanely.)

Sikhs strive to uphold the role of women as being equal to men. As a result, women are encouraged to develop their spiritual lives through prayer, song, and attendance at the gurdwara. Women participate equally in and perform all ceremonies, including baptism.

Sikhs assert that theirs is a very practical religion that aims to improve the world by direct action—including, for example, working to improve the environment and to achieve social justice for all. This belief in the potential for improving the world embodies another dominant Sikh virtue: optimism. Sikhs believe that no matter how difficult things are, God has given them the blessings they need to turn the situation toward the good.

Sikh Virtues and Vices

Sikh Virtues	Sikh Vices
Truth (including righteousness, honesty, justice, impartiality, and fair play)	**Lust** (produces shame and misery)
Contentment (freedom from ambition, envy, greed, or jealousy)	**Anger** (leads to arguments and violence)
Patience (all trials will end; all difficulties will pass away)	**Greed** (tempts us to acquire more than we need)
Perfect Faith (life often offers difficult tests; perfect faith prevents despair)	**Attachment** (all Earthly love is transient; only God is eternal)
Compassion (considering another's sorrow as one's own)	**Pride** (leads to conceit, vanity, jealousy, and arrogance)

The Sacrament of *Langar*. Sikhs run community kitchens to provide food for fellow Sikhs and all visitors. Members of the gurdwaras donate the food for the kitchens. The intent is to feed all who gather, no matter what their background.

Family Life

Sikhs believe that all adults should marry, if possible. They consider family life to be of the highest honour. Sikhs maintain that family life, lived with virtuous behaviour and sincere faith in God, leads to salvation. It is in the family that young Sikhs are taught the beliefs and moral code of Sikhism. Divorce is not encouraged in Sikhism, but it is permitted, especially on grounds of cruelty, adultery, or change of religion. Second marriages after divorce are permitted. Remarriage after the death of a spouse is actively encouraged. Because Sikhs believe sex outside marriage is wrong, young Sikhs are often discouraged from dating.

Check Your Understanding

1. In your own words, list some of the main teachings of the Sikh moral code. What is the purpose of the moral code?
2. Summarize the Sikh view of the status of women.

Think About It

3. In small groups, make a list of ways that Sikh teachings might make it difficult for young Sikhs living in Canada today. How might the teachings make life easier?
4. Using the Internet, find a list of the seven Catholic virtues and vices. How does this list compare with the Sikh list above? With a partner or in small groups, suggest reasons for the differences.

Making It Personal

5. What principles are so important to you that you would be willing to risk your life for them?

Interreligious Dialogue

Sikhism and the Catholic Church

Catholics Meet Sikhs. A representative of the Vatican meets with Sikh leaders at the Golden Temple.

Sikhs take pride in their tradition of interreligious tolerance. A dialogue between Sikhs and Catholics began recently. The first official encounter took place in New York in 2006. Meetings in London, Mexico, and Washington have followed. Catholics and Sikhs have committed themselves to meeting regularly to discuss matters of common concern. As the head of the Sikh delegation, Dr. Manohar Singh, said,

> The universal message of Sikhs respects pluralism and we welcome our Catholic friends with open arms. This dialogue is an opportunity for our communities to begin a conversation at the highest level on how we may be able to work with each other in trust and friendship to make this world a more peaceful and just place for all.

The first encounters were intended to raise the level of trust and mutual understanding. As the Vatican representative, Monsignor Machado, said, "The Catholic Church at the highest level appreciates this dialogue with the Sikh community. Sikhs respect us, not suspect us."

Profile: Yogi Bhajan

In September of 1968, a very unusual Sikh visitor arrived in Toronto from India. His name was Harbhajan Singh Puri, but he became known to millions worldwide as Yogi Bhajan. Yogi Bhajan was born on August 26, 1929, in the part of the Punjab province that would be given over to Pakistan in the 1947 partition. As a young boy, he attended a Catholic convent school. He began training in yoga when he was only 8 years old, and was proclaimed as a master of *Kundalini*—an ancient and secret form of yoga—when he was just 16.

After a successful career in the Indian government, Yogi Bhajan was convinced by a friend and former student, the Canadian High Commissioner to India, to immigrate to Canada. It became his mission to teach the ancient discipline of *Kundalini* yoga to the Western world. His goal, he said, was to "create teachers, not to gain students."

His stay in Toronto was brief. He had been invited to teach at the University of Toronto, but when his sponsor died, the job disappeared. During what was to have been a weekend trip to Los Angeles, Yogi Bhajan met a group of young people who practised an alternative lifestyle. Rather than dismissing their ideals and beliefs, Yogi Bhajan saw them as authentic spiritual seekers. He offered them the teachings of *Kundalini* yoga, meditation, and philosophy as alternatives to experimenting with drugs.

He soon became known for his 3HO movement, which stated that it was the birthright of all people to be "Healthy, Happy, and Holy." The movement became so popular that it developed into a corporation, which now boasts more than 300 centres in 35 countries. Yogi Bhajan's work and ministry culminated in the founding of 3HO SuperHealth, a drugless drug rehabilitation program that blends the ancient yogic wisdom of the East with Western medicine.

An excellent model of Sikh acceptance and a champion of religious unity, Yogi Bhajan met with leaders of all faiths to encourage dialogue, including two popes, Aboriginal elders, the Dalai Lama, and two Archbishops of Canterbury. In 1972, Yogi Bhajan visited Pope Paul VI and suggested to him that he bring together leaders of all religions for friendship and dialogue. After the death of Paul VI, Yogi Bhajan continued his relationship with the Catholic Church, visiting and developing a friendship with Pope John Paul II.

In 1986, John Paul II convened the Assisi Conference, a gathering of the world's religious leaders much like the one Yogi Bhajan had proposed 14 years earlier. Although he could not attend in person, Yogi Bhajan participated in a companion ceremony held in Los Angeles on the same day.

Yogi Bhajan became co-president of the World Fellowship of Religions in 1974. In 1986, during the United Nations Year of Peace, he established the first International Peace Prayer Day for people of all faiths. This celebration continues to this day and has spread to countless sites around the world, including the University of Toronto.

Yogi Bhajan. Yogi Bhajan in Los Angeles, California

In 1995, Yogi Bhajan received the Courage of Conscience Award for his work in promoting peace between religions. When he died in 2004, members of the United States Congress passed a rare bipartisan resolution honouring his life and work.

Throughout his ministry, Yogi Bhajan was a champion of women's rights. His personal motto was, "If you can't see God in all, you can't see God at all."

Fast Fact

The Peace Abbey Multi-Faith Retreat Center in Sherborn, Massachusetts, awards Courage of Conscience Awards to people who have promoted the causes of peace and justice, non-violence, and love.

Check Your Understanding

1. What is *Kundalini*?

Think About It

2. Work with a partner or in small groups. Choose two other religious leaders profiled in this textbook. Compare and contrast what they did to encourage religious unity with what Yogi Bhajan did.

Making It Personal

3. Imagine that you are starting an organization to promote healthy, balanced living, such as 3HO. What three qualities would you promote as being essential for balanced living? What would your slogan or motto be?

Skill Focus: How to Argue Persuasively

Whether you are writing an essay or preparing for a debate, knowing how to present a point of view and argue persuasively is an essential skill. Here are some suggestions for organizing your argument so that you can present it in the most effective way.

1. Determine your point of view or your position on the topic. Be clear and specific on the subject.
2. Determine the reasons for your position. Why do you think that way? Do you really believe in your position?
3. Find facts and examples that support your opinion. Consider a range of sources: research from websites, books, and articles from newspapers and online sources. If you know someone who is associated with the viewpoint or position you are defending, consider interviewing or e-mailing that person to request more information. When you have collected the information, make sure to put it in your own words. If you are quoting your interview subject, make sure that you clearly indicate that by using quotation marks.
4. When you start to write an essay or prepare an oral presentation, explain your position clearly and briefly in your opening sentences or remarks.
5. Present your facts and examples in a clear and logical way, so that readers or listeners can easily follow your line of thinking. If you are writing an essay, reread it carefully before you finalize it, checking for errors or spelling mistakes. Too many errors, even if they are small, can give readers the impression that you have given little thought to your work.
6. Sum up your argument in the last few sentences. Leave your readers or listeners with something to think about, something that might change their minds if they support a position opposite to yours.

What I Have Learned

In this chapter, I learned about

- the contribution of Sikhism to Canada
- the origin of Sikhism in India
- the history and importance of Guru Granth Sahib, the sacred text of the Sikhs
- the major rituals, prayers, worship, and festivals through which Sikhs express their faith
- the concept of God in the lives of Sikhs
- Sikh teachings of morality
- the role of the family
- the state of interreligious dialogue between Sikhism and the Catholic Church

Sikh Prayer

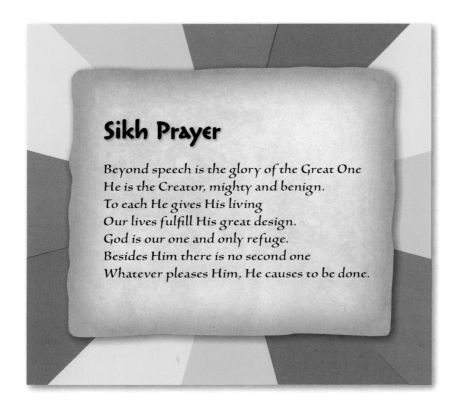

Beyond speech is the glory of the Great One
He is the Creator, mighty and benign.
To each He gives His living
Our lives fulfill His great design.
God is our one and only refuge.
Besides Him there is no second one
Whatever pleases Him, He causes to be done.

Chapter 10 Modernity and Religion

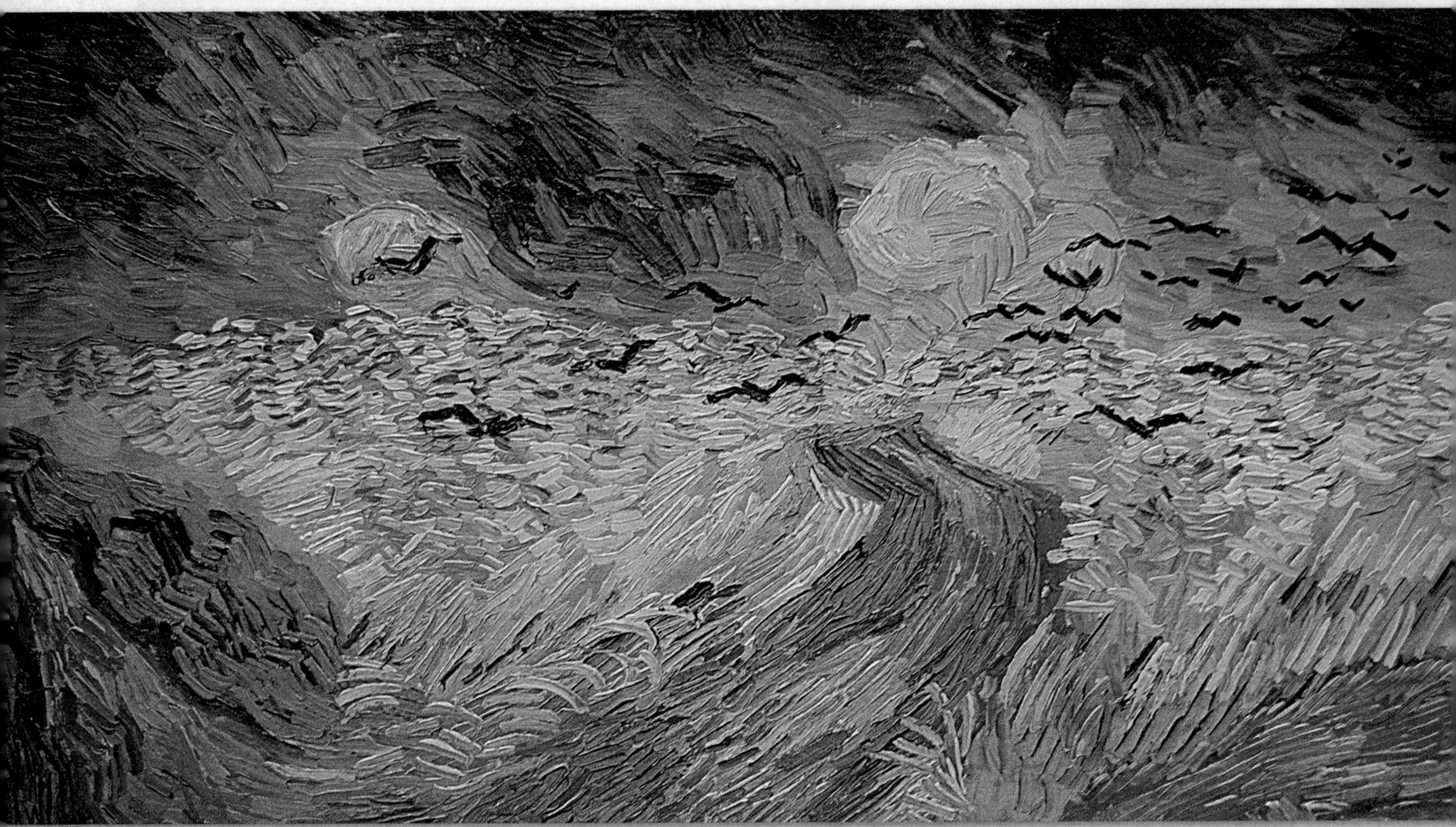

"Sagan's argument is straightforward. We exist as material beings in a material world, all of whose phenomena are the consequences of physical relations among material entities."

—Richard Lewontin

The Power of Materialism. In his review of fellow scientist Carl Sagan's *The Demon-Haunted World: Science as a Candle in the Dark,* biologist Richard Lewontin summarizes Sagan's belief that everything that exists is material or physical, and that the spiritual does not exist. **What is your response to this belief and to the term "atheist"?**

The Power of Nature. In his 1890 painting *Wheatfield with Crows*, Dutch artist Vincent van Gogh explored a subject that he painted regularly: the power of nature. Describing this and other paintings, van Gogh wrote to his brother: "They are vast fields of wheat under troubled skies, and I did not need to go out of my way to try to express sadness and extreme loneliness ... I almost think that these canvases will tell you what I cannot say in words, the health and restorative forces that I see in the country." **Compared with art of previous periods, art of the modern world refers less often to the power of God and more often to other subjects. Why do you think this is so? Think of other works of art and popular culture. What subjects do they explore?**

What You Will Learn

In this chapter, you will learn about

- movements, trends, and beliefs in modern times as they relate to religion
- the terms modernity, globalization, secular, secularism, secularization, rationalism, agnostic, atheist, humanism, secular humanism
- the origins and basic beliefs of secularism and what it means to live in a secular world
- how religion has responded to modernity
- how world religions have been changed by their interaction with modernity and globalization
- the Church's evaluation of modernity as expressed in the Second Vatican Council

Canada and Religions Today

Like everything else, religions shift and change with time. Religions underwent a radical transformation in the period of history we call modern times; that is, the last 500 years. What happened to us, as modern people, and what happened to religion in the modern age as it affects us in Canada is the topic of this chapter.

Since Canada's Confederation in 1867, there has been no official state religion in Canada. Yet, as recently as 50 years ago, most Canadians thought of Canada as a Christian nation. In the 1800s and the first half of the 1900s, Christianity heavily influenced most areas of Canadian life. As a result, people tended generally to agree about what was right and wrong.

There is still much today that reminds us of the influence of Christianity on Canadian society:

- Our legal and ethical systems are largely based on Judaeo-Christian teachings.
- We hear major public figures asking God to bless this country.
- Several provinces have Catholic schools.
- The landscape is dotted with churches.

However, over the past 50 to 60 years, the influence of Christianity has declined. Here are some signs of that change:

- The idea that individuals should be able to decide for themselves what is right and wrong has gained support. This viewpoint, which is known as secular humanism, will be explained later in this chapter.
- Laws no longer require stores and other businesses to close on Sunday to reflect the Christian belief that God declared the seventh day to be a day of rest.
- Popular culture reflects an increasingly secular world, often downplaying and sometimes mocking religiously grounded standards of right and wrong.
- A greater number of people in Canada say they have no religion. Prior to 1971, only 1 percent of Canadians said that they had "no religion." By 2001, that percentage had risen to 16.2 percent, which represents approximately 4.8 million people.

Percentage of People in Canada with "No Religious Affiliation" or "No Religion," 2001 Census

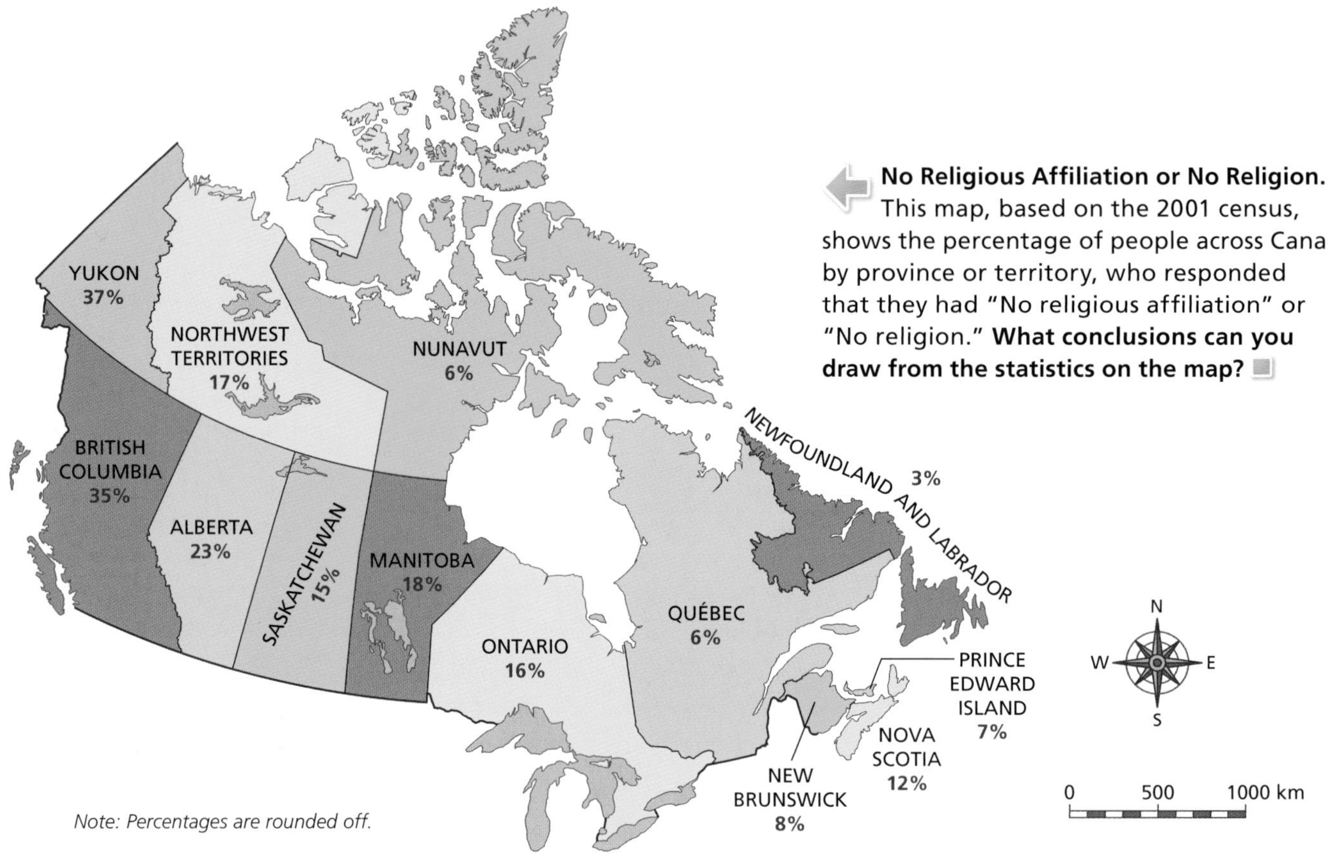

No Religious Affiliation or No Religion. This map, based on the 2001 census, shows the percentage of people across Canada, by province or territory, who responded that they had "No religious affiliation" or "No religion." **What conclusions can you draw from the statistics on the map?**

Defining Modernity

Fast Fact

We define the period from around 1500 to the present as "modern times." Our time is still part of modern times, although we sometimes also call our time "postmodern."

Globalization

The interdependence of societies throughout the world because of developments in business, communication, science, and ethics

Modernity, or modern times, refers to a period of history that started around 1500 and continues to the present. The modern era brought about enormous shifts in ways of thinking and acting that changed the world as it was into the world we know today. For our purposes, this period began with the journeys of exploration and leads to what we call **globalization**. Globalization is the idea that people, countries, and businesses throughout the world are interconnected and interdependent because of developments in politics, economics, communication, science and technology, and ethics.

Before modern times—from the fifth century to the beginning of the sixteenth century—the Catholic Church played a dominant role in all areas of people's existence in Europe: politics, the economy, education, the sciences, and morality. The Church formed the centre of life. Throughout European society—and despite local differences—religion was the central and sole source of meaning and morality for people. In life, religion, politics, the economy, education, the sciences, and morality were not seen as separate.

About 500 years ago in Europe, it was almost unthinkable for someone not to believe in God. The same was true among Europeans who first travelled to Canada. Today, this lack of belief is becoming more common. What changed? How can we understand this change? For answers, we must take a look at movements that developed over the past 500 years and how religion came to be seen as separate from other areas of life.

The Hockey Sweater. In this well-known story by Québécois writer Roch Carrier, young Roch wants a sweater of his favourite hockey player, Maurice Richard of the Montréal Canadiens. His mother orders it from a department store catalogue, but to his horror, the department store sends him a Maple Leafs sweater instead. The story highlights the differences between Catholic francophone and largely Protestant anglophone Canadian society. **What aspects of life do you see connected in this image from the National Film Board's version of the story?**

Check Your Understanding

1. On a timeline for Canadian history, note and briefly describe
- the role of religion in Canada now
- the role of religion in Canada 50 to 60 years ago

2. On a timeline for world history spanning 1000 CE to now, note
- modern times
- the role of the Catholic Church up to 1500

Think About It

3. Think about the story of *The Hockey Sweater* and then about your daily life and stories and movies you know. What signs do you see of the influence of Christianity in daily life and popular culture? Share your ideas in a small group and summarize them for the class.

Making It Personal

4. In your own life, what challenges do you see to living a spiritual life? Write your thoughts in a journal entry.

The Story of Modernity

As you saw in Chapter 5, Christianity faced many changes with the end of the Middle Ages and through modern times. The sixteenth and seventeenth centuries saw

- the breakup of the unity of the Western Christian Church
- the founding of new Protestant churches
- the Peace of Augsburg, which determined that European rulers could decide on an official religion for the state and all people in it
- the creation in England of a national Protestant church—the Anglican church

During the sixteenth and seventeenth centuries, changes were taking place in geography and economics:

- an outburst of journeys of discovery by Europeans in search of lands previously unknown to them
- trade in these lands, new goods, and a greater appetite for wealth
- a new type of economy that eventually evolved into what we now call capitalism

A Closer Look

The Anglican Church—or Church of England—is an example of a national church with its administrative centre in the country of its origin. Historically, many national churches had connections to the state government. In contrast, in modern times, many churches have no connection to the state; the United Church of Canada is an example. The Catholic Church is not a national church. Its spiritual and administrative centre is in Rome, and all Catholic churches throughout the world are interconnected.

A Seventeenth-Century Map of the World. Sixteenth- and seventeenth-century map makers did not have accurate knowledge of the world beyond European borders. Exploration allowed Europeans to see the Earth in a new way. **How would explorers expand a Christian European vision from local to global?**

Changes were also taking place on the political scene. The first nation-states began to break the absolute power of kings and emperors. Their citizens questioned whether kings and emperors received their power from religion or from God. The first stirrings of a government by the people and for the people—democracy—became noticeable. This change meant that kings and emperors no longer received their power from religion or from God. The sixteenth century was a turbulent time, with many conflicts and much unrest.

King Louis XVI and Queen Marie Antoinette of France. The political changes of the sixteenth and seventeenth centuries would eventually lead to the end of many monarchies. The most dramatic example was the execution of Louis XVI and Marie Antoinette during the French Revolution. In modern times, kings were no longer seen as representatives of God. Power belonged to the people. Religion and politics changed forever.

Defining Secular

All the areas of life in Europe that had been nurtured and overseen by the Church—such as the economy, politics, and the sciences—began to develop on their own, increasingly separate from the Church and religion. The different areas of human action and interaction also became separated from each other:

- economy from politics
- politics from religion
- science from the Bible

Each area developed independently, so that in time each evolved into a distinct discipline—political science, economics, biology, physics, chemistry, theology and religious studies, and so on—at universities. The aspects of life that had been seen as so intertwined that they were inseparable were, actually, being separated. Some aspects of life were now being considered **secular**—separated from religion.

Secular

Of this world; not religious or sacred; "secular" comes from the Latin word meaning "of the time"; the term comes from the contrasting belief in God being eternal, existing outside of time

In God We Trust. One example of separation was the separation between religion and the government in the United States. The First Amendment to the U.S. Constitution states: "Congress shall make no law respecting an establishment of religion, or prohibiting the free exercise thereof ..." and Thomas Jefferson later referred to that as the "separation of church and state." Ironically, "In God We Trust" was made the official motto of the United States in 1956, and it appears on all currency.

At the same time, politics, economics, the sciences, and ethics looked less and less to the Bible or to the Church for direction. Instead of accepting things on authority (such as the teachings of the Church or the Bible), people were encouraged to find for themselves the reasons why things are the way they are. Science—not religion—began to provide the foundation of truth. These changes did not happen all at once. In some cases, they involved intense conflicts. These conflicts were most evident in science.

Check Your Understanding

1. On a web diagram, summarize key historical changes in religion, politics, geography, and economics during modern times.
2. With a partner, create a definition and example of "secular" in your own words.

Think About It

3. Create a brief biographical sketch of a key historical figure in modern times and comment specifically on his or her religious beliefs. How does this person reflect his or her times?

Making It Personal

4. For questions about life or contemporary issues, where have you turned for information and guidance?

The Rise of Science and Reason

Fast Fact

From the sixteenth century to the present, scientists, theologians, and Christians have often been at odds about the age of the world, evolution, and ways of interpreting the Bible.

Rationalism

The attitude of accepting reason as the supreme authority in matters of opinion, belief, and conduct

Empirical

Based on experiment and observation as opposed to revelation of religion

Modern times have involved a growing emphasis on a scientific way of knowing—what can be seen in the material world, what can be proven through observation, and what can be understood through reason. It became more and more accepted that people should not accept anything as true unless they had observable and measurable reasons to hold something to be true. Everything, it was felt, has a reason for its existence. It is the task of science to discover and communicate these reasons. The movement called **rationalism** was a new and distinct way of thinking.

Galileo

One early example of conflict between scientists and theologians was in the case of Galileo. Galileo Galilei (1564–1642) was an Italian astronomer who made many discoveries and was the first to study celestial bodies using the telescope. Using **empirical** evidence, Galileo defended the view of the universe as revolving around the Sun, not Earth. Before Galileo, this heliocentric (Sun-centred) view had been rejected by the Church and unproven by observable and measurable methods.

Eventually, the Catholic Church forced Galileo to withdraw his heliocentric view—at least publicly. He spent the last years of his life under house arrest.

Agnostics and Atheists

With the increased emphasis on science, proof from the observable

world, and questioning of authority, people in modern times have increasingly questioned the existence of God (**agnostics**) and have often flirted with denying God's existence and questioning the need for religion. Because God cannot be known empirically (in other words, there is not a measurable, observable reason or cause for God's existence) it became possible for some individuals (**atheists**) to act and think as if God did not exist.

Galileo. In 1633, Galileo was ordered to Rome to stand trial on suspicion of **heresy**.

Agnostic

From the ancient Greek word meaning "not to know"; a person who believes that God may exist, but that humans cannot know it with any certainty

Atheist

From the ancient Greek word meaning "no God"; a person who does not believe in God, or in any other higher power or reality

Heresy

A belief or practice that is contrary to doctrine

STANLEY KRAMER presents
SPENCER TRACY
FREDRIC MARCH
GENE KELLY
"INHERIT THE WIND"
...IT'S ALL ABOUT THE 'MONKEY TRIAL' THAT ROCKED AMERICA...
DICK YORK · DONNA ANDERSON
FLORENCE ELDRIDGE
STANLEY KRAMER
UNITED ARTISTS

Inherit the Wind. In 1926, a Tennessee high school teacher named John Scopes was taken to court for teaching that humans evolved from earlier primate species and were not created, as the Bible taught. Teaching anything other than the biblical account was illegal in the state. The trial is a famous example of the clash between science and religion. The case was retold in the 1960 movie *Inherit the Wind*.

Fast Fact

Galileo was one of the first to be involved in the struggle between biblical and scientific truth. During the eighteenth century, Church authorities accepted the fact of heliocentrism. In 1992, the Church publicly accepted that it had been wrong about Galileo.

A Closer Look

In hindsight, the Church now realizes that it confused biblical truth and scientific truth. During Galileo's time, the Church did not know how to deal with a source of truth that seemed to contradict biblical truth. It took until the twentieth century before theologians began to make clearer distinctions between biblical and scientific truths.

Make It Your Own: Atheism Symbol

All religions have sacred symbols that represent their central beliefs. Even atheism has a symbol! This is the symbol of the American Atheist Society. Can you think of what the symbol might stand for? What does it remind you of? What kinds of associations does it suggest to you? If you did not know that it was an atheist symbol, what kind of organization would it remind you of?

American Atheist Society. This is the symbol of the American Atheist Society.

Activities

1. Share your ideas with a partner about the American Atheist Society symbol. What are your associations with the symbol? Does your partner agree or disagree? If you wish, research the symbol on the Internet.
2. The symbol is black and white. Imagine that the symbol was in colour. What colours would you suggest and why?

Fear of the Unknown. Early explorers—such as those on this sixteenth-century ship—had to overcome the fear of the unknown and concerns about what could happen to them while they were isolated from the rest of the world. One of the things they feared was sea monsters.

Expanding Knowledge and Worldviews

At the same time that science was expanding knowledge of the world and focusing many thinkers on the material world, exploration and trade were expanding the world that Christian Europeans knew, exposing them to new ideas and ways of living, and leading the way for colonial expansion and immigration. These changes led to the multicultural and religiously diverse reality we have today.

Immanuel Kant. The influential German philosopher Immanuel Kant (1724–1804) was the first to explore the limits of reason. He argued that scientific knowledge and religious knowledge are distinct. Science cannot say anything about God. **Do you agree with Kant's conclusion?**

Check Your Understanding

1. With a partner, summarize what you have learned on pages 314 to 316 about
   - conflicts over scientific knowledge
   - the meanings of "agnostic" versus "atheist"
   - the impact of exploration and trade

Think About It

2. What current issues do you think raise questions of reason (for example, questions involving scientific knowledge) and faith?

Making It Personal

3. Imagine undertaking your own journey of discovery—for example, a space voyage to the planet Mars. Describe your feelings as you move farther away from all you know and closer to your goal.

Skill Focus: Analyzing Cause and Effect

A cause is something (an event, a situation) that makes another event happen. The resulting situation is the effect, or the impact of the cause. Using a fishbone diagram to analyze causes can be helpful, especially if there are many possible causes for an event and its resulting impact. In a fishbone diagram, the horizontal line points toward the effect. The diagonal lines represent the kinds of causes that led to the effect. For example, in this example of a partially completed fishbone cause-and-effect diagram to the right, the effect is the Protestant Reformation in Germany. The categories are: People, Places, and Actions.

Only some possible answers are supplied in the diagram. There are many others. What other historical figures (religious and state) might have been involved at this time? Were other countries involved? What other events might have led up to the Protestant Reformation?

Cause and Effect

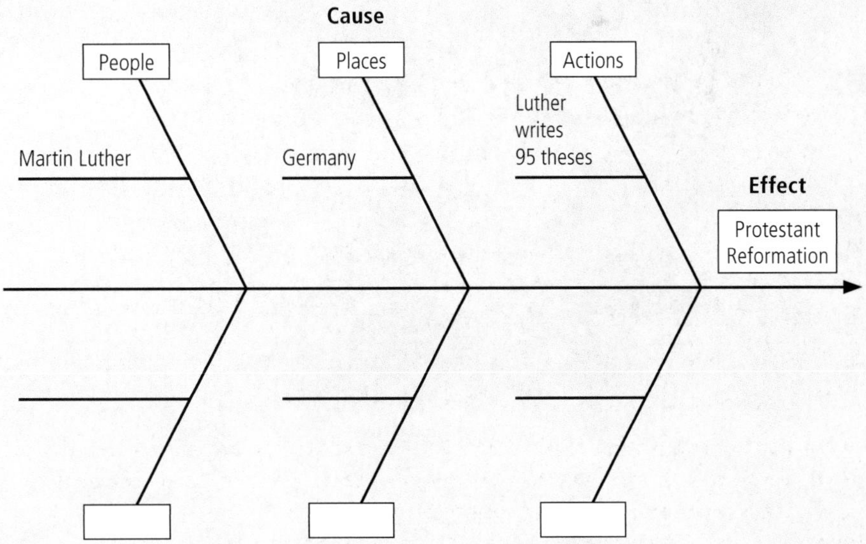

An Example of a Partially Completed Fishbone Diagram Showing Cause and Effect. Using graphic organizers like the one above will help you organize your thinking before you write an essay or prepare an oral presentation.

The Enlightenment, Humanism, and Secularism

La Grande Arche de la Fraternité. La Grande Arche de la Fraternité in Paris, a monument to humanism, was built to mark the two hundredth anniversary of the French Revolution. The bloody revolution overthrew the French monarchy and established a republic. The arch celebrates the humanism without God that is one of the characteristics of the French Revolution.

In the eighteenth century, many thinkers focused on questioning traditional authority and structures, on reason and scientific knowledge, on the individual, and on freedom. The movement is sometimes called the Enlightenment or the Age of Enlightenment. Both the French Revolution and the American Revolution arose from this movement.

Other movements and philosophies developed in the years following, including a new philosophy called humanism. At the same time, secularization—the movement to separate aspects of life as secular or religious—was continuing.

- **Humanism** is a philosophy or worldview that upholds the importance of human life, reason, and justice. Humanism affirms human dignity and the importance of ethics.
- **Secularism** is, generally, the belief that governmental practices and institutions should exist separately from religion or religious beliefs; it is a principle of promoting secular ideas or values in either public or private settings over religious ways of thought. This term was first used in the nineteenth century.
- **Secularization** is the process of separating public institutions and popular culture from religious institutions and philosophies.

Humanism can be described as Christian humanism or secular humanism. You will explore both of these belief systems in the coming pages.

Humanism

A philosophy or worldview that upholds the importance of life, reason, justice, and ethics; humanism affirms human dignity

Secularism

A way of thinking and approaching the world that separates religion from other areas of life; for example, government and schools

Secularization

Rejection of the influence of religion in other areas of life; for example, in schools or in public life

A MONSTER SCIENCE CREATED
But Could Not Destroy!
FRANKENSTEIN
Starring BORIS KARLOFF as The MONSTER

Frankenstein. As scientific knowledge expanded, theologians and other thinkers asked questions about its impact on human lives and what could (and should) be done with that scientific knowledge. In 1818, Mary Wollstonecraft Shelley wrote the story of Frankenstein, in which a scientist combines corpses and brings them to life.

Fast Fact

Mary Wollstonecraft Shelley was a writer during the Industrial Revolution. During the Industrial Revolution (in England first in the late eighteenth century, then in Europe, North America, and eventually the rest of the world), new technologies such as steam engines made factories possible. Many people moved away from rural areas to towns and cities. However, Shelley and many writers of her time turned to nature. What role, do you think, should science play in life?

Check Your Understanding

1. On the world history timeline you created earlier, add details and events of modernity. What happened as a result of these events?
2. With a partner, take turns defining and asking questions about the following terms:
   - humanism
   - secular
   - secularism
   - secularization

Think About It

3. In a small group, brainstorm a list of possible cause-and-effect relationships—from the reasonable to the ridiculous. Then write them as headlines for a newspaper or news website using language that underlines cause and effect. Share your headlines with your class and display them in the classroom.
4. The story of Frankenstein was a response to the time in which it was written and was later retold in movies. What is one current movie that you think expresses well a key concern of your time? Present your choice in a movie poster.

Making It Personal

5. Have you ever felt that you are living your life as if there is no God? Explain.

Christianity in Modern Times

From its dominant position during the Middle Ages, Christianity had a hard time letting go of its influence over politics, economics, science, and ethics. As the diagram below shows, whereas religion once unified these areas of life, now these areas are seen as separate, and religion is one of many social systems.

Although the social functions of politics, economics, science, and ethics are now independent in many ways, they interact whenever they overlap with another function. Religion still speaks to issues in the other areas. The Church continues to let its voice be heard whenever it considers that human dignity, human life, and justice are at stake. For example,

- in economics, the Church speaks out about harm to the poor
- in politics, Catholics would speak out if the Canadian government were to reinstate capital punishment

Many people, on seeing that religion has become one social system among several others, conclude that religion is declining. However, as we will see, religion is not in decline.

The Interrelationship of Religion and Other Spheres of Life

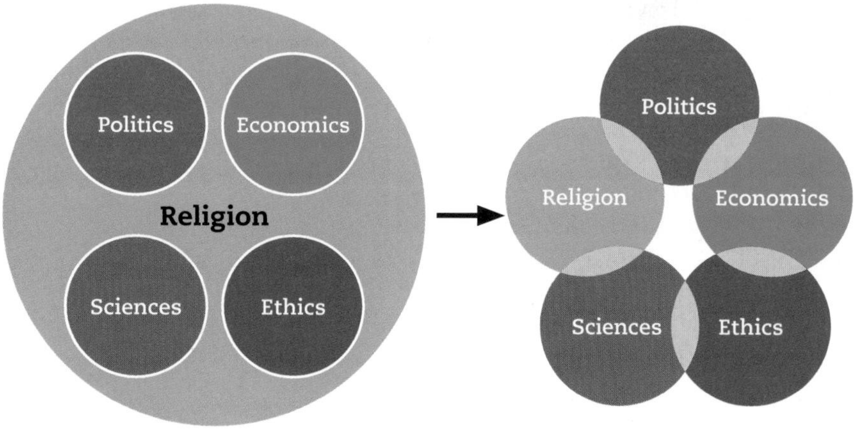

Christianity and Other Spheres of Life. The first diagram shows how Christianity encompassed all of the various areas of life in the Middle Ages. The second diagram shows what has happened in modern times. Now, religion is one of many different social systems.

Capital Punishment. In 1976, after years of debate, capital punishment was removed from Canada's *Criminal Code*. The last executions in Canada took place in 1962—both for murder—at the Don Jail in Toronto. **What do you think were the arguments made against the death penalty?**

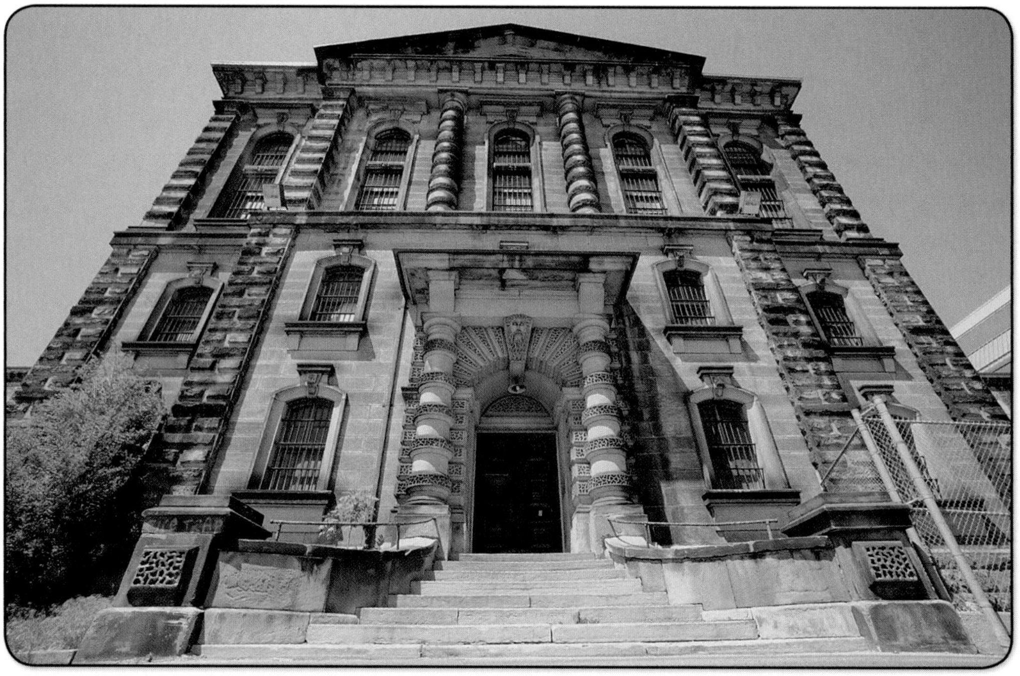

Secular Humanism

The Church's Role. **On a drive through a town like this one in Québec, what inferences could you draw from the size and location of this church in relation to the rest of the town? What does this tell you about the importance of religion? About the connection between religion and other spheres of life?**

Fast Fact

Christian humanists uphold the dignity of the human person, human life, and happiness *in light of Christian teaching.* In contrast, secular humanists uphold the dignity of the human person, human life, and happiness, but do not believe that God, gods, or the supernatural play any role in human life.

As you read on page 318, secularization is a process of separating aspects of life so that those that had been under the overall topic of religion are now "secular"—of this world, without reference to God. Out of this cultural process has grown a way of life that is called "secular." In this section, we will examine some of the beliefs of this secular way of life as represented by secular humanism.

Secular humanists believe that the dignity of the human person, human life, and happiness are achieved through human reason and effort alone. They reject the belief that God or the supernatural plays a role in moral reflection and decision making. While secular humanism has its foundations in classical Greek philosophy, it did not emerge with an organized philosophical system until the 1980s.

Secular humanism is a worldview that shares many humanist beliefs with Christian humanism, but it has general beliefs that distinguish it from faith-based humanism. To start looking at secular humanism, here is a brief overview of its general beliefs:

Secular Humanism: General Beliefs

Belief	Features of Belief
Life	• The main concern is for this life, not for the hereafter. Secular humanists can commit to improving life through science and technology, education, health care, and art. • Life is a constant, progressive search for objective truth. If we do not have the answers and the know-how today, we will in the future. The future will be better than the past. • The main concerns of humans are fulfillment, growth, and creativity for both the individual and humankind.
Reason	• To find solutions to human problems and answers to human questions, people should use critical reason, factual evidence, and scientific methods of inquiry—not faith and mysticism. • With reason, an open exchange of ideas, goodwill, and tolerance, humans can build a better world for themselves and future generations.
Individual Authority	• Each individual must weigh and test dogmas (doctrine or body of beliefs), ideologies, and traditions (religious, political, social, or economic)—not simply accept them on the word of an outside authority, such as the Church or the Bible.
Ethics	• Ethical conduct is based on workable individual, social, and political principles. • Ethics can be evaluated by how useful they are in enhancing human well-being and individual responsibility.

Secular Humanism. These are some of the general beliefs of secular humanism.

Check Your Understanding

1. Describe two outcomes of the changed role of religion in society during modern times.
2. In your own words, explain the following terms:
   - secular way of life
   - Christian humanism
   - humanism
   - secular humanism

Think About It

3. Discuss in a group and then hold a brief informal debate about the following topic: today, the media (including the Internet) have more impact on what teens think is right and wrong than does any other single source.
4. In a small group, review the general beliefs of secular humanism outlined on this page. What initial responses, reactions, and questions do you have? What are possible implications of each belief? Note your ideas on a chart.

Making It Personal

5. Take a look at the main concerns listed for secular humanists. To these concerns, what would you add or subtract as *your* main concerns?

NEL

Secular Humanism's Beliefs

Secular humanists present several arguments to support their belief system. We will look at each of them in turn before offering a reply to these arguments.

Belief: Secular Humanism Is about Humans Coming of Age

In modern times—as politics, the economy, the sciences, and ethics broke away from religion—some people thought that

- the era of religion was coming to an end
- religion would necessarily disappear as a way of understanding human life and meaning
- giving up religion was part of this new, enlightened time, where only the **rational** and the scientific counted

As evidence, they pointed to what they saw as the general decline of religion as a force in people's lives: "The more progressive and enlightened people have let go of religion," they said. "These people live by reason. Religion belongs to the past." This view is common today among secular humanists.

Belief: Religion Provides a Sense of Security

Secular humanists believe that life ends with death and that it takes courage to let go of the security that religion provides. Secular humanists consider the consolation of religion to be an illusion and an escape from life's difficulties. They believe that we humans—without the promise of a reward in an afterlife—should work to improve our lives and the lives of those around us. They accept that without religion, there is no transcendence: nothing bigger than us to guide us on our way in a life that is often difficult. Secular humanists believe that it takes more courage to accept life without God than to live with faith in a loving God.

Belief: Secular Humanism Values Authenticity

In modern times, the focus shifted away from humans in community to humans as individuals. For secular humanists, being "authentic" means being true to yourself as an individual. They believe that identity is no longer linked to belonging to a community or being a

Fast Fact

Secular humanism argues that religion is a stage in humanity to grow out of and that there is no afterlife; it all ends with death.

Rational

Describes a way of knowing on the basis of causes; everything has a reason, or cause

Auguste Compte. Auguste Compte (1798–1857) viewed religion as a stage of human history—the infancy stage—but religion would be left behind in the final stage of history, the scientific age.

Individualism. In the 1970s, popular culture in North America encouraged young people to "do their own thing" and become "themselves" through individual efforts, including self-help therapies. **What similar messages do you see in popular culture now?**

child of God, but is about being at one with yourself. For secular humanists,

- we need to express ourselves *as individuals*
- all of us have our own way of realizing who we are—this is the task of life
- people are seen as individuals before they are seen as part of a community

Belief: Secular Humanism Is Based on Human Reason

Modern times have put tremendous emphasis on

- observable facts, scientific knowledge, and reason
- questioning authority, rules, and regulations
- the individual and his or her freedom

Modernity was all about freedom from external restraints. To be authentic, people were to be inner-directed. They were to be true to themselves, not to the rules and regulations imposed from the outside.

Since revelation was not based on reason or on self-evident, rational truths, religion came to be seen as not scientific, not rational. In fact, religion was frequently branded as "irrational." In contrast, the secular view saw itself as representing the rational and the scientific.

Fast Fact

Most of the current ethical theories of secular institutions such as the Canadian government, corporations, schools, and universities are an attempt to apply reason to human actions.

Belief: Ethics Should Be Based on Reason

Secular humanists often paint a very negative image of Christian ethics. For many secular humanists, religion has inflicted terrible suffering, especially on those who stray from the "right" path. Secular humanism sees this suffering as often resulting from the use of revealed truths in religion. The use of revelation, they say, is an attack on human freedom. Secular humanists, therefore, seek ethics based not on revelation but on reason, and thus try to apply reason to human actions. Here are two examples:

- ethics based on utilitarianism—the idea that what is ethical must be useful to the individual, contributing to the person's well-being and greatest happiness and pleasure, not necessarily to the common good
- the human rights tradition—including the ideas that all humans have a number of inherent rights and freedoms, that these are first of all individual rights, and that governments must protect these rights against infringement

Signing of Canada's New Constitution. Here, Queen Elizabeth officially signs Canada's new Constitution, which included the *Canadian Charter of Rights and Freedoms*, on Parliament Hill in 1982.

Check Your Understanding

1. Give three reasons why secular humanism rejects religion.
2. How does secular humanism define authenticity? Explain how secular humanism sees religion as inauthentic.
3. Visually present secular humanists' beliefs about secular humanism, reason, and ethics.

Think About It

4. Secular humanism presents the belief that humans have an unlimited capacity to shape reality. List the positive and negative consequences if this were true. What paintings, movies, TV shows, or songs present this idea?

Making It Personal

5. Explain what you consider to be an authentic life. Is living an authentic life important to you? Explain.

The Religious Reply to the Beliefs of Secular Humanists

This chapter has explored beliefs and arguments of secular humanism. Now let us turn to the response of religion, in particular the response of the Catholic Church and Christianity.

Religious Reply: Modern Times and Secular Life

First, secular humanists speak from a modern perspective and their belief system is a fact of modern times. In disagreeing with secular humanists, the Catholic Church does not reject modernity. The Church has been deeply influenced by modernity and has acknowledged developments in these times—for example, the importance of the individual and the rights that must be given to each human being. However, the Church does not accept that human beings must remove God from their lives (that is, live secular lives) in order to flourish. In the Church's view, individual rights are best respected through faith in God.

To understand the place of religion in modern times, we will look at each of the arguments on the previous pages in turn.

Religious Reply: Religion in the Twenty-First Century

Research does not support the secular humanist belief that religion is in decline in the twenty-first century. The problem is how to define "religion." As you have read, in modern times, religion and politics, religion and science and technology all began to act separately. Religion became more independent and began to find its own sphere of action in society. From having one dominant religion, the West now found itself with many religions. There are at least four classifications of religion today:

- organized religion
- religious movements, sects, and cults
- state religion
- folk religion

"Only God ... meets the deepest longings of the human heart ... By no human law can the personal dignity and liberty of man be so aptly safeguarded as by the Gospel of Christ which has been entrusted to the Church."
(The Constitution on the Church in the Modern World, #41)

Bahai Temple. Bahai Lotus Temple in Delhi, India. The Bahai faith was founded by Bahaullah of Tehran, in Persia (now Iran). Key beliefs of this faith are unity, one God, and one human race.

Each category is explored on pages 327 to 330. These many forms and classifications show that religion has branched out in different directions, just as the sciences, politics, economics, and other spheres have done. So, although a growing number of Canadians surveyed have indicated that they follow "no religion," religion in all its forms is still a vibrant social system.

Religious Reply: Humans Search for What Religion Offers

As you read on page 323, secular humanists believe that life ends with death and that religion is false security. However, they do not appreciate the fact that religion offers consolation. For humans to know that there is a God who loves and takes care of them, and that they can pray to God anytime, makes humans feel less alone in the struggles of life. It is comforting to know that in death they will be welcomed into God's house.

While secular humanists do not look for consolation in a world beyond this life, few humans succeed in sticking to only rational practices. That is why the Age of Enlightenment—modernity at its most pure—was followed by the Age of Romanticism (1800–1850). This was the age in which Mary Wollstonecraft Shelley wrote about Frankenstein; her husband, poet Percy Bysshe Shelley, wrote of love, nature, the imagination, freedom, and humanism; and their contemporaries seemed to rebel against a focus on reason and science alone. Romanticism rediscovered the power of feeling and was filled with music, art, and literature that evoked emotions of attachment not to reason, but to nature, and beyond nature to the cosmos. Feeling takes us beyond order, structure, and rationalism—the bleakness of life—and allows us to touch a realm of freedom and beauty that brings us deep joy and fulfillment.

Our time, in all its secularity, continues this search for something that goes beyond the individual and the purely secular. Music is one way of searching: concerts bring forth feelings of sharing in a common beauty and a common humanity. People are looking for wholeness, peace, joy, and health. While they may not want to be part of organized religions, they are in search of spirituality—matters of the spirit or soul. This quest overrides the purely secular view and leads people to a deeper understanding of life.

Environmental Effort. These volunteers help to clean up the environment by picking up garbage. Turning to nature in the environmental movement is one spiritual approach.

Organized Religion

Organized religions—such as Judaism, Christianity, Islam, Hinduism, Buddhism, and Sikhism—all have their own well-developed systems of rituals and beliefs. The fact that a new religion like the Bahai faith formed in the mid-1800s is evidence that organized religion continues to grow in the modern era.

Religious Movements, Sects, and Cults

New religious movements have appeared in modern times. They came into being when the faith and practices of the organized religions were seen as out of step with modern life. People within organized religions often formed splinter groups or sects that responded to some spiritual, political, or social need. These are known as religious movements.

Organized Religion around the World. Christianity is practised in countries throughout the world. Organized religions, such as Christianity, have given a form to their beliefs and practices through art, buildings, books, rituals, and so on.

Fundamentalist Movements

Some groups have responded to secular challenges to traditional religions by breaking off from the mainstream to create fundamentalist branches of their religions. They see themselves as radically at odds with secular culture and globalization. In their opposition, fundamentalist movements will often take a specific concern, such as modesty for women in Islam, and make it central, such as the wearing of the *burka*.

Fundamentalists believe that religious truth is to be found solely in their own religious movement. Such fundamentalist attitudes exist within all organized religions, including Hinduism, Islam, and Christianity. Some Christian groups, for example, stress a strict or literal interpretation of the scriptures (such as the creation of the world in six days) and categorically reject the value of other religions or beliefs. **Fundamentalism** can be a response to secular challenges to traditional religions. Fundamentalists see things in absolute terms. They believe that their view is right and all others are wrong and dangerous, leading the world to ruin.

Fundamentalism

A form of religion in which groups or subgroups with a strict interpretation of religious scripture hold those beliefs as absolute authority and beyond human interpretation or adaptation

Fundamentalists are unwilling to enter into—or perhaps, to be more precise, incapable of entering into—dialogue of any kind with those who disagree with them or hold different views. Fundamentalists are most concerned about their own identity and believe that dialogue is not permissible with those who do not share their own views.

Fundamentalists are often very selective about what they believe. What they accept and reject is largely decided by the charismatic leaders they tend to follow. Often these leaders introduce their highly personal emphasis on what is to be believed, and their followers are bound to these teachings.

Standing Buddha. This is one of two enormous statues of standing Buddhas. The statues were carved into the side of a cliff in the Bamyan Valley in central Afghanistan in the sixth century. The Buddhas were destroyed in 2001 by Islamic fundamentalists called the Taliban, who governed Afghanistan, after the Taliban declared the statues to be idols. Idols are prohibited in Islamic *shariah* law. The destruction is an example of fundamentalist intolerance of other religions' beliefs and practices.

Sects and Cults

Sects and cults are other religious reactions to the challenges of modernity. Both organized religion and secular groups often refer to some of these movements in a negative way. Opposition to sects and cults has come from the fact that they are very different from organized religion. Often they are breakaway groups from organized religion.

Religious cults tend to be headed by charismatic leaders who claim either to have a divine nature or to receive divine revelations. These people are often authoritarian and require blind obedience from their followers. Often, followers are controlled harshly, leaving them physically and psychologically vulnerable. In a cult, the followers are put under constant pressure to accept the worldview of the leader, which makes members fully subject to him or her. The worldview often includes the belief that the end of the world is near and that all people outside the cult are a threat or are evil.

Some people—often in their late teens or in their 20s—join cults in their personal search for happiness and belonging. When individuals are going through a difficult transition, they are vulnerable. Members feel supported and carried by the cult and its strong leader, and so are ready to accept the full package of teachings and indoctrination. In some cases, members break off relationships with parents and friends. Life outside the cult is considered dangerous.

Whether we agree with the views of these new movements or not, each is

- a religious movement
- in its own way, an attempt to live the mystery of life and to understand the world

In an age when people remark on a decline in religion, the growth of these new religious movements shows that religion is still flourishing today.

The Order of the Solar Temple. The Order of the Solar Temple was based in Québec and Switzerland. One of its founders was Luc Jouret (shown here). The cult wanted to "correct notions of authority and power in the world" and to help humanity prepare for the coming again of Jesus Christ as a solar god-king. Many of this cult's members committed suicide in 1994 because they believed in "death voyages" that would take them to a new life on the star Sirius.

State Religions

A third form of religion today is politicized religion. In this situation, the state and its laws authorize and privilege the beliefs and practices of a particular religion. The particular religion sets the agenda for the nation, making religion an arm of the state, or the state an arm of religion. In these cases, the state sets rules derived from the chosen religion for all the people. In this way, a particular religion becomes an unavoidable part of people's lives, whether they embrace its beliefs or not. Religion is not a social system on its own. It remains linked to other social systems—politics, economics, and ethics—just as all aspects of life in Western Europe before the modern era were linked to the Catholic Church.

States and Their Religions

Example States	State Religions
Zambia, Russia	Christianity
Iran, Saudi Arabia, Indonesia	Islam
Israel	Judaism
Thailand and Myanmar (Burma)	Buddhism

Halloween. Halloween probably came from an old Celtic feast marking the end of harvest time. The Celtic peoples believed that the boundary between the dead and the living was dissolved on this day. Because the dead and the spirits were thought to wander about, people wore masks and dressed up as spirits and ghosts to appease them.

Folk Religion

Another classification of religion today is folk religion. Practices that are rooted in folk religion—more ancient or traditional religions—exist beside practices of organized religions or religious movements.

Many of these practices go back to pre-Christian times. Even though organized religion may have opposed them, they have survived and remain popular. No religion claims these celebrations, yet they have a religious tinge to them. They are often tied closely to a religious feast and they often were (and remain) ways of living the mystery attached to the feast.

These folk practices include those associated with

- Halloween
- aspects of Christmas—not the birth of Jesus, but the lights, the gifts, Santa Claus
- aspects of Easter—not the resurrection, but the Easter Bunny and the eggs
- New Year's Eve—the fireworks
- Valentine's Day
- Carnival
- Thanksgiving
- Groundhog Day

Make It Your Own: Cults

Often, young people are attracted to cults at a time of life when they are under great pressure to leave adolescence behind. During this time of becoming an adult, young people experience a period of searching and develop greater self-awareness. Cults seem to give a kind of security because they do not expect people to deal with these issues alone. For these and other reasons, both organized religion and secular groups tend to view religious sects and cults negatively.

Activities

1. With a partner or in a small group, discuss some of the stressful situations that could make a young person feel vulnerable to the influence of a cult.
2. Choose one of the stressful situations you discussed in question 1 and suggest strategies for overcoming it. If you wish, make a poster to show ways of solving the problem.

Check Your Understanding

1. Use a visual organizer to outline and define classifications of religion.

2. With a partner, summarize the responses to the ideas that religion is in decline and that it offers false security.

Think About It

3. Some people argue that the 15 percent increase in people indicating "no religion" on the census form between 1971 and 2001 (see page 309) is a sign that religion is in decline. Based on the religious reply to the beliefs of secular humanism on the previous pages, discuss in a small group whether you think religion is in decline. Explain your conclusions.

Making It Personal

4. In a journal, describe what experiences you have had—or know about—of different classifications of "religion" or of other searches for meaning and purpose in contemporary life. For example, have you ever taken part in a folk religion celebration? What made the experience "religious"?

NEL

Religious Reply: Secular Humanism Is Itself a Belief

The story of secular humanism is one that some humans tell themselves. It is a belief. Like any ideology, secular humanism has certain values and beliefs. Many secular humanists believe that their view is more scientific and rational than Christianity is. After all, they say, science has not been able to find evidence for the existence of God. Thus, they believe that there is no God and that humans are totally free—in control of their own thought processes and fully responsible for themselves.

Yet, secular humanism is no more rational than faith in God. Both depend on a belief that is not scientifically proven. In other words, secular humanism has no more empirical evidence for its point of departure (there is no God and humans are entirely free) than Christianity has for its point of departure (the belief that humans are creatures of God).

Religious Reply: Secular Humanists Are Neither More Authentic nor Free

One of the most seductive feelings that modernity brought was freedom—liberation from institutions, authorities, the Bible, and anything else that demanded obedience. Humans tried to be authentic, to be true to themselves, to create their own meaning for life, to authorize themselves to do what is right and good. Yet, how do we determine what is right and good? We need to look to an authority we trust. Secular humanists, like all people, must turn to role models, to the past, to tradition, to what others hold out to be right and good. They turn to authority—for example, to secular institutions such as many modern governments, their laws, and their secular schools.

Christianity Compared to Secular Humanism

Christianity	Secular Humanism
key belief—humans are creatures of God	key belief—there is no God
absence of God cannot be proven scientifically	presence of God cannot be proven scientifically

In contrast, Catholics have always searched for—and continue to search for—the meaning of life in the Bible. They find meaning, authority, and authenticity in the Bible and in the Church. In Christian Europe, a person's authentic self existed through relationship with God and being part of the Church. The authentic self was the person who was relational. To be authentic was to be in a relationship with another—especially with God and with the community of the Church. In the Catholic tradition, a person is never an isolated individual. A person is identified by his or her relationships.

In a statement he made before he became pope, Benedict XVI accepted the secular thesis that separated Church and state. However, he warned that this did not mean that God must be kept out of the decisions of the state. A state, he said, should not act as if there is no God. It is not irrational to believe in God: faith and reason are healthy partners.

"The name 'atheism' covers many very different phenomena. One common form is the practical materialism which restricts its needs and aspirations to space and time. Atheistic humanism falsely considers man to be 'an end to himself, and the sole maker, with supreme control, of his own history.'"

(Catechism of the Catholic Church, #2124)

Pope Benedict XVI on Faith and Reason. Pope Benedict XVI has spoken of faith and reason a number of times. Faith, he says, is compatible with human reason, but is not based on human reason. Reason is a gift to all humans, religious or not. The Church values this gift, but is not limited by it.

Religious Reply: Ethics Based on Reason Are Insufficient

To find moral guidance, Christianity draws on the inherent dignity of the human person as being in the image of God, and turns to the Sermon on the Mount that Jesus gave. In contrast, secular humanism draws on principles such as the following:

- the universality principle—follow a rule only if you think it should apply to all humans
- the utilitarian principle—actions are moral when they are useful; that is, when they contribute to human happiness

However, applying these principles has not led to consensus.

Although the Catholic Church never endorsed the 1948 United Nations Universal Declaration of Human Rights, the Church

- has praised the efforts to arrive at declarations of human rights and freedoms and praised the declaration itself
- has created its own statement of human rights, based on the dignity of each person as the image of God

In a letter he wrote in 1963, Pope John XXIII noted that what he thought was lacking in the UN Declaration was

- the emphasis on the social nature of the human person
- the need to counterbalance rights with duties

Check Your Understanding

1. In your own words, summarize
- how secular humanism is a belief
- the religious response regarding authenticity and freedom
- the Church's response to the UN Universal Declaration of Human Rights

Think About It

2. In Canada, three general arguments against the death penalty were made:
- Someone might be wrongfully convicted.
- The state should not take the lives of individuals.
- The death penalty might not deter crime.

In a small group, discuss the arguments, identify which ones are based on religious grounds and which ones attempt to apply reason, and share your responses to them.

3. Do you think a life based solely on reason is possible? Create a poster to express your response.

Making It Personal

4. Explain how religion has helped you or someone you know to find meaning in life. Tell this story in a testimonial, either anonymous or signed, and share it on a bulletin board.

Catholics and Modernity

Over the past 500 years, there have been many religious reactions to modernity, especially when modernity became secularist and atheistic. Because modernity tried to find explanations for things and to govern without referring to God, tensions arose between the Catholic Church and modernity.

There are many examples where the Catholic Church opposed certain aspects of modernity; for example, when the Church opposed scientific discoveries made by astronomers in the sixteenth and seventeenth centuries. However, the Church has had positive reactions to modernity, too. The most memorable occasion was Pope John XXIII's 1958 speech in which he declared his desire to hold an ecumenical council to bring the Church into our time. This "opening of the windows" of the Church became the Second Vatican Council (1962–1965).

Two documents of the Second Vatican Council in particular spoke of the need to update the Church in the face of the challenges of modernity:

- *The Constitution on the Church in the Modern World*
- *The Declaration on Religious Freedom*

The Constitution on the Church in the Modern World

The Constitution on the Church in the Modern World was a document not only for Catholics but for all people. It begins by saying that "the joys and the hopes, the griefs and the anxieties" of all, especially the poor, are the joys and hopes, the griefs and anxieties of the followers of Christ. With this belief in mind, the document reflects on the way humans see themselves today: the wonder we feel about our

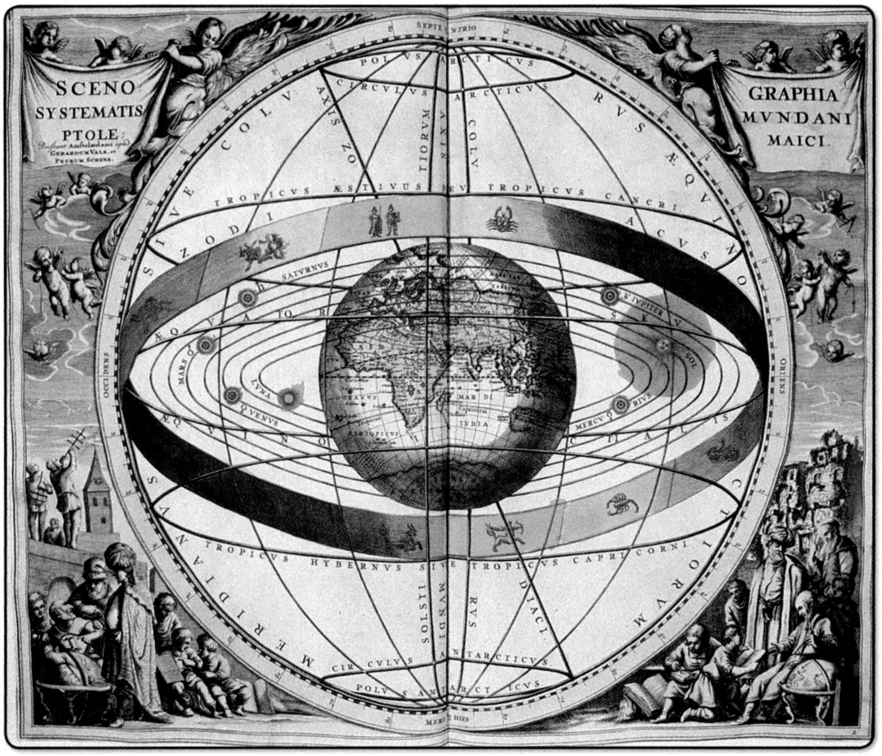

Geocentric Solar System. In the Middle Ages, Earth was understood to be the centre of the solar system, as shown in this medieval drawing.

own discoveries, the wonder we feel about our power, the anxiety we have over the place and role of humans in the universe, our questions about the meaning of all our striving, and the ultimate destiny of everything.

The *Constitution* affirms some of the main ethical beliefs of modernity, such as the dignity of the human person, the goodness of the human body, the accomplishments of the human mind, the affirmation of moral conscience, and the excellence of liberty. However, the document also

- points to the capacity of humans to sin and to abuse these immense gifts
- speaks at length about atheism

A Closer Look

The *Constitution* says:

> Modern atheism often takes on a systematic expression which, in addition to other causes, stretches the desires for human independence to such a point that it poses difficulties against any kind of dependence on God.

Dependence on God, the document says, is seen as the equivalent of thwarting freedom, as if humans and God are in some sort of competition. Against these views, the document affirms that recognizing God is not hostile to human dignity.

A Closer Look

The *Declaration* states:

> It is in accordance with their dignity as persons—that is, beings endowed with reason and free will and therefore privileged to bear personal responsibility—that all [people] should be at once impelled by nature and also bound by moral obligation to seek the truth, especially religious truth.... However, [people] cannot discharge these obligations in a manner in keeping with their own nature unless they enjoy immunity from external coercion as well as psychological freedom.

In 2006, Pope Benedict XVI elaborated on religious freedom as follows:

> Since religion is also organized in visible structures, as is the case with the Church, it should be recognized as a form of public community presence. This also implies that every religious denomination (provided it is neither in opposition to the moral order nor a threat to public order) be guaranteed the free exercise of the activities of worship—spiritual, cultural, educational and charitable—of the believing community.

To sum up, the document, on the one hand, affirms the many accomplishments of modernity. On the other hand, it warns against seeing the gift of reason and freedom outside of God's attachment to us in the person of Jesus Christ. The Church is not outside of the concerns and joys of today's women and men.

The Declaration on Religious Freedom

The *Declaration on Religious Freedom* is a landmark document. Although constitutional law in many countries had already recognized this right, the Church had never before proclaimed that everyone has the right to religious freedom. In the declaration, this right is accepted as an official teaching of the Church.

The issue of freedom as a gift from God is also important—so important, in fact, that the Church can never allow faith to be forced or coerced. God calls freely, and people must respond only in freedom. This is a matter not only for the Church, but also for governments.

It's OK to Be a Believer. When religion played a dominant role in most aspects of life in the Western world, it was controversial to take the secular position. It took courage for people to say that they no longer believed in God. Today, many people would argue that the reverse is true—that it takes more courage to say that you are a believer. **Do you agree with this statement?**

Check Your Understanding

1. The Catholic Church both affirms and critiques modernity. Explain the Church's major concern about modernity.
2. Explain in your own words how the document *The Constitution on the Church in the Modern World* defines atheism. Add this definition to your earlier definition of the word.
3. Explain why, according to the Church, having religious freedom is important.

Think About It

4. Lena's parents give her a hard time if she says she does not want to go to church. Does the statement on freedom of religion apply in her case? Discuss in a small group and present your conclusions to the class.
5. With a partner, consider why some people choose atheism. Write a short paragraph summarizing your conclusions.

Making It Personal

6. In a poem, drawing, or paragraph, express the personal challenge of living a religious life in modern times.

What I Have Learned

In this chapter, I learned about

- the changed role of religion in Canada
- movements, trends, and beliefs within modern times as they relate to religion—including secularism; rationalism; exploration, trade, migration, and globalization; atheism and agnosticism; humanism; and secular humanism
- what it means to live in a secular world
- the origins of secularism
- the development of religion as a social function alongside other functions, such as economics and politics
- beliefs and arguments of secular humanism
- religious responses to secular humanism
- the human search for meaning and purpose within contemporary culture
- the Church's evaluation of modernity as expressed in the Second Vatican Council

Growing Seed

"The kingdom of God is as if someone would scatter seed on the ground, and would sleep and rise night and day, and the seed would sprout and grow, he does not know how. The earth produces of itself, first the stalk, then the head, then the full grain in the head. But when the grain is ripe, at once he goes in with his sickle, because the harvest has come." (Mark 4:26–29)

Living Faith Today

The Many Faces of the World. We hold that these persons were all equally loved into existence by the one God. How must we live this faith today? One of the ways is to maintain a constant conversation and dialogue between peoples and religions. One of the ways is the kind of dialogue of world religions that happened in 1986, in Assisi, Italy, the birthplace of St. Francis.

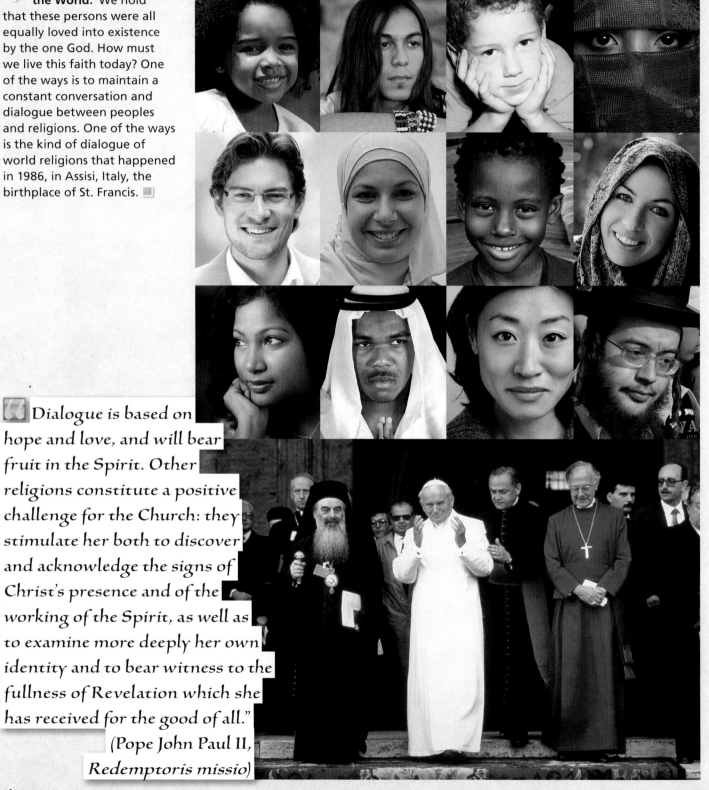

"Dialogue is based on hope and love, and will bear fruit in the Spirit. Other religions constitute a positive challenge for the Church: they stimulate her both to discover and acknowledge the signs of Christ's presence and of the working of the Spirit, as well as to examine more deeply her own identity and to bear witness to the fullness of Revelation which she has received for the good of all."

(Pope John Paul II, *Redemptoris missio*)

What You Will Learn

In this chapter, you will learn about

- the challenge of living faith in a multi-religious world
- the human search for God
- examples of people of faith and integrity
- ways of being involved in interreligious dialogue
- the dialogue of theological exchange
- the dialogue of religious experience
- the dialogue of everyday life
- the dialogue of action

Personal Recollection

Sarah Howard. Sarah Howard is a student at McGill University in Montréal.

I was born into a family that could be considered "different" in that we uphold two faiths: Christianity and Judaism. My father comes from an Irish-Catholic background, whereas my mother was brought up in an Orthodox Jewish household. Instead of favouring one religion, my parents decided it would be important to honour both religions and raise their children to take part in two faith traditions: Christian and Jewish.

This decision has meant that throughout my life, we have celebrated traditions from the Christian calendar as well as the Jewish calendar every year. Through the years, I have come to realize that the Christian and Jewish traditions are highly comparable. The two religions put enormous emphasis on similar values, namely those of tradition, remembrance, and family.

The first snowfall of every winter season, for some, marks a highly anticipated countdown to the Christmas holidays. In the Jewish faith, Hanukkah is celebrated during the wintertime. My family celebrates both holidays. Ironically, my mother has always been the one to make sure that the Christmas tree is properly decorated, while my father usually takes charge in lighting the Hanukkah candles. In doing so, my parents have taught me the value of drawing connections and recognizing the similarities between both of our religions.

For instance, consider the fact that for Christians, Christmas is a festival of lights, since the birth of Christ is interpreted as bringing light to the world. For Jews, Hanukkah is also a festival of lights, since the candles of the menorah are lit as a symbol of the victory of the Maccabees and the rededication of the Temple in Jerusalem. As a result of our own efforts and the existing connections, our family has successfully been able to blend both traditions.

—Sarah Howard

Living Faith Today

Diversity. How might living in a society with such diversity be a challenge? A benefit? An opportunity?

Sarah's story on page 337 raises many questions. She and her family seem to have found a way of "upholding two faiths." In her family, both Catholic and Jewish feasts are celebrated. However, as her story unfolds, it becomes obvious that they remain two different faith traditions. Sarah's family is not living one religious tradition. It would be difficult to avoid the claim of the Catholic Church that Christ is *the* light of the world. Much as we might admire what Sarah and her family are doing to live with two religious traditions, they show the challenge of living in a world with many religions.

Canada Today

Many Canadians grow up in intercultural and interreligious families—more than ever before. They are already living on a family scale what is one of the great challenges and opportunities of our time: the creative interaction of religions, beliefs, rituals, values, and traditions. This interaction raises many questions:

- How do religious people live together with respect?
- How do religious people live surrounded by others with different beliefs, rituals, and values without losing their own faith?
- How can living side by side with other religions become an opportunity to be enriched by each other and not a cause for division?

Faith as Human

Around the world, faith—or the possibility of faith—plays a large part in what it means to be **human**. A huge proportion of the world's population belongs to a religion. Only 16 percent identify themselves as "non-religious" and half of that number are "theist"—they believe in God, gods, or some other divine being.

Why do humans search for God or the **transcendent**? What makes humans religious? What is it about human beings that causes almost all of us to identify with some form of faith or religion?

Aristotle said that because humans can think, they are different from any other creature on Earth. Aristotle's definition emphasizes human intelligence. We are capable of thinking about things. We imagine, solve problems, and have emotions. We communicate using language. Language shapes our beliefs, values, and traditions. We use our imaginations to create literature, paintings, sculptures, movies, songs, and web pages. Not only are humans creative, we are also social: we need each other.

Many other definitions of what it means to be human developed from Aristotle's definition. St. Thomas Aquinas, for example, accepted Aristotle's definition; he also identified humans as having the ability to use reason.

Throughout human history, men and women have continued to try to define what it means to be human. They have asked where we came from, what sustains us, what is the meaning of life, and where we go after we die. As the world's religions show, something within humans makes them search for God.

World Religions, 2005

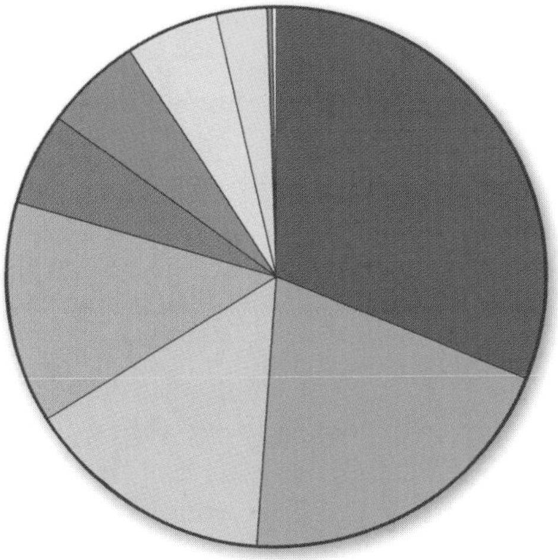

Christianity	33%
Islam	21%
Non-religious (answering "none," "no religious preference"; 8% of this total have theistic beliefs)	16%
Hinduism	14%
Indigenous and Aboriginal spirituality	6%
Chinese traditional	6%
Buddhism	6%
Other	3%
Sikhism	.36%
Judaism	.22%

Note: Total adds up to more than 100% due to rounding up and use of upper-end estimates for each group.

World Religions, 2005. This pie chart shows the proportion of people who follow different religions in the world.

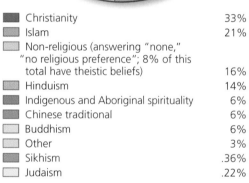

Homo Sapiens. *Homo sapiens* means "wise human." The evolution of intelligence in humans is a key element of how we understand what it means to be human.

Human

A rational animal who is physical, spiritual, social, creative, and emotional

Transcendent

Something beyond comprehension or a reality beyond the material universe

"I am … wonderfully made."
(Psalm 139:14)

Aristotle. Aristotle was an ancient Greek philosopher who lived from 384 to 322 BCE. He defined a human being as "a rational animal." **Why do you think this definition has stood for more than 2000 years?**

A Closer Look

St. Thomas Aquinas (1225–1274) used the philosophy of Aristotle to understand and explain Catholic beliefs and teachings about the meaning of human life. He also used the teachings of the Muslim Aristotelian scholars Avicenna and Averroes, and the Jewish philosopher Maimonides. Aquinas was an early model of an interreligious theologian. He was also a Doctor of the Church—someone whose teaching has been accepted publicly by the Church.

St. Thomas Aquinas

Humans and Mystery

Human intelligence is constantly at work, trying to understand the world around us. Our natural curiosity makes us problem solvers. We develop technologies, tools, and skills to help us in everyday life. When humans do not understand something, their curiosity prompts them to find a way to understand. However, human existence is surrounded by things that are beyond our understanding—by **mystery**. Humans face mystery in various ways: human reason, creativity, and revelation.

Human Reason

There is much that we do not understand about ourselves, the world, and the divine. One of the most powerful ways of exploring what we do not know is the scientific method. As you read in Chapter 10, the use of science to explain the material world has been an increasing focus in modern times. The Catholic Church believes that humans can arrive at some knowledge of God using reason. The study of God by using only human reason is called "natural theology."

Creativity

Another way that humans face mystery is through creativity. This is the way of artistic imagination expressed in painting, sculpture, music, drama, literature, poetry, and other creative arts.

Revelation

Many religions—including Christianity—believe that the intimate mystery of God cannot be uncovered by human reason. Only God can reveal God, they say. They present a God who is revealed to an inspired leader, to a community, or in written texts, such as the Tanakh, Bible, or Qur'an. In this case, God's mystery is explored by studying texts. Each religion represents a human response to what it believes to be a direct encounter with, or **revelation** of, the Ultimate Mystery.

Mystery

A religious truth that is wholly unknown or beyond the human capacity to understand; something concealed that causes wonderment

Revelation

God's act of making known something about God that was partially or completely unknown

Exegesis. The process of studying a sacred text for revelation is called "exegesis."

NEL

Mohandas Gandhi. Gandhi said of religion: "I see no poverty in the world of tomorrow, no wars, no revolutions, no bloodshed. And in that world there will be a faith in God greater and deeper than ever in the past. The very existence of the world, in a broad sense, depends on religion. All attempts to root it out will fail."

Make It Your Own: Religious Mystery in Art

The Creation of Adam. One of Michelangelo's most thought-provoking paintings is found on the ceiling of the Sistine Chapel in the Vatican. It depicts the creation of Adam. Adam reaches out to God and God reaches out to Adam, yet they do not touch. God desires to be with Adam but leaves a distance. Adam desires to be with God, stretching out his hand, but he does so without straining, contrary to God whose whole being is yearning for Adam. It seems that God is inviting Adam to simply lift his finger, as if God's desire for humanity is greater than humanity's desire for God, but God leaves us free to answer. That is our dignity and the challenge. **What else do you see in this picture about the relationship between God and humans?**

Christianity has a long tradition of art that expresses the divine—from early Christianity, through the Middle Ages and the Renaissance, and to the present. This textbook has many examples of art that expresses the divine.

Activities

1. Look at samples of religious art in this textbook, online, or on the multimedia CD to see what moves you and what seems the strongest expression of mystery. Be prepared to describe your responses.
2. Think of your own creative activities. In these activities, have you ever discovered something that goes beyond reason? Describe your experiences.

Check Your Understanding

1. Identify the characteristics of what it means to be human.

2. What are three human approaches to mystery? Of the three, which one best helps humans to uncover mystery? Explain.

Think About It

3. How does the fact that more than 84 percent of the world's people believe in a higher power or reality support or challenge your own views of belief in God?

Making It Personal

4. a) Outline how each aspect of being human listed below can be found in your own life:

- rational
- social or cultural
- physical
- creative
- spiritual
- emotional

b) Your Catholic school is set up according to the Catholic understanding of what it means to be human. Identify which department, activity, or subject at school addresses each aspect of being human.

You and Interreligious Dialogue Today

In a world where most people consider themselves to be religious but also where one religion is so different from another, how should a person live as a member of one religious tradition? How is one to live as a Catholic in a multi-religious world? The table below lists two possible approaches to living as a member of a religious tradition.

Approaches to Religion

Some people say that …
because religions cannot seem to agree on the most basic questions, and because religious beliefs have led to so much conflict, it is time to abolish religion.
Others say that …
because all religions, beneath their differences, seem to be saying the same thing, let us concentrate on what they have in common and drop all the rest.

Neither of the approaches in the table to the left has had much success. In the Church's 2000-year history, Catholics have used two approaches to other religions:

- The first approach, called the mission approach, was to proclaim the Gospel to other nations and peoples, inviting them to worship the God revealed by Jesus.
- The second approach—really an extension of the first—was to enter into dialogue with other religions, to search for truth together. That is the main point of exploring world religions: to discover the faith of others and, in that faith, to find traces of God's Holy Spirit.

Living the Christian faith in the twenty-first century means being willing to be part of this marvellous journey of bringing this world together.

In his parable of the Good Shepherd, Jesus reached out to those whom he said "do not belong to this fold," meaning those who were not his disciples. He was ready to lay down his life for *all* so that there would be "one flock" and "one shepherd" for humanity. This unity of humanity is the challenge of the Catholic faith in the twenty-first century. This chapter explores how you might become involved in this great dialogue that will define the lives of Catholics and all peoples in this century.

"By dialogue, we let God be present in our midst, for as we open ourselves to one another, we open ourselves to God."

(Pope John Paul II, "Address to Other Religions," Madras, February 5, 1986)

St. Paul in Athens. St. Paul's attempt to connect the Unknown God of the Greeks with the God he knew in Jesus is the first known example of Christian interreligious dialogue.

St. Peter's Basilica. The Basilica of St. Peter in Rome has become a symbol of the Catholic Church. People stream to it from all over the world. It has truly become a gathering place of people from all nations. **How does the Catholic Church take part in this mission for humanity to be one?**

"I must bring them also, and they will listen to my voice."

(John 10:16)

Aboriginal Circle Meeting in Kamloops, British Columbia. The circle is a symbol of dialogue. **What does the circle say about the participants of a dialogue? What have you learned from discussions in a circle?**

The Necessity of Dialogue

There are dangers if Catholics do not take part in dialogue. In some places in the world, the result could be misunderstanding, mistrust, division, violence, or even war. In a multicultural and multi-religious society such as Canada, where people from many traditions live side by side, Catholics must interact respectfully and vigorously with people of all faiths and cultures.

Types of Dialogue

In this final chapter, we take another look at the four types of interreligious dialogue discussed in Chapter 1:

- the dialogue of theological exchange
- the dialogue of religious experience
- the dialogue of everyday life
- the dialogue of action

We begin with a review of some of the guidelines for dialogue. We will then explore the four types of dialogue.

Dialogue: Some Guidelines

For interreligious dialogue to be honest, it must be rooted in both

- a deep knowledge and love for one's own religion and faith
- a deep respect for the faith and beliefs of others

Catholics bring their own faith tradition in all its richness, and their questions, to the interreligious dialogue table. While they listen with respect to the other religion and arrive at a deeper understanding, they gain at the same time a deeper appreciation and enrichment of their own faith. Interreligious dialogue is not a debate, not a question of scoring points; it is an honest search for truth and goodness.

Interreligious dialogue shows us that faith offers the world wisdom that has been passed down through the ages from our ancestors. In particular, all religions offer our modern world three things: community and tradition, guidance and ritual, and justice and service.

NEL

What All Religions Offer Our Modern World

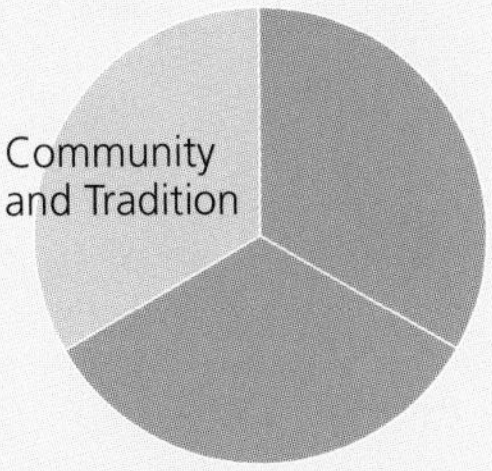 Community and Tradition	**Community:** Religion tells us we are not alone. The community of believers is there to help us, to celebrate with us in times of joy, and to share our sorrows.
	Tradition: Religion offers us the wisdom, teachings, and traditions of those who lived and died before us. By turning to these traditions, we can learn from the wisdom of faith ancestors.
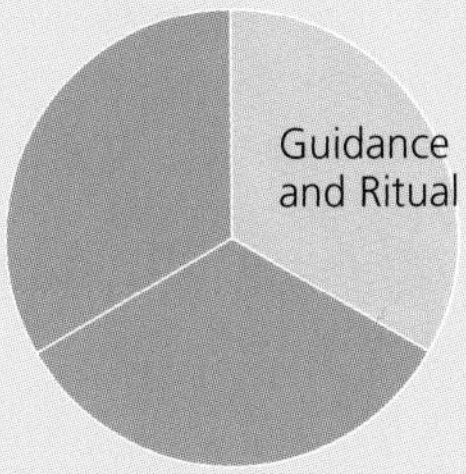 Guidance and Ritual	**Guidance:** Religion gives us the vision as well as the laws, rules, and moral principles that human beings need to live. In this way, humans are guided by the collective wisdom of previous generations.
	Ritual: Rituals allow believers to be open to God or Ultimate Reality by engaging in the acts of worship of their community.
 Justice and Service	**Justice:** Religion reminds us that all human beings have a right to live life to the fullest. The "good life" is not just the privilege of the few, but the right of all. Religion calls us to right the wrongs we encounter in economic, social, gender, and ecological injustice.
	Service: Religion reminds us to love others as much as we love ourselves. We are not in this world alone. Nor are we in this world to take care only of ourselves. Religion calls people to a life of service to others, especially to those who are poor or sick. We use what we have to help those who are in need.

Diwali. Diwali is celebrated with treats, which are traditionally given as gifts during the five-day Hindu festival of light. This participant from a community in the Greater Toronto Area in Ontario holds a tray of popular treats.

Catholic Student Service. Religion calls people to a life of service to others. These Canadian Catholic students participate in a food drive in their community.

Check Your Understanding

1. a) Summarize in jot notes
   - the mission approach
   - the dialogue approach
   - why dialogue is necessary

   b) In the form of an e-mail or Twitter message, rewrite your notes as an invitation to dialogue.
2. Create a poster summarizing guidelines for authentic dialogue and three things religions offer.

Think About It

3. With a partner or in a small group, examine a list of occupations. For each occupation, identify and explain two reasons why a Canadian with each job should have some understanding of other people's cultures and religions.
4. In what ways is your school answering the call of faith to make this world a better place? In a small group, investigate the opportunities for service in your school and post your results.

Making It Personal

5. Remember a time when you had a conversation that brought you closer to another person. Name three things about the conversation, the person, or the place that helped bring about that closeness.

Skill Focus: Comparing and Contrasting

Part of interreligious dialogue is examining faith traditions for what is the same (or similar) and what is different. For example, Sarah Howard (on page 337) noted that both Judaism and Christianity use light as a symbol of remembrance, and she states that the two faith traditions are "highly comparable." Finding common ground or a shared approach to a key question in life can help people of different faiths build bridges of understanding. At the same time, examining for what is the same, similar, and different can help avoid jumping to false conclusions.

Faith traditions have so many differences that they should all be abolished.	OR	Faith traditions are saying the same thing so all differences should be forgotten.

Activities

1. Practise the skill of comparing (finding what is the same or similar) and contrasting (finding what is different) using a Venn diagram.

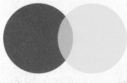

Venn Diagram

2. Here are some key words and phrases to look for when you are analyzing text or research to find comparisons or contrasts:
   - On the one hand … on the other hand …
   - Both ___ and ___ believe … ___ and ___ have some similarities: …
   - However, they also have some key differences: …
3. Summarize the Venn diagram in speech or writing using some key words and phrases. As a final review of your summary, consider the key words and phrases you have chosen: do they carefully represent what is the same, similar, and different?

You and the Dialogue of Theological Exchange

The dialogue of theological exchange usually takes place between scholars from different religions. Together, they explore theological and philosophical questions. These experts study their own religion for many years before becoming part of such a dialogue. To take part in interreligious dialogue, they must be open to examining difficult issues with respect and understanding.

By taking part in the study of other religions, you have in some way become part of this theological exchange. You have explored the main beliefs, rituals, values, and feasts of other religions. You have learned to appreciate how members of other religions experience what transcends or goes beyond the human aspect of life. If, as a Catholic, you wish to participate further in this dialogue, you must keep a few principles in mind:

1. You bring to this dialogue the story of your own faith. It is not to deny your own story that you engage another religion. For Catholics, their faith in Jesus Christ and the salvation he offers are not in question. Any dialogue begins with your own faith.
2. A dialogue is not a debate. A dialogue is a conversation about truth and human solidarity. Out of a dialogue, there should be no winners and losers, but a deeper appreciation of the dignity of the human person and human society in light of God. At the same time, you must be open to a prophetic voice within the dialogue. Like the prophets of Israel, this voice makes you aware of your inner resistance to change and of what blocks you from being open to other religions. You must realize that to be open to others is one way of being true to your faith and tradition. Like every faith, Catholic faith needs to examine constantly whether it remains true to its core beliefs. The Church, at the same time holy and in need of being purified, always follows the way of renewal.
3. Those who enter into dialogue desire that a new humanity before God will emerge from it. By breaking the barriers between religions, it is hoped that all humans can say "we" in a fuller way. We are all children made in the image of the same God.

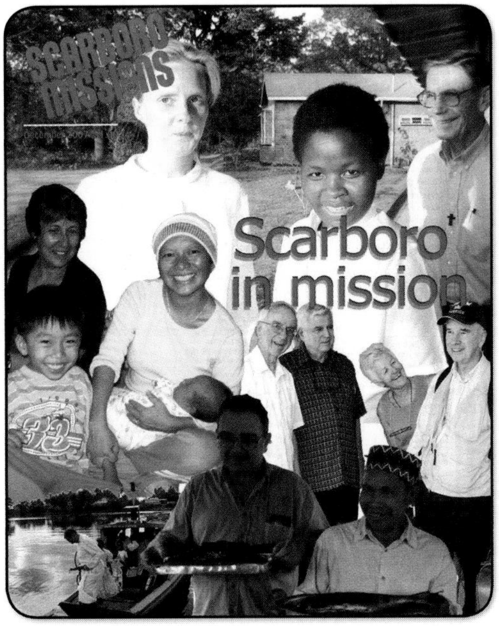

Scarboro Missions. The Scarboro Foreign Missions Society was founded in 1918 by a Toronto priest, Fr. John Fraser. The initial purpose of the society was to train and send missionary priests to China. However, this religious community has since put much of its energy into interfaith dialogue.

A Closer Look

Today, Scarboro Missions holds workshops, prayer meetings, dialogues on world religions, and gatherings of diverse people doing things together. The society's magazine, *Scarboro Missions,* provides information on the interreligious activities going on in Canada.

A Closer Look

We call someone who truly recognizes all others as fellow human beings without reservation an "ecumenical person" or a "catholic" (with a small "c"). The word "catholic" comes from the ancient Greek words *kata* and *holis*. It means universal or including or embracing everyone. A catholic is one who lives in relation to the whole world.

Political Dialogue. Many other areas in our lives would benefit from the principles of dialogue that have been discussed on the preceding pages. Three of the leaders of federal political parties are shown in a televised debate during the 2008 federal election. **What principles of religious dialogue would you recommend politicians use to discuss and solve the problems facing Canada today?**

Check Your Understanding

1. Explain what is meant by the dialogue of theological exchange.
2. To the poster you created on page 346, add a summary of the three principles for dialogue.

Think About It

3. Think back to a political debate you have seen. Use the skill of comparing and contrasting to examine interreligious dialogue and political debates.

Making It Personal

4. What would it mean for you to be a "catholic" in the sense given on this page? Note your ideas in a journal entry before sharing two or three key ideas in a small group.

You and the Dialogue of Religious Experience

What Is a Religious Experience?

A second type of dialogue involves the exchange of religious experiences. Each world religion and spiritual tradition is based on unique experiences of God or of what transcends, or rises above, human existence. The dialogue of religious experience is a discussion between members of different religions about their experiences of faith.

Religious experiences are difficult to describe. This is because a religious experience forms and gives an identity to the one who has the experience. Here are some examples:

- a short but intense experience of a deep underlying unity of all things
- exhilarating freedom from whatever is keeping someone from opening his or her heart to God
- the joy of knowing that you are loved unconditionally
- the desire to live in difficult circumstances to help others
- the peace of saying "yes" to life in the midst of sadness

These are all experiences of the sacred.

Religious experiences may come early in life, much later, or perhaps not at all. For some, these religious experiences are found in a monastery, a quiet chapel, or a full church. However, the experiences are not always clearly religious. Such experiences can take place on the way to school, in the classroom, in the beauty of nature, when someone we love dies, or in the intensity of a loving relationship. These experiences, often called mystical experiences, are a central feature of all religious traditions.

Fast Fact

A religious experience is an experience of the divine and is unique to the individual. Religious experiences can be as varied as the people who have them.

The Miracle of Birth. Religious experiences may come when we hold a baby.

Profile: St. Thérèse de Lisieux

Thérèse de Lisieux (1873–1897) is a saint who experienced God at a young age. When Thérèse was 4 years old, her mother died, at which point her eldest sister, Pauline, became like a second mother to Thérèse. When Pauline later decided to become a nun and left home, Thérèse felt abandoned. In 1887, when Thérèse was 14, she thought that other students at school were picking on her and she became very ill. She wrote, "When I began to cheer up, I'd begin to cry again for having cried." She felt trapped in a vicious circle. However, Thérèse had an experience of God while meditating on Paul's hymn of love in the Letter to the Corinthians (12:31–13:8). It was such a strong experience of love that afterwards she realized that her vocation in life was to love.

In the most ordinary chores of daily life in the convent, Thérèse tried to bring joy and love. She said:

> Love proves itself by deeds, so how am I to show my love? Great deeds are forbidden me. The only way I can prove my love is by scattering flowers and these flowers are every little sacrifice, every glance and word, and the doing of the least actions for love.

Thérèse's was a spirituality of the "little way." Countless people around the world practise her "little way" of love.

Thérèse died at the age of 24. In 1997, Pope John Paul II named her a Doctor of the Church—one of only three women to be so honoured.

St. Thérèse de Lisieux. Thérèse once said, "I will spend my heaven doing good on Earth." **What did Thérèse mean by this statement? How could you say the same thing in your own words?**

Mysticism

The word "mysticism" refers to the experience of, and seeking communion with, the Ultimate Reality or Supreme Being. Although often linked to highly devout people, mysticism touches most people at least once in their lives. Mysticism teaches us that God, or the Divine Reality, is more than a concept to be understood, debated, and read about. God, or the Divine Reality, is also to be experienced.

Love

One way of understanding this idea is to look to another experience in human life: love. Love is a spiritual reality that is common to us all, something we all desire. We can spend hours talking to our friends or family about what love is. We can see many examples of love all around us. We can read about love. Scholars, psychologists, philosophers, and theologians can all help us to define and analyze the nature of love. Yet, none of these approaches can measure up to our direct experience of love in our lives. When we love someone, what we experience often cannot be put into words or be defined.

The Divine

The same is true of the divine. A mystical experience is a direct experience of the divine. A mystic is a person who seeks, or experiences, a direct connection with the divine.

The Beauty of Nature. A religious experience may come in the beauty of nature.

Meditation. There are many schools of mysticism in the world. Each one offers distinct paths to—and teachings from—mystical experiences. One way to search for the divine through mysticism is meditation.

The Experience of Mysticism

Mystical experiences have a number of common aspects shared by people of different religions.

Because mysticism is common to all religions, it is one of the important areas of interreligious dialogue. While Catholics do not seek mysticism for itself, Catholics have adopted and integrated some mystical practices of other religions within their own search for God. To listen to the voice of the Spirit in other religions may give insight into the Catholic experience of God in Christ.

Across Canada, groups from different religions gather to listen to each other's spiritual experiences. Our experience of the divine as direct and actively present in our lives—whether from ordinary experiences, from daily prayer life, or from grand mystical experiences—connects us all, no matter which religion we follow.

Mystical Experience

Mystical Experience

- **Vision:** A direct experience of divinity that has its impact through the senses
- **Reality:** An experience of reality that is beyond worldview, perception, interpretation, and judgment
- **Internal realization:** A deep sense of the connection of one's inner self with the divine reality
- **Bliss:** An experience of great joy beyond everyday understanding

Mystical Experience. Mystical experiences come in many forms. Here are only some examples.

A Closer Look

Many Christians use repetitive prayer, such as the Jesus prayer ("Lord Jesus, have mercy on me") or similar phrases, or meditate on sayings of Jesus, such as these:

> *The greatest among you will be your servant.*
> *All who exalt themselves will be humbled, and all who humble themselves will be exalted.*
>
> *(Matthew 23:1–12)*

> *A lawyer asked him a question to test him. "Teacher, which commandment in the law is the greatest?" He said to him, "You shall love the Lord your God with all your heart, and with all your soul, and with all your mind." This is the greatest and first commandment. And a second is like it: "You shall love your neighbour as yourself." On these two commandments hang all the law and the prophets.*
>
> *(Matthew 22:35–40)*

Kabbalists and Hasidic Jews value the role of mysticism in living the Jewish faith. Many meditate on these sayings from the Book of Proverbs in the Old Testament:

> *Trust in the Lord with all your heart,*
> *and do not rely on your own insight.*
> *In all your ways acknowledge him,*
> *and he will make straight your paths.*
> *Do not be wise in your own eyes;*
> *fear the Lord, and turn away from evil.*
> *It will be a healing for your flesh*
> *and a refreshment for your body.*
>
> *(Proverbs 3:5–8)*

In Sufi Islam, the whirling dervishes try to enter a meditative state that opens them to a direct mystical experience. Here is a pearl of wisdom from the great Islamic mystic Mawlana Jalal ad-Din Muhammad Balkhi (1207–1273). He is best known as Rumi:

> *The Prophet said that God has declared,*
> *"I am not contained in aught above or below,*
> *I am not contained in earth or sky, or even*
> *In highest heaven. Know this for a surety,*
> *O beloved!*
> *Yet am I contained in the believer's heart!*
> *If ye seek me, search in such hearts."*
>
> *(Rumi, Masnavi I Ma'navi)*

Buddhist monks use chant and meditation to bring about a mystical experience. They often meditate on a saying from the Dhammapada (423 verses of scripture attributed to the Buddha):

> *Let a man overcome anger by love, let him overcome evil by good;*
> *let him overcome the greedy by liberality,*
> *the liar by truth!*
> *Speak the truth, do not yield to anger;*
> *give, if thou art asked for little;*
> *by these three steps thou wilt go near the gods.*
>
> *(Dhammapada 223–224)*

Some Aboriginal groups practise vision quests, in which a mystical experience comes in the form of a vision. For example, in their quest for vision, the Tewa (Pueblo Aboriginal people) from New Mexico have used the following prayer:

> *O, our Mother the Earth, O our Father the Sky,*
> *Your children are we, and with tired backs*
> *We bring you the Gifts you love,*
> *Then weave for us a garment of brightness,*
> *May the warp be the bright light of evening,*
> *May the fringes be the falling rain,*
> *May the border be the standing rainbow.*
> *Thus weave for us a garment of brightness,*
> *That we may walk fittingly where birds sing,*
> *That we may walk fittingly where grass is green,*
> *O our Mother the Earth, O our Father the Sky.*

Hindu monks practise asceticism and meditation as spiritual preparation for mystical communion with the divine. They often meditate on a saying of the Bhagavad Gita:

> *Without hatred for any creature, friendly and compassionate, free from possessiveness and egoism, indifferent to pleasure and pain, enduring,*
>
> *Contented, ever the self-controlled yogin, certain of purpose, his mind and intelligence concentrated on me, he who is devoted to me is dear to me.*
>
> *(Bhagavad Gita 12.13–14:*
> © Oxford University Press*)*

Check Your Understanding

1. What are common aspects of the mystical experiences of all religions?

Think About It

2. From the Bible or from lives of the saints, what two or three mystical experiences are most memorable to you? In writing or a short presentation, summarize one experience and comment upon why it is so memorable.

3. With a partner, look at the sayings to note similarities and differences. What questions and comments do you have about the collection of mystical sayings?

Making It Personal

4. Have you talked about a spiritual or religious experience with a friend? If so, describe your conversation. If you have not, how might you take part in a dialogue of religious experience?

Dialogues of Theological Exchange and Religious Experience

To explore dialogue further, here are two examples of dialogue to consider, compare, and contrast.

Dialogue of Theological Exchange: Father Bede

Father Bede Griffiths lived his life in surrender. He once said that the hardest thing to do is to let go of our egos. Yet he was convinced that "the surrender of the ego is the only way of life." That is how he began a lifelong friendship with Hinduism.

Born Alan R. Griffiths in 1906 in England, the young Father Bede excelled at school. He received a scholarship to Oxford University, where he studied English literature and philosophy. During that time, he was disillusioned by the excesses of modern life in the Western world and decided to live a simple life.

After he graduated from university, he and a couple of friends bought a country cottage and began to live away from urban life, dependent on nature and nature's bounty. They found great inspiration for their lifestyle in scripture.

After reading the writings of Cardinal John Henry Newman, Griffiths was received into the Roman Catholic Church in 1931. He became a Benedictine novice and took the name "Bede." He was ordained a priest in 1940. His monastic clothing, called a habit, was a sign for him of putting on Christ, and his new name showed that he "had become a new man in Christ."

Father Bede was restless in European monasteries. He was always looking for a spiritual and life experience other than the one offered by Western culture. Finally, in 1955, his superiors allowed him to go to India. Over time, he undertook a serious study of and dialogue with Hinduism. He dressed in orange robes and took the Sanskrit name of Swami Dhayananda (bliss of compassion). He gradually enriched his

Father Bede Griffiths. According to Father Bede Griffiths, "The surrender of the ego is the only way of life."

Ashram. Students are learning at Maharishi Mahesh Yogi's Ashram in India. An ashram is a place of quiet and retreat, often in a forest, where a spiritual master has gathered a group of people together to live a spiritual life.

Christian life by incorporating within it his experiences of the Vedanta, the philosophy of Hinduism that is expressed in its earliest writings. During these years he wrote 12 books on Hindu–Christian dialogue. Bede Griffiths died as a Catholic monk in 1993 at an ashram (spiritual retreat and learning centre) in India.

During his life, Father Bede lived the "loss of self" by striving to be a *sanyasi*—someone who gives up everything in order to stop seeing himself or herself at the centre of everything. Father Bede believed that only when we let go of the self-centred self can we open ourselves to our true centre: God. Father Bede saw this search for God taking place within the very soul of the person, beyond selfishness and ego.

Dialogue of Religious Experience: Sister Elaine MacInnes

Sister Elaine MacInnes was born in Moncton, New Brunswick, in 1924. In her mid-30s, she decided to become a member of Our Lady's Missionaries, an order of Roman Catholic nuns founded in Canada in 1949.

In 1961, her order sent her to Japan to start a Catholic Cultural Centre. While in Japan, Sister Elaine was accepted as a disciple of Yamada Koun Roshi, one of the greatest Zen teachers of the twentieth century.

Zen is a type of Buddhist meditation that seeks to lead someone to a direct insight into the unity of all things. Zen meditation often uses *koans*, or short riddles, to grow in the art of silence. Sister Elaine found this type of meditation helpful in her Christian meditation.

Zen, as Sister Elaine explains, is a living tradition that is transmitted from one living master (a *roshi*, meaning "old teacher") to students. In 1980, Yamada Roshi granted the title of *roshi* to Sister Elaine. She became one of only a handful of Catholics who have ever received this great honour and responsibility. There are perhaps 100 *roshis* alive today.

After 17 years in Japan, Sister Elaine was sent to the Philippines to work in a poor rural community where many of the people were malnourished. To help them feed themselves, she started a pig farm. In the Philippines, she also had the idea of teaching Zen meditation's calming influence to political activists who were jailed during the repressive government of Ferdinand Marcos (1965–1986).

Sister Elaine incorporated Zen practice within her own Catholic faith, and found that the practice of Zen meditation helped her as a Catholic. For her, Zen is about silence and spirit and spirituality. She says, "Spirituality is spirit in action, empowered by what you do with the fires burning within."

Sister Elaine is the leader of the Toronto-based charity Freeing the Human Spirit. Their volunteer teachers bring meditation and yoga to those in prison. These safe and therapeutic disciplines help lessen the power of the ego, which leads to offending behaviour, and helps inmates improve their power of concentration and self-esteem. The program also gives them a way of interacting with the sacred. In 2001, Sister Elaine was invested as an Officer of the Order of Canada in recognition of her work.

Sister Elaine MacInnes. "I started Zen to know the Japanese people better, but I continued it as a personal discipline in the development of my own spirituality, and finally chose it as my service to others."

You and the Dialogue of Everyday Life

The third type of dialogue, the dialogue of daily life, deals with the challenges and opportunities we face each day in a multicultural society. We live in a society where our friends, neighbours, and loved ones may come from cultural or religious backgrounds different from our own. The dialogue of everyday life is based on the ordinary day-to-day interaction of people of different religions. The dialogue of everyday life takes place in schools where people of different religions study together, in the community, and at work. In larger cities, we find neighbourhoods filled with cafés, restaurants, shops, and services of diverse cultures. We meet each other on the street, in shopping malls, and through TV, radio, newspapers, and the Internet.

Ethnic Restaurants. Many decades ago, most Canadians from all ethnic backgrounds would not have considered eating unfamiliar food that they had not grown up eating. Now ethnic restaurants like the ones shown here are popular across Canada. **What opportunities for dialogue can you imagine in your own community?**

Interreligious Marriage. This interreligious couple is taking part in a traditional Korean Paebaek marriage ceremony.

Fast Fact

Interreligious marriages are one example of how dialogue among religions takes place in a multicultural society.

These many ways of interacting with each other offer a great opportunity to engage in the dialogue of everyday life. The bonds of trust and understanding that are built through everyday interactions can make interreligious dialogues possible.

One of the more intense types of dialogue of everyday life takes place in marriages between members of different faiths or cultures. Sarah Howard's example of growing up in an interreligious family (see page 337) is becoming a more and more common one.

Team Sports. Team sports are another opportunity for the dialogue of everyday life.

"Doing" Dialogue

We must keep in mind both cautions and opportunities as we seek to appreciate other people's faith traditions.

Cautions

False comparisons and contrasts: As we look at the faiths and traditions of others, we can easily fall into making false comparisons and contrasts. For example, we can compare the best of one faith with the worst of another faith. We might look at the religious devotion of some Muslim youth and compare it

Students and Places of Worship. Catholic students learn about Buddhism at a Buddhist temple.

with people of our own tradition who do not practise their faith. When we do this, we risk under-appreciating our own faith tradition and glorifying another's. Partial understandings or misrepresentations harm dialogue.

However, comparing faith traditions in both their positive and their negative expressions gives us an honest picture. What that picture reveals to us is that, although humans are complex and limited, we all struggle to understand ultimate meaning and goodness.

Peace Rally. Mother Teresa drew more than 20 000 people to a peace rally at Varsity Stadium in Toronto. If we contrast the peace and justice language of our own faith tradition with a call to violence found in the writings of some other traditions, we run the risk of overglamorizing our own faith and devaluing the faith of others.

A Closer Look

The Canadian Council of Christians and Jews (CCCJ) promotes interfaith understanding and dialogue. The CCCJ was founded in 1947 by a group of prominent Christian and Jewish Canadians from social and business communities. The organization's goal is to develop a Canadian society without prejudice and discrimination, a society that celebrates diversity, difference, and inclusion. The CCCJ works mainly through education, research, communication, and community building.

In 1947, the CCCJ established the Canadian Centre for Diversity, which provides programs that teach Canada's youth how to overcome fear and prejudice through information, education, and involvement. The programs bring together young people from a range of cultural and ethnic communities.

Youth from many cultures discover that it is possible to foster equality by building bridges of understanding and trust. The CCCJ recognizes that this trust is built in these ways:

1. by knowing what others feel, think, and believe
2. by sharing in each person's unique story
3. by hearing, respecting, and appreciating those stories

Relativism

The belief that knowledge, truth, and morality are only opinions of individuals and therefore do not necessarily hold for others

Religious relativism: Exploring others' faith traditions and cultures can lead us to a sense that any belief system is acceptable, that one religion is as good as another. In this way, we think of learning about other faiths as similar to going through a department store with all sorts of products on display so that we can pick and choose—or ignore. Because religions are so many and varied, we may think that committing ourselves to any one religion is impossible. We run the risk of judging religions by what we like in other faiths and our own, and setting aside what we do not like, and ultimately ending up with no religion at all. The problem here is that we have set ourselves up as judges of what is truth. We have made the truth subjective. However, in religion there is a truth beyond ourselves that calls us.

Christians believe that Jesus is the truth. And, although Christians do not always live up to the truth, it is by remaining faithful to the truth that they can explore it in depth and develop a rich and life-giving spirituality. From a solid commitment to our own faith tradition, we can then enter into a much more fruitful dialogue with other religions. That is the lesson passed on to us by the monks Thomas Merton (see Chapter 8) and Bede Griffiths (discussed in this chapter). In contrast, if we use what we discover in other traditions to deny the validity of our own faith, then we abandon the truth passed on in our own traditions and through our ancestors in faith.

Opportunities

Interreligious dialogue gives us the opportunity to search for truth as a constant in all religions. We can deepen our appreciation of our own tradition as we see it reflected in the faith traditions of other people.

Multicultural society challenges us to meet difference with respectful curiosity, not fear. Likewise, our curiosity in interreligious dialogue can lead us to a deeper understanding of how we, and others, view the world. We can also find many points of similarity among religions and beliefs when we engage in honest and respectful dialogue.

Curiosity, openness, and willingness to grow, then, are key to relating to

Common Ground. Searching for the common ground helps bring people closer together. This is an extremely important dynamic in the Canadian mosaic.

those we meet from other traditions. Our modern society provides many opportunities for us to learn about the cultures and religions of the people we live with on a daily basis. Our task is to find out how we can interact and respond in a way that

- brings the best of our traditions together and
- challenges our assumptions regarding other people's practices, beliefs, and customs

Dialogue of Everyday Life: The Monks of Tibhirine

In March 1996, seven Trappist monks from the monastery Notre Dame de l'Atlas in Tibhirine, Algeria, were killed by a violent group that claimed to be speaking for Islam. With their deaths, a remarkable story and example of a dialogue of everyday life came to light.

In 1990, Algeria had descended into a spiral of violence. No one was safe. Several nuns and priests had already been killed. The Trappist monks in Tibhirine themselves were visited by an armed band on Christmas Eve in 1994. The armed group left when the monks said it was a holy day for them.

The monks could have moved away. Many advised them to look for a safer place. However, they stayed—mainly after the Bishop of Algiers asked them to remain faithful to the very reason they had come to Algeria in the first place: to be a Christian presence in a Muslim country.

The Trappists had been in Algeria since 1934. At first, the monastery had been very much like any in Europe. It was well provided for, very European, and not integrated into the Atlas region of Algeria. However, that changed: over time, the monastery let go of its wealth. It gave away its property and set up a community garden for the village.

Gradually, the monks had begun to see themselves as "worshippers in the midst of a nation of worshippers." The Muslims respected them for their life of poverty for the sake of God. Muslims, too, know the need to do God's will. An Algerian priest, Father Becker, said of the monks: Theirs was "a message of poverty, of abandonment in the hands of God and men, of sharing in all the fragility, vulnerability and condition of forgiven sinners, in the conviction that only by being disarmed will we be able to meet Islam and discover in Muslims a part of the total face of Christ."

The Bishop of Algiers convinced them to stay, to give courage to the small number of Algerian Christians and to the local population. The bishop and the monks wondered what effect their leaving would have on the Muslim neighbours in the village. The monks had created many ties with the Muslim villagers. The bishop asked, "Could they leave them all of a sudden? Poverty, yes, that too has different forms. Wouldn't it be a poor showing indeed to leave … when the neighbours have none? What kind of poverty is that … to be poor only as long as it is convenient to be poor?"

After listening to the bishop, each monk was asked to make a decision. As the monks' leader, Christian de Chergé met privately with them, each monk told him, "I am not at peace with the decision to leave." Not long after this, another band of militants took the monks hostage and, after two weeks, killed them.

At the burial, the local Muslims as well as *imams* (mosque prayer leaders) from the area came to say goodbye. In an emotional scene, they insisted on closing the graves of the seven monks. The monastery is now deserted. The local people guard it. The monastery has been left untouched out of respect. The people had come to regard the monks as brothers and elders in their faith.

Trappist Monks. These Trappist monks at the Notre Dame de l'Atlas monastery in Tibhirine, Algeria, survived a massacre in 1996.

A Closer Look

Christian de Chergé, the prior (leader) of the Trappists, wrote a beautiful testament a year before he died. Anticipating his death, he asked for peace for his murderer and wrote, in part:

> Obviously, my death will justify the opinion of all those who dismissed me as naïve or idealistic: "Let him tell us what he thinks now." But such people should know that my death will satisfy my most burning curiosity. At last, I will be able—if God pleases—to see the children of Islam as He sees them, illuminated in the glory of Christ, sharing in the gift of God's Passion and of the Spirit, whose secret joy will always be to bring forth our common humanity amidst our differences.

The Monks of Tibhirine. This photo shows four of the seven monks who were killed: Christian de Chergé (standing left), Luc Dochier (standing second from right), Christophe Lebreton (sitting left), and Michel Fleury (sitting right). At their monastery, Notre Dame de l'Atlas in Tibhirine, the seven monks learned to live together and interact with the local Muslims, gaining their respect and admiration. **What do these monks teach us about everyday dialogue?**

Check Your Understanding

1. List and describe examples and the opportunities of engaging in interreligious dialogue.
2. Summarize and illustrate with examples cautions for engaging in interreligious dialogue.

Think About It

3. Considering opportunities, cautions, and methods used by the Canadian Centre for Diversity for building trust, work in a small group to brainstorm ideas for dialogue in your community. Discuss your ideas and choose one to develop into a proposal for interreligious dialogue.

Making It Personal

4. Have you ever changed your opinion about another person after you had an opportunity to spend time together? Describe your experience.

You and the Dialogue of Action

The fourth form of dialogue is the dialogue of action. This dialogue takes place when people of different religions respond together to

- make neighbourhoods safe
- help poor or unemployed people
- provide help in times of crisis
- address another need or a situation of injustice

Common to all religious faiths is the desire to make the world a better place. All religions have teachings that deal with **social justice**. In recent years, religions have worked together to further social justice. A good Canadian example is the Interfaith Social Assistance Reform Commission, which tries to reduce poverty and make housing available to people with lower incomes.

Another example comes from Asian bishops who live in countries where Catholics are a minority. These bishops, more than any others, have urged the Church to enter interreligious dialogue. During the Second Vatican Council, they were instrumental in bringing about *The Declaration on the Relation of the Church to Non-Christian Religions.* They insisted that they—and we—could be Church only if a threefold dialogue takes place: dialogue with the poor, their cultures, and other religions.

They knew that, to understand the Gospel, one must listen to and act with the many victims of injustice, learn from the spiritualities and cultures that have nurtured their peoples for so long, and talk with one another about religion.

Habitat for Humanity. These Habitat for Humanity volunteers and future homeowners are working together to build a home in Scarborough, Ontario. Habitat for Humanity is an ecumenical Christian ministry.

Social justice

The practice of giving every person an opportunity to have fair and equal rights to take part in the social, educational, and economic benefits of a society

Dialogue Web

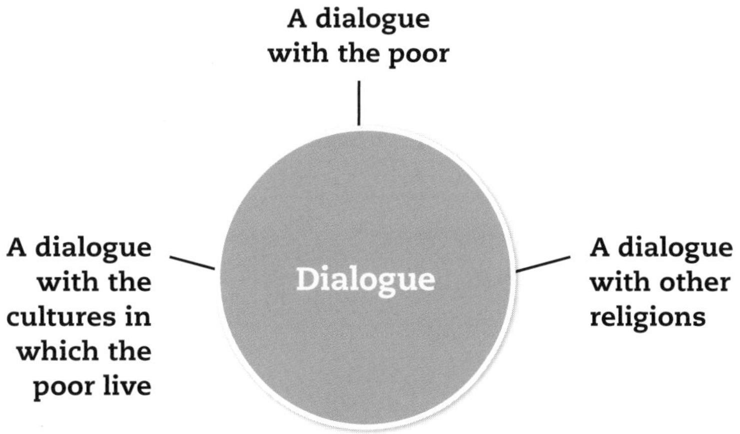

Dialogue Web. This dialogue web shows the three ways the Church can use dialogue to communicate with people of other faiths, cultures, and living standards.

A Closer Look

There are many examples of individuals undertaking dialogue of action. Here are some:

- Mohandas Gandhi (1869–1948), a Hindu, taught the practices of non-violence (*ahimsa*) and civil disobedience. He used these practices to draw attention to injustice and in India's movement for independence from Britain.
- Martin Luther King, Jr. (1929–1968) was inspired by Gandhi and rooted in the Christian faith. He struggled for equal rights for Blacks in the United States, for the end of racial segregation, and against the Vietnam War.
- Archbishop Oscar Romero (1917–1980) had a religious experience and went on to fight for justice and the end of violence in El Salvador. He was killed for his political convictions as he celebrated Mass.
- The Dalai Lama (1935–), a Tibetan Buddhist monk, has lived a message of non-violence and hope through his struggle for Tibet's right to have a level of independence within China.
- Dorothy Day (1897–1980), Blessed Mother Teresa (1910–1997), and Jean Vanier (1928–) are examples of people whose Christian beliefs led them to serve the poor and abandoned. Dorothy Day did so with the poor and homeless in New York City. Mother Teresa worked with the poor, sick, orphaned, and dying street people in India and elsewhere. Jean Vanier founded group homes (L'Arche) for people with developmental disabilities.

Martin Luther King, Jr.

The Dalai Lama

Dorothy Day

Pope Benedict XVI

During Mass when he was installed as pope in 2005, Pope Benedict XVI offered the following words about the role of the Catholic religion in the world:

> There are so many kinds of desert. There is the desert of poverty, the desert of hunger and thirst, the desert of abandonment, of loneliness, of destroyed love. There is the desert of God's darkness, the emptiness of souls no longer aware of their dignity or the goal of human life. The external deserts in the world are growing, because the internal deserts have become so vast. Therefore the earth's treasures no longer serve to build God's garden for all to live in, but they have been made to serve the powers of exploitation and destruction. The Church as a whole and all her pastors, like Christ, must set out to lead people out of the desert, towards the place of life, towards friendship with the Son of God, towards the one who gives us life, and life in abundance.

Pope Benedict XVI. Pope Benedict XVI called on the Church to respond to the injustices of our time.

Check Your Understanding

1. Explain to a partner the meaning of the term "dialogue of action" and note at least three examples.
2. What does Pope Benedict XVI identify as being one of the main concerns of people of faith today?

Think About It

3. Identify someone or a group whose faith moves them to make the world a better place. Describe this person or group, their efforts, challenges, and successes in a short profile.

Making It Personal

4. Suggest ways you can be involved in the "dialogue of action."

A Call to Action

In a speech to the Vatican Diplomatic Corps in 2003, where many of the world's religions were represented, Pope John Paul II raised a number of issues that could serve as a starting point for a dialogue of action in a multi-religious world.

All people today—from all different religious traditions—live in a world where there is much fear. The pope mentioned acts of terrorism that can strike at any time and anywhere, the turmoil caused by war, oppression and violence between peoples, new deadly diseases, and the irresponsible use of Earth's resources. The question is, what can we do together? What can your school do? What can you personally do? The pope suggested some action points. As you read each of the following six action points, note how you could participate as an individual and how your school could participate.

1. Respect for the rule of law. Life within society—particularly international life—is best protected by properly legislated laws. Laws are necessary to guarantee the security and the freedom of individual citizens and of nations. It is important, therefore, to respect these rules of conduct.

2. Change. Change depends on each of us. Everyone can develop within himself or herself the potential for faith, for honesty, for respect for others, and for commitment to the service of others.

Change. From chrysalis to butterfly, every change is a challenge. The challenge among religions is to live respectfully and creatively with others.

3. Say "yes" to life! Respect life itself and individual lives. Everything starts here, for the most fundamental of human rights is the right to life. If life is truly a treasure, we need to be able to preserve it and to make it bear fruit without distorting it. In other words, saying "yes" to life means saying "no" to

- everything that attacks the dignity of every human being, beginning with that of unborn children
- all that weakens the family, the basic cell of society
- all that destroys in children the sense of striving, their respect for themselves and others, the sense of service

Children and Poverty. In Canada, 1.6 million children (23 percent) live in poverty. **What steps might you and your school take to reduce child poverty?**

4. Be in solidarity with others. In a world with so much information, communication remains difficult. Humans have to learn to talk with one another and to listen to one another. It is important to spare no effort to ensure that everyone feels responsible for the growth and happiness of all. Our future is at stake.

An unemployed young person, a person with a disability who is marginalized, elderly people who are uncared for, and people in countries that are captives of hunger and poverty—all humans are our brothers and sisters.

Solidarity. Solidarity comes in many forms. Everyone has a right to decent living conditions. When social or economic conditions—such as job layoffs at the General Motors plants in Oshawa, Ontario (shown here)—make earning a living difficult, solidarity reaches beyond each one's religion. There are no boundaries here. **What can you as an individual do to help others in need? How can you ask for help if you are one of those in need?**

5. Think of others before yourself. Struggle to move away from a world of privilege and comfort to a world where you consider and include others. The lifestyle of the prosperous and their patterns of consumption must be reviewed in light of how this behaviour affects people in other countries.

Selfishness today shows itself in the indifference of prosperous nations toward less developed nations. All peoples are entitled to receive a fair share of the goods of this world and of the know-how of the more advanced countries—for example, by making generic medicine available for people with HIV/AIDS in Africa.

Homeless People. A homeless man in Montréal bows his head as he sits by his dog. **What needs to change in society to give everyone a place to live?**

6. Say "no" to war and violence. War is not always inevitable. It is always a defeat for humanity. Always search for international law, honest dialogue, solidarity between states, and the noble exercise of diplomacy to resolve differences. Too many today still place their trust in nuclear weapons and rely on violence.

The solution is never terrorism or armed conflict. Military victories are not a solution. War is never just another means that one can choose to settle differences between nations. Only as the very last option and with very strict conditions may war be undertaken.

Youth Violence. Violence of any kind is a sign of weakness. The best approach is to find ways of working together to remove the conditions of violence, such as child poverty, inadequate social housing, lack of youth programs, unemployment, and so on. **How can you avoid situations of violence (for example, bullying, name-calling, gang formation) in your school?**

Check Your Understanding

1. Explain the meaning of the dialogue of action.

Think About It

2. Discuss how the six points of Pope John Paul II help people of different religions to act together to create a better world.

Making It Personal

3. Take each of the six areas mentioned by Pope John Paul II (Change, Say "yes" to life!, Respect for the rule of law, Be in solidarity with others, Think of others before yourself, Say "no" to war and violence) and explore what you or your school community can do to improve dialogue.

Dialogue of Action: Sister Susan Moran

Sister Susan Moran is the founder of Out of the Cold, an interfaith program. When she was honoured with the Order of Canada in 2006, she said: "I'm here because of all the beautiful, suffering people who are now my sisters and brothers. It is through them that I've learned such love and compassion."

A first flash of inspiration for the Out of the Cold program came from students. Sister Susan was chaplain at St. Michael's College High School in Toronto. One day she heard about students who had befriended a homeless man named George, who regularly slept on the grass in front of the school. The students were bringing him clothing, blankets, and food. Sister Susan herself saw George shortly thereafter and they talked briefly. However, that was the only time Sister Susan had an opportunity to get to know the man who would influence her for the rest of her life. George got into a fight and was beaten up so badly that he died in hospital.

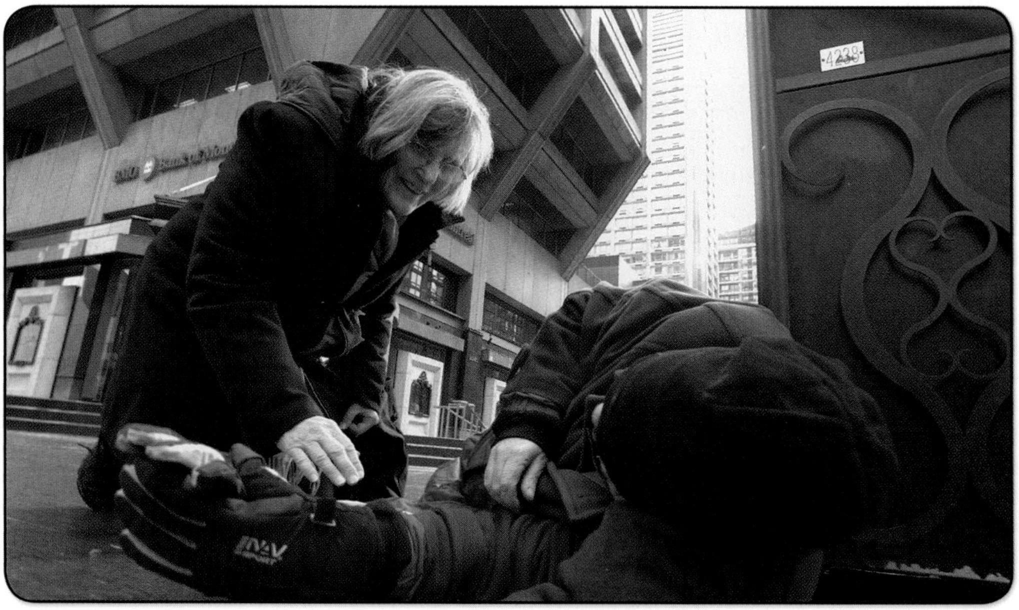

Sister Susan Moran. Sister Susan Moran talks with a homeless person in Toronto. Each night, hundreds of people seek shelter in one of the centres for the homeless. Many more decide to sleep out in the open.

The students were in shock. It was probably the first time they realized how hard it was to live on the street. They began a discussion with Sister Susan about homelessness. They wanted to do something.

Sister Susan began by contacting churches and faith groups in Toronto. She asked them whether they would help create a temporary solution to homelessness by opening the doors of their churches and synagogues. Initially, the plan was that volunteers from each different faith group would

- open their worship space one day a week for 23 weeks
- provide food and hospitality to their guests

With volunteers acting together and faith groups combining their efforts, they could make a difference.

The idea that began in 1987 caught on. Soon there were all kinds of faith groups taking part. By 2009, Out of the Cold had spread to 19 faith groups in Toronto and had chapters in other Canadian cities.

Conclusion

After this long journey through our own religion and the major religions and the Aboriginal spiritual traditions found in Canada, we ask once again the question we started with: How can Catholics relate to other religions?

The same question could be asked of Muslims or Buddhists or any other religious people. Not all faith groups respond in the same way. In this textbook, however, we have not asked what others ought to do, but mainly how the Catholic tradition sees its mandate.

What have Catholics learned from Jesus and their faith concerning this question? What stands out most is how Catholics must not be neutral to others. Catholics believe that they are their brothers' and sisters' keepers, and that they must care for all people. This taking care comes from an experience of how deeply God cares for humanity. Catholics are convinced that their experience of God in Jesus Christ is not addressed only to them, for their individual benefit. They also have a responsibility for others. Part of their faith is a call to mission. What God revealed in Jesus Christ must

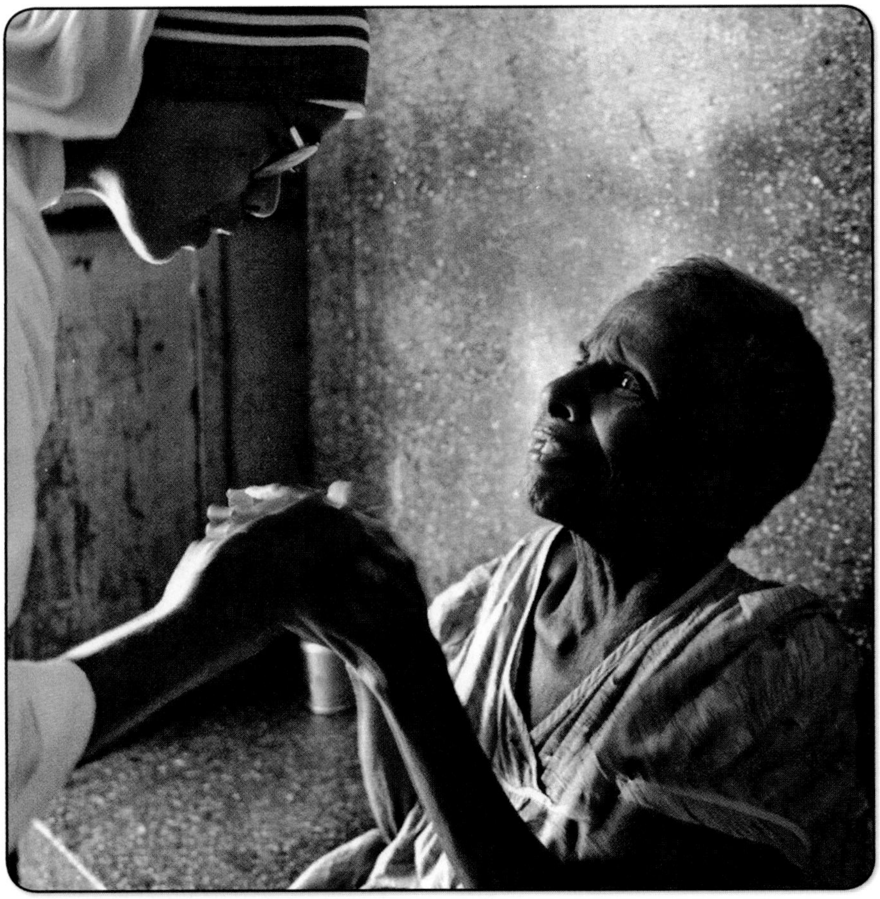

Outflow of Love. Sister Juditha shows affection toward the destitute and dying at the Prem Dan Home in Calcutta. The home was founded by Mother Teresa's Missionaries of Charity.

be brought to the nations—not as a search for power, not by force, but as an outflow of love and hope for peace among people. In the words of St. Thérèse, "Let us love, since that is all our hearts are made for."

As a last word, let us remember what the Second Vatican Council said of how Catholicism relates to other religions:

> **The Catholic Church rejects nothing that is true and holy in these religions.** She regards with sincere reverence those ways of conduct and of life, those precepts and teachings which, though differing in many aspects from the ones she holds and sets forth, nonetheless often reflect a ray of that Truth which enlightens all.... The Church, therefore, exhorts her sons [and daughters], that through dialogue and collaboration with the followers of other religions, carried out with prudence and love, and in witness to the Christian faith and life, they recognize, preserve, and promote the good things, spiritual and moral, as well as the socio-cultural values found among these ... [people] (*Declaration on the Relation of the Church to Non-Christian Religions*, #2).

What I Have Learned

In this chapter, I learned about

- the challenge of living faith in a multi-religious world
- what it means to be human and the human search for God
- ways of being involved in interreligious dialogue
  - the dialogue of theological exchange
  - the dialogue of religious experience
  - the dialogue of everyday life
  - the dialogue of action
- examples of people of faith and integrity

The Golden Rule. The Golden Rule appears in slightly different versions in almost all religions. It beautifully summarizes that human beings are indeed one another's keepers.

Pronunciation Guide

This key will help you pronounce unfamiliar terms used in *World Religions: A Canadian Catholic Perspective.* The vowel symbols correspond to the boldfaced vowels shown in the English words in the box below.

Syllables are indicated by spaces. **Boldfacing** indicates the syllable with the main stress.

ā	face	ī	pie
a	cat	i	pin
ă	pot, car	ō	go
ē	see	o	or
e	end	ou	how
ə	about, pizza, her	ū	cool
		u	put

Ahimsa	ă **him** sə
Algonquin	al **găng** kin
Allah	ăl **lă**
Amrit	**ăm** rēt
Anatta	ă **nut** ə
Anicca	ə **nik** ə
Animism	**an** ə mizəm
Anishinabe	a nish i **nă** bā
Anti-Semitism	**an** tē **se** mi tizəm
Ardas	**ăr** dăs
Ashkenazim	ash kə **na** zəm
Athapaskan	a thə **pas** kən
Atman	**ăt** măn
Aum	om
Avatar	**a** vă tăr
Bahai	bə **hī**
Baisakhi	**bī** sa kē
Beothuk	bē **ă** thik
Bhagavad Gita	**bug** văd **gē** tə
Bodhisattva	**bou** dē **săt** wă
Brahma	**bră** mə
Brahman	**bră** mun
Catechesis	ka tə **kē** sis
Chrismation	kris **mā** shən
Dharma	**dăr** mə
Diaspora	dī **as** por ə
Du'a	**dū** ă
Dukkha	**dū** kə
Ecumenical	e kyə **me** ni kəl
Eid ul-Adha	**ēd** ul ad **hă**
Eucharist	**yū** kə rist
Evangelism	**i van** jə lizəm
Glooscap	**glū** skap
Gurdwara	**gərd** wă ră
Guru Granth Sahib	**gū** rū grant **să** hib
Guru Nanak	**gū** rū **nă** nuk
Hadith	hă **dēth**
Haggadah	hă gă **dă**
Haida	**hī** də
Hajj	hăj
Halakhah	hă lă **kă**
Halal	hă **lăl**
Haram	hă **răm**
Haramandir	hăr **mun** dăr
Hasidism	**hă** si dizəm
Haudenosaune	hō dē nō **shă** nē
Hijab	**hē** jăb
Hijra	**hij** ră
Ichthus	**ik** thəs
Iconoclasm	ī **kă** nə klazəm
Imam	i **măm**
Inuit	ē nū **ēt**
Inuksuk	ē **nūk** sūk
Iroquoian	i rə **kwă** ən
Jihad	jē **hăd**

Kaaba	**kă** bă
Kabbalah	kə **bă** lə
Keshdhari	**kīsh** dă rē
Khalsa	**kăl** sə
Khanda	**kăn** də
Kirpan	**kēr** pun
Kootenayan	kū tə **nā** ən
Kosher	**kō** shər
Langar	**lun** găr
Mahayana	ma ha **yă** nă
Mandala	**mun** də lə
Mandir	**mun** dēr
Manitou	**ma** ni tū
Menorah	mə **no** rə
Métis	**mā** tē
Mezuzah	mə zə **ză**
Mi'kmaq	**mē** gə măg
Mishnah	**mish** nə
Mitzvah	**mits** vă
Moksha	**măk** shă
Mul Mantra	**mūl man** trə
Murti	**mūr** tē
Nam	năm
Nirvana	nər **vă** nə
Ojibwa	ō **jib** wā
Parshad	**păr** shăd
Patka	**put** kə
Piegan	**pē gan**
Potlatch	**păt** lach
Puja	**pū** jə
Qur'an	ko **răn**
Quraysh	ko **rāsh**
Ragi	ră **jē**
Ramadan	ră mă **dăn**
Rosh Hashanah	**rōsh** hă **shă** nə
Sahajdhari	**să** huj dă rē
Salat	săl **ut**
Salishan	**sā** lish ən
Samsara	săm **săr** ə
Sangha	**sung** gə
Sawm	soum
Schism	skizəm
Seder	**sā** dər
Sephardim	si **făr** dəm
Shabbat	shă **băt**
Shahadah	shă **hă** dă
Shakti	**shuk** tē
shaman	**shā** mən
Shariah	shă rē **ă**
Shema	shmă
Shi'ite	**shē** īt
Shiva (Hindu deity)	**shē** və
Shoah	**shō** ă
Shofar	shō **făr**
Siddhartha Gautama	**sid** harth **gă** tum
Sioux	sū
Sufi	**sū** fē
Sunna	sū **nă**
Sunni	**su** nē
Sura	**sū** ră
Syncretism	**sing** krə ti zəm
Talmud	**tăl** mud
Tanakh	tə **năk**
Tawhid	**tăw** hēd
Theravada	tār ə **vă** dă
Tlingit	**kling** kit
Torah	**tor** ə
Tripitaka	trē **pi** tə kă
Tsimshian	**chim** shē ən
Umma	ūm **mă**
Upanishad	ū pa **nē** shad
Vajrayana	**vuj** ră **yă** nă
Veda	**vā** də
Vishnu	**vish** nū
Wakashan	wă **kash** ən
Yom Kippur	**yăm** ki **pūr**
Zakat	**zā** kat
Zionism	**zī** ə nizəm

Glossary

Chapter 1

Multicultural Consisting of multiple ethnic groups, cultures, languages, and religions

Multiculturalism A policy and law that recognizes and supports the diversity of a nation's or province's population

Religious pluralism The co-existence of many religions in a society; Canada, India, and the United States are examples of countries where religious pluralism exists

Salvation A word meaning, literally, "made whole" or "made healthy"; Catholics use this term to describe how people are made whole in Christ and freed from the power of sin and death; salvation is a gift from God, not something that people can obtain for themselves

Syncretism The attempt to blend the beliefs and practices of different religions into one system

Tolerance An attitude that recognizes the right of others to think, live, or worship according to their own beliefs

Chapter 2

Assembly For Christians, a gathering of baptized people for liturgy or worship in the name of Christ; the assembly is also called the "congregation" or the "Church"

Catechesis Word meaning "teaching"; a catechist is a person who teaches about the faith

Chrismation When a baptized person is confirmed by anointing the person with chrism (holy oil)

Holy Describes what is spiritually whole, sound, virtuous, or acceptable to God

Myths Stories of how things came to be

Philosophy Literally, "love of wisdom"; the study of what is true, good, and beautiful in human existence, the use of reason to seek truth and knowledge

Sacred Describes what has been set aside as holy in a religious ritual, such as the water blessed in baptism and made holy by the words of the priest

Theology The study of God

Triduum The three days of Holy Thursday, Good Friday, and Easter

Vigil A time of staying awake and waiting before a great feast; at the Easter Vigil, Christians stay awake with Jesus in the tomb to be present at his resurrection

Chapter 3

Assimilate Absorb one group into the culture of another

Elders Aboriginal men or women who are recognized, respected, and consulted for their wisdom, experience, knowledge, background, and insight; an elder is not necessarily one of the oldest people in the community

Indigenous Refers to native, original, or earliest known inhabitants of a region

Shaman An Aboriginal spiritual leader

Chapter 4

Ashkenazim Central and Eastern European Jews and their descendants

Covenant An agreement of mutual faithfulness, like a contract or alliance, between two parties; "I will be your God and you shall be my people"; the agreement binds the parties together with mutual privileges and obligations

Diaspora The scattering of Jews outside of Israel in both ancient and modern times

Halakhah "Laws" or "the path"; the oral tradition of Judaism

Holocaust The systematic killing of over six million Jews before and during World War II

Messiah A word meaning "the anointed one"; the word "Christ" comes from the Greek word meaning the same thing

Mitzvah Religious or moral path that Jews must follow; the plural form is "mitzvot"

Prayer of Sanctification A prayer to make something sacred

Revelation The act of showing, or revealing, something that was hidden

Righteous Describes one who is just, or who is in a right relationship with God

Secular Jew An ethnic Jew who is not religious

Sephardim Primarily Spanish, Portuguese, and North African Jews and their descendants

Shabbat Hebrew word meaning "Sabbath"

Shiva A seven-day period of mourning

Shoah From the Hebrew word for "catastrophe," "calamity," or, as it is usually translated, "holocaust"; it refers to Nazi Germany's deliberate attempt to exterminate the Jewish race between 1933 and 1945

Talmud The compilation of written interpretation of the oral Torah (the *Halakhah*); after the second defeat of the Jews by the Romans in 135 CE, the rabbis began to write down and interpret this oral Torah

Tanakh Hebrew word for the sacred writings of Judaism; the word is formed from the first Hebrew letter of the three parts of the Jewish scriptures (what Christians call the Old Testament): Torah, Neviim, Ketuvim

Zionism A movement that began in the nineteenth century for the purpose of creating a Jewish state in what is now modern Israel; today, "Zionism" refers to strong support for the State of Israel

Chapter 5

Apostles Followers of Jesus who were sent forth to bring the Gospel to others; the 12 especially chosen from among the disciples by Jesus

Disciple Literally, a student; here it means a follower of Jesus

Ecumenical movement (Also called "ecumenism") The movement toward unity among the Christian churches; "ecumenism" comes from the Greek word meaning "the whole inhabited world" and reflects Jesus's desire that his word be spread to the whole of the human race

Evangelist A writer of a Gospel of the New Testament

Icon A sacred image (in a painting or carving, for example) of Christ and the saints used in devotion and other religious rituals

Iconoclasm Breaking icons (images used in religious worship)

Orthodox Word meaning "those who believe correctly" or "those who glorify God correctly"; Orthodox Christians' origins coincide with the origin of Christianity

Schism A separation, but not a full break, of two churches on the basis of a dispute over beliefs or practices

Speaking in tongues Vocalizing a string of syllables in religious practice; in Greek, the term is *glossolalia*, which means literally "gift of tongues"; it is believed to be the gift of holy language from the Holy Spirit

Chapter 6

Allah Arabic word for God; Muslims worship the same God as Christians and Jews, but some of the revelations are interpreted differently. The word "Allah" is a unique word because it is genderless. It is neither masculine nor feminine.

Bedouin A nomadic or wandering tribesperson of the Arabian, Syrian, or North African deserts

Eid al-Fitr (Also spelled Eid ul-Fitr) A celebration that takes place at the end of Ramadan, which is a period of fasting and reflection; the festival is often referred to as Eid (pronounced EED)

Hajj Arabic word meaning "pilgrimage"; the pilgrimage to Mecca that Muslims are asked to make at least once in their lifetime, if they are healthy and can afford it

Halal Permissible; usually refers to foods that are allowed

Hijab Arabic word for "cover"; a scarf that covers most or all of a woman's hair

Hijra Arabic word meaning "migration"

Imam A Muslim leader of prayer and giver of sermons in the mosque

Khalifa The Muslim duty of stewardship that lies at the heart of Muslim ecological ethics; although *khalifa* refers to other areas of responsibility, it is used to make the point that certain destructive environmental actions, such as polluting water and wantonly killing animals, are forbidden

Mosque A place where Muslims gather for group worship

Muslim A believer in Islam

Nasheeds Music that is traditionally sung a cappella, accompanied only by the beat of a large drum; *nasheeds* often consist of religious stories and recitations of the Qur'an in Arabic

Patriarchal society Society in which women are defined by their relationships to men (father, husband, uncle, brother, or son)

Polytheist A believer in more than one god

Shi'ite Muslims who believe that leadership of the Muslim community should be passed down through the direct descendants of the Prophet; Shi'ites form the majority of the population in Iraq and Iran

Sufi A Muslim who uses mysticism to gain a special understanding of Allah that goes beyond rational thought; Sufis can be Sunni or Shi'ite

Sunni Muslims who believe that community leaders do not have to be descended from the Prophet. The name Sunni comes from Sunna, which is a collection of the words, actions, and practices of Muhammad, as taken down and transmitted by his inner circle of family and friends. Sunnis make up the majority of the world's Muslim population.

Umma The Muslim community

Zakat The Muslim obligation to pay 2.5 percent of one's wealth to the needy

Chapter 7

Ahimsa The principle of non-violence

Ascetic Someone who practises severe self-discipline or abstains from physical pleasures for religious purposes

Atman The true self

Avatar A deity who has descended into the world in earthly form

Bhagavad Gita A sacred Hindu story about Prince Arjuna and Krishna

Brahman The supreme cosmic force

Caste A traditional Hindu social level or class

Deities Images of the God in many forms

Dharma One's personal code of conduct relating to family and society; one's duty

Guru Wise teacher

Karma The law of cause and effect, of one's actions having an impact on one's future life

Mandir A Hindu temple

Mantra Sacred sounds, words, or phrases, repeated in ritual

Maya Illusion

Moksha Freedom or liberation from *samsara*, or the cycle of rebirth

Murti An image of a Hindu deity

Puja Hindu worship ceremony

Ramayana A Hindu epic about Prince Rama and Sita

Samsara The law of birth, death, and rebirth, or the process of reincarnation

Sanskrit The language of ancient India

Untouchables In the traditional Hindu social levels, the lowest outsider class

Upanishads Sacred scriptures; the final dialogues ending the Vedas

Vedas Early sacred scriptures of Hinduism

Yoga Hindu path (or discipline) to liberation

Chapter 8

Ascetic Someone who practises severe self-discipline or abstains from physical pleasures for religious purposes

The Buddha The founder of Buddhism, Siddhartha Gautama; teachers who fully understand the nature of mind and reality are also called Buddhas

Enlightenment A state of perfect happiness and understanding; unconditional compassion for all beings

Karma The law of cause and effect, of one's actions having an impact on one's future life

Mandala A visual object, usually in the form of a circle, that can be used as an aid for focusing in meditation

Mantra A word or phrase that is chanted as an aid to meditation

Merit The idea in Buddhism that a person can be reborn in a form closer to enlightenment if he or she accumulates merit; wholesome deeds and intentions can add to a person's merit

Nirvana The end of personal suffering and the experience of unchanging peace

Samsara The law of birth, death, and rebirth, or the process of reincarnation

Chapter 9

Amrit Ceremonial water used in Sikh rituals

Gurdwara Sikh place of worship

Guru A prophet and teacher

Kirpan Small sword or dagger

Turban Head covering worn by male Sikhs

Chapter 10

Agnostic From the ancient Greek word meaning "not to know"; a person who believes that God may exist, but that humans cannot know it with any certainty

Atheist From the ancient Greek word meaning "no God"; a person who does not believe in God, or in any other higher power or reality

Empirical Based on experiment and observation as opposed to revelation of religion

Fundamentalism A form of religion in which groups or subgroups with a strict interpretation of religious scripture hold those beliefs as absolute authority and beyond human interpretation or adaptation

Globalization The interdependence of societies throughout the world because of developments in business, communication, science, and ethics

Heresy A belief or practice that is contrary to doctrine

Humanism A philosophy or worldview that upholds the importance of life, reason, justice, and ethics; humanism affirms human dignity

Rational Describes a way of knowing on the basis of causes; everything has a reason, or cause

Rationalism The attitude of accepting reason as the supreme authority in matters of opinion, belief, and conduct

Secular Of this world; not religious or sacred; "secular" comes from the Latin word meaning "of the time"; the term comes from the contrasting belief in God being eternal, existing outside of time

Secularism A way of thinking and approaching the world that separates religion from other areas of life; for example, government and schools

Secularization Rejection of the influence of religion in other areas of life; for example, in schools or in public life

Chapter 11

Human A rational animal who is physical, spiritual, social, creative, and emotional

Mystery A religious truth that is wholly unknown or beyond the human capacity to understand; something concealed that causes wonderment

Relativism The belief that knowledge, truth, and morality are only opinions of individuals and therefore do not necessarily hold for others

Revelation God's act of making known something about God that was partially or completely unknown

Social justice The practice of giving every person an opportunity to have fair and equal rights to take part in the social, educational, and economic benefits of a society

Transcendent Something beyond comprehension or a reality beyond the material universe

Index

C

N

O

P

Photo/Text Credits

CREDITS
This page constitutes an extension of the copyright page. We have made every effort to trace the ownership of all copyrighted material and to secure permission from copyright holders. In the event of any question arising as to the use of any material, we will be pleased to make the necessary corrections in future printings. Thanks are due to the following authors, publishers, and agents for permission to use the material indicated. All material © copyright its respective owner.

VISUALS
(t)=top (b)=bottom (m)=middle (l)=left (r)=right

Chapter 1. 2: NASA GPN-2000-001138 **3:** Monkey Business Images/Shutterstock **4:** (br) Fallsview/Dreamstime (l) Don MacKinnon/Getty (tr) © Toronto Star/GetStock **6:** (br) REUTERS/Todd Korol/Landov (l) © Tony Bock/Toronto Star/GetStock (tr) © 4loops/iStockphoto **8:** (b) Michael Bann/Shutterstock (c) thefinalmiracle/Shutterstock (r) © Aman Khan/iStockphoto (tl) Mikhail Levit/Shutterstock **9:** (b) White/Photolibrary (t) Bill Wittman **11:** © jan middelveld/iStockphoto **12:** Brasiliao/Shutterstock **14:** (b) © Mary Evans Picture Library/The Image Works **15:** (b) David Máška/Shutterstock (t) Mosaic depicting Foliage and a Mask, Byzantine (mosaic)/Great Palace Mosaic Museum, Istanbul/The Bridgeman Art Library **16:** (b) © The Art Gallery Collection/Alamy (t) Erich Lessing/Art Resource, NY **17:** © Alinari/The Image Works **18:** © Mary Evans Picture Library/The Image Works **19:** STANISLAV FILIPPOV/AFP/Getty **20:** REUTERS/Vincenzo Pinto **21:** © David Lees/CORBIS **23:** DONATELLA GIAGNORI/Maxppp/Landov **25:** Francois Lochon/Time Life Pictures/Getty **26:** Michel de Broin **27:** (b) Chen Leopold, Sulhita, Sulha Peace Project, Feb 27–Mar 2, 2007 (t) The Canadian Press (Michele Chabin)

Chapter 2. 30: Bill Wittman **31:** Courtesy the Dufour family **32:** Monseigneur de Montmorency-Laval (1623–1708) Bishop of Canada (oil on canvas), French School, (17th century)/Société des Missions Etrangères, Paris/Lauros/Giraudon/The Bridgeman Art Library **35:** (bl) Panaspics/Shutterstock (bml) © Steve Crise/CORBIS (bmr) detail of Last Supper, Christ and St John (w/c on paper) Chinese School, (19th century)/Photo © Boltin Picture Library/The Bridgeman Art Library (br) © Charity Borg/iStockphoto (t) Mark Brayer/artizans. Please visit the Artizans website. **36:** Courtesy Allan Moon **37:** Juan Manuel Silva/age fotostock/Photolibrary **38:** (l) Vladimir Melnik/Shutterstock (m) Regien Paassen/Shutterstock (r) Bill Wittman **40:** Bishop Paul-André Durocher **42:** (all) Bill Wittman **43:** (l) © Nancy Sheehan/Photo Edit (r) Rob Melnychuk/JupiterImages, a division of Getty **44:** (b) © Wojtek Kryczka/iStockphoto (t) Bill Wittman **45:** Bill Wittman **46:** Elena Elisseeva/Shutterstock **47:** "Celebrating the mystery of Christ throughout the year" (adapted), Liturgical Chart in *Born of the Spirit* series, copyright © Concacan Inc. All rights reserved. Reproduced with permission of the Canadian Conference of Catholic Bishops. Please visit the CCCB website. **48:** © National Gallery, London/Art Resource, NY **49:** (b) Bill Wittman (t) Gisele Bauche **50:** Sorin Popa/Shutterstock **51:** *Mary, a Mother's Sorrow,* copyright 2006 Janet McKenzie. Please visit Janet McKenzie's website. **52:** Nagy Melinda/Shutterstock **53:** (bl) Andrew Burke/Lonely Planet Images/Getty (r) Bill Wittman (tl) AP/The Canadian Press (Khalid Mohammed) **54:** Catechesis of the Good Shepherd Association of Canada **55:** Bildarchiv Preussischer Kulturbesitz/Art Resource, NY **56:** (b) The Art Archive/Gianni Dagli Orti (tl) Bill Wittman (tr) Reproduced by courtesy of the University Librarian and Director, The John Rylands University Library, The University of Manchester **58:** Trinity medal, recast version of original made in 1544 now in Domschatz, Trier (gold), Reinhart, Hans (c.1500/10–81)/Kunsthistorisches Museum, Vienna, Austria/The Bridgeman Art Library **59:** (bl) Alexey Stiop/Shutterstock (br) © Massimo Listri/CORBIS (t) ZanyZeus/Shutterstock **60:** © David Cooper/GetStock **61:** Bill Wittman **63:** (b) Bill Wittman (c) Courtesy of Adrianna Edwards, Focus Strategic Communications Inc. (t) Glenda M. Powers/Shutterstock **64:** Bill Wittman

Chapter 3. 66: Angel of the North by Blake Debassige **67:** Reproduced with permission of Eva Solomon, CSJ, D. Min., Sister of St. Joseph of Sault Ste. Marie, Assembly of Western Catholic Bishops—Standing Committee on Aboriginal Affairs **68:** (t) Toronto Sun/The Canadian Press (Paul Henry) (b) © Keith Levit/GetStock **69:** (bl) Winnipeg Free Press/The Canadian Press (Joe Bryksa) (br) Whitehorse Star/The Canadian Press (Jeff Korenko) (t) Rob vanNostrand, PerfectPhoto Photography **71:** (b) © Bill Brooks/GetStock (m) Hope, P/Parks Canada (t) © David Lewis/iStockphoto **73:** (b) Glenbow NA-5719-4 (t) Library and Archives Canada, Acc. No. 1989-492-2 **74:** (b) AP Photo/The Canadian Press (Pier Paolo Cito) (t) The Canadian Press (Fred Chartrand) **75:** (b) © Toronto Star/Russell/GetStock (t) Courtesy of Char Deslippe **76:** (b) Mastio1/Shutterstock (t) The Canadian Press (Kevin Frayer) **78:** © Shaun Lowe/iStockphoto **79:** (b) Brockville Recorder and Times/The Canadian Press (Darcy Cheek) (t) Bill Wittman **80:** (b) © Joe Sohm/GetStock (t) Marilyn Angel Wynn/Nativestock **81:** Courtesy Bill Frisinger **82:** (b) kathmanduphotog/Shutterstock (t) Mona Makela/Shutterstock **83:** (b) Jostein Hauge/Shutterstock (t) Marilyn Angel Wynn/Nativestock **84:** (b) Trueman/Library and Archives Canada/C-014106 (t) John E Marriott/All Canada Photos/Photolibrary **85:** David A. Barnes/GetStock **86:** *The Healing Rock* by Métis artist Natalie Rostad **87:** *Raven and The First Men* by Bill Reid. Courtesy UBC Museum of Anthropology, Vancouver, Canada **89:** (b) Cliff LeSergent/GetStock (t) Corel **90:** Nancy Carter/North Wind Picture Archives/Photolibrary **91:** (b) TCPI/The Canadian Press(Adrian Wyld) (t) Bryan and Cherry Alexander Photography **92:** Courtesy of Allan Novak, *Loving Spoonfuls* **93:** Bill Wittman **94:** (l) The Martyrs' Shrine, Midland, Ontario (r) The Canadian Press (Andy Clark) **95:** Fumoleau/NWT Archives/N-1995-002: 1547

Chapter 4. 98: Richard T Nowitz/age fotostock/Photolibrary **99:** Jessica Rose **100:** Joseph Rabin/Library and Archives Canada/PA-103552 **101:** © Toronto Star/GetStock **104:** Mikhail Levit/Shutterstock **105:** The Art Archive/São Paulo Art Museum Brazil/Gianni Dagli Orti **107:** The Canadian Press (Paul Chiasson) **108:** © Toronto Star/GetStock **109:** (l) Imagno/Contributor/Hulton/Getty (r) The Canadian Press (M. Kathleen Kelly) **110:** © Bill Aron/Photo Edit **111:** Three Lions/Getty **112:** (b) RussianArchives/Abamedia (t) © Mark Pink/GetStock **113:** (l) Laski Diffusion - Wojtek Laski/Contributor/Getty (r) Kordcom/age fotostock/Photolibrary **114:** © Karen Benzian/GetStock **115:** Hans Pinn/GPO/Getty **116:** (b) Lauree Feldman/Index Stock Imagery/Photolibrary (t) John Phillips/Time Life Pictures/Getty **117:** © Bill Aron/PhotoEdit **118:** Andy Crawford/Dorling Kindersley/Getty **119:** Howard Sandler/Shutterstock **120:** (t) DAVID FURST/AFP/Getty (b) Photography by Choco Studio **121:** (b) © Bill Aron/PhotoEdit (t) Keith Levit **122:** (l) Christopher Poliquin/Shutterstock (m) Pumba1/iStockphoto (r) Tetra Images/Photolibrary **123:** © Pascal Deloche/Godong/CORBIS **124:** (b) Comstock/Getty (t) Ron Zmiri/Shutterstock **128:** *Garden of Eden* (oil on canvas), Bruegel, Jan the Elder (1568–1625)/Galleria Doria Pamphilj, Rome/Alinari/The Bridgeman Art Library **133:** vadim kozlovsky/Shutterstock **134:** © bonnie jacobs/iStockphoto **136:** The Bridgeman Art Library/Getty **137:** © Leland Bobbé/CORBIS **139:** © Copyright: the Estate of William Kurelek **140:** (l) AP Images/The Canadian Press (Matt Sayles) (r) © Keith Levit/Alamy 43: AP Photo/The Canadian Press (Herbert Knosowski)

Chapter 5. 146: © 2004 Werner Forman/TopFoto/The Image Works **147:** Courtesy of Gary Mak **149:** (b) The Canadian Press (Sean Kilpatrick) (t) © Nuvista/Dreamstime **150:** © Hanan Isachar/GetStock **151:** © SERDAR YAGCI/iStockphoto **152:** The Crucifixion of St. Peter, 1600–01 (oil on panel), Caravaggio, Michelangelo Merisi da (1571–1610)/Santa Maria del Popolo, Rome, Italy/The Bridgeman Art Library **153:** (l) AridOcean/Shutterstock **155:** © Hospitalera/Dreamstime **156:** Jozef Sedmak/Shutterstock **157:** MS 58 fol.27v Introductory page to the Gospel of St. Matthew, Book of Kells, c.800 (vellum), Irish School, (9th century)/© The Board of Trinity College, Dublin/The Bridgeman Art Library **158:** (b) St. Paul Preaching at Athens (cartoon for the Sistine Chapel) (PRE RESTORATION), Raphael (Raffaello Sanzio of Urbino) (1483–1520)/Victoria & Albert Museum, London, UK/The Bridgeman Art Library **159:** (l) © Mary Evans Picture Library/The Image Works (r) The Art Archive/Gianni Dagli Orti **160:** North Wind Picture

Archives **161:** (b) © The Print Collector/GetStock (t) Jose Antonio Moreno/age fotostock/Photolibrary **162:** © Mary Evans Picture Library/The Image Works **163:** Dima Korotayev/Epsilon/Getty **164:** © Roger-Viollet/Topham/The Image Works **166:** (l) © Csld/Dreamstime (r) North Wind Picture Archives **167:** Time Life Pictures/Mansell/Time Life Pictures/Getty **168:** © GFC Collection/GetStock **169:** (b) Library of Congress USZC4-8327 (t) © Sean Cayton/The Image Works **171:** © DeA Picture Library/Art Resource, NY **173:** St. Charles Borromeo (1538–84), Archbishop of Milan, Dolci, Carlo (1616–86)/Palazzo Pitti, Florence/The Bridgeman Art Library **174:** Anthony Correia/Shutterstock **175:** (b) © BRIAN HARRIS/GetStock (t) Flower Pentecostal Heritage Center **176:** Kevin Winter/Getty **178:** Bill Wittman **180:** Gasper Furman/Shutterstock **181:** Keystone/Getty **182:** REUTERS/Alessandro Bianchi/Landov **183:** Sean_Warren/iStockphoto **184:** Courtesy of Kairos Canada

Chapter 6. 186: Guenter Fischer/imagebroker.net/Photolibrary **187:** Caroline Penn/Imagestate RM/Photolibrary **188:** TODD KOROL/Reuters/Landov **190:** Sufi/Shutterstock **191:** (b) braedostok/Shutterstock (t) © Kazuyoshi Nomachi/CORBIS **192:** © Joanna B. Pinneo/Aurora Photos/GetStock **193:** Reza/Getty **196:** (flag) Kgtoh/Dreamstime **197:** (l) Courtesy Allan Moon (r) mypokcik/Shutterstock **198:** (b) © Studio DL/CORBIS (t) Pars/Abacapress/The Canadian Press (Shahin) **199:** (b) ayazad/Shutterstock (t) © Gordon Sinclair/Alamy **200:** ayazad/Shutterstock **201:** (b) Paula Bronstein/Getty (t) © JLImages/GetStock **202:** (b) © BAZUKI MUHAMMAD/Reuters/CORBIS (t) lordet/Shutterstock **203:** (b) archana bhartia/Shutterstock (tl) © Richard Melloul/Sygma/CORBIS (tr) Steve Raymer/Asia Images RM/Photolibrary **205:** (b) Salem Alforaih/Shutterstock (t) © Richard Lautens/GetStock **207:** A.G.E. Foto Stock/First Light **208:** © Arpad Benedek/iStockphoto **209:** (b) © murat $en/iStockphoto (t) © Toronto Star/GetStock **210:** MAHMOUD ZAYAT/AFP/Getty **211:** The Virgin and Child, from a Johnson Album no. 14 vol. 2, Mughal, c.1630 (gouache on paper with gold border of cockscomb flower/British Library, London, UK/© British Library Board. All Rights Reserved/The Bridgeman Art Library **212:** © Christopher Herwig/Aurora Photos/GetStock **213:** Heba Amin **214:** Steve Vidler/Imagestate RM/Photolibrary **215:** (b) The Canadian Press (Adrian Wyld) (t) REUTERS/Khaled al-Hariri/Landov **217:** (b) © Ryan McGinnis/GetStock (t) from the film *The Peace Tree* by Mitra Sen **218:** (bl) Jane Sweeney/Robert Harding Travel/Photolibrary (br) Marc van Vuren/Shutterstock (tl) Le Journal de Montréal/The Canadian Press (Luc Belisle) (mt) Harry Maynard/Cusp/Photolibrary (rt) Distinctive Images/Shutterstock **219:** Distinctive Images/Shutterstock **220:** (b) Pippin Lee (t) Courtesy ISNA Halal Certification Agency **221:** Glenn Baglo/The Vancouver Sun **222:** © CSI Productions/GetStock **223:** © Gianni Giansanti/Sygma/CORBIS **224:** (b) Courtesy WestWind Pictures/Canadian Broadcasting Corporation (t) REUTERS/Osservatore Romano/Landov **226:** REUTERS/Osservatore Romano/Landov

Chapter 7. 228: (l) Anyka/Shutterstock (r) Yan Simkin/Shutterstock **229:** Courtesy of Michael Harrison **231:** (bl) Yan Simkin/Shutterstock (br) Alvaro Leiva/age fotostock/Photolibrary (t) Courtesy Vinay and Sanjli Gidwaney **233:** (b) Francis Bacon/Axiom/Photolibrary (t) © Mike Goldwater/GetStock **234:** Hu Xiao Fang/Shutterstock **235:** Pixeazee/Dinodia **237:** Paul Cowan/Shutterstock **238:** Vakhrushev Pavel/Shutterstock **239:** Pietro Scozzari/age fotostock/Photolibrary **241:** Imagestate Media Partners Limited - Impact Photos/Alamy **242:** Shailesh Nanal/Dreamstime **243:** (b) Courtesy Everett Collection (t) Courtesy of Himalayan Academy, Kauai's Hindu Monastery **245:** (l) © Louise Batalla Duran/GetStock (m) © ArkReligion/Alamy (r) Shalini Saran/Photolibrary **246:** (bl) © Helene Rogers/GetStock (bm) © Stuart Forster/GetStock (br) © david pearson/GetStock (mt) © ArkReligion/GetStock (tl) © ArkReligion/Alamy (tr) ErickN/Shutterstock **248:** Andrew Errington/Photographer's Choice/Getty **250:** (t) Mahesh14/Dreamstime **252:** Luca Tettoni/Robert Harding Travel/Photolibrary **253:** Plush Studios/Blend Images/JupiterImages, a division of Getty **254:** © Toronto Star Archives/GetStock **256:** (b) Paul Prescott/Dreamstime (t) © Classic Image/GetStock

Chapter 8. 258: (b) © Kathy Konkler/iStockphoto (t) Piers Cavendish/Imagestate RM/Photolibrary **259:** Courtesy of Les Miller **260:** (b) The University of Toronto (tl) Courtesy of Shambhala Sun magazine. Please visit the Shambhala Sun website. (tr) Russell Gordon/Aurora Photos **261:** © Leonard de Selva/CORBIS **262:** V Muthuraman/Photolibrary **264:** Valery Shanin/Shutterstock **265:** © Toronto Star/GetStock **266:** Davidstudio2008/Dreamstime **267:** Neil Emmerson/Robert Harding World Imagery/Getty **268:** (b) Roderick Chen/First Light/Getty (t) Halifax Chronicle-Herald/The Canadian Press (Darren Pittman) **269:** (t) AND Inc./Shutterstock **270:** The Canadian Press (Andrew Vaughan) **271:** (l) © Toronto Star/GetStock (r) © Lindsay Hebberd/CORBIS **272:** (l) © Neal Preston/CORBIS **273:** (b) Todd Korol/Aurora Photos (t) Anthony Ricci/Shutterstock **275:** (b) BESTWEB/Shutterstock (t) Stringer/AFP/Getty **278:** A Chederros/Onoky/Photolibrary **279:** © Richard Ross/CORBIS **281:** The Canadian Press **282:** MarFot/Shutterstock

Chapter 9. 284: © Yadid Levy/GetStock **285:** Courtesy of Michael Harrison **286:** © Keith Beaty/GetStock **287:** (br) Bill Pugliano/Getty (t) Rob Straight/Vancouver Sun **288:** (t) © ArkReligion/GetStock **289:** © ArkReligion/GetStock **290:** © zennie/iStockphoto **291:** B P S Walia/Photolibrary **292:** © ArkReligion/GetStock **294:** (bl) Photos India RF/Photolibrary (br) © Tim Page/GetStock (t) © ArkReligion/GetStock **296:** Indu Arora **297:** (b) © India Images/GetStock (t) AP/The Canadian Press (Altaf Qadri) **298:** Toronto Star/The Canadian Press (David Cooper) **299:** (l) © Andrew Stawicki/GetStock (r) © ArkReligion/GetStock **300:** From BASTIAN D. *PRISMS OF FAITH* STUDENT TXT GRADES 7–9. © 1988 Nelson Education Ltd. Reproduced by permission. Please visit the Cengage permissions website. **302:** (l) © The Toronto Star/GetStock (r) © ArkReligion/GetStock **303:** © Paul Doyle/GetStock **304:** STR/AFP/Getty **305:** © Lisa Law/The Image Works

Chapter 10. 308: *Wheatfield with Crows*, 1890 (oil on canvas), van Gogh, Vincent (1853–90)/Van Gogh Museum, Amsterdam, The Netherlands/The Bridgeman Art Library **311:** *The Sweater* ©1980 National Film Board of Canada. All rights reserved. **312:** Bildarchiv Preussischer Kulturbesitz/Art Resource, NY **313:** (b) © Feng Yu/iStockphoto (t) Josef Hauzinger/The Bridgeman Art Library/Getty **315:** (b) Courtesy Everett Collection (t) North Wind Picture Archives **316:** (bl) *Flying Fish Meet in the Torrid Zone*, from *'Americae Tertia Pars...'* (coloured engraving), de Bry, Theodore (1528–98)/Service Historique de la Marine, Vincennes, France/Lauros/Giraudon/The Bridgeman Art Library (br) ppl/Shutterstock (t) Courtesy of the American Atheists Society **318:** Alexander Mul/Shutterstock **319:** Courtesy Everett Collection **320:** © Rick Eglinton/GetStock **321:** Yves Marcoux/First Light/Getty **323:** (l) Hulton Archive/Stringer/Getty (r) Michael Ochs Archives/Stringer/Getty **324:** © Ron Bull/GetStock **326:** ARTEKI/Shutterstock **327:** (b) Krzysztof Dydynski/Lonely Planet Images (t) © Maigi/Dreamstime **328:** AP/The Canadian Press **329:** (b) © Sandra O'Claire/iStockphoto (t) AFP/Getty **331:** © Cbeckwith/Dreamstime **333:** © 2009 Photos, a division of Getty Images. **334:** Stockbyte/Getty

Chapter 11. 336: (b) Francois Lochon/Time Life Pictures/Getty (grid, clockwise from tl) Studio1One/Big Stock Photo; CREATISTA/Shutterstock; Jules Studio/Shutterstock; Andrew Taylor/Shutterstock; Aron Brand/Shutterstock; paul prescott/Big Stock Photo; iofoto/Shutterstock; photographhunter/ Big Stock Photo; Diana Lundin/Shutterstock; Yuri Arcurs/Shutterstock (mr) Blacqbook/Shutterstock (ml) Ramzi Hachicho/Shutterstock **337:** Reprinted with permission of Michael Skinner **338:** Steve Mason/Photodisc/Photolibrary **339:** (l) D. Gifford/Photo Researchers, Inc. (r) Dhoxax/Shutterstock **340:** (l) *St. Thomas Aquinas Reading*, c.1510–11 (fresco), Bartolommeo, Fra (Baccio della Porta) (1472–1517)/Museo di San Marco dell'Angelico, Florence, Italy/The Bridgeman Art Library (r) Christopher Futcher/Shutterstock **341:** (b) david5962/Shutterstock (t) Time & Life Pictures/Getty **343:** (l) Library of Congress LAMB, no. 1239 (AA size) [P&P] (r) © S. Greg Panosian/iStockphoto **344:** © Emily Riddell/GetStock **345:** (b) Bill Wittman (t) © Toronto Star/GetStock **347:** Courtesy of Scarboro Missions Magazine **348:** The Canadian Press (Tom Hanson) **349:** sonya etchison/Shutterstock **350:** © Humberto Olarte Cupas/GetStock **351:** (l) © Dan Driedger/iStockphoto (r) Tan, Kim Pin/Shutterstock **353:** Painting by 'Richart' Richard Proulx Copyright © 2005 **354:** Dilip Banerjee/The India Today Group/Getty **355:** (b) Corey Wise/Lonely Planet Images (t) Freeing the Human Spirit **356:** (b) Rana Faure/White/Photolibrary (t) © Adam Kazmierski/iStockphoto **357:** (b) © David Cooper/GetStock (t) Reprinted with permission of Michael Skinner **358:** Laura DeSantis/White/Photolibrary **359:** Thomas Eagle **360:** AP Photo/Zebar **361:** © Simon Hayter/GetStock **362:** (l) ASSOCIATED PRESS (m) Vladimir Wrangel/Shutterstock (r) Lee Lockwood/Time Life Pictures/Getty **363:** REUTERS/Jerry Lampen/Landov **364:** (b) The Canadian Press (Darryl Dyck) (t) Sergey Goruppa/Shutterstock **365:** (bl) © Tatianatatiana/Dreamstime (br) Monkey Business Images/Shutterstock (t) The Canadian Press (Nathan Denette) **366:** © Colin Mcconnell/Toronto Star/GetStock **367:** AP Photo/John Moore **369:** Reprinted with permission of Paul McKenna

TEXT

Biblical passages throughout this textbook were retrieved from the online oremus Bible Browser, which displays the *New Revised Standard Version Bible: Anglicized Edition*, copyright 1989, 1995, Division of Christian Education of the National Council of the Churches of Christ in the United States of America. Used by permission. All rights reserved.

Chapter 1. 20, 24, 25, 27, 29: Excerpts from Papal speeches: © Libreria Editrice Vaticana, reprinted with permission.

Chapter 2. 40: Profile courtesy of Bishop Paul-André Durocher **51:** Anna Akhmatova. "Crucifixion." Poem from *Requiem 10: Poems of Anna Akhmatova*, selected and translated by Stanley Kunitz with Max Hayward. Toronto: Little, Brown and Company, 1973, p. 113. Reprinted with permission of Darhansoff Verrill Feldman, Literary Agents. **57:** Apostles' Creed, from the Catechism of the Catholic Church, Chapter 3, Article 2, The Credo.: © Libreria Editrice Vaticana, reprinted with permission. **65:** The Lord's Prayer, retrieved from the online oremus Bible Browser, which displays the *New Revised Standard Version Bible: Anglicized Edition*, copyright 1989, 1995, Division of Christian Education of the National Council of the Churches of Christ in the United States of America. Used by permission. All rights reserved.

Chapter 3. 66: Chief Yellow Lark. "Oh, Great Spirit." Lakota prayer, circa 1887. Accessed online. **71:** Quote from Art Solomon in A Closer Look feature: accessed online **79:** Brave Buffalo excerpt source: Mails, Thomas E. *Fools Crow: Wisdom and Power*. San Francisco: Council Oak Books, 1991, p. 124. **92:** (br column) Source: *Report of the Royal Commission on Aboriginal Peoples*, Vol. 1. Ottawa: Indian and Northern Affairs Canada, 1996, p. 680. **95:** Rene Fumble. "Missionary." *Here I Sit*. Toronto: Novalis, 2004, pp. 44–45. Reprinted with permission. **96:** Arthur (Art) Solomon. "Renaissance." Reproduced with permission of Eva Solomon, CSJ, D. Min., Sister of St. Joseph of Sault Ste. Marie, Assembly of Western Catholic Bishops—Standing Committee on Aboriginal Affairs. **97:** Reprinted by permission from *Black Elk Speaks: Being the Life Story of a Holy Man of the Oglala Sioux, The Premier Edition* by John G. Neihardt, the State University of New York Press © 2009, State University of New York. All Rights Reserved.

Chapter 4. 98, 102, 117, 126, 127, 130, 132, 135: Jewish scripture excerpts source: *Tanakh: the Holy Scriptures*: the New JPS Translation according to the Traditional Hebrew Text. Philadelphia: The Jewish Publication Society, 1985. **142, 143:** Excerpt from Papal speech: © Libreria Editrice Vaticana, reprinted with permission. **145:** Source: Wikipedia

Chapter 5. 159: Source of Irenaeus text: Schaff, Philip. *The Apostolic Fathers with Justin Martyr and Irenaeus*. Retrieved online from Christian Classics Ethereal Library (11 September 2009). **159:** Source of Polycarp text: *The Epistles of Ignatius and Polycarp*. WK Clementon, ed. Brighton: Baldwin, Cradock and Joy, 1827. Retrieved online. **179:** Excerpt from Papal letter: © Libreria Editrice Vaticana, reprinted with permission. **185:** Source: Vincent Donovan. *Christianity Rediscovered*. Maryknoll, New York: Orbis Books, 1993. Reprinted with permission of the publisher.

Chapter 6. 186, 209, 210, 211, 212, 223: Source of excerpts from the Qur'an: *The Qur'an: A Modern English Version*, trans. Majid Fakhry, Reading, UK: Garnet Publishing, 1997. Reprinted with permission. **193:** Source of excerpt about equality: Akbar S. Ahmed. *Islam Today: A Short Introduction to the Muslim World*. London: I.B Tauris, 1999, p. 21. **198, 209, 210:** Quotes from Vatican online archives and papal speeches in Catholic Connection features: © Libreria Editrice Vaticana, reprinted with permission. **213:** Source: Michael A. Sells. *Early Islamic Mysticism: Sufi, Quran, Miraj, Poetic and Theological Writings*. New York: Paulist Press, 1996, p. 169. **216:** Source: Indepth: Islam, Fatwa FAQ CBC News online, June 15, 2006. Reprinted with permission. **219:** A Closer Look source: Katherine Bullock, "The Hijab Experience of Canadian Muslim Women." Originally published in the March/April 1998 issue of *Islamic Horizons* magazine. **221–222:** Douglas Todd/*The Vancouver Sun* **225:** Quote from *Relationship of the Church to Non-Christian Religions*: © Libreria Editrice Vaticana, reprinted with permission. **227:** From *Teachings of Rumi*, by Andrew Harvey, © 1999 by Andrew Harvey. Reprinted by arrangement with Shambhala Publications Inc., Boston, MA. Please visit the Shambhala website.

Chapter 7. 228, 237, 250: Source of Hindu scripture excerpts: *Bhagavad Gita*. W.J. Johnson, trans. Oxford University Press, 1994. **238:** (bl column) Reprinted by permission, from *The Upanishads*. Translated by Swami Nikhilananda, published by Ramakrishna-Vivekananda Center of New York. **238:** (tl column) Bede Griffiths. *A New Vision of Reality: Western Science, Eastern Mysticism and Christian Faith*. Springfield, Illinois: Templegate Publishers, 1990, p. 60. **240:** (tl) Source: Wendy Doniger. "The Hymn of Purusha." *The Rig Veda: An Anthology*. London: Penguin, 1981, p. 30. Reprinted with permission of Penguin Group UK. **250:** Source of Bhagavad Gita 9.34: from page 43 of *Bhagavad Gita*. W.J. Johnson, trans. Oxford University Press, 1994. Reprinted by permission of Oxford University Press. **251:** Source: Wendy Doniger. *The Rig Veda: An Anthology*. London: Penguin, 1981, p. 279. **254:** Quote from Second Vatican Council in A Closer Look feature: © Libreria Editrice Vaticana, reprinted with permission. **254:** Source of Gandhi excerpt: Mohandas Gandhi, "Fellowship and Toleration," in *Liberating Faith: Religious Voices for Justice, Peace, and Ecological Wisdom,* ed. Roger S. Gottlieb (Lanham, Maryland: Rowman & Littlefield Publishers, Inc., 2003), p. 93. **256:** (r column) Excerpt source: *Christ in India: Essays Towards a Hindu–Christian Dialogue*. New York: Charles Scribner's Sons, 1967, p. 99. **257:** Source: Wendy Doniger. *The Rig Veda: An Anthology*. London: Penguin, 1981, p. 25. Reprinted with permission of Penguin Group UK.

Chapter 8. 258: Three Jewels text source: Bhikkhu Nanamoli. Bhikkhu Bodhi. ed. *The Middle Length Discourses of the Buddha: A New Translation of the Majjhima Nikaya*. Boston: Wisdom Publications, 1995, Sutta 4, paragraph 35, p.107. **280:** Excerpt from Vatican Council II: © Libreria Editrice Vaticana. **280, 281:** Excerpt from Pontifical council and papal speech: © Libreria Editrice Vaticana, reprinted with permission. **283:** From *The Way of the Bodhisattva*, by Shantideva, translated by the Padmakara Translation Group, ©1997, 2006 by the Padmakara Translation Group. Reprinted by arrangement with Shambhala Publications Inc., Boston, MA.

Chapter 9. 284: Source, Khushwant Singh. *Hymns of the Gurus*. Penguin Books India, 2003, p. 111. Reprinted by arrangement with the publisher. **304:** Source, Interreligious dialogue: Paul McKenna *Scarboro Missions Magazine*. "Sikh–Christian dialogue: First U.S. Catholic–Sikh National Consultation." January/February 2007. **307:** Source, Khushwant Singh. Hymns of the Gurus. Penguin Books India, 2003, p. 111. Reprinted by arrangement with the publisher.

Chapter 10. 325 (r), **333, 334** (A Closer Look): Quote from Vatican online archives: © Libreria Editrice Vaticana, reprinted with permission. **331:** Quote from Catechism of the Catholic Church: © Libreria Editrice Vaticana, reprinted with permission.

Chapter 11. 336, 343: Excerpt from Papal speech: © Libreria Editrice Vaticana. **352:** (Tewa prayer) Herbert Spinden. "Translated Songs of the Tewa." New York: Brooklyn Museum, 1933, p. 94. Reproduced with permission. **352:** Source of Bhagavad Gita 12:13–14: from page 56 from *Bhagavad Gita* by Johnson, WJ, edited by Johnson, WJ (1994). By permission of Oxford University Press. **352:** Source of Sufi Islam excerpt: Maulana Jalalu-'d-din Muhammad Rumi, *The Masnavi I Ma'navi*. Abridged and Translated by E.H. Whinfield [1898]. Retrieved online. **352:** Source of Dhammapada: Accessed online via The Internet Sacred Text Archive **359:** Source of Fr. Becker excerpt: "Legacy of Slain Monks." *Zenit News*, 28 March 2006. Accessed online. **59:** Source of monk's excerpts: John W. Kiser. *The Monks of Tibhirine: Faith, Love, And Terror in Algeria*. New York: St Martin's Press, 2002. **363:** Quote from Papal speech: © Libreria Editrice Vaticana, reprinted with permission. **368:** Quote from Declaration on the Relation of the Church to Non-Christian Religions: © Libreria Editrice Vaticana, reprinted with permission.